Taking the High Road

A Guide to Effective and Legal Employment Practices for Nonprofits

2nd Edition

by Jennifer Chandler Hauge and Melanie L. Herman

Copyright © 2006 Nonprofit Risk Management Center

ISBN 1-893210-21-9

Nonprofit
Risk Management
Center

About the Nonprofit Risk Management Center

The Nonprofit Risk Management Center is dedicated to helping community-serving nonprofits prevent harm, conserve resources, preserve assets, and free up resources for mission-critical activities. The Center provides technical assistance on risk management, liability, and insurance matters; publishes easy-to-use written materials; designs and delivers workshops and conferences; and offers consulting help in the areas of policy development, risk assessment, and risk management program design.

The Center is an independent nonprofit organization that doesn't sell insurance or endorse specific insurance providers. For more information on the products and services available from the Center, call (202) 785-3891 or visit our Web site at **www.nonprofitrisk.org**. Additional Center Web sites are available at: www.MyRiskManagementPlan.org, www.RiskManagementClassroom.org and www.NonprofitCARES.org.

Nonprofit Risk Management Center
1130 17th Street, N.W., Suite 210
Washington, DC 20036
(202) 785-3891
Fax: (202) 296-0349
www.nonprofitrisk.org

Staff

Sheryl Augustine, *Customer Service Representative*
Melanie L. Herman, *Executive Director*
Barbara B. Oliver, *Director of Communications*
John C. Patterson, *Senior Program Director*

George L. Head, Ph.D., *Special Advisor*

Acknowledgements

The Nonprofit Risk Management Center is grateful for the support of the Public Entity Risk Institute (PERI), which provided a generous grant to support the cost of publishing this book. PERI is a tax-exempt nonprofit whose mission is to serve public, private and nonprofit organizations as a dynamic, forward thinking resource for the practical enhancement of risk management. For more information on PERI, visit the organization's Web site, www.riskinstitute.org.

This publication is designed to provide accurate and authoritative information in regard to the subject matter covered. It's distributed with the understanding that the publisher isn't engaged in rendering legal, accounting, or other professional service. If legal advice or other expert assistance is required, the services of a competent professional should be sought. From a Declaration of Principles jointly adopted by a Committee of the American Bar Association and a Committee of Publishers.

Table of Contents

Sidebars

The use of the ✍ signifies the availability of a hyperlink to the source reference (e.g. statute, factsheet) in the online edition of *Taking the High Road*. Consult the online edition in order to gain ready access the source material.

Introduction

"Employees are our most valuable asset," is an organizational cliché. It's also a true statement. An equally true statement is that employees can be a nonprofit's liability, both by their specific actions and by not sharing the vision of the organization's leadership. Managing an organization well requires being mindful of both sides of this conundrum: assets and liabilities. The nonprofit sector can claim no exception to this advice. In fact, when the *higher moral purpose* that typically distinguishes the nonprofit sector is taken into account, it's even more important for managers of nonprofit organizations to be attentive to taking the high road.

There are both practical and ethical imperatives for this advice. Minimizing risk comprehends both dimensions. Often overlooked, however, is the desirability of having a workforce that believes in the moral correctness and benevolence of the organization and its leadership. Arguably, the employees in such a workforce will be more motivated and productive. Probably more important is the organizational commitment that ensues from such an environment. Every organization will eventually face difficult times. And every manager will eventually have to make difficult and sometimes controversial decisions. What better way to ensure that the organization maintains as much equilibrium as possible during these difficulties than to have a workforce that truly believes in the values and moral correctness of the organization. Treating employees well affirms the values and provides an important subliminal message about how employees should treat others (clients, co-workers, and the organization itself). Taking the high road better ensures the long-term health of the organization to cope with the ills that it will almost certainly encounter at some point.

Defining "The High Road"

Dignity. Respect. Compassion. Fairness. Accountability. Consideration. These familiar words describe important values in *any* workplace. And they represent *essential* values in a nonprofit work environment. These values represent a basic formula for reducing the risk of employment-related mishaps, disputes, claims and lawsuits. These and other undesirable events disrupt the flow of mission-related work and threaten a nonprofit's ability to focus all or most of its resources on meeting client or community needs.

Throughout this book we refer to a wide range of recommended practices in the employment arena. In each case the advice goes beyond what a nonprofit employer is legally required to do. Our goal is to help nonprofit leaders adopt policies and practices that put their organizations on a high road with regard to their relationship with paid employees.

Unfortunately, in an attempt to run their organizations "like a business" some nonprofit leaders have overlooked the importance of legally prudent employment practices or have adopted confining employment practices inconsistent with the organization's charitable mission. This book serves as a global positioning system (GPS) to help get your organization's policies and practices back on track. Back on a decidedly *nonprofit*—yet, a legally compliant and feasible—track. Your nonprofit's employment practices should reflect the values and caring your organization demonstrates to its clients, while offering sound, reliable policies on which your employees can rely.

The advice in this book is drawn from a variety of sources, beginning with the authors' experience advising nonprofits of varying sizes and missions about many aspects of human resources management. Each of the authors has spent more than a decade helping individual nonprofits fine-tune their employment policies. The authors have delivered hundreds of workshops and presentations on employment topics to audiences of nonprofit leaders. Additional sources for the information in this book include published resources on employment topics, periodic newsletters published by law firms specializing in the employment arena, and insurance providers that underwrite employment practices liability coverage. As a guide to legal and effective employment practices, this book will provide a roadmap for avoiding claims alleging illegal or wrongful conduct, and avoiding liability in the face of a claim. Taken as a whole, we believe that this book provides practical and feasible advice for strengthening your employment practices. We hope that adherence to the guidance in this text will enable your nonprofit to operate with confidence regarding its employment practices. Operating within the bounds of federal, state and local labor laws is only a starting point.

Ten Rules of Effective Employment Practices

Several themes repeat throughout the book. We summarize them here with explanations. These *rules* provide an essential foundation for an organization committed to compassionate and legal employment practices.

1. Always put key employment policies in writing.

Written policies are your first line of defense when a current or former employee questions the legality or appropriateness of a policy or its application. Written policies also serve as an invaluable reference point when questions about your practices are raised: "When do I start accruing vacation leave? Is it permissible to make personal long-distance phone calls and use the organization's postage machine?" Most legal advisors to nonprofits urge the adoption of written employment policies. On occasion an attorney will state that written policies are a dangerous trap, and it's better not to commit policies to writing. While there are downsides (namely the risk that your written policy will be used against you), the benefits outweigh the risks by a mile. The upsides include:

❑ *Written policies provide a starting point for consistency.* They represent an effective way to communicate a common message to all employees. Each person receives the same information about the nonprofit's position on various topics. Written policies help you avoid the risk that individual supervisors will apply a personal interpretation to your policies, resulting in the inequitable treatment of employees. Written policies are comforting to employees and provide a sense of the nonprofit's commitment to fairness.

❑ *Written policies provide admissible evidence* of the organization's policies. Should your nonprofit ever need to defend its employment practices in court or at an administrative hearing, you'll want to refer to your written policies as evidence of your legal conduct. Don't risk the chance of liability for unlawful employment practices simply because you were unable to prove that a lawful policy existed and was followed.

❑ *Written policies establish the business-related reason for an employment action,* reducing the possibility that the employer's conduct will be challenged as subjective and discriminatory.

Caution: Establishing, but not following your written policies is a recipe for disaster. Equally troublesome is permitting supervisors to put their own spin on policies when they deal with employees.

2. Communicate and disseminate without delay.

Written employment policies that are a nonprofit's best kept secret are of little use. New employees should be schooled in the nonprofit's policies as soon as practicably possible. Some employers send the employee handbook along with the offer letter; others distribute the handbook at the employee orientation session held on the first day of employment. From a bound manual to a file on the nonprofit's intranet, the method of dissemination should fit the culture of your organization. Getting this vital information into the hands of employees is of great importance. Repeatedly telling the story, year in and year out, will help ensure that the policies are truly learned and followed. These methods provide valuable opportunities for ongoing dialogue about "what we believe."

3. Size matters; form may not.

A multivolume treatise on employment rules is of minimal use and may create unintentional risks for the nonprofit. A manual that attempts to answer every conceivable question that could arise during an employee's tenure is likely to be ignored. A handbook that's written in legalese will confuse most, if not all employees, leaving them wondering about the organization's policies and effectively unable to comply. The handbook or policy manual must be a reasonable length to ensure its effectiveness and strict adherence. It must be written in plain language that will be understood by all. Two questions that you should ask about every section in the handbook include:

❑ Does every employee need to know this information?

❑ Will every employee be able to understand this policy?

Employment gurus don't always agree whether or not an organization's employment-related policies should be consolidated in a single handbook or policy manual. Some argue that a policy manual or compilation should be limited to critical policy information, and that other information about the workplace, such as etiquette, benefits information, vacation accrual, and issues subject to change and frequent updating should be maintained in a separate document or simply circulated periodically to staff in written memos. The authors don't find this distinction particularly compelling. More important in our view is that an employee handbook or personnel policy manual 1) be circulated to all staff, 2) include important policy issues, 3) contain only commitments the nonprofit is willing and able to keep, and 4) be reviewed annually by counsel to ensure that outdated information is removed and current policies, procedures, and new statutory requirements are incorporated.

Of almost equal importance to putting employment policies in writing is the need to obtain a written confirmation from each employee that he/she has read, understands, and agrees to abide by the rules of the workplace as presented in the policy manual or handbook. When new policies are developed, the handbook should be revised and redistributed, or a separate document describing a new policy should be circulated. In either case, each employee should sign an Acknowledgment Statement that she/he received the revised (or new) policy, and the signed Acknowledgment Statement should be kept in the employee's personnel file.

4. Involve the board.

An additional tenet of safe and effective employment practices is appropriate board involvement. Some nonprofit boards report very little involvement, preferring instead to delegate to a Personnel Committee responsibility for reviewing and adopting employment policies. Adopted policies are then implemented by paid staff. This framework may be most appropriate and effective in a relatively mature nonprofit, with a governing/policy-making board that regularly delegates key areas of policy development to committees and implementation to staff. To make this approach work, it may be necessary for the committee to include subject matter experts, such as employment counsel or human resources professionals as committee members.

Another approach is to encourage more active involvement and awareness by the full board due to the significant risks posed by the employment of paid staff. With employment-related claims representing an estimated 85 percent or more of all claims filed under directors' and officers' liability policies, employment missteps place both an organization and its individual directors at risk. State and federal volunteer protection/immunity laws provide no safe harbor, because they specifically exclude intentional wrongs and claims alleging violations of civil rights law—exactly the type of claims alleged by employees or former employees against their employer. Therefore, keeping the entire board apprised of the nonprofit's employment policies may be appropriate. Under this latter approach the board may review and ratify employment policies developed by the CEO/executive director in consultation with an employment attorney and human resources director. The board may further inquire about the organization's policies and procedures during its regular meetings, and suggest the development of a training program and complaint procedure to ensure the timely correction of prohibited activities, such as harassment. This framework grants permission to the board to ask the CEO about specific employment policies and practices or even to review potentially volatile employee matters. In a start-up or a nonprofit where the board attends to program and service delivery, as well as policy-setting and governance, members of the board may be tapped to research employment practices of similar nonprofits and draft policies for board consideration.

With the exception of their role as direct supervisor of the executive director (or other chief staff member) it's never appropriate for a nonprofit board, or certain members of the board, to step out of an advisory role and into the driver's seat.

5. Strive for fairness.

The fair application of employment policies is vital to reducing employment-related risks. While true for employers in the business and government sectors, it's especially true in the nonprofit sector, where many employees have high expectations about their employer's compassion, sensitivity and fairness. The expectation that they will be treated fairly may be one of the tradeoffs an applicant accepts when foregoing more lucrative opportunities in the private sector. It's neither costly nor unnecessarily time-consuming to strive for and achieve fairness. Employers who dishonor the commitment to fairness discredit the nonprofit sector and foster cynicism. Defining fairness isn't an easy task. It means affording employees respect, courtesy, equal treatment and opportunities, a forum to seek redress of grievances, and, except when a serious violation of workplace rules or ethics has occurred, notice of poor performance and an opportunity to improve prior to discharge. Striving for fairness is the essence of a sound risk management program, as employers with the policies previously referenced are less likely to be dragged into court or held liable for unlawful or negligent employment practices. And, as we pointed out at the beginning of the introduction, this commitment to fairness won't go unnoticed by the employees and will pay dividends at critical points in the organization's future.

6. Be wary of contract-like promises.

At the heart of the debate over whether or not policies should be in a handbook format is consideration of whether or not employee handbooks seriously impair the revered at-will employment relationship governing most workplaces by creating a contractual obligation between employee and employer. This topic is explored in detailed in the section on *employment at will*.

The viewpoint of this text is that written employment policies are essential. However, simply reiterating and using large print to remind employees about their at-will status in no way diminishes the obligations an employer may create through oral and written promises to employees. Contractual or contract-like obligations may be created when an employer makes a promise to its employees. Every nonprofit employer should recognize this and exercise caution in adopting policies or making promises the organization may not be able to live with. Minor alterations in many employment policies can remove or minimize the contract trap. For example, an appropriate progressive discipline policy should give management the *discretion* to place a poor performer on a time-based probation, but not *require* that management do so. Remember that even casual representations such as, "I would like to see you retire from this place," may be interpreted as a promise of lifetime employment and subject the employer to liability for an unfulfilled promise.

7. Strive for consistency.

Enough emphasis can't be placed on the importance of achieving consistency in employment practices. This is closely related to (and is the technical implementation of) the value of fairness. Just as sound risk management requires that every activity be viewed through a *lens of safety*, safe employment practices require that the application of a policy in a particular instance be subject to a *consistent-treatment* test. This test can be achieved by asking, "How have other employees in this situation been treated?" "If the employee in question were a man instead of a woman, would I be reducing this position to part-time status?" or "If this employee were a finance director instead of a mailroom clerk, would I be firing him for sleeping on the job?" The perception of disparate treatment leads to countless claims and lawsuits against employers, including nonprofits. The consistent-treatment test may help a nonprofit manager who is caught up in the emotionally-charged atmosphere of a termination avoid missteps and resulting litigation. The best way to ensure consistency is to involve an objective third party—such as another manager or board member or outside legal counsel—who can review the situation before the nonprofit takes adverse action.

8. Stay mission-focused and strive for efficiency.

The employment practices reviewed in this book shouldn't be viewed as distracting management from an organization's core mission. While it's true that any policy takes time to develop and implement, the real time waster for a community-serving nonprofit is defending a lawsuit. By focusing on the preventive medicine of sound, defensible employment practices, the nonprofit will be reducing the risk of employment litigation and its accompanying expense, heartache, worry, and distraction.

Staying mission-focused sometimes leads a nonprofit to negotiate a monetary settlement or termination agreement with an employee to avoid a lawsuit. It isn't uncommon to resist settling a dispute when the nonprofit believes it hasn't done anything wrong. However, a negotiated settlement is frequently the best outcome in an employment case. The cost of defending an employment claim can be substantial. The cost of defense counsel is only the beginning; lost personnel time, damage to the nonprofit's reputation in the community, a decline in staff morale, and a rise in insurance premiums can far exceed the lawyer's fee for services. Since the nonprofit's mission is to serve its constituency, preservation of resources to ensure that the nonprofit will be there in the future to continue its service to the community should be paramount. On the other hand, merely acceding to the demands of a difficult employee can have a different cost: the demoralizing effect on the workforce. When an organization consistently takes the high road, it makes sense to defend the values of the organization. Each case will have to be judged on the merits and in consideration of the *costs* of settling or persisting.

9. Honesty is always the best policy.

Always be honest and tell the truth in dealing with prospective and current employees. Never exaggerate a position's duties or responsibilities to attract a desirable candidate, or give someone a false reason for an adverse employment action (such as telling them that they're being laid off due to budgetary constraints when they're being terminated for incompetence). Commit to providing honest appraisals of performance, and empower supervisors in your organization to conduct appraisals in a timely manner. Dishonesty or delay heightens the risk of litigation. An employee who isn't told why he or she is being fired is likely to assume the firing was illegal. Don't let employees second-guess the nonprofit's motives. Honesty, however difficult to hear or deliver, is the best policy.

10. Resist the urge to hurry; allow time to get a second opinion.

Just as increasing speed to 20 mph above the speed limit isn't guaranteed to get you to your destination quicker (an accident would add hours to the trip or perhaps derail your plans altogether), sound employment practices require patience and respect for timing. In Chapter 7, read why providing a poor performer with time to address his deficiencies minimizes the likelihood of a lawsuit, and why it's never a good idea to terminate an employee on the spot. Similarly, it makes no sense to hurry the development of an employee handbook that will invite legal challenge. Allow policy development the time, care, and feeding it deserves. Resolve to administer employment practices with deliberation and to follow the sound risk management practices described throughout this book.

Also remember to never go it alone. Creating and administering defensible, compliant and appropriate employment policies requires expert help. No nonprofit of any size should establish employment policies and procedures without the assistance of an employment lawyer licensed in the state where the nonprofit does business. We invite you to consider the policy frameworks and sample forms included in this book, but offer extreme caution about the downsides of proceeding without legal counsel. Your organization's mission and services are too important to jeopardize by a misstep in this risky area of operations. The materials in this book should serve as a refresher, a starting point for discussion with employment counsel, or a reminder about issues to discuss with other experts or stakeholders. Nonprofit managers and volunteers are widely regarded as creative resource developers. It takes creativity and commitment to secure donations of equipment, funds, and services to support charitable activities. Similarly, learn as much as possible about effective and legal employment policies, including the specific laws that apply in the state where the organization operates, and you'll reduce the cost of a legal review and make the organization an enviable client.

To a large extent, this book is about regaining your footing as a manager. It's about easing out of the fast lane and reclaiming the higher moral ground for you and your organization. It's about dealing with your employees fairly and honestly. Treating people right doesn't mean lowering your standards. On the contrary, it's making the standards known and giving your employees the opportunity to live up to them.

Every manager has to discipline or even terminate an employee from time to time. By following the guidelines in this book, you can approach these difficult tasks with more confidence and the knowledge that you can back up your words and actions.

Doing the *right* thing is often the smartest thing from a legal perspective, too. In this text you'll learn how to apply the Fundamental Fairness Formula, an aid to decision-makers faced with discipline, termination, or day-to-day employee performance dilemmas. This formula not only will protect your nonprofit from liability, but will ensure that management treats staff fairly.

Your organization will run better too. How often has it been said that our reward is the journey and not the destination. Think of your organization's mission as a journey. Taking shortcuts may save a little time, but at what cost? We all know that sometimes the seemingly shortest path may cost precious time and resources in the long run. The journey will be more rewarding and the results produced by your nonprofit more satisfying when you and your fellow managers focus on taking the high road.

—*Jennifer Chandler Hauge and Melanie L. Herman*

Chapter 1

What Is Employment-at-Will?

In essence *employment-at-will* means that either the employee or the employer may initiate separation of employment 'for good cause, bad cause or no cause at all' with or without notice to the other party. Consequently, in an employment-at-will relationship an employee can decide to quit anytime, and an employer can decide to hire someone today and fire them tomorrow, 'just because.' Absent some other factor, such as breach of a contract, violation of a recognized public policy, or the existence of an illegal discriminatory motive for the discharge, the termination of an at-will employee at any time, for any reason, is perfectly legal.

Bear in mind, the biggest risk by far in human resource management is the termination of an employee. Despite the prevalence of the employment-at-will doctrine around the country,[1] there are still many ways that an employee can challenge an employer's decision to end the employment relationship. Preserving employment-at-will gives a nonprofit the flexibility it needs to conclude that some staff members aren't contributing to the furtherance of the organization's mission—perhaps a staff member is draining the organization of resources without adding value—or is simply unable to follow the directions provided by his or her supervisor. Terminating an employee is both difficult and unpleasant, but at times it's necessary in order for a nonprofit to act responsibly. Upholding the public trust and meeting the promises made to funders requires staff terminations from time to time. Making sure that a nonprofit has employment-at-will as one of its defenses is a basic and essential risk management strategy.

Risk Management to Preserve Employment-at-Will

The *employment-at-will* doctrine doesn't negate the need for nonprofit employers to exercise extreme caution when implementing decisions that negatively affect an employee. Two common danger zones are:

❑ Failing to recognize that policies or language, verbal or written, can inadvertently erode or cancel the employment-at-will relationship by creating a contractual right to continued employment.

❑ Taking action that negatively affects employees (including the decision to terminate employment) without taking into consideration the possibility of a challenge based on a claim of discrimination, retaliation, or violation of public policy.

> **Defining Employment-at-Will**
>
> Either the employee or the employer may terminate the employment relationship, at any time and for any reason, except a reason specifically prohibited (illegal) under state or federal law.
>
> *Source: Nonprofit Risk Management Center*
>
> "…when an employee doesn't have a written employment contract and the term of employment is of indefinite duration, the employer can terminate the employee for good cause, bad cause, or no cause at all."
>
> *Source: Shane and Rosenthal,* Employment Law Deskbook, *Section 16.02 (1999).*
>
> "The employment-at-will doctrine provides that both the employer and the employee can end the employment relationship at any time without notice or reason."
>
> *Source: www.workplacefairness.org*

Risk management involves identifying risks and taking action steps to avoid, modify or accept (retain) risk. One obvious risk management step that shouldn't be overlooked is asking an employment lawyer to review the nonprofit's employment handbook. Often a quick look at the handbook can tell the lawyer volumes about vulnerabilities in the nonprofit's human resources management practices. Simply changing the language in an employee handbook can be the catalyst for important discussions with management and the board of directors about practices that should be changed to protect the nonprofit. Often the changes are simple: Adding a prominently placed disclaimer at the front of a handbook, in bold face, set apart from other text, is often the easiest and most important change resulting from the legal review of a handbook. In many court cases the presence of a prominent disclaimer has tipped the balance of the court's decision in favor of the employer.

---

1 With the exception of Arizona and Montana, employment-at-will is the recognized "public policy" in all states. In Montana, employees can only be terminated for "good cause." The definition of "good cause" in the <u>Montana Wrongful Discharge from Employment Act</u> includes a reasonable, job-related ground for dismissal based on a "failure to satisfactorily perform job duties."

In Arizona, the <u>public policy of the state</u> identifies that the employment relationship is contractual in nature, however, the law specifically provides that either the employer or employee may terminate the employment relationship at any time, *unless* there is a written, signed contract to the contrary.

Even though employment-at-will is the *default* relationship between employer and employee in all but two states (Montana and Arizona), words or actions by the nonprofit's leaders can weaken or completely eliminate employment-at-will: Examples: 1) a supervisor's verbal promise that, "You won't lose your job unless we close our doors," 2) references to *permanent employment* in a handbook, or 3) written policies that mandate that employees give their employer notice prior to resignation. Each of these circumstances gives an employee grounds to argue that being discharged (or how the discharge occurred) was a violation of employee's rights.

Written or verbal promises of job security can supersede employment-at-will, locking the employer into even unintended promises made to employees. Consequently, most nonprofits go to great pains to reinforce the employment-at-will relationship by managing employees' expectations about job security from *day one*. These nonprofits make sure that the employment application and all written documents provided to employees, such as policy manuals, summaries of benefits and employee handbooks have a *disclaimer* prominently displayed, informing employees of the employment-at-will relationship. Prudent nonprofits also regularly enlist assistance from an employment law specialist to make sure that the nonprofit stays up to date with changes in the law and that documents provided to employees don't contain explicit promises or language that could cause an employee to conclude that employment was anything but *at-will*.

What employment-at-will means:

It's possible to terminate an employee for a trivial issue or for no reason at all and not violate state or federal law.

Nonprofit employers, like other employers, have the ability to hire and fire employees based on the needs and resources of the organization and the preferences of management.

What employment-at-will doesn't mean:

Firing an employee on a whim is okay, even with a prominent employment-at-will policy.

There is no need to tell an employee the reason for his or her termination. *In fact, when employees aren't told or don't understand why they were terminated, they're much more likely to conclude that there was an illegal reason for their termination.*

Exceptions and Limitations to Employment-at-Will

Limitations on an employer's right to terminate an employee typically arise from three major sources: federal and state laws (statutory rights), employee handbooks or other documents distributed by the employer to all employees (contractual rights), or court decisions finding that an employee was wrongfully discharged for a reason that violated the public policy of the state (common law rights).

Federal and state anti-discrimination and anti-retaliation laws prohibit an employer from taking any action that adversely impacts an employee if the reason for the action is because the employee:

1. is a member of a *protected class* (that's race, age, sex, religion, ethnicity, etc.); or

2. acted in a manner protected by law (such as filing a workers' compensation claim, or a complaint of sexual harassment) and the employer's motivation for taking the action was *retaliation.*

Under common law, courts have recognized and enforced an employee's right not to be terminated from employment if it would violate public policy (For example, it would violate the public policy of a state to terminate an employee who reported illegal conduct at the workplace.) or because the employer's conduct violated an implied covenant of *good faith and fair dealing* or caused the employee to rely on the employer's promise, to the employee's detriment.

Under contract theory, courts have found that language in employee handbooks or benefit plan documents (for example, references to *permanent* employment) can create a contract, whether expressed or implied, that employment is something other than *at-will*.

Any of these theories can be used to challenge a decision to terminate an employee, even if the employee is an employee-at-will. Because an employee-at-will can claim that the *real* reason for the termination was an illegal reason, or that the termination was in breach of a contract, or in violation of public policy, whether or not employment was at-will. Due to the success of wrongful termination claims in all states, employers have adapted their workplace procedures to incorporate strategies and policies that reduce the risks of wrongful discharge claims. We explore these strategies in more detail in the next section.

Caution! Erosion of Employment-at-Will Through Creation of an Implied Contract

Employer Handbooks and Manuals

Employers often use handbooks and manuals to inform employees of their employment policies and to enforce their at-will policies. Although no express employment contract exists, courts have held that handbooks and manuals can be implied contracts if the language creates an impression that employees can only be dismissed for cause. The employee must be aware of the handbook provisions at the time of the discharge to rely on them in a lawsuit. Consequently, when a nonprofit changes its policies and distributes a new employee handbook it's important to ensure that every employee receives the new version of the policy manual. Even employees who are out of work on leave should receive a new manual, by mail using a method that provides proof of delivery.

> **States Recognizing Implied Contract Based on Handbook Statements Include:**
>
> Alabama, Alaska, Arizona, Arkansas, California, Colorado, Connecticut, Delaware, Hawaii, Idaho, Illinois, Indiana, Iowa, Kansas, Kentucky, Maine, Maryland, Massachusetts, Michigan, Minnesota, Mississippi, Missouri, Montana (by statute), Nebraska, Nevada, New Hampshire, New Jersey, New Mexico, New York, North Dakota, Ohio, Oklahoma, Oregon, Pennsylvania, South Carolina, South Dakota, Tennessee, Virginia, Washington, West Virginia, Wisconsin and Wyoming.

Some courts have found that a handbook or manual may create not only a right not to be discharged except for cause, but also an obligation on the part of the employer to follow certain procedures—even where an employee is discharged for cause. For example, when an employer includes a detailed description of progressive discipline procedures, the handbook may create an impression that the employer will follow every step in the procedures before terminating an employee. If the employee is summarily discharged without all steps being taken—even if the employee's conduct warranted dismissal—courts have found that the employer breached an implied contract to follow all disciplinary steps described in the manual prior to discharging an employee.

The primary way to minimize the likelihood that a court or arbitrator will find that handbook provisions amount to an implied contract is to include an unambiguous prominent disclaimer, on the first page of the handbook, stating that the handbook or other documents don't create contractual rights, and that the employment relationship is at-will. Any procedures that describe disciplinary steps should always be clearly described as *guidelines*, to be used at the nonprofit's discretion. The disclaimer should also address the fact that the nonprofit has the right to make changes to its personnel policies and that the new policy manual supersedes any prior manuals.

Example of an at-will disclaimer:

DISCLAIMER—IMPORTANT NOTICE ABOUT YOUR EMPLOYMENT

Employment with Nonprofit is *at-will*, which means that either you or Nonprofit may terminate your employment at any time, for any reason, with or without notice. The policies and practices described in this employee manual are provided to you for guidance only, but don't constitute a contract of employment. Neither this handbook nor any other documents circulated to employees, nor any verbal representations constitute contracts. No supervisor or employee except the executive director has the authority to enter into an employment agreement, express or implied, with any employee. These policies supersede any policies that may have been distributed previously. Your signature on the acknowledgement is a certification that you have received a copy of these policies as updated. These policies are subject to change at any time at the discretion of Nonprofit.

Handbook Errors to Avoid

The following are examples of employee handbook mistakes that may give an employee sound footing to claim wrongful discharge based on the breach of an implied contract:

❏ Language implying that if an employee makes it through the introductory work period (inappropriately called the *probationary period*) the employee is somehow less vulnerable to termination

❏ The use of the phrase *permanent employee* anywhere in the handbook

❏ The absence of a disclaimer about employment-at-will status, or a disclaimer that's so buried in the text that it isn't *prominently* displayed

❏ A narrowly defined list of reasons for termination that implies that an employee can only be terminated for the reasons itemized on a list

❏ A verbal promise from a supervisor that the employee will have a job *as long as they want* or similar assurances of continued employment

❏ Language stating that termination can only be *for cause*

❏ A definite list of disciplinary actions, usually described as *progressive discipline* that could be interpreted as requiring that all the steps, or certain of the steps, *must* be followed prior to termination, or that the discipline described must be applied in a *certain order* prior to termination.

Verbal Promises

As a precautionary measure, any supervisory employee involved in hiring should be trained not to make promises about future job tenure. Courts in 34 states have held that *an employer's oral statements can create an enforceable contract for employment.* For example, statements to a prospective employee that he will have a job (i) 'as long as your performance is adequate' or (ii) 'as long as you do the job' were found to create a standard that employees could only be terminated (i) if their performance was inadequate, or (ii) if they failed to complete their job duties.

Employee Handbooks: Risk Management 101

Having written workplace policies and procedures that are legally up to date and easy to follow is as important as having adequate insurance. Policies that are clearly communicated to staff and consistently applied serve to safeguard against improvised solutions that can result in a lawsuit. Written policies are the starting point for ensuring that personnel dilemmas are resolved consistently and fairly. Moreover, several federal laws and many state laws require that workplaces distribute or post certain written policies. Up-to-date, legally sound personnel policies are so significant that many insurance companies, funders and potential board members look to a nonprofit's personnel policies as a bellwether of security—or risk. Many accreditation standards require that personnel policies be reviewed regularly. To ensure that the nonprofit's policies are current, schedule a policy review on a regular basis.

Revising or drafting policies is generally authorized by the chief staff executive or board of directors that designates a staff person or special task force to lead the project. Some nonprofits have standing personnel or human resource committees charged with responsibility for the project. Compare current practices to the written policies. Are we doing what we say we'll do? is a basic but important question to explore. Ultimately, after changes are made and the draft has been reviewed by legal counsel, the board of directors should formally approve the revised policies and charge the chief staff executive with making employees aware of policy changes and distributing the policies to all employees.

Whatever changes are made, from revising how vacation time is calculated to reinforcing that employment is at will, a nonprofit employer should always communicate the changes to employees *well before* they're implemented. Any time rights or benefits are taken away, not only is it helpful to give the employees as much notice as possible, but employees should each sign an acknowledgment that they understand that the new policies supersede any former policies or procedures. The nonprofit should notify supervisors first, via a revised policy statement, then notify each employee by memorandum, and follow that up by distributing a copy of the revised, updated employee handbook or policy manual. Employees should each sign and date an acknowledgment that they received the updated handbook or manual. The signed acknowledgement should be maintained in each employee's file.

The Public Policy Exception to Employment-at-Will

Several states recognize a cause of action for violation of public policy when an employer terminates an employee because the employee has engaged in conduct that's considered part of our civic duty, such as reporting an unsafe condition or exercising the right to join the National Guard. In states that recognize a public policy exception to employment-at-will, an employee can state a cause of action for wrongful discharge as a result of actions such as:

❏ Refusing to commit illegal or unethical acts, as directed by an employer

❏ Testifying before a public body

❏ Performing a civic duty such as military service or jury duty or serving as a witness

❏ Exercising legal rights, such as filing a complaint of discrimination or submitting a claim for workers' compensation benefits

❏ Reporting the wrongful conduct of an employer (*whistleblowing*).

Protections for Whistleblowers

The most sweeping exception to employment-at-will in the public policy category is the protection afforded to *whistleblowers*. This exception began as a common-law exception, but has rapidly become law in many states. Whistleblower laws in various states prohibit employers from retaliating against employees for reporting or complaining about a violation of law or public policy. Some states, such as Montana and New Jersey, protect whistleblowers from retaliation if the employee only *has a reasonable or good faith belief that the employer is engaged in illegal conduct*. Other states, such as New York and Pennsylvania, restrict the protections to whistleblowers to situations where *the employer has actually engaged in illegal conduct or violated a regulation*.

In several states the law explicitly protects employees who refuse to go along with their employer's requests that they engage in activity that they reasonably believe to be in violation of law. In other states, case law reaches a similar conclusion. In *Yanowitz v. L'Oreal USA, Inc.* (Cal. 2005), an employee who never complained of discrimination, but instead refused to go along with what she believes to be her employer's discriminatory conduct, was protected from discharge under the California Fair Employment and Housing Act.

SAMPLE -

Employee Protection (Whistleblower) Policy

If any employee reasonably believes that some policy, practice, or activity of [Name of Nonprofit] is in violation of law, a written complaint must be filed by that employee with the Executive Director or the Board President.

It's the intent of [Name of Nonprofit] to adhere to all laws and regulations that apply to the organization and the underlying purpose of this policy is to support the organization's goal of legal compliance. The support of all employees is necessary to achieving compliance with various laws and regulations. An employee is protected from retaliation only if the employee brings the alleged unlawful activity, policy, or practice to the attention of [Name of Nonprofit] and provides the nonprofit with a reasonable opportunity to investigate and correct the alleged unlawful activity. The protection described below is only available to employees that comply with this requirement.

[Name of Nonprofit] won't retaliate against an employee who in good faith, has made a protest or raised a complaint against some practice of [Name of Nonprofit], or of another individual or entity with whom [Name of Nonprofit] has a business relationship, on the basis of a reasonable belief that the practice is in violation of law, or a clear mandate of public policy.

[Name of Nonprofit] won't retaliate against employees who disclose or threaten to disclose to a supervisor or a public body, any activity, policy, or practice of [Name of Nonprofit] that the employee reasonably believes is in violation of a law, or a rule, or regulation mandated pursuant to law or is in violation of a clear mandate or public policy concerning the health, safety, welfare, or protection of the environment.

My signature below indicates my receipt and understanding of this policy. I also verify that I have been provided with an opportunity to ask questions about the policy.

_____   _____
Employee Signature   Date

States with Individual *Whistleblower* Laws and Those that Recognize a Public Policy Exception to Employment-at-Will Based on Whistleblower Activity

The state laws noted here are subject to constant review and revision in state legislatures. This summary should therefore be used for reference purposes, rather than as a definitive guide.

Alabama: The workers' compensation law in Alabama prohibits discharging employees because they've filed written notice of willful and intentional violations of safety rules. See Ala Code § 25-5-11.1

Alaska: The Alaska Human Rights Act, AS 18.80.220(a)(4) applies to private employers and prohibits retaliation against employees who oppose or file complaints about unlawful employment practices. Employers may not discharge or discriminate against employees who file a safety complaint. In addition, the implied covenant of good faith and fair dealing is recognized in Alaska and could be applied to protect an employee who reports an unsafe or illegal condition and is disciplined or discharged as a result.

Arizona: The Employment Protection Act, Ariz. Rev. Stat. §§ 23-1501 provides employees with broad protections against retaliatory discharge for exercising their lawful rights or filing complaints if they hold a reasonable belief that their employer is in violation of the state Constitution or some other regulation or law. Employees are also protected if they refuse to engage in unlawful activity. In order to receive protection from retaliation, employees must disclose the information to someone in management whom the employee has reason to believe has the authority to act on the information in an effort to prevent the transgression of law.

California: California's Whistleblower Protection Act is a broad anti-retaliation statute that prohibits employers from taking any disciplinary step to intimidate or prevent an employee from reporting a reasonable belief that there has been a violation of state or federal law. The California Attorney General maintains a hotline for reports. Cal. Lab. Code §1102.5(b). Employers must **post** a notice for employees explaining their rights under the law. See Cal. Lab. Code §1102.8

Connecticut: Employers may not discharge, discipline or otherwise penalize employees because they report to a public body a violation or suspected violation of any state or federal law or regulation or municipal ordinance or regulation. Employees who participate in hearings may also not be intimidated or retaliated against. Conn. Gen. Stat. § 31-51m . Also the Connecticut Fair Employment Practices Act prohibits retaliation against any employee who complains of discrimination. See Conn. Gen. Stat. § 46a-60(a)(4)

Delaware: Employers may not discharge, discipline, intimidate or otherwise negatively impact the conditions or terms of employment of any employee who files a report of a violation of local, state or federal law, rule or regulation. Similarly, employees can't be retaliated against for filing workers' compensation claims, or discrimination claims. The Whistleblowers Protection Act, 19 Del. C. § 726 ; 19 Del. C. § 735(b) and 19 Del. C § 1701 et seq. Additionally, under the Delaware False Claims Reporting Act, Del. Code *tit. 6 § 1208 employers may not harass, threaten,* retaliate against, discharge or discriminate against employees who exercise their rights under the act or participate in investigations or provide testimony against their employers.

Florida: Employers may not discharge or threaten to discharge employees for disclosure or threatened disclosure of violations of a law, rule, or regulation to the appropriate government authority; or for testifying before a government authority about a violation of law; or for objecting to or refusing to participate in activity that's in violation of a law, rule or regulation. Employees must bring the activity, policy, or practice to the attention of a supervisor or the employer in writing, and afford the employer a reasonable opportunity to correct the activity, policy, or practice. See Florida Stat. Ann. § 448.102

Hawaii: Employers may not threaten to discharge, discharge or otherwise discriminate against employees because they or someone acting on their behalf reported or are about to report to the employer or to a public body, a violation of suspected violation of law, rule, ordinance, or regulation, or a contract, (unless the report is false). Employers are similarly prohibited from retaliation against employees who are requested by a public body to provide testimony or participate in an investigation, hearing or inquiry. See Hawaii Rev. Stat. § 378-62

Idaho: The Idaho Human Rights Act, Idaho Code §§ 67-5901 et seq. prohibits employers from retaliation against individuals who oppose or complain about discrimination or cooperate with investigations of discrimination.

Illinois: The Illinois Whistleblowers Act, 740 ILCS 174/1 et seq. has 3 provisions prohibiting employers from: 1) making any rule or policy that prevents employees from disclosing information to a government or law enforcement officer if the employee has reasonable cause to believe that the disclosure is of a violation of state or federal law; 2) retaliating against employees who disclose information to a government or law enforcement agency when they've reasonable cause to believe that the information discloses a violation of law; and 3) retaliating against employees who refuse to participate in any activity that would result in a violation of any state or federal law. Also Illinois recognizes the public policy exception to at-will employment such that it would violate state law to discharge an employee in retaliation for the employee reporting a safety violation or violation of a criminal statute.

Indiana: Employers are prohibited from discharging employees who have filed complaints, testified in any proceeding or exercised any right under the Indiana Safety & Health Act. See Indiana Code § 22-8-1.1-38.1

Iowa: Employees are protected under the Iowa Civil Rights Act, Iowa Code § 216.11 ✎ from retaliation for reporting or participating in proceedings that identify violations of the Iowa Civil Rights Act or potential violations of the act. Employees are also protected from retaliation for reporting alleged workplace safety violations. Iowa also recognizes the public policy exception to employment at will.

Kansas: Employers are prohibited from retaliating against employees who make complaints or report violations of discrimination. Kansas Stat. Annot. 40-2209(i) ✎ ; Court cases in Kansas have recognized an exception to at-will employment when discharge is based on an employee's good faith complaint of violations or alleged violation of laws or regulations relating to health, safety or general welfare. See *Palmer v. Brown*, 242 Kan. 893, 752 P. 2d 685 (Kan 1986).

Louisiana: Employers with 20+ employees (each working 20+ weeks) are prohibited from retaliating against an employee who, in good faith and after advising the employer, discloses or threatens to disclose or testifies about any unlawful conduct or violation environmental law, rule, or regulation, or provide information or testify in any investigation of a violation by their employer or any other employer with whom their employer does business. Employees are also protected when they object or refuse to participate in an unlawful activity at the workplace. See La. Rev. Stat. Ann. §§ 23:967, 30:2027, ✎ and 42:1169. ✎

Maine: Employers are prohibited from retaliating against employees who report a violation of state or federal law or rule or report a condition or practice that endangers the health or safety of any individual. Employees must have reasonable cause to believe that a violation or condition exists. Employees must report the violation/omission to their employer first before reporting to a public body unless the employee has a specific reason to believe that reporting wouldn't result in prompt correction. See 26 Maine Rev. Stat. Ann. § 832, 833(1), § 833(2) ✎

Employers must Post **a notice** provided by the Maine Department of Labor that informs employees of their rights and has the telephone number of the DOL on it. See 26 Maine Rev. Stat. Ann. § 839 ✎

Michigan: Under the Michigan Whistleblowers Protection Act, employers may not retaliate against employees who report, or are about to report, a violation or suspected violation of a federal or state law or regulation to a public body, unless the employee knows the report is false. See MCL 15.362 ✎

Minnesota: Employers may not retaliate against employees who make a report/claim in good faith, or violations or suspected violations of law, to either the employer or government official. The Minnesota Human Rights Act, Minn. Stat. Ann. §§181.932 and 363A.04 ✎ also protects employees who are requested to testify or who participate in investigations of unlawful activity. Employees who make good faith reports when they believe that an accepted health care standard has been violated are also protected. The law protects the identity of employees making the reports.

Mississippi: Mississippi recognizes an exception to employment-at-will when an employee is discharged in retaliation for refusing to participate in illegal acts or when employees are discharged for reporting illegal acts of any employer, another employee or anyone else. See *McArn v. Allied Bruce-Terminix Co.*, 626 So. 2nd 603, 607 (Miss. 1993).

Missouri: Missouri common law recognizes an exception to employment-at-will based on a violation of public policy, such as in the case of an employee discharged for reporting or opposing a violation of law or illegal activity. The Missouri Human Rights Act, Rev. Stat. Mo. § 213.070 ✎ and the workers' compensation statute, Rev. Stat. Mo. § 287.780 ✎ , contain provisions that prohibit retaliation against employees who exercise their rights under those laws.

Montana: Employers may not discharge employees in retaliation for reporting a violation of *public policy* which is defined as a policy in effect at the time of discharge concerning the public health, safety, or welfare. See Montana Wrongful Discharge Act, Mont. Code. Ann. §§ 39-2-901 et seq. ✎

Nebraska: Employers that have 15+ employees for 20+ weeks in the current or preceding calendar year are prohibited from retaliation or discharging employees who have "opposed any practice or refused to carry out any action unlawful" under state or federal law. See Neb. Rev. Stat. 48-1114(3). ✎

Nevada: Employers with 15+ employees for 20+ weeks in the current or preceding calendar year are prohibited from discriminating (discharging, demoting, disciplining, harassing, denying promotions, etc.) against employees who have disclosed a violation/filed a claim under the state's equal employment law or because the employee testifies, assists with or participates in an investigation relating to the state's equal employment opportunity law. See Nev. Rev. Stat. 449.205 and 449.207, ✎ and 613.310 through 613.435 ✎

New Hampshire: Under the New Hampshire Whistleblower's Protection Act, employers are prohibited from retaliation against employees who report violations of law or rule adopted by the state, or federal government. Employees who refuse to engage in illegal activity are also protected. New Hampshire Rev. Stat. Ann. 275-E. ✎ Employers must POST a notice of the Act's protections. See New Hampshire Rev. Stat. Ann. 275-E7 ✎

New Jersey: New Jersey has several separate laws prohibiting retaliation against employees for reporting violations of law, including the Conscientious Employee Protection Act, (CEPA) N.J.S.A. § 34:19-3 ✎ which prohibits retaliation against an employee who files a complaint with a public body provided that the employee has brought the violation to the attention of a supervisor and afforded the employer a reasonable opportunity to correct the violation; A notice of employees' rights under CEPA must be **posted**. New Jersey also recognizes a public policy exception to employment-at-will that protects employees from discharge for refusing to participate in illegal conduct or conduct that violates a clear mandate of public policy or that the employee has a reasonable belief violates public policy. See *Pierce v. Ortho Pharmaceutical Corp.*, 84 N.J. 58 (1980).

New Mexico: Employers may not retaliate against employees who seek benefits under or file complaints under or testify about violations of New Mexico's workplace safety regulations under New Mexico's workers' compensation or OSHA laws; N.M. Stat. Ann. § 50-9-25 ☜ and § 52-1-28.2 ☜ ; Employers also may not retaliate against any employee who opposes any unlawful discriminatory practice in violation of the New Mexico Human Rights Act. See N.M. Stat. Ann. § 28-1-7 ☜

New York: Employers are prohibited from retaliating against employees who disclose or threaten to disclose to a supervisor or public body a violation of law or regulation that creates a danger of public health or safety provided that the employee has brought the violation to the attention of a supervisor and afforded the employer a reasonable opportunity to correct the violation. Employers may also not retaliate against employees who participate in investigations or refuse to participate in violations of law. N.Y. Lab. Law §§ 215. 740 and 741 ☜ ; A separate law, the Health Care Workers Protection Act, prohibits employers from retaliating against employees who disclose or threaten to disclose to a supervisor or public body an activity, policy or practice that the employee reasonably believes constitutes improper patient care. N.Y.Civ. Serv. Law § 75b. New York City also has a separate law that prohibits employers from discriminating against, threatening or harassing employees who are victims of domestic violence, or for the exercise of their lawful rights.

North Carolina: Employers are prohibited from retaliating against employees for exercising their rights under anti-discrimination health and safety, workers' compensation and wage and hour laws or workers who are positive for the sickle cell trait. N.C. Gen. Stat. §§168A-10 ☜ ; North Carolina also recognizes the public policy exception to employment-at-will. See *Lenzer v. Flaherty*, 106 N. C. App. 496 (1992).

North Dakota: Employers are prohibited from retaliating against employees who file good faith reports of violation or suspected violations of law, participate in investigations or refuse to participate in activity at the workplace that the employee has an objective good faith belief are in violation of local, state, or federal law. N. D. Cent. Code § 34-01-20 ☜ ; Employers are also prohibited from retaliating against any employee who has opposed any unlawful discriminatory practice or who in good faith has filed a complaint, testified, assisted or participated in an investigation, or litigation action. See N.D. Cent. Code § 14-02.4-18 ☜

Ohio: Employers are prohibited from reporting violations of state or federal law that are likely to cause imminent risk of physical harm to persons or a hazard to public health or safety. See Ohio Rev. Code § 4113.52 ☜ .

Oklahoma: Oklahoma recognizes the public policy exception to employment-at-will.

Oregon: Employers are prohibited from discriminating or retaliating against employees who report criminal activities or initiate civil proceedings against their employers, Or. Rev. Stat. 659A:233 ☜ ; or who report safety violations or unhealthy working conditions or exercise their rights under state workers' compensation statutes, Or. Rev. Stat. 654.062(5)(a) ☜ ; laws, and Or. Rev. Stat. 659A.040 ☜ .

Rhode Island: Employers are prohibited under the Rhode Island Whistleblowers' Protection Act, R.I. Gen. Laws §§ 28-50-1 et seq. ☜ , from retaliating, threatening or otherwise discriminating against employees because they or someone on their behalf reports or is about to report to a public body a violation that the employee knows or has reason to reasonably believe has occurred or is about to occur. Employees who participate in investigations or to participate in unlawful acts are also protected. Employers are required to **post** a notice.

South Dakota: Social service agencies, schools, and community service providers are prohibited from retaliating against any staff member who files a good faith report of violation of law or regulations, abuse or neglect or exploitation of children. SDLC 27B-8-43 ☜ ; and 28-1-45.7 ☜ ; Employers of social workers, counselors or anyone else in a position to advise clients concerning abortion, are prohibited from retaliating against staff members for the advice they provide; SDCL 34-23A-11 ☜ ; Employers may not retaliate against any employee who brings charges or gives information against an employer or testifies on matters of sex discrimination in wages SDLC 60-12-21 ☜ ; Employers may not discharge employees in retaliation for filing a workers' compensation claim. SDLC § 62-1-16 ☜ .

Tennessee: Tennessee recognizes the cause of action for *retaliatory discharge* in cases where an employer discharges an employee *solely* for refusing to participate in or remain silent about *illegal activities* that are in violation of criminal or civil codes in the state or federal laws or any regulation that protects the public welfare, health or safety, but the statute applies to the state and public employees only (not private nonprofits). See Tenn. Code Annot. § 50-1-304 ☜ .

Texas: An employer commits an unfair labor practice if the employer discriminates or retaliates against a person who opposes a discriminatory practice, or makes or files a complaint, or testifies, assists or participates in any manner in an investigation of discrimination. Texas Labor Code § 21.055 ☜ . Additionally, health care facilities may not retaliate, discharge, suspend or otherwise discipline or discriminate against employees for reporting to their supervisor, the state or a law enforcement agency that their employer is in violation of a law a rule adopted under health and safety codes or the Board of Mental Health and Mental Retardation, or the Commission on Alcohol and Drug Abuse. Health care facilities must prominently **post** in English and a second language that staff are protected from discrimination or retaliation for reporting a violation of law. See Health & Safety Code § 161.134(a) and (j) and § 242.133.

Utah: Employers are prohibited under the Utah Occupational Safety and Health Act from discharging or discriminating against employees who file complaints or institute proceedings, or testify or exercise any rights under the Act. Utah Code § 34-6-203 ; The Utah Antidiscrimination Act prohibits employers from retaliating against an employee who opposes any illegal discrimination. See Utah Code § 34A-5-102(17) .

Vermont: The Vermont Healthcare Whistleblower's Protection Act 21 Vt. Stat. Ann. § 507 prohibits hospitals and nursing homes from retaliating against employees who report a violation of law, a medical error, or improper standard of patient care and also prohibits retaliation against employees for objecting to or refusing to participate in any activity, policy, or practice of the hospital or nursing home that the employee reasonably believes is in violation of the law or constitutes improper quality of patient care.

Virginia: Employers may not discharge or discriminate against employees who file safety complaints, testify or exercise their rights under safety and health provisions. See Va. Code 40.1-51.2.1

West Virginia: Employers may not retaliate or discriminate against employees who have opposed any practices or acts or unlawful discrimination or because they've filed a complaint, testified, or assisted in any proceeding concerning unlawful discrimination. West Virginia recognizes the public policy exception to employment-at-will; employers will be liable for wrongful discharge if their motivation for discipline or discipline is in violation of public policy. See W. Va. Code § 5-11-9 ; See *Kanagy v. Fiesta Salons Inc.*, 208 W. Va. 526, 541 S. E. 2d 616 (2000).

Wisconsin: Employers are prohibited from retaliation for the exercise of their rights under state and federal law, such as filing complaints of discrimination, attempting to enforce a right permitted by law, testifying or assisting in law enforcement actions under state labor law standards or laws, such as child labor, wage and hour claims and prevailing wage rate claims. Employees are protected if their employer takes an adverse employment action against them due to the belief (even if incorrect) that the employee had taken such action or exercised rights under law. Wis. Stats. §§ 111.31 et seq., ; (also retaliation prohibited against health care workers for filing reports of violations of health care standards) Wis. Stats. §146.997 (3) .

Wyoming: Employers are prohibited from discharging or discriminating against employees who report safety violations or participate in ISHA investigations. Wyo Stat. § 27-11-109 ; Wyoming recognizes the public policy exception to employment-at-will in the context of an employee who was discharged for exercising rights under the state workers' compensation law. See *Greiss v. Consol. Frieghtways Corp. of Delaware*, 882 F. 2d 461 (10th Cir. 1989).

Federal Law Whistleblower Protections

Federal law also protects whistleblowers from retaliation. The Anti-Competitiveness and Corporate Responsibility Act of 2002, better known as the Sarbanes-Oxley Act, includes a prohibition against retaliation in cases where an employee has reported wrongdoing. The whistleblower protection of Sarbanes-Oxley arose from a situation in which an employee raised concerns about accounting practices and was terminated as a result. As with many of the state whistleblower protection laws, Sarbanes-Oxley doesn't require that there actually be a violation of law or public policy—only that the whistleblower has a reasonable belief or suspicion of wrongdoing. Retaliation against an employee in violation of the Sarbanes Oxley Act can result in criminal penalties. Most of the provisions of the Sarbanes-Oxley Act only pertain to public companies, with two exceptions. One of the exceptions is the prohibition against retaliation. For more information about the Sarbanes–Oxley Act and how it impacts nonprofits, visit the Web site of The Independent Sector (www.independentsector.org/issues/sarbanesoxley.html).

Regardless of whether your state has its own whistleblower protection legislation, to ensure compliance with Sarbanes Oxley Act, *every nonprofit should have a written whistleblower protection policy*, and should raise awareness among board and staff through training on the policy that retaliation is prohibited. A suitable policy should identify someone or several people to whom complaints must be directed. It might be appropriate to designate a board member. Some nonprofits select someone outside the organization to serve as an independent ombudsman. Two sample whistleblower policies appear below. The first is a generic "employee protection" policy that could be adapted to meet the requirements of nonprofits in most states. The second complies with the special requirements of the Conscientious Employee Protection Act in New Jersey.

Whistleblower Policy for New Jersey Nonprofits
The New Jersey Conscientious Employee Protection Act Policy Statement*

If any employee reasonably believes that some policy, practice, or activity of NONPROFIT is in violation of law, a written complaint must be filed by that employee with the Executive Director or the Chairperson of the Board of Trustees.

NONPROFIT won't retaliate against an employee who, in good faith, has made a protest or raised a complaint against some practice of NONPROFIT or of an employee of NONPROFIT on the basis of a reasonable belief that the practice is in violation of law, or a clear mandate of public policy.

NONPROFIT will also not retaliate against employees who in good faith, have made a protest or raised a complaint against some practice of NONPROFIT, or of another individual or entity with whom NONPROFIT has a business relationship, on the basis of a reasonable belief that the practice is in violation of law, or a clear mandate of public policy.

NONPROFIT also won't retaliate against employees who disclose or threaten to disclose to a supervisor or a public body, any activity, policy, or practice of NONPROFIT that the employee reasonably believes is in violation of a law, or a rule, or regulation mandated pursuant to law or is in violation of a clear mandate or public policy concerning the health, safety, welfare, or protection of the environment.

Employees are protected from retaliation only if the employee brings the alleged unlawful activity, policy, or practice to the attention of NONPROFIT and provides NONPROFIT with a reasonable opportunity to investigate and correct the alleged unlawful activity.

*This sample policy was provided by the Pro Bono Partnership. For more information, visit *www.probonopartnership.org*.

Other Theories Creating an Exception to at-Will Employment

Covenant of Good Faith and Fair Dealing

This doctrine assumes that there is a *covenant* of good faith and fair dealing inherent in every employment relationship that would prohibit an employer from discharging an employee in bad faith. The vast majority of courts have rejected this type of claim.

The implied covenant of good faith and fair dealing has been interpreted to mean either that employment decisions are subject to a just-cause standard or that terminations motivated by malice or discrimination are prohibited. Courts rejecting the theory have held that it's too great an undertaking for courts to determine an employer's motive for terminating an employee. Other courts simply take the position that the implied covenant claim is nothing more than a thinly veiled effort to circumvent the at-will employment doctrine.

Whether or not your state recognizes a covenant of good faith and fair dealing, surely any nonprofit wants to deal fairly and decently with its employees. Consequently the lesson to be learned is that managing an employee's expectations is equally as important as treating them with respect and dignity. If the discharge takes the employee by surprise or feels *unfair*, there is a greater chance that an employee will bring a lawsuit. Even if the lawsuit is eventually rejected by a court, the harm will have already been done.

Detrimental Reliance

Detrimental reliance is a theory that permits a plaintiff to collect damages from someone who made a promise upon which the plaintiff relied to his detriment. Although successful claims of detrimental reliance are rare, a cause of action could be available to an employee where all of the following conditions are present:

❑ A promise of employment or continued employment is extended to an employee in unambiguous terms.

❑ It's foreseeable that the employee will rely on the promise.

❑ The employee in fact relies on the promise, and takes action that causes him expense or inconvenience as a result. *Example*: Bikes for Kids, located in San Francisco, avidly pursues, recruits and hires Eager Beaver to start work as Executive Director, on May 1. Eager resigns from his job, sells his home in Pennsylvania, and moves to San Francisco to start work. On May 2, Bikes for Kids decides they made a mistake, and Eager is terminated.

In such circumstances employees may be able to recover out-of-pocket costs caused by their reliance on assurances of employment made to them by their employer.

Tort theories

The least applied—and weakest—of the common-law exceptions to employment-at-will are the tort theories of intentional infliction of emotional distress and defamation. Note that volunteers can't generally rely on protection from state or federal laws that only protect *employees*, but they can successfully seek redress for a perceived wrong, such as a discharge, by pursuing a tort law claim. Although specific risk management issues relating to volunteers are beyond the scope of this text, the authors encourage nonprofit managers to take a risk management approach in forming and managing relationships with volunteers. It's prudent to review volunteer management policies and practices in the context of all the principles outlined here, and treat volunteer staff in some cases just as you would professional paid staff.

Intentional Infliction of Emotional Distress and Defamation

The tort of intentional infliction of emotional distress was created to compensate individuals who are victims of conduct deemed by society as extreme and outrageous. To succeed with this type of claim an employee must assert that the employer acted outrageously, causing the employee emotional distress. Similarly, to succeed with a defamation claim an employee must show that his employer knowingly communicated false information, intending to do the plaintiff harm. Both these claims are difficult to prove and may end up being dismissed, but if the facts warrant it, they're often tacked onto a lawsuit to give color to the allegations. Sadly, some of these legal maneuvers are justified by employers' callous approaches to terminating employees. *Lesson learned*: Treat employees with respect, even when they're being ushered out the door. When an employee is humiliated or yelled at during the termination process, or when the employee's belongings are thrown in a box that's left outside the door, a lawsuit should come as no surprise.

Why Put a Nonprofit's Employment Policies in Writing?

As discussed in the introduction, written policies and procedures are the starting point for defensible, consistently applied and ultimately effective employment practices in every nonprofit. There is no substitute for committing the organization's policies to writing. Written employment policies serve several important purposes:

❏ *Written policies ensure consistency.* They represent an effective way to communicate a common message to all employees. Each person receives the same written statement of policy. The organization can avoid the risk that various supervisors will interpret a policy differently, causing inequitable treatment of employees. Employees are likely to feel that they're being treated fairly if the same standards are applied consistently.

❏ *Written policies provide admissible evidence* of the nonprofit's business practices in the event that the organization needs to defend its practices in court or at an administrative hearing. Many employers have been held liable for unlawful employment practices when they were unable to prove that a policy or business practice existed. The absence of written policies leaves a nonprofit needlessly vulnerable to legal challenges.

❏ *Written policies establish the business-related reason for an employment action*, reducing the possibility that the employer's conduct will be challenged as subjective and discriminatory.

It's critical to establish a foundation for managing an employee's expectations. Written policies communicate expectations in ways that an employee orientation can't. There is no more important time to manage employees' expectations than during the early stages of the employment relationship. Establishing at-will employment in addition to expectations for professional dress, work hours and performance goals—should happen as soon as possible.

In Chapter 2 we will explore risks to be aware of, and risk management policies important for nonprofits to implement during the hiring process.

Chapter 2

Staffing the Nonprofit Workplace

The most obvious *legal* risk in hiring is illegal discrimination. There is another equally serious risk—that the wrong person will be hired. The second risk is actually more likely to occur than the first, and its practical ramifications more insidious. If a nonprofit makes a poor hiring decision, the organization will have to decide somewhere down the line whether to terminate the employee, or alternatively to invest significant time in counseling, training, and rehabilitating a *poor hire*. If the employee is terminated, another liability risk rears its head—the possibility of a lawsuit or administrative claim alleging wrongful discharge or discrimination. To avoid that risk, the nonprofit may decide to tough it out with the under-performing employee, not realizing that the nonprofit is then vulnerable to additional, equally serious risks: less efficient operations because of poor performance; damage to the morale of co-workers, to reputation, client relations, or relationships with funders; and in the worst cases, physical injury to clients or third parties caused by the ill-chosen employee. Consequently, successful hiring decisions are critically important. In this chapter of *Taking the High Road,* we'll explore the risk management strategies that can reduce the risk of making a poor hiring decision and minimize a nonprofit's liability for the staffing choices that must be made during any hiring process.

Avoiding Discrimination in Hiring

The federal law that protects employees from most forms of illegal discrimination is Title VII of the Civil Rights Act of 1964 known as, Title VII ✎ . There are actually a host of laws which together make up the federal civil rights protections we know today. Title VII prohibits discrimination in employment on the basis of race, color, religion, sex, and national origin. There are additional federal laws that protect employees and applicants based on age, disability, pregnancy and veteran status, to name just a few. Each state has its own anti-discrimination laws. In some cases, the state laws provide more protection than the federal laws.

Federal Law Prohibitions Against Discrimination

The following federal laws in conjunction with Title VII prohibit discrimination in employment (or any employment decision) on the basis of age, sex, religion, race, color, national origin, pregnancy, disability or the appearance of disability and veteran status: The Americans with Disabilities Act (ADA), the Age Discrimination in Employment Act (ADEA), the Pregnancy Discrimination Act (PDA), the Equal Pay Act, and the Employee Retirement Income Security Act (ERISA) plus the Immigration Reform and Control Act (IRC), Executive Orders and regulations impacting government contractors, These federal laws prohibit discrimination, reverse discrimination and retaliation. Here's a summary of the most applicable federal laws and their protections:

Title VII of the Civil Rights Act of 1964 ✎
(Applies to employers of 15 or more employees)

Title VII makes it illegal to base employment decisions, such as hiring, promotions, demotions, pay practices, and terminations, on the characteristics of race, color, religion, sex (*sex* includes the prohibition against sexual harassment), and national origin; also prohibits harassment against an employee because of these characteristics.

Age Discrimination in Employment Act ✎
(Applies to employers of 20 or more employees)

The ADEA protects employees age 40 years of age or older from discrimination in employment. The *Older Worker Benefits Protection Act (OWBPA)* amended the ADEA to specifically make it illegal for employers to use an employee's age as a basis for discrimination in benefits (including health, and life insurance and severance pay) and retirement. As with the ADEA, OWBPA only protects people 40 years and older.

Americans with Disabilities Act of 1990
(Applies to employers of 15 or more employees)

The ADA prohibits discrimination against qualified individuals with a disability (those who with or without accommodation are capable of performing the essential functions of the position). Those who are protected include: currently disabled individuals, persons having a record of impairment, persons who are perceived as having impairment or those who are related to or associated with persons who are disabled/perceived as disabled.

Pregnancy Discrimination Act of 1978
(Applies to employers of 15 or more employees)

The PDA defines sex discrimination under Title VII as including childbirth, pregnancy and related conditions, and makes it illegal to refuse to hire on the basis of pregnancy. There may be exceptions, such as when the employee is immediately unavailable, for example. hiring an accountant during tax season who is unavailable in April. The PDA doesn't bar employers from requiring pregnant employees to meet objective standards of performance as long as those expectations and policies are applied equally to other employees.

Equal Pay Act

The Equal Pay Act prohibits paying different compensation to men and women for similar jobs, unless based on a *reasonable factor other than sex.*

Employee Retirement Income Security Act (ERISA)

The law known as ERISA regulates pension plans and also prohibits discrimination in order to avoid paying benefits, for example, discharging an employee just before his pension vests.

Immigration Reform and Control Act of 1986 (IRCA)

The IRCA prohibits discrimination in hiring based on citizenship, national origin, language spoken, or appearance as a non-American citizen.

Uniformed Services Employment and Reemployment Rights Act (USERRA)

The USERRA prohibits workplace discrimination against individuals because of their service in the Armed Forces, the Reserves, the National Guard or other uniformed services. USERRA prohibits an employer from denying any benefit of employment on the basis of an individual's membership, application for membership, performance of service, application for service or obligation for service in the uniformed services. A poster explaining employees' rights under USERRA must be displayed at the workplace, whether or not any employee is currently serving in the military. The poster may be downloaded from the DOL Web site: www.dol.gov/vets/programs/userra/USERRA_Private.pdf#Non-Federal.

Special Laws for Government Contractors

Nonprofits that receive federal funding, or state funding through federal programs, are generally subject to special nondiscrimination obligations that require government contractors to refrain from discrimination and in some cases to implement affirmative action programs.

Executive Order 11246

(Applies to federal contractors and subcontractors with contracts over $10,000; employers with 50 or more employees and at least $50,000 in contracts.) This Executive Order requires federal contractors and subcontractors to adhere to equal employment opportunity clauses incorporated into all government contracts. Employers with 50 or more employees and contracts exceeding $50,000 must:

❏ develop a written affirmative action compliance program;

❏ refrain from discriminating against employees or applicants on the basis of race, national origin, color, religion or sex; and

❏ take affirmative action to employ and advance qualified minorities and women.

The Rehabilitation Act of 1973 ✐
(Applies to government contractors and subcontractors with contracts over $10,000.)

Requires federal contractors and subcontractors to take affirmative action with respect to qualified individuals with disabilities, and refrain from discriminating against disabled individuals. Employers must:

❑ develop a written affirmative action compliance program which includes hiring goals and timetables;

❑ refrain from discriminating against employees or applicants on the basis of disability; and

❑ take affirmative action to employ and advance qualified individuals with disabilities.

Vietnam Era Readjustment Assistance Act of 1974 ✐
(Applies to government contractors and subcontractors with contracts over $25,000)

Requires covered federal government contractors and subcontractors to take affirmative action to employ and advance in employment specified categories of veterans protected by the act and prohibits discrimination against such veterans.

State Anti-Discrimination Laws

All 50 states[2] have laws prohibiting discrimination in some form in the workplace. Many of the state laws are more extensive in their coverage than the federal anti-discrimination laws. Additionally, many of the state laws apply to employers with fewer than 15 employees, which means that for smaller nonprofits, awareness of your state anti-discrimination laws is crucial. Be aware that these state laws are subject to constant review and revision in state legislatures. Therefore, this text should be used for reference purposes, rather than as a definitive guide. In many states, religious institutions and charitable and educational institutions controlled by or affiliated with religious institutions are exempt or partially exempt. Special attention should be given to the categories that are highlighted in boldface. These are protections afforded by specific state laws that are broader than those afforded under parallel federal laws.

Summary of State Anti-Discrimination Laws

The state laws noted here are subject to periodic review and revision in state legislatures. This summary should therefore be used for reference purposes, rather than as a definitive guide.

Alabama: The only protected category of discrimination that's prohibited by state statute is age. See Code of Alabama, Industrial Relations and Labor Title 25-1-22. ✐

Alaska: The Alaska Human Rights Law generally covers employers with one (1) or more employees, *but nonprofit, "fraternal, charitable, educational, or religious associations or corporations" are excluded from coverage.* See Alaska Stat. §18.80.300. ✐

Private employers may not discriminate in employment on the basis of race, religion, national origin, color, age, physical or mental disability, sex, **marital status, changes in marital status**, pregnancy, or **parenthood**, when the "reasonable demands of the position don't require distinction on those grounds."

Arizona: The Arizona Civil Rights Act applies to employers with 15 or more employees in each of 20 calendar weeks of the year and prohibits employment discrimination against any individual on the basis of race, color, religion, sex, age, disability or national origin. The act doesn't prohibit employers from giving preferential treatment to Native Americans because the individual is a Native American living in or on a reservation. The law doesn't forbid discrimination on the basis of religion, sex, age, or national origin *when it's a bona fide occupational qualification.* See Ariz. Rev. Stat. Ann. § 41-1463 et seq. ✐

Arkansas: The Arkansas Civil Rights Act of 1993 applies to employers with 9+ employees for at least 20 weeks in the year, and prohibits employment discrimination on the basis of race, religion, national origin, gender, (includes pregnancy, childbirth, or related medical conditions) or the presence of any sensory, mental, or physical disability. See Ark. Stat. Ann. § 11-4-601. ✐

> ### State Anti-Discrimination Laws Often Provide Broader Protection
>
> In most states, state-specific laws have expanded the federal civil rights' protections by specifying that *marital status* is a protected category, and that *sexual preference or sexual orientation* is also protected. Some state laws specifically prohibit sexual harassment. While the federal law only protects employees age 40 or older, in many states the definition of the protected category for age discrimination is persons age 18 or older. Other states specifically protect smokers and nonsmokers from discrimination in employment, while still others prohibit discrimination on the basis of the employee's lawful use of alcohol and tobacco while off-duty and off-site. In New Jersey, the law has been interpreted to prohibit reverse age discrimination. Consequently, you should be familiar with the applicable laws in your state and municipality and recognize that those laws may expand or redefine the federal definition of *protected class*.

---

2 Alabama and Mississippi don't have comprehensive anti-discrimination laws governing private employees. Alabama's law only applies to employers that receive state funding and only addresses disability discrimination; Mississippi's anti-discrimination law only applies to public employees.

California: The California Fair Employment and Housing Act applies to employers with five (5) or more employees and prohibits employment discrimination on the basis of race, religion, creed, color, national origin, **ancestry**, physical handicap, (employers with 15 or more employees), **medical condition, marital status**, sex, **sexual orientation**, pregnancy, or age (40 or older). Other prohibitions: sexual harassment, and **forbidding an employee to wear pants on account of sex**. Note that a 2004 California state law ☞ requires employers to offer **sexual harassment training** to all supervisory employees and independent contractors every two years. See Cal. Gov't. Code §§ 12900 et seq.[3] ☞

Colorado: The Colorado Anti Discrimination Act of 1957, as amended prohibits private employers with two+ employees from discrimination in employment on the basis of disability, race, religion, color, sex, age, national origin, **ancestry, marital status**, or pregnancy. Colo. Rev. Stat. §§ 24-34-301 et seq. ☞ . Note that under Colorado law, "harassment isn't an illegal act unless a complaint is filed with the appropriate authority at the complainant's workplace and such authority fails to initiate a reasonable investigation of a complaint and take prompt remedial action if appropriate." See Colo. Rev. Stat. § 24-34-402.

Connecticut: The Connecticut Fair Employment Practices Act prohibits employers with three (3) or more employees from discrimination on the basis of race, color, religious creed, age (up to age 70), sex (including **sexual orientation**, sexual harassment, pregnancy, **child bearing capacity, sterilization, fertility, and related medical conditions**), **marital status**, national origin, **ancestry**, present or past history of mental disability, mental retardation, **learning disability**, physical disability, including blindness, and **previous arrest or conviction records**. See Conn. Gen. Stat. §§ 46a-51 et seq. ☞

Delaware: The Delaware Fair Employment Practices Act prohibits employers with four (4) or more employees from discrimination on the basis of race, **marital status, genetic information**, color, age (up to age 70), religion, sex, or national origin. A separate statute prohibits discrimination on the basis of disability and another prohibits the state from giving funds to employers which discriminate on the basis of sex. See Del. Code Ann. tit. 19 §§ 710 et seq. ☞

District of Columbia: The District of Columbia's Human Rights Act applies to all employers and prohibits employment discrimination on the basis of race, color, religion, national origin, sex, age (18 or older), **marital status, personal appearance, sexual orientation, family responsibilities**, pregnancy, (childbirth or related medical conditions) handicap, **matriculation** or **political affiliation**—unless the employer can demonstrate a "business necessity." Employers are also required to give reasonable time off for religious accommodation. See D.C. Code §§ 1-2501 et seq. ☞

Florida: The Florida Civil Rights Act, Fla. Stat. Ann. § 760.01 et seq. ☞ prohibits employers with 15 or more employees from discrimination against any individual because of race, color, religion, sex, national origin, age, handicap, or **marital status**. A separate law prohibits discrimination against individuals who have the sickle cell trait. Fla. Stat. Ann. §§ 448.075 ☞ ; *Note:* In Florida, the State Attorney General can bring an action against an employer for discrimination in a place of public accommodation.

Georgia: The Georgia Fair Employment Practices Act only applies to **public employers** (not private nonprofits) and prohibits employment discrimination on the basis of race, color, religion, national origin, age (ages 40 through 70), sex, and handicap. Ga. Code. Ann. Sections 45-19-20; A separate law, the Georgia Equal Employment for Persons With Disabilities Code, Ga. Code Ann. § 34-6A-1 to 6 ☞ bars discrimination against any person with a disability that doesn't restrict that person's ability to perform the job in question.

Hawaii: The Hawaii Fair Employment Law applies to all employers and prohibits employment discrimination on the basis of race, sex (includes pregnancy, childbirth and related conditions), age, religion, color, **ancestry** ☞ , **sexual orientation**, disability, **marital status**, or **arrest and court records**. See Haw. Rev. Stat. §§ 378 et seq. ☞

Idaho: The Idaho Human Rights Act, Idaho Code §§ 67-5901 et seq. ☞ (applies to employers with 5+ employees) and the Idaho Civil Rights Act, Idaho Code §§18-7301 et seq., ☞ (applies to all employers) together prohibit employment discrimination on the basis of race, color, religion, national origin, handicap, association with persons with disabilities, sex, (includes pregnancy) or age (40 or older).

Illinois: The Illinois Human Rights Act applies to employers with 15 or more employees for 20 or more calendar weeks in the year, and prohibits employment discrimination on the basis of race, color, religion, national origin, **ancestry**, citizenship status, pregnancy, **arrest record**, age (40 or older), sex, **sexual orientation**, handicap, **marital status**, or **unfavorable discharge from the military**. Illinois Human Rights Act, 775 ILCS 5/1-101 ☞ . A recent amendment makes it illegal to discriminate against individuals on the basis of **sexual orientation**, defined as "actual or perceived heterosexuality, homosexuality, bisexuality, or gender-related identity, whether or not traditionally associated with the person's designated sex at birth." Additionally, sexual harassment is prohibited.

The Right to Privacy in the Workplace Act prohibits discrimination against employee for the use of lawful products off-premises during nonworking hours. See Ill. Rev. Stat. ch. 68 Sections 1-101-1-103. ☞

---

3 As of January 1, 2006, all California employers with 50 or more employees or contractors have been required to provide training for all supervisors within six months of their hiring, consisting of at least two hours of classroom or other effective interactive training regarding sexual harassment by a person with expertise and knowledge in this area. The training must include practical guidance and examples regarding state and federal laws, including identifying, preventing and correcting sexual harassment, discrimination and retaliation and the remedies available to victims of such behavior. The training doesn't have to be completed in two consecutive hours. For more information, see the text of the regulations, modified 6/20/06: www.fehc.ca.gov/pdf/modified_6-20-06.pdf.

Note: The Illinois Attorney General is empowered to bring a lawsuit against an employer when the attorney general finds a "pattern or practice" of discrimination at the workplace.

Indiana: The Indiana Civil Rights Law applies to employers with six (6) or more employees and prohibits employment discrimination on the basis of race, religion, color, sex, handicap, national origin, or **ancestry**. State law also prohibits discrimination in employment on the basis of age (40 through 70), and **prohibits discrimination against smokers**. See Ind. Code. Ann. §§ 22-9-1-1 et seq.

Iowa: The Iowa Civil Rights Act applies to employers with four (4) or more employees, and prohibits discrimination in employment on the basis of age (**18 or older)**, race, pregnancy, creed, color, sex, national origin, religion, or disability (including AIDS). See Iowa Code. Ann. §§ 216.6.

Kansas: The Kansas Act Against Discrimination applies to employers with four (4) or more employees and prohibits discrimination in employment on the basis of race, religion, color, sex, disability, national origin, or **ancestry**. The Kansas Age Discrimination in Employment Act prohibits discrimination against **persons age 18 or older**. See Kan. Stat. Ann. §§ 44-1001 et seq.

Kentucky: The Kentucky Civil Rights Act applies to employers with eight (8) or more employees in each of 20 calendar weeks of the year, and prohibits discrimination in employment on the basis of race, color, religion, national origin, sex, pregnancy, age (40 or older), or disability (applies to employers with 15+ employees), including AIDS, or **because the individual is a smoker or non-smoker**. Kentucky has a state law similar to Executive Order 11246, prohibiting the state from contracting with any employer which discriminates on the basis of race, color, sex, age, religion, or national origin. A separate statute prohibits discrimination on the basis of physical handicap. In Kentucky, **it's illegal to request that employees waive their rights under state or federal laws, nor may employers demand that employees agree to arbitrate possible claims rather than litigate those claims under state or federal law**. See Ky. Rev. Stat. Ann. §§ 344.010 et seq.

Louisiana: The Louisiana Fair Employment Practices Law applies to employers with 20 or more employees in each of 20 calendar weeks of the year, and prohibits discrimination in employment on the basis of race, color, religion, creed, age, disability, sex (including pregnancy), or national origin. See La. Rev. Stat. § 23:301.

Separate state laws also prohibit discrimination on the basis of **smoking**, La. Rev. Stat. § 23:966 **pregnancy, childbirth and related conditions**, (applies to employers with 25+ employees) La. Rev. Stat. Ann. § 23:342 or because an individual has the **sickle cell trait**, La. Rev. Stat. Ann. § 23:352 ; or on the basis of **genetic information** or the fact that the employee has requested genetic information. See La. Rev. Stat. Ann. § 23:368.

Maine: The Maine Human Rights Act applies to all employers and prohibits discrimination in employment on the basis of race, color, sex, **gender identity**, physical or mental disability, religion, **ancestry**, national origin, pregnancy, or age. Me. Rev. Stat. Ann. tit. 5, §§ 4684 et seq. ; Maine has a state regulation, similar to Executive Order 11246 requiring that all contracts with the state include a provision prohibiting employment discrimination on the basis of race, color, religious creed, sex, national origin, **ancestry**, age, or handicap.

Maryland: The Maryland Fair Employment Practices Act applies to employers with 15+ employees in 20 or more calendar weeks of the year and prohibits discrimination in employment on the basis of race, color, religion, sex, pregnancy, age, national origin, **ancestry, familial status, marital status, sexual orientation, genetic testing**, or physical or mental disability. See Md. Ann Code art. 49B, §§ 1-30.

Massachusetts: The Massachusetts Fair Employment Practices Act applies to employers with six (6) or more employees and prohibits discrimination in employment on the basis of race, color, religious creed, national origin, **ancestry**, age, sex, pregnancy, **sexual orientation, veteran status, results of genetic testing**, or physical or mental handicap. A separate statute prohibits discrimination in employment against persons aged 40 or older. See Mass. Gen. Laws c. 151B 4(1) et seq.

Michigan: The Michigan Civil Rights Act applies to all employers and prohibits discrimination in employment on the basis of religion, race, color, national origin, **ancestry**, age, sex, **sexual orientation**, pregnancy, **height, weight, familial or marital status or genetic information that's unrelated to ability to perform the job**. See Mich. Comp. Laws Ann. § 37.2101 et seq.

A separate law, The Persons with Disabilities Civil Rights Act (PDCRA) requires employers to accommodate applicants and employees with disabilities unless the employer can show that the accommodation would impose an undue hardship. See Mich. Comp. Laws § 37.2202.

Minnesota: The Minnesota Human Rights Act, Minn. Stat. Ann. Section 363.01 et seq. applies to all employers and prohibits employment discrimination on the basis of race, color, creed, religion, **ancestry**, national origin, sex, **sexual orientation**, pregnancy, **marital status, status with regard to public assistance**, disability, age, or **membership or activity in a local commission**.

A separate state law similar to Executive Order 11246 prohibits employment discrimination by contractors on the basis of race, color, or creed. Another law prohibits discrimination in hiring on the basis of the **off-duty use of lawful consumable products, including food, alcoholic and nonalcoholic beverages and tobacco**.

Mississippi: Mississippi employers may not discriminate against any person on the basis of past or present participation in the military. See Miss. Code. Ann. § 33-1-15.

There is no other anti-discrimination law applicable to private employers other than a law which imposes a $250 fine on employers that unlawfully interfere "with the social, civil, or political rights of any of its employees or agents." See Miss. Code Ann. § 79-1-9.

Mississippi has no comprehensive Fair Employment Practice Act. Therefore, nonprofits in Mississippi which have more than 15 employees are governed only by Title VII and other federal laws. Mississippi also has a separate law which prohibits discrimination against **smokers**.

Missouri: The Missouri Human Rights Act applies to employers with six (6) or more employees and prohibits employment discrimination on the basis of race, color, creed, religion, national origin, sex, **ancestry**, age, or handicap, including AIDS or AIDS-related illnesses or the **lawful use of tobacco, or alcohol products off the employer's premises during non-working hours**. Mo. Rev. Stat. §§ 213.010 et seq. ; Missouri has a separate law that makes it illegal to discriminate against anyone who tests positive for AIDS/HIV. See Mo. Rev. Stat. §191.665(1).

Montana: The Montana Human Rights Act doesn't apply to charitable nonprofit corporations, but normally applies to employers with one or more employees and prohibits employment discrimination on the basis of race, creed, religion, color, national origin, age, physical or mental handicap, **ancestry, marital status**, sex, or pregnancy. Mont. Code Ann § 49 ch 2 ; **A separate law** prohibits discrimination based on the use of lawful products during nonworking hours. See Mont. Code Ann. § 39-2-313.

Nebraska: The Nebraska Fair Employment Practices Act applies to employers with 15+ employees in each of 20 calendar weeks and prohibits employment discrimination on the basis of race, color, religion, sex, pregnancy, disability, **marital status**, or national origin. Neb. Rev. Stat. §§ 48-1101 et seq. ; It's illegal in Nebraska to advertise for a job opening indicating a preference in hiring that discriminates against any of the categories above. Neb. Rev. Stat. § 48-1101 ; A separate law prohibits discrimination on the basis of **AIDS**. See Neb. Rev. Stat. § 20-168, 169 , and age.

Nevada: The Nevada Fair Employment Practices Act applies to employers with 15+ employees and prohibits employment discrimination on the basis of race, color, religion, sex, pregnancy, age (40 or older), disability, or national origin. Nev. Rev. Stat. §§ 613 et seq. ; (The prohibitions of the act don't apply if the employer is located on or near an Indian reservation and has announced a policy to give preferential treatment to Native Americans living on or near a reservation.) The Nevada law's requirements don't explicitly require employers to make accommodations for religious beliefs or observances. See *Balint v. Carson City, Nevada* 180 F. 3d 1047 (9th Cir. 1999).

New Hampshire: The New Hampshire Law Against Discrimination *doesn't apply to nonprofit charitable, educational, or religious corporations*. Otherwise the state law applies to employers with six (6) or more employees and prohibits employment discrimination on the basis of sex, **and sexual orientation**, age (18 or older), pregnancy, race, color, **marital status**, physical and mental disability, religious creed, or national origin. The statute also prohibits sexual harassment. See N.H. Stat. Ann. §§ 354-A:1 et seq.

New Jersey: The New Jersey Law Against Discrimination applies to all employers and prohibits employment discrimination on the basis of race, creed, color, religion, national origin, **ancestry,** age (over 18), disability, **marital status, military status,** sex, **affectional or sexual orientation, atypical hereditary cellular blood traits**, or handicap. New Jersey Stat. Ann. §§ 10.5-1 et seq. ; A separate law also prohibits discrimination against **smokers and nonsmokers.** See New Jersey Statutes Ann. § 34:6B-1.

New Mexico: The New Mexico Human Rights Act, N. M. Stat. Ann. §§ 28-1-7 (a) et seq. applies to employers with four (4) or more employees and extend protections against discriminations on the basis of: age, race, color, national origin, **ancestry, religion,** sex, physical or mental handicap or serious medical condition; for employers with 50 or more employees, spousal affiliation is a protected category, and for employers with 15 or more employees, **sexual orientation and gender identity** is a protected category. A separate law prohibits discrimination against **smokers**. See New Mexico Stat. Ann. §§ 50-11-3.

New York: The New York Human Rights Law applies to employers with 4+ or more employees, and prohibits employment discrimination on the basis of age (18 or older), race, creed, color, national origin, **religion,** sex, **sexual orientation**, pregnancy, disability, **genetic predisposition, or carry status, military** or **marital status,** or **certain criminal offenses or lawful off-duty conduct.** New York Human Rights Law, Art. 15, §§ 296 et seq. ; New York City law prohibits employers from discriminating based on actual **or perceived** age, race, creed, color, national origin, or **ancestry, religion,** sex, disability, marital status, **military status, sexual orientation**, or **citizenship** status; also **real or perceived status as a victim of sexual assault or domestic violence.** See NYC Admin. Code § 8-107(1).

> **New York City:** The law also requires employers in New York City to make accommodations for such victims in the implementation of leave of absence policies.

North Carolina: The North Carolina Equal Employment Practices Act applies to employers with 15+ or more employees and states that discrimination on the basis of race, religion, color, national origin, age, sex, or handicap is contrary to public policy. Separate laws prohibit discrimination against qualified individuals with a handicap. N.C. Gen. Stat. §168A-1 ; and on the basis of **AIDS, HIV infection, the sickle cell trait**. See N.C. Gen. Stat. § 95-281 and of **genetic testing** N.C. Gen. Stat. § 95-28.1A.

North Dakota: The North Dakota Human Rights Act applies to all employers and prohibits discrimination on the basis of race, color, religion, sex (including pregnancy, childbirth and related conditions), national origin, age (40 or older), mental or physical disabilities, **marital status, or status as to public assistance or participation in lawful activities during nonwork hours that don't conflict with essential business interests of the employer.** See N.D. Cent. Code §§ 14-02.4-01 et seq.

Ohio: The Ohio Fair Employment Practices Law applies to employers with 4+ employees and prohibits employment discrimination on the basis of race, color, religion, sex, pregnancy, national origin, handicap, age, or **ancestry**. See Ohio Rev. Code Ann. § 4112.02 et seq.

Oklahoma: The Oklahoma Civil Rights Act applies to employers with 15+ or more employees in each of 20 weeks during the calendar year, and prohibits employment discrimination on the basis of sex, race, color, religion, national origin, age (40 or older), or disability "unless such action is related to a bona fide occupational qualification, reasonably necessary to the normal operation of the employer's business or enterprise." See Okla. Stat. Ann. tit. 25 § 1303.

Oregon: The Oregon Fair Employment Practices Act applies to all employers and prohibits employment discrimination on the basis of race, religion, color, sex, pregnancy, **childbirth, related medical conditions, expunged juvenile records,** national origin, **ancestry, marital status,** age (18 or older), or **personal association with protected group members, or for having reported violations of the state public health law, testified before the legislature or filed workers' compensation claims.** The law also prohibits discrimination based on physical or mental handicap, **nepotism, and the use of tobacco products off-duty**. See Or. Rev. Stat. §§ 659.010 et seq.

Pennsylvania: The Pennsylvania Human Relations Act applies to employers with four (4) or more employees (and applies to independent contractors) and prohibits employment discrimination on the basis of race, color, religious creed, **ancestry**, age, sex, pregnancy, national origin, disability, **high school equivalency certification, or opposition to abortion or sterilization**. See Pa. Stat. Ann. tit. 43, §§ 951 et seq. ; The City of Philadelphia Fair Practices Code prohibits employment discrimination based on **sexual orientation/gender identity,** as well as race, religion, sex, national origin, or ancestry.

Rhode Island: The Rhode Island Fair Employment Practice Act applies to employers with four (4) or more employees and prohibits employment discrimination on the basis of race, age (40 or older), color, religion, sex, **sexual orientation**, **gender identity or expression, disability,** or **country of ancestral origin**. See R.I. Gen. Laws §§ 28-5-1 et seq.

South Carolina: The South Carolina Human Rights Affairs Law applies to employers with 15+ employees in each of 20 or more calendar weeks and prohibits employment discrimination on the basis of race, religion, color, sex, (including pregnancy, childbirth and related conditions), age (40 or older), national origin and disability. S.C. Code Ann. §§ 1-13-10 et seq. A separate law prohibits discrimination based on the **use of tobacco outside of the workplace**. See S.C. Code Ann. § 41-1-85

South Dakota: The South Dakota Human Relations Act applies to all employers and prohibits employment discrimination on the basis of race, color, creed, religion, sex, **ancestry,** disability, **specifically including blindness or partial blindness,** or national origin. See S.D. Codified Laws Ann. § 20-13-10

Tennessee: The Tennessee Human Rights Act, Tenn. Code Ann. § 4-21-101 et seq. applies to employers with 8+ employees and prohibits employment discrimination on the basis of race, creed, color, religion, sex, age (over 40), national origin, and **ancestry**. Sexual harassment is prohibited in the workplace. Also it's a crime to intimidate or harass a person based on race, color, ancestry, religion or national origin. See Tenn. Code Annot. § 39-17-309.

Texas: The Texas Commission on Human Rights applies to employers with 15+ employees in each of 20 or more calendar weeks and prohibits employment discrimination on the basis of race, color, creed, disability, religion, sex (pregnancy, childbirth and related conditions), national origin, age (40 or older), or disability. See Tex. Lab. Code Ann. § 21-051, 21.101, 21.105, 21.106, 21.108, 21.110.

Utah: The Utah Anti-Discrimination Act applies to employers with 15+ employees in each of 20 calendar weeks and prohibits employment discrimination on the basis of race, color, sex (pregnancy, childbirth, and related conditions), age (40 or older), religion, national origin, or disability. *The state statute specifically defines who is "qualified" for a position: one who "possesses the education, training, ability, moral character, integrity, disposition to work, adherence to reasonable rules and regulations, and other qualifications required by an employer for any particular job, job classification, or position to be filled."* See Utah Code Ann. §§ 34A-5-102, 106 et seq.

Vermont: The Vermont Fair Employment Practices Act applies to all employers and prohibits employment discrimination on the basis of race, color, religion, national origin, sex, **sexual orientation, ancestry, place of birth**, age (18 or older), **AIDS,** or **physical or mental conditions.** Sexual harassment is prohibited in the workplace. Vt. Stat. Ann. Tit. 21 §§ 495-520(d)

Virginia: The Virginia Human Rights Act applies to all employers and prohibits employment discrimination on the basis of race, color, religion, national origin, sex (includes pregnancy, childbirth and related medical conditions), age, **marital status,** or disability.

Contractors with the state government in excess of $10,000 may not discriminate on the basis of race, religion, color, sex, or national origin, unless those categories are bona fide occupational qualifications. Va. Code. Ann. §§ 2.2-3900 et seq.

Washington: The Washington Law Against Discrimination applies to employers with eight (8) or more employees[4] and prohibits employment discrimination on the basis of race, creed, color, national origin, **ancestry**, sex, pregnancy, **marital status**, age (40 or older), **sensory,** mental or physical disability, **use of a trained guide dog by a person with a disability,** or **arrest or conviction record**. A separate regulation prohibits discrimination on the basis of **HIV infection unless the absence of HIV infection is a bona fide occupational qualification for the job in question**. Wash. Rev. Code §§ 49.60.180. Discrimination against independent contractors is covered under a separate provision.

West Virginia: The West Virginia Human Rights Act applies to employers with 12 or more employees and prohibits employment discrimination on the basis of race, religion, color, national origin, **ancestry**, sex, pregnancy, age (40 or older), **blindness,** or handicap. A separate law prohibits discrimination against applicants and employees who **use tobacco products off the employer's premises during nonworking hours**. W. Va. Code §§ 5-11-1 to 5-11-19

Wisconsin: The Wisconsin Fair Employment Act applies to all employers and prohibits employment discrimination on the basis of age (40 or older), creed, race, color, handicap, sex (including sexual harassment), pregnancy, **marital status,** national origin, **arrest or conviction record, ancestry, sexual orientation, membership in the military** or **genetic testing**. A separate state law parallel to Executive Order 11246 prohibits employers receiving state funds from discriminating on the basis of age, race, religion, color, handicap, **physical condition, developmental disability**, national origin, and engaging in **off-duty use of lawful products**. Wis. Stat. Ann. §§ 111.31.1 et seq.

Wyoming: The Wyoming Fair Employment Practices Act applies to employers with two (2) or more employees and prohibits employment discrimination on the basis of age (40 through 70), sex, race, creed, color, national origin, **ancestry**, or handicap or based on the **use or non-use of tobacco products outside of the course of employment**. Wyo. Stat. 27-9-101 to 27-9-108

A Word About Independent Contractors and Consultants

While independent contractors or consultants aren't employees, and should be classified differently from employees, several states have determined that the states' **anti-discrimination laws** also protect independent workers. States that have extended the protection of anti-discrimination laws to independent workers include: New Jersey, Pennsylvania, Washington State, and others. In direct contrast, some states specifically don't extend protection from discrimination in employment to independent contractors, for example, California.

Fourteen states have determined that the engagement of independent workers **must be reported** to the state Department of Labor in accordance with the state's **new hire reporting procedures**. Violation in some states will incur a penalty of $25 per employee or contractor who isn't reported; many states have no penalty at all. States where employers are required to report newly engaged contractors include: Alabama, Alaska, California (if the contractor is paid over $600), Connecticut (if the contractor is paid over $5,000), Iowa (under certain conditions), Massachusetts (if the contractor is paid over $600), Mississippi, New Hampshire, Nevada, New Jersey (under certain conditions), Ohio, Tennessee, Texas, and Washington.

What's different about the treatment of independent contractors? Contractors or consultants are independent workers. They aren't employees, thus they shouldn't receive a W-2. Instead, assuming they earn compensation in excess of $600 annually, the nonprofit should issue an IRS Form 1099 to the independent worker. Because they aren't employees the nonprofit doesn't have the obligation to withhold taxes from earnings (for example, FICA, social security contributions and state payroll taxes).

❑ In most states independent workers aren't covered by workers' compensation insurance. They should be clearly informed that they're responsible for their own insurance coverage so that they don't claim they **are** employees in order to have insurance coverage when they're injured on the job.

❑ It's very important for the nonprofit to insist on a written agreement with the independent worker before the start of assignment. The agreement outlines the nature of work to be performed, and addresses the factors that distinguish the worker from an employee of the nonprofit.

---

4 In 2000, the Washington Supreme Court gave employees of small employers that would normally be exempt from the state's Law Against Discrimination, a right to sue for discrimination based on sex and other protected classifications. The case opened the door for employees at organizations with fewer than eight employees to bring claims for wrongful termination in violation of public policy, effectively exposing **every employer** in Washington to risk of discrimination claims based on common law. *Roberts v. Dudley*, 140 Wn.2d 58, 993 P.2d 901 (2000).

❏ Finally, the compensation of the independent worker should be reviewed either by the board of directors, or by senior management, in a documented process that concludes that the compensation to the contractor for the work performed is reasonable for the services rendered.

❏ As with any vendor providing services to the nonprofit, when the consultant or independent contractor is a board member or an immediate family member of a board member, there can be an appearance of undue influence/conflict of interest. Consequently, it's especially critical for the nonprofit's policy on conflict of interest to be activated and followed when considering the engagement of any contractor or consultant who has a relationship (business or personal) to a board or staff member.

Best Practices in Hiring and Employment Practices

The Equal Employment Opportunity Commission (EEOC) is the enforcement body that will challenge an employer's hiring or employment practices when a discrimination complaint is lodged by an employee, a former employee or an applicant. The EEOC is also in the business of helping employers *avoid* acting in a discriminatory manner. In this way, the EEOC can be seen as a nonprofit's risk management partner. Guidelines and fact sheets published by the Department of Labor and available on the EEOC's Web site are very helpful. Among the most helpful information recently made available is the EEOC's 2006 Compliance Manual ✍ (April 2006) that describes common pitfalls and best practices for employers striving to avoid discriminatory practices.

The 2006 Compliance Manual provides a list of the following best practices:

❏ Develop a strong Equal Employment Opportunity policy that's championed by senior management.

❏ Train all supervisors and senior staff on the policy.

❏ Enforce the policy and hold supervisors accountable for enforcement.

❏ Make employment decisions in a transparent manner and document them.

❏ Recruit, hire and promote with equal employment opportunity in mind and implement practices that widen and diversify the pool of applicants.

❏ Monitor equal employment opportunity by conducting self-assessments.

❏ Create objective, job-related qualification standards for each position.

❏ Identify and remove barriers to equal employment opportunity, such as word-of-mouth recruiting in nondiverse workplaces.

❏ Monitor hiring, compensation and performance appraisals for patterns of potential discrimination or apparent discriminatory practices.

❏ Provide training and professional development opportunities to encourage staff members' growth in their positions and opportunities for advancement.

❏ Promote a culture of diversity and inclusiveness.

❏ Encourage open communication and dispute resolutions.

❏ Prohibit retaliation and make every employee aware of the policy.

The most significant recent change in civil rights enforcement is reflected in the EEOC admonition that *supervisor training* is a best practice. The prevalence of supervisory training in the workplace is credited with the reduction in the number of cases of sexual harassment in recent years. California has been a leader in this area with its state law mandate that all employers with more than 50 employees provide sexual harassment training to supervisors every two years.

Promoting a Culture of Inclusiveness

Ironically, most nonprofits are intuitively aware of the value of ethnic diversity in a nonprofit workplace, and the importance of reflecting, from the board of directors on down, the communities served by the nonprofit. Actually having a diverse workforce is often difficult when your staff is small in number. Even if your nonprofit doesn't have the luxury of dozens of staff members with varied backgrounds, striving to promote a culture of inclusiveness is a worthy goal. There are many ways in which discrimination can be almost imperceptibly present: in work assignments (Do we only give certain people certain types of assignments?) performance measures (Do we hold certain types of people to different standards?) training and offering constructive feedback (Do we mentor some employees more than others?), and grooming standards (Do we overlook the personal expressions, such as tattoos or facial hair, of some employees but not others?).

With regard to hiring and promotions, the EEOC Compliance Manual stresses that job standards and minimum qualifications with respect to educational background and experience must be consistent with business necessity and specifically related to the job at issue. Employers should review job requirements and descriptions without regard to who is presently doing that particular job. Instead they should identify the requirements for anyone who might hold that position.

The EEOC's Compliance Manual highlights that the use of homogenous recruiting practices, such as word-of-mouth and announcing position openings in the same tried and true publications, are particularly susceptible to claims of inhibiting workplace diversity.

Small Nonprofits Beware

Awareness of state anti-discrimination laws is important for small nonprofits because most of the state statutes apply to employers with one or more employees, while Title VII and related federal laws only apply to those nonprofits with 15 or more employees. Example: Delaware considers an "employer" for purposes of discrimination laws to be someone who employs four or more employees. In some states, protections are extended for some types of discrimination when the workplace reaches a certain size, but not others.

Race and Color Harassment

In recent years, the concept of harassment that violates Title VII's standards of workplace equality has focused less on sexual harassment and more frequently on harassment based on a person's race or color. In surveys conducted in 2004 and 2005, sexual harassment claims fell 11 percent from 2003 levels; with 90 percent of employers reporting that training on sexual harassment policies regularly occurred at the workplace. In contrast, race and color harassment claims rose considerably in the same period, with only 56 percent of employers responding that training was offered. Race and color harassment is unwelcome conduct that unreasonably interferes with a person's work performance or creates an intimidating, offensive or hostile work environment. To be actionable as a violation of law, the alleged harassment must be so severe or pervasive that it alters the alleged victim's terms and conditions of employment, as evaluated from the perspective of a reasonable person in the victim's position. For conduct to be unwelcome, the victim may not have solicited or incited the conduct. It makes sense to raise awareness among staff that in subtle or overt ways, a person's conduct or words can be perceived as unwelcome harassment and can therefore violate the nonprofit's EEO policy. Training the entire workforce to be more sensitive to race and color harassment is a logical first step to reduce this risk.

Be Sensitive to Religious Accommodations

Remember that Title VII of the Civil Rights Act of 1964 prohibits discrimination based on religious beliefs and practices. Employees and applicants whose dress, hairstyle, beards, prayer requirements and Sabbath and holy day observances are required by their religious beliefs, generally can't be forced to choose between their religious practices and their jobs. As with requests to accommodate a disability, employers must make an effort to negotiate with an employee to find a *reasonable accommodation* for his or her religious practices. The legal standard is that an accommodation is reasonable as long as it doesn't impose an *undue hardship* on the nonprofit's business operations. According to federal standards, almost any additional expense or administrative burden can be found to impose an *undue hardship* on an employer.

Religious accommodations frequently are achieved by rearranging work schedules to permit employees time off to pray or attend religious services, or by modifying a dress code, such as by permitting an employee to wear head coverings or long robes.

Retaliation is also prohibited. Remember that an employee's exercise of rights to practice his or her religion may not result in adverse personnel actions.

Employers may not require employees to participate in, or refrain from participating in, religious activity as a condition of employment. Even faith-based nonprofits generally can't make membership in a certain organized religion a qualification for employment unless it can be shown that being of a certain religion is a *bona fide* qualification of employment. Employers can be vulnerable to a claim of *disparate impact* discrimination if they treat individuals more or less favorably because of their religious beliefs. This can arise when a nonprofit outwardly favors persons of one religion over another, or permits some types of personal expression at work, such as body art, but not other expressions that are religious in nature. In general, unless an undue hardship results, a nonprofit should permit employees to express their religious views through their customs or dress. This tolerance needs to be balanced, because there is a risk that co-workers could find that religious practices by one employee create a *hostile environment* (thereby exposing the nonprofit to the risk of a claim of illegal harassment). Consequently, nonprofits should:

- Have a written policy that explains that illegal harassment isn't just about sexual harassment, but includes harassment based on religious beliefs and practices.

- Educate employees about the policy.

- Include a mechanism for employees to bring a complaint or grievance to management's attention if they believe a violation of the policy has occurred.

- Take all claims of harassment based on religion seriously and investigate thoroughly.

- Emphasize in the policy and in staff training that no retaliation will be permitted against any employee as a result of the exercise of their religious beliefs, or because they've raised a claim that they've been harassed or discriminated against because of their religious beliefs or practices.

- Document all requests for accommodations and the negotiations that ensue to reach a reasonable accommodation for the employee's religious practices.

Violation of the Americans with Disabilities Act

The Americans with Disabilities Act of 1990 (ADA) ✍ creates employer obligations at the hiring stage. The very process of applying for a job must be accessible to persons with special needs. Applicants with disabilities must be evaluated on the basis of their qualifications for the position without consideration of their disability. The Department of Labor's checklist ✍ for hiring persons with disabilities emphasizes these important points:

- Make sure that no questions seeking disability-related (or medical-related) information are posed on the written application or during the interview process.

- Treat applicants with disabilities the same way you would treat any other applicant.

- Make sure that the hiring process is accessible to persons with disabilities, which means that if there are forms to fill out, persons with sight impairment may need an accommodation. Similarly, an applicant with a physical impairment might not be able to attend pre-hire training sessions if they're held in a nonaccessible facility.

- Have a written job description available for all applicants. That way, if someone with a hidden disability reads the job description and realizes that their impairment will impact their ability to perform the job duties, the applicant can raise the issue and the employer and applicant can then discuss potential accommodations. This is a permissible way for the issue to come up—it's **not** permissible for an employer to **ask** whether an applicant has a disability.

Recent Developments in Discrimination Claims: Gender Identity

The protected class of *sexual orientation* shields homosexuals and heterosexuals or those perceived as being homosexual or heterosexual, from discrimination. The newest protected class to emerge in recent years is *gender identity*, which expands the concept of sexual orientation to include self perception or the perception of someone else as to a person's identity as a male or female, as a result of their appearance, dress, or physical characteristic, whether or not they're consistent with the person's biological gender at birth. In a few states and several municipalities around the country the term *gender identity* has specifically been added to the list of protected categories in anti-discrimination laws.

Eight states and the District of Columbia prohibit discrimination based on sexual orientation *and, as recently expanded,* to gender identity—California, Hawaii, Illinois, Maine, Minnesota, New Mexico, Rhode Island, Washington State and the District of Columbia. Nine other states limit the prohibition to *sexual orientation*—Connecticut, Maryland, Massachusetts, Nevada, New Hampshire, New Jersey, New York, Vermont and Wisconsin. The courts in eight states have interpreted existing law to extend protection to transgendered persons even though the law doesn't include the phrase *gender identity*— Connecticut, Florida, Illinois, Hawaii, Massachusetts, New Jersey, New York and Vermont. Additionally, nine states have executive orders or state government personnel regulations prohibiting discrimination on the basis of sexual orientation and/or gender identity, although these regulations are only applicable applies to public employees—Alaska, Arizona,

Age Discrimination: How Old Is Old?

Under federal law, age 40 is *old*. A plaintiff claiming a violation of the federal law against age discrimination can only succeed if she/he is 40 or older. However, in some states, it doesn't matter how old the plaintiff is, as long as the alleged reason for the adverse employment action is based on age. A case in point: In New Jersey a 28 year old was denied a promotion to loan officer in a bank because he looked too *young*.) Other examples:

Massachusetts requires that in order to establish a prima facie case of age discrimination under state law, there must be an age difference of at least five years between a plaintiff and a younger person who replaced the plaintiff. *Knight v. Avon Products, Inc.*, 438 Mass. 413 (Ma. January 10, 2003)

The *Minnesota Human Rights Act* (MHRA) prohibits employers from discriminating against employees based on age. The protected class includes any person *over the age of majority*. Thus, unlike the federal Age Discrimination in Employment Act (ADEA), which only protects employees age 40 or older, the MHRA protects individuals age 18 or older.

Colorado, Delaware, Indiana, Louisiana, Michigan and Montana, and Pennsylvania. The Human Rights Campaign maintains a comprehensive 50-state chart of the states' positions on this emerging area of protection from civil rights violations.

There are a few states where gender identity is specifically **not** a protected category (such as Texas and Kansas); and some (such as Minnesota) that define gender identity more narrowly than others as *biological gender* rather than self-perceptions of gender.

Consequently, it's becoming more common for claims to be brought by transgendered persons or transsexuals, either on the basis of gender or sexual orientation discrimination or on the basis of *disability* discrimination under the ADA. Several states (such as New Jersey, California, Connecticut, Hawaii, Florida, Illinois, Massachusetts and Vermont) have case law precedent or administrative law decisions that provide protection in employment specifically for transgendered persons or transsexuals because of the conclusion that persons in those categories suffer from the disability of *dysphoria* (discomfort with one's gender/sex as biologically assigned).

The analysis of whether an employer has discriminated against an employee may hinge on whether the employer provided reasonable accommodations for the employee. For example, the California Labor Code requires employers to permit their employees to dress consistently with the employee's gender identity, while in Minnesota, where gender identity is defined more narrowly, employers may restrict restroom and locker room use based on biological gender.

Breach of Contract Claims

Another hiring risk involves communications made to applicants that may create an unintended employment contract. Such communications could be in writing, such as in an offer letter, or earlier, on the application form, or verbally, during the interview or job negotiations. In your eagerness to find the right candidate, you may say something you will regret later. These include promises that can't be kept, such as assurances to new employees about benefits, conditions of employment, wages, time off, or the length of employment. Such promises can result in a breach of contract claim when the employer fails to deliver the promised benefits. To protect against the risk of a breach of contract claim based on promises made during the hiring process, consider adding a Certification paragraph (See the example that follows) to your employment application.

Truth in Hiring

Just as the nonprofit is expected to stand by what it offers an applicant, the applicant is expected to provide honest and accurate information during the hiring process. While there are many reasons for rejecting an applicant for a position at your nonprofit, dishonesty or providing misleading information at any stage of the hiring process are among the most defensible reasons for rejecting an applicant. Thus, every nonprofit application for employment should include not only a disclaimer stating that employment is *at will*, but also a statement that the applicant understands that providing false or misleading information during the hiring process is grounds for refusal to hire or termination. Such certifications are commonly referred to as a *truth clause*.

Using a certification and authorization statement on an application for employment is an excellent risk management strategy. In one fell swoop the employer can obtain authorization to conduct background checks, ensure grounds for dismissal if the candidate has been untruthful, make it easier to obtain reference information and underscore the at-will nature of employment.

Certification

By my signature below, I certify that this information is accurate and complete. I understand that giving incomplete or false information during the hiring process is a serious matter and is grounds for dismissal and forfeiture of related benefits. I authorize [Name of Nonprofit] and any of its authorized representatives to investigate any and all of the information contained in this application and to conduct a thorough background check as to my suitability for employment, including a criminal background record check.

I understand that if hired, my status will be that of an employee at will, with no contractual right, express or implied, to remain in [Name of Nonprofit]'s employ for any specific length of time. I understand that my employment may be terminated, with or without cause, or notice. I understand that no one has the authority verbally to change these terms and that only a written agreement signed by me and the CEO of [Name of Nonprofit] can change the at-will nature of my employment. I have read and understand and agree to the provisions of this application for employment with [Name of Nonprofit].

I give my permission to my past employers to provide information regarding my performance history to [Name of Nonprofit]. I hereby consent to and authorize persons employed by my former employer(s) to disclose any information they consider relevant to a potential employer of mine with respect to my work history and/or performance on the job, and I knowingly waive any claim for disparagement, defamation, slander or libel against my former employer(s) for sharing such information with [Name of Nonprofit].

Signed: _____   Date:_____

Keep in mind when evaluating an applicant's qualifications for a particular position that considering any of the characteristics of a protected category, whether defined by the applicable state or federal law, is impermissible. The only exception to this rule is when the protected characteristic is a *bona fide occupational qualification.*(*Example:* Being female is considered a legitimate, bona fide occupational qualification for the position of attendant in a women's locker room. A male applicant for the position can be rejected simply because of his gender.) Public and private safety can also create exceptions. For instance, the Americans with Disabilities Act provides a narrow exception which permits employers to turn down a qualified applicant with a disability if the applicant would pose a direct threat to the safety or health of the applicant or other individuals in the workplace. This exception has been interpreted narrowly. In general, hiring decisions shouldn't be based on any characteristics that are listed in the state or federal laws as protected categories.

State law guidelines must be followed when asking applicants questions during the selection process, whether on the application or in the interview. In states with no published guidelines, follow the rule-of-thumb *to ask only those questions that are truly job-related.* An appropriate risk management strategy in hiring is to base selection decisions on the applicant's qualifications and to document that the chosen applicant was more qualified than others considered for the same position. When a nonprofit can demonstrate that an applicant was selected because he or she was the most qualified—not because others were discriminated against—the nonprofit is in the strongest position to defend against allegations of illegal discrimination.

Many nonprofit managers wonder what questions are impermissible in job interviews with candidates. Two dozen states have published guidelines for *pre-employment inquiries* that set forth examples of the questions which employers may and may not ask in the pre-hire stage. The West Virginia Pre-Employment Inquiry Guide is provided on the next page as a representative sample of these resources.

A Word of Caution for New York Employers

Under the New York State Human Rights Law, Executive Law Section 296 (10), supervisors and managers, as *agents* of employers, may be held *individually* liable for violating the religious accommodation law.

A Case in Point

In one recent case, an employee was fired right before the Sabbath. He claimed that his termination was motivated by religious discrimination. As proof that his employer had engaged in *harassing* conduct on the basis of his religion, he offered that his employer had ordered pizza with pork sausage topping for a staff lunch, knowing that he could not eat pork. As it turned out, the complaining employee's employer had a legitimate business reason for terminating him (and evidence to support that reason), and the plaintiff was ultimately unsuccessful in his claim of wrongful discharge. However, the facts of this case highlight that something as seemingly innocuous as a staff lunch can come back to haunt an employer who isn't sensitive to religious practices. (See *EEOC v. Rite Aid Corp.*, No. 03- CV-777 (D. Del., Dec. 12, 2005).

West Virginia Pre-Employment Inquiry Guide

The prime consideration for any job is the ability to perform it.

Pre-employment inquiries (interviews and applications for employment)

Subject	Lawful inquiries/requirements	Unlawful inquires/requirements
Age	Are you 18 or over? Whether the applicant meets the minimum age requirement set by law; if required as a bona fide occupational qualification (BFOQ); or after hire, if inquiry serves a legitimate record-keeping purpose	That applicant state age or date of birth. That applicant produce proof of age (birth certificate, baptismal record). Specifications such as "young," "college student," "recent college graduate," "retired person."
Arrests & convictions	Inquiries about convictions that bear a direct relationship to the job and have not been expunged or sealed by the courts. Consideration should be given to the nature, recentness and rehabilitation. This inquiry should be accompanied by a disclaimer which states that *a conviction record will not necessarily be a bar to employment.*	
Citizenship, birthplace	After employment, verification of legal right to work (all new hires).	Whether applicant, parents or spouse are naturalized or native-born US citizens. Birthplace of applicant, parents or spouse. Requirement that applicant produce naturalization papers.
Credit and financial records	The employer is bound by federal law (PL 91-0508) to inform the applicant, in writing, that if financial or credit investigations are made, the applicant may make written requests as to the nature and scope of such investigations.	
Dependents		Inquiries regarding the number and ages of children; what child care arrangements have been made; family planning.
Disability	Whether applicant is able to perform the essential functions of the job with or without reasonable accommodation. That applicant demonstrate how she/he would perform the job and with what accommodation(s). After a job offer, but before hire, require medical examination for all similarly situated entering employees.	Requirement that the applicant take medical examination or provide information about workers' compensation claim(s) before a job offer. General inquires into the applicant's state of health or the nature and severity of a disability.
Drivers' license	Inquiry, if driving is necessary to the job	Inquiring if all applicants have a valid driver's license regardless of job.
Education	What academic, professional or vocational schools attended; course of study, degree or certificate earned	Dates of elementary/high school attendance. Nationality, racial or religious affiliation of any school attended by the applicant.
Federal W-4 form		This is not to be completed by an applicant until after the hire because it requests information that is unlawful during the pre-employment process.
Marital status		Whether applicant is single, married, divorced, widowed, etc.; Mr., Mrs., Miss, Ms.; inquiries regarding the names and ages of spouses or children.
Military status	Job-related inquires into military experience in the US Armed Forces or state militia (e.g., branch, occupational specialty)	Inquiries regarding foreign military experience. Type of military discharge. Request for copy of military discharge or military discharge number.

Subject	Lawful inquiries/requirements	Unlawful inquires/requirements
Name	Whether the applicant has used another name (for the purpose of verifying past work record)	Inquiries or comments about the name which would reveal applicant's lineage, national origin, marital status, etc. (e.g., maiden name?) Mr., Mrs., Miss, Ms.?
National origin	What languages applicant reads, speaks or writes fluently if relevant to the job or if required as a bona fide occupational qualification.	Inquiries regarding: applicant's nationality, ancestry, lineage or parentage; nationality of applicant's parents or spouse; maiden name of applicant, wife or mother.
Photograph	May be requested after hire (for identification).	Request before hire.
Polygraph, lie detector		Require test to be taken as condition of employment.
Pre-employment survey	If this section is completed by the applicant, this page is to be kept separate from the application and is to be detached before the application is handled by the person conducting the interview or the person making the employment decision.	
Professional associations	Inquiries regarding memberships in job-related clubs and organizations. Applicants may omit those which reveal the race, religion, age, sex, disability, etc. of applicant.	Requesting the name of all organizations, clubs, associations to which the applicant belongs. Inquiries regarding how the applicant spends his/her spare time.
Race, color, height, weight		Inquiries regarding: applicants' race; color of applicant's skin, eyes, hair or other questions directly or indirectly indicating race or color; applicant's height or weight (unless based on legitimate job need).
References	Inquiring by whom was applicant referred. Requesting names of person willing to provide professional or character references. Making job-related inquiries of references.	Requiring the submission of religious references. Inquiries of references which would elicit information on applicant's race, color, national origin, age, marital status, disability or sexual orientation.
Relatives		Name, address, relationship of person to be notified in case of emergency. This information may be requested only after hire.
Religion	Inquiries regarding the normal hours of work. After hire, inquires regarding religious accommodations.	Inquires regarding applicant's religious denomination or affiliation or religious holidays observed. Any inquiry which would indicate or identify religious customs or holidays observed.
Sex	Inquiry only if required as a bona fide occupational qualification.	Inquiries regarding: applicant's sex; Mr., Mrs., Miss, Ms.; if applicant is expecting, planning a family or used birth control.
Sexual orientation		Any inquiry concerning an applicant's heterosexuality, homosexuality or bisexuality.

State Guidelines on Pre-Employment Inquiries

The following states have published resources to assist employers with identifying what questions are impermissible during the hiring process. Download or order the guidelines for your state and review these materials with staff members at your nonprofit whose responsibilities include interviewing prospective employees.

The state laws noted here are subject to periodic review and revision by state legislatures. This summary should therefore be used for reference purposes, rather than as a definitive guide.

Alaska: Alaska Department of Labor and Workforce Development, *Alaska Employer Handbook*, "Pre-Employment Questioning," page 82.

California: Although the guide isn't currently downloadable, it can be ordered from The California Department of Fair Housing Web site. ✎

Colorado: Colorado Civil Rights Division, Publications, *Preventing Job Discrimination.* ✎

Idaho: *Pre-Employment Inquiry Guide.* ✎

Indiana: The University of Indiana has compiled a comprehensive chart of permissible and impermissible questions to ask in an interview with an applicant in Indiana. ✎

Iowa: Iowa Workforce Development, *Successfully Interviewing Applicants.* ✎

Kansas: Kansas Human Rights Commission, *Guidelines on Equal Employment Practices: Preventing Discrimination in Hiring.* ✎

Maine: Maine Human Rights Commission, Publications, *Pre-Employment Inquiry Guidelines.* ✎

Maryland: *Guidelines for Pre-Employment Inquiries Technical Assistance Guide.* ✎

Massachusetts: Massachusetts Commission Against Discrimination, *Pre-Employment Inquiries Fact Sheet.* ✎

Michigan: Michigan Civil Rights Commission, *Pre-Employment Inquiry Guide.* ✎

Minnesota: Minnesota Department of Human Rights, *Hiring, Job Interviews and the Minnesota Human Rights Act.* ✎

Missouri: Commission on Human Rights, Missouri Department of Labor and Industrial Relations, *Pre-Employment Inquiries.* ✎

Nevada: Nevada Equal Rights Commission, *Pre-Employment Inquiry Guide.* ✎

New Hampshire: *Guidelines for Pre-Employment Inquiries Technical Assistance Guide.* ✎

New York: New York State Division of Human Rights, *Rulings on Inquiries (Pre-Employment).* ✎

North Dakota: North Dakota Department of Labor, Human Rights Division, *Employment Applications and Interviews.* ✎

Oregon: Oregon Bureau of Labor and Industries, Civil Rights Division, *Fact Sheets, Pre-Employment Inquiries.* ✎

Pennsylvania: Pennsylvania Human Relations Commission, Publications, *Pre-Employment Inquiries.* ✎

Rhode Island: Department of Labor and Training, *Employer Handbook.* ✎

South Dakota: South Dakota Division of Human Rights, *Pre-Employment Inquiry Guide.* ✎

Utah: *Pre-Employment Inquiry Guide.* ✎

Washington: Washington Small Business Development Centers, *Frequently Asked Questions and Answers on Human Resources.* ✎

West Virginia: Bureau of Employment Programs, *Pre-Employment Inquiry Guide.* ✎

Wisconsin: Wisconsin Department of Workforce development, Civil Rights Division Publications, *Fair Hiring & Avoiding Loaded Interview Questions.* ✎

The Hiring Decision: Risk Management Strategies

1. **Determine the minimum qualifications of the open position.** The minimum qualifications should be described on a written job description that lists the physical requirements (if any) for the position, as well as the minimum qualifications in education or experience. Having a written job description that describes the minimum qualifications, including physical requirements, will reduce the risk that an applicant will be successful claiming that an illegal factor was used to disqualify the applicant.

2. **Determine who is an applicant for an open position.** You don't have to consider everyone who sends an unsolicited letter or résumé for an open position as an applicant. Generally only those individuals who meet the minimum qualifications for the position need to be considered applicants. If the nonprofit's hiring procedures require applicants to fill out an application form, then only those individuals who have submitted a complete application form should be considered formal applicants for an open position. This will narrow the pool of people who the nonprofit has to decide between—and reduce not only the paperwork, but also the nonprofit's potential liability for discrimination in hiring.

3. **Be consistent:** In order to document that the hiring decision was based on legitimate grounds, the nonprofit should be able to show consistency in its hiring procedures, specifically that the same application process and the same interview questions were asked of every candidate for a given position.

4. **Use job-related criteria to make hiring decisions:** If asked, "Why was this person hired?" make sure that your nonprofit can articulate a job-related reason. Identifying the business-related reason why one individual was hired but not another could be the cornerstone of your defense against a claim of discriminatory hiring.

Interviews are commonly used to determine who to hire. They are arguably the most subjective screening tool. To avoid the appearance of discrimination, it's helpful if interviews are conducted by more than one staff member. A script can be helpful in making certain that all applicants are asked the same questions. It's also advisable to educate staff members who conduct interviews in interview techniques to understand which questions raise liability concerns. No matter where they're maintained, notes by interviewers should be restricted to job-related comments or impressions of the applicant's qualifications for the position.

To safeguard against subjective comments being included in an applicant's file, **never** make notes on résumés or cover letters. Ideally, the interviewer will make notes only on the script of the interview questions posed to each applicant.

In one celebrated case, an interviewer noted "no jew" on the top of a candidate's résumé. The candidate was applying for a position in a department store. The interviewer's notation was meant to indicate that the candidate did not want to work in the "jewelry department," however the jury didn't buy that story when the department store failed to hire the plaintiff and he sued for religious discrimination.

Questions Not to Ask During the Hiring Process

There are many facts that might be useful to know about someone who is already employed but shouldn't be considered during the hiring process. The nonprofit can always find out these details after the hiring decision has been made, but not before. In general, no employer should make inquiries, either on an application or in an interview, concerning the following topics:

❏   *The age of the applicant, their birth date or when they graduated from college or high school.* You *may* ask what schools the applicant has attended, how many years the applicant attended each school, and whether a degree was awarded. Even though employers can't ask about age directly, asking whether an applicant is of *majority age* is permissible and important for students who might be working with a nonprofit as an intern or volunteer, since being of majority age might be a minimum qualification. Note that requiring proof of age should happen *after* the job offer has been extended, not before, in order to avoid any claim that the employer discriminated against an applicant on the basis of age.[5]

❏   *How long the applicant has lived at his or her current address.* You *may* ask whether the applicant has recently moved from another state or municipality.

❏   *The name of the applicant's place of worship, or religious leader.* Any discussion of religion is out of bounds unless the nonprofit is affiliated with a religious institution and being supportive of, or practicing that religion is a job requirement.

❏   *Whether the applicant would like to be called Ms., Miss or Mrs., or what the applicant's maiden name was, or whether the applicant is married, divorced, single, or who resides with the applicant.* You *may* ask whether the applicant has ever used any other name and what that name was.

❏   *How many children the applicant has, what schools the children attend, their school schedules, or what childcare arrangements will be made.*

❏   *How the applicant will get to work,* unless owning a car is a bona fide requirement of the job.

❏   *Whether the applicant owns or rents a residence.*

❏   *Any information relating to the applicant's bank or personal financial matters, including whether the applicant has any loans outstanding or whether the applicant has ever had wages garnished.* (Such information can be obtained from a credit history report.)

❏   *Whether the applicant has ever been arrested.* Check your state law before making inquiries into criminal records. Several states have laws that limit access to, the use of, or inquiries into an applicant's criminal records. It isn't appropriate to base a hiring decision on arrests, since an arrest doesn't necessarily result in a conviction. You *may* ask whether an applicant has ever been convicted of a crime *as long as* follow-up questions are asked to determine whether the conviction is *relevant* to the position.

5 New York law requires employers to maintain "proof of age" of employees claiming to be between 18 and 25 years old. See N.Y. Labor Law § 135(2). The amendment, which took effect December 15, 2005, states that the required proof of age must be in the form of: (1) a driver's license; (2) a certificate of age issued by an "employment certificating official"; or (3) other government-issued documentation. Previously, employers were permitted, but not required, to demand proof of age from employees claiming to be over 18. Note that requiring proof of age should happen after the job offer has been extended, not before, in order to avoid any claim that the employer discriminated against an applicant on the basis of age.

Trend Spotter: Leased Employees/Professional Employer Organizations (PEO's)

Leased employees are employees of a third party (the leasing company or PEO), but work at a nonprofit in a specific capacity, usually defined by the contract with the leasing company. Leasing firms carry a few or all staff members of a workforce on the leasing company's payroll, and handle all the withholding, paperwork, and human resources administration issues, freeing the traditional employer from many human resources burdens. This option is growing in popularity, although it isn't widely used in the nonprofit sector. Occasionally one will hear about a nonprofit leasing a worker with a specialized skill set, or an executive director or financial officer during a time of transition. This arrangement appears to relieve the traditional employer of liability for employment law claims, including wrongful discharge claims. Yet, several courts have found that employees who work under the direction and control of the on-site employer are deemed the common law employees of that employer, not the leasing company. At the very least the nonprofit employer will be considered the joint employer with the leasing company. This means that *both the nonprofit and the leasing company* will have various legal responsibilities under federal and state employment laws for the leased employees. Even if the contract with the leasing company is structured so that the leasing company handles many of the traditional roles of an employer, the nonprofit always retains liability for claims of discrimination and for the safety of employees in the workplace. Leased employees also are included in any *count* for coverage and nondiscrimination purposes if they've worked for the nonprofit for more than one year.

Q: How long should we keep applicants' files?

A: Employers that are federal contractors with over $10,000 in federal funding must keep applicants' files for two years in accordance with the federal requirements for affirmative action plans. After two years, it's safe for all employers to discard applicants' résumés, cover letters and application forms. If your nonprofit is keeping statistics on applicants (which is required of certain federal contractors), make sure to transfer any required information onto EEO data forms prior to discarding the information.

❏ *Whether the applicant has ever served in the military.* In some states military status is a protected category, but in those states you *may* ask applicants to provide a copy of his or her discharge from the military, if you ask every applicant the same question and preface the request with: *if applicable.*

❏ *Whether the applicant can speak or write any foreign languages, unless doing so is a bona fide job requirement.*

❏ *What clubs the applicant belongs to, or how he or she spends her spare time.*

❏ *Whether the applicant is for or against any candidate for public office, what political party she or he belongs to, or whether he or she is for or against unions.*

❏ *How many days the applicant missed work in the last year and whether the applicant filed any workers' compensation claims at his or her previous place of employment.* You *may* tell the applicant what the expectations are for attendance and ask about the applicant's ability to meet those expectations, as long as the questions aren't designed to elicit disability-related information. For instance, you *may* ask, "How many Mondays and Fridays did you take off last year which weren't approved days off?"

❏ *Whether the applicant has any disabilities, impairments, recurring illnesses, whether she or he has ever been hospitalized, treated by a psychiatrist, psychologist, or counseled for any mental condition; whether the applicant has had any major illness or about any health-related concern, mental or physical.* You *may* ask the candidate whether he or she is capable of performing all the job duties of the written job description. You should give a written description to the candidate to review.

❏ *Whether the applicant uses lawful drug and alcohol products, smokes, takes any prescription drugs, has ever been addicted to drugs, or alcohol, is undergoing treatment for addiction disorders, or substance abuse.*

❏ *Whether the applicant is good at handling stress or has ever demonstrated any physical response to stressful working conditions.* You *may* ask what the applicant does to respond to stress or what the applicant considers to be a stressful work experience, in an effort to elicit whether the applicant is qualified to handle a particularly stressful job. If too many questions on this subject are asked, it appears that the questions are designed to elicit disability information.

❏ *Questions about an applicant's former employers or acquaintances that elicit information specifying the applicant's race, color, religious creed, national origin, ancestry, physical handicap, medical condition, marital status, age, or sex.* You *may* ask for names of persons willing to provide professional and/or character references for the applicant.

❏ *Questions about arrests or convictions unless state law clearly permits the questions, and the employer is prepared to document that evaluation of past criminal activity was conducted without any regard to race or color, and that there is a business reason to make the inquiry.* Blanket exclusions of applicants on the basis of convictions and arrests are prohibited by the EEOC on the basis of race or color discrimination. An employer may justify its decision not to hire an applicant on the basis of past criminal conduct if the conduct was particularly egregious or is related to the job duties of the position sought.

Questions to an Applicant with a Disability

With respect to an applicant with a disability, employers *may* ask the following questions, *if* the employer reasonably believes that the disability may affect the applicant's ability to perform the job duties of the position:

❏ Whether the applicant needs any particular accommodation to participate in the hiring process.

❏ Whether the applicant can describe or demonstrate how the job duties would be performed.

❏ Whether the applicant would be willing to provide medical documentation of the disability so that the employer can assess whether a medical professional has identified functional limitations.

Despite the reasonableness of the employer's belief that the disability might affect job performance, if the applicant denies that the disability will affect job performance, the employer *may not* pursue the matter.

Questions Relating to Nationality and Eligibility to Work in the United States

The Immigration Reform and Control Act of 1986 (IRCA) and Title VII prohibit discrimination on the basis of national origin and race. Many state anti-discrimination statutes list *ancestry* as a protected category. Consequently, the time to ask about an applicant's ability to work in the United States *isn't* during the hiring process, but after a decision has been made to extend a job offer to the applicant. Job offers should be contingent upon the candidate's verification of authorization to work in the United States. Employers *shouldn't* ask any questions during interviews or on applications having to do with national origin, including what language is normally spoken in the applicant's home. Similarly, there should be no questions on the application form or in the interview about ethnicity or national origin, even if required as identifying information for affirmative action plans, state or federal contracts or funders. Gathering this information can be done after the decision to offer employment to the candidate, or on a separate form with a statement that, "providing such information is voluntary and won't be considered in the employment decision."

Don't ask if an applicant is a U.S. citizen, unless being a citizen is a bona fide occupational qualification. Generally what the employer really needs to know is whether the applicant is legally eligible to work in the U.S. Assume every candidate does have work authorization, but require proof of authorization *after* the offer of employment has been extended.

Don't ask applicants to provide a recent photograph during the pre-hire stage, since personal appearance isn't normally job-related.

Verification of Authorization to Work in the United States

After the decision to hire has been made then it's the employer's obligation to verify that the newly hired employee is authorized to work in the United States by having the employee complete an I-9 form. Employees must present original documents, except for birth certificates, which may be certified copies. The I-9 form may be downloaded from the U.S. Department of Homeland Security Web site along with helpful information about the process of verifying work authorization. This process must be strictly followed for *every* candidate who is offered employment, and ideally the documentation of each employee's

---

Developing Written Job Descriptions Step by Step

Here is a guide for drafting written job descriptions, which should be developed for every position. A written description spelling out the essential functions of the position is useful to protect a nonprofit from claims that the organization violated the Americans with Disabilities Act. A detailed, written job description is also a helpful tool to engage the applicant in meaningful discussion during the interview, and to protect the employer in the event the employer decides to reject the applicant or later discharge an employee on the basis that the applicant or employee failed to meet the minimum qualifications for the position. Furthermore, a written job description is essential as a starting point for evaluation whether an employee is fulfilling the job duties expected of him/her, and therefore essential to an effective performance evaluation process.

The written job description should clearly articulate:

Job Title: Give the job a name that's descriptive of the job duties as well as the relative level of importance of the position in the nonprofit's administrative structure. Don't assign an inflated or lofty title to compensate for noncompetitive compensation.

Job Classification: Identify whether the position is exempt or non-exempt, part time or full time, regular, temporary or a substitute position. Independent contractors and consultants shouldn't have a position description, but instead a contract that sets forth the nature of their services for the nonprofit.

Job Purpose Statement: Give the name of the department or position of the supervisor to whom the position reports and provide a description of how the position fits into the mission of the organization. Ask: Why does this position exist? What does the employee in this position spend most of his or her time doing?

Essential Functions: Describe all physical functions that are essential to the position's successful performance, such as driving a van or active care of infants and toddlers, including lifting children, holding arms overhead, getting up and down off the floor, and aiding children on the playground.

Job Responsibilities: List the major job activities, if possible listing those which are more significant first.

Minimum qualifications or requirements: List any skills or abilities that are critical to successful job performance. List educational degrees, licenses, registrations, certifications, and other credentials that fulfill the minimum requirements for the position. Ensure that these requirements are job-related and truly necessary, not just the characteristics of the person presently holding the position.

authorization to work in the USA will be placed in a separate file, labeled: INS Work Authorization, so that if the INS audits the workplace, all the files relevant to the investigation are easily accessible in one place. Maintaining separate records makes it less cumbersome to cooperate with the audit and also restricts the investigation to the segregated files, which should shorten the time of the investigation, as well as limit what the INS investigates. Section 274 ☛ of the Immigration Naturalization Act provides for penalties for each worker that the government finds employed without proper paperwork demonstrating authorization to work in the United States. Consequently the penalties can be very steep. If your nonprofit is audited by the INS, this is the time to hire legal counsel who can negotiate with the INS to reduce the fines. There is a *good-faith* defense that may be asserted in situations where the employer took steps to verify worker status, but may have been fooled by a worker's false identification, or inadvertently overlooked a required step in the process. Even with the possibility of a good faith defense, the risk of expensive penalties is quite high unless the nonprofit diligently follows procedures and maintains comprehensive records.

Hiring Practices That Affirm a Commitment to Equal Treatment and Fairness: EEO and Affirmative Action Distinguished

Every nonprofit should have an EEO (equal employment opportunity) statement in its employee handbook stating the policy that the nonprofit will adhere to state and federal anti-discrimination laws[6]. However, not every nonprofit is required to have an Affirmative Action Plan (AAP). Affirmative action is the commitment to actively recruit and retain a diverse workforce that's statistically balanced, as well as to actively recruit certain protected classes of workers identified by the federal government. An AAP is a policy document that mandates recordkeeping and statistical review, action plans and timetables, to ensure a statistically balanced workforce. Depending on the number of employees at the workplace and the level of government funding, a federal or state contractor may be required to have an AAP as a condition of receiving funding. The requirement of an AAP means that the nonprofit must keep track of statistics that provide a profile of the workforce by race, gender, veteran status, national origin, disability and other protected categories. Statistics must be kept on both the current workforce and on individuals who apply for positions with the nonprofit.

The organization must have a written Equal Employment Opportunity policy statement in its employee handbook that refers to adherence to affirmative action if the nonprofit:

❑ Has a contract with any funder, including a municipal, state or federal government, that states in the funding proposal or contract that an affirmative action policy is required; or

❑ Receives $10,000 or more in federal funding as a contractor or subcontractor.

Government Contractors: Special Rules for Nondiscriminatory Practices

Executive Order 11246 ☛ provides that when an employer receives more than $10,000 in federal funding, whether as a contractor or subcontractor, the employer must have a policy not to discriminate as follows:

"…The contractor won't discriminate against any employee or applicant for employment because of race, color, religion, sex, or national origin. The contractor will take affirmative action to ensure that applicants are employed, and that employees are treated during employment, without regard to their race, color, religion, sex or national origin. Such action shall include, but not be

---

6 An Equal Employment Opportunity statement is required under federal law (Title VII) for nonprofits with 15 or more employees; however many state anti-discrimination laws apply to workplaces with fewer than 15 employees, therefore, having an EEO policy is a best practice no matter what the size of the nonprofit.

limited to the following: employment, upgrading, demotion, or transfer; recruitment or recruitment advertising; layoff or termination; rates of pay or other forms of compensation; and selection for training, including apprenticeship. The contractor agrees to post in conspicuous places, available to employees and applicants for employment, notices to be provided by the contracting officer setting forth the provisions of this nondiscrimination clause."

Executive Order 11246 doesn't require that employers undertake any special statistical analysis or recordkeeping, but it does require that the nonprofit maintain nondiscriminatory employment policies and that the employer posts a notice (www.dol.gov/esa/regs/compliance/ofccp/fsvevraa.htm) of compliance with Executive Order 11246. Executive Order 11246 also requires that the nonprofit include a statement in any advertisements for available positions that: "…all qualified applicants will receive consideration for employment without regard to race, color, religion, sex or national origin."

Vietnam Era Veterans Readjustment Act

Similarly, if your organization is a federal contractor or subcontractor and receives at least $25,000 in federal funds, the Vietnam Era Veterans' Readjustment Assistance Act (www.dol.gov/esa/regs/compliance/) requires that employers: "… provide equal opportunity and affirmative action for Vietnam era veterans, special disabled veterans, and veterans who served on active duty during a war or in a campaign or expedition for which a campaign badge has been authorized."

Federal Contractors with $50,000 in Federal Funding and over 50 Employees

If your organization employs at least 50 employees and receives at least $50,000 in funding as a contractor or subcontractor of the federal government, your organization will fall under federal regulations found at 41 C.F.R. Section 60-1 et seq., ☞ that require a written AAP. The regulations also require that the employer keep tract of hiring statistics and workplace demographics by completing an equal employment survey annually.

The written plan should describe that the employer will maintain and report statistics on an EEO survey on an annual basis that include:

❏ A detailed analysis of the employer's current workforce by race and sex;

❏ An analysis of whether minorities, special disabled veterans, or females are statistically underrepresented or underused in the workforce;

❏ The establishment of guidelines for recruiting and hiring in job categories in which minorities or females are underrepresented;

❏ Action programs necessary to achieve the stated goals and to remedy identified problems areas; and

❏ Timetables for achieving these goals.

The Office of Federal Contract Compliance (OFCCP) ☞ is the enforcement agency that monitors compliance with the regulations, sends out the EEO surveys (generally only to employers with 100+ employees) and also conducts random audits to test whether federal grantees are in compliance. The survey asks for information pertaining to a contractor's Affirmative Action Program and summary data on personnel activity and compensation. Note that the Office of Federal Contract Compliance is most likely to conduct an audit for compliance with Affirmative Action Plans if the nonprofit employs more than 100 employees.

If your nonprofit is considering bidding on a government funded project, the pieces of the AAP must be in place within 120 days of receiving a contract for the nonprofit to qualify for the contract with the government. If you already have a government contract, make sure an internal audit is conducted to assess compliance. If the OFCCP pays your nonprofit a visit, you can be sure that any missing requirements, such as the AAP, will be exposed.

E-Mail Interviews: Is Saving Time Worth It?

Along with the upside of Internet-based hiring is the downside of e-mail or Internet-based interviews. Some employers—in an attempt to reduce the cost of the recruitment process—elect to conduct preliminary candidate interviews online. An important consideration is that e-mail interviews eliminate the opportunity for the interviewer to gauge the integrity of the applicant by reading visual cues and body language. It's easy to misinterpret the tone of an e-mail or instant message, or draw inappropriate conclusions due to the brevity of a statement. In-person interviews, while time-consuming, are likely to offer greater insights into an applicant's suitability for a position at a nonprofit.

Experienced human resources directors and nonprofit managers with long track records of hiring are well aware that dishonesty isn't uncommon among applicants. Whether the applicant exaggerates her or his qualifications on an application or résumé, or tells an outright lie during the interview, hiring personnel should be aware that an applicant's written and oral statements may not be the whole truth. An estimated 30 percent of all résumés contain material misstatements, while a much larger number (perhaps as high as 70 percent) may contain exaggerated statements concerning responsibilities at prior positions. An excellent opportunity to test the truthfulness of claims made in writing is during the in-person interview.

A sample Affirmative Action Plan can be found at the following Web site: www.dol.gov/esa/regs/compliance/ofccp/pdf/sampleaap.pdf.

Negligent Hiring

Hiring someone who has a history of injuring others, such as someone with a criminal conviction for child abuse, sexual assault or violent crimes, can result in legal liability to the nonprofit on the theory of *negligent hiring* or *negligent retention*. In most states, employers are responsible for employee crimes or accidents if the nonprofit *knew or should have known* that the employee posed a threat of harm to others. Negligent hiring claims arise when an employee injures a co-worker or a third party, and the injured party claims that the employer never should have hired the employee in the first place, or should have fired the employee once the employer realized that the employee was potentially dangerous. This claim might occur when a child-serving agency fails to conduct a thorough background check and hires a felon who has served time for child molestation. When that employee abuses a child in the nonprofit's care, the nonprofit may be held responsible for negligently hiring the child abuser. Similarly, if complaints are raised about an employee's conduct with children, but the nonprofit doesn't fire that employee, the nonprofit risks a lawsuit that the nonprofit knew, or should have known, that the employee was a danger to children. The legal claim will be that the nonprofit was negligent in retaining the employee—in essence, that the nonprofit should have fired the employee after the initial complaint. Avoiding claims of *negligent retention* is accomplished by thorough and consistent screening, conscientious supervision, and not tolerating employees who place consumers or the nonprofit at risk. Screening employees effectively is a grave responsibility—selection of the wrong employee can result in severe liability for a nonprofit.

Q: Can you contact a reference whose name wasn't given to you by an applicant?

A: Yes! If the applicant has given written authorization to verify information about their background, you should feel comfortable checking references you haven't received. This may not be necessary in the case of an applicant who has provided appropriate references. This may be very important if not essential when an applicant has failed, without explanation, to provide suitable professional references (for example, most recent supervisor). Remember that you are trying to find the best match for an important position in your nonprofit. You owe it to your clients and other staff and volunteers to put on your Sherlock Holmes cap and approach people who may be able to provide valuable insight on the applicant's suitability.

Reference Checking Options

Checking an applicant's references is a time-consuming but worthwhile risk management task. Consistency in the nonprofit's background checking procedures is very important. Checking references in a haphazard manner is asking for trouble. There are at least three basic approaches to checking references:

❑ meeting with the applicant's references,

❑ telephoning the applicant's references, and

❑ requesting a written response by mail or e-mail.

A personal meeting may elicit the most information, because the person checking the reference can interpret the facial expressions and body language of the person providing the reference. This approach may not be practical, however.

Speaking to a former employer on the telephone is a common method of checking references, although frequently former employers won't divulge any information without a written release from their former employee. A conversation provides an opportunity to interpret the vocal inflections of the person providing the reference, perhaps revealing more than the written word.

Getting information in writing may be the most challenging, because former employers are often reluctant to release information in writing without authorization from their former employee due to the liability risks involved for the employer.

Risk Management Tip: Obtain Written Authorizations for Reference Checks

Many nonprofits have difficulty getting helpful information from previous employers because the employers don't want to be sued by former employees for defamation of character resulting from a negative reference. As a result most advisors to nonprofits stress that the nonprofit should have a policy of only releasing the bare minimum when contacted to verify employment history of a prior employee. However, if a previous employer only verifies dates of employment, job title and compensation, this is *not* enough information for another nonprofit that's checking references to conclude that the candidate passes muster.

Keep in mind that references are among the most valuable screening tools at a nonprofit's disposal. Few employers would attempt to place an applicant in a key position without first checking that applicant's professional references. However, the growing tendency of employers to refuse to provide references has made reference getting unnecessarily difficult. As an employer considers how to improve its success in reference getting, an important first step is obtaining permission from the applicant.

Many nonprofits require applicants to sign a written authorization and release, which both authorizes the nonprofit to check references, and gives any prior employers permission to provide information on the applicant's qualifications for employment by promising that the applicant won't bring a lawsuit if negative information is disclosed. The form should include a specific waiver of the right to sue both the previous employer and the nonprofit seeking the information.

Negligent Reference Giving

An employer owes a former employee a duty to exercise reasonable care when communicating facts about his or her work history to a prospective employer. Employers can be held liable for providing *negligent references*, if they *either* share information that results in harm to the former employee (which could result in the employee filing a defamation claim) *or* withhold information about a former employee's propensity for violence (when doing so results in harm to a third-party.) While there is a risk to the nonprofit for sharing information, there is also a risk for withholding important information that would prevent future harm. Without proper guidance about safe reference giving, a nonprofit employer is vulnerable to claims. With a thoughtful approach providing the backdrop for reference giving, nonprofit leaders can and should provide references on former employees. There are several practical and feasible risk management tools that nonprofits can use to heighten the safety of reference-giving practices.

State Reference Immunity Laws Protect Employers

Thirty-five states have enacted legislation that creates an immunity shield to protect an employer who gives or receives employment history information about a candidate for employment. In Minnesota, "no communication of a statement furnished by the employer to the employee may be made the subject of any action for libel, slander, or defamation by the employee against the employer." In these states employees may not bring a lawsuit against their employer for providing negative employment history except in certain circumstances, as specified in the statute. The Minnesota statute provides that an employee or former won't have a cause of action unless, "…the information was false and defamatory; and the employer knew or should have known the information was false and acted with malicious intent to injure the current or former employee." Minn. Stat. Ch. 181.967 ✎

The online version of *Taking the High Road* contains a detailed summary of state reference immunity laws. Consult this resource for information on your state's law.

Reference Authorization Forms

Not all states have adopted laws that protect reference-givers, and the immunity available in 35 states only provides protection after a lawsuit has been filed by a disgruntled employee or former employee. It's preferable to avoid a lawsuit for defamation in the first place. Therefore, it's useful to employ a strategy that will minimize the risk of the nonprofit being a target in litigation. One such strategy is to ask all applicants to sign a *reference authorization form*, which the employer provides to the applicant's former employer(s). The purpose of the form is to release the prospective employer from any liability associated with seeking and obtaining information about the prospective employee. See the sample that follows to better understand how such a release might be worded.

SAMPLE--

Authorization for Employment Reference and Release of Information

To Whom it May Concern: I hereby authorize [Name of Nonprofit] to conduct a thorough background check on my qualifications for employment and I specifically authorize any representative of [Name of Nonprofit] to obtain information from my former employer(s), or other sources, pertaining to my qualifications for employment and employment history. I also authorize [Name of Nonprofit] to contact my current employer
[__ Yes __ No].

This authorization is executed with the full knowledge and understanding that the information is for use by [Name of Nonprofit] in evaluating my qualifications for employment.

I hereby release [Name of Nonprofit], its directors, officers, and agents, and my current or former employer(s), including agents, officers, directors and employees of my current and former employer(s), both individually and collectively, from any and all claims of liability for damages of whatever kind, including, but not limited to, invasion of privacy, slander or defamation of character, which may at any time result to me, as a result of compliance with this Authorization for Employment Reference and Release of Information, or any attempt to comply with it.

Should there be any question about the validity of this authorization, you may contact me as indicated below.

This Authorization will continue in effect for 90 days from the date of signature. A photocopy of the authorization shall have the same force as the original.

Signature of applicant _____   Contact telephone: _____

- -

Four-Step Process for Checking Applicant Information

Here's a very simple system for verifying information provided by an applicant:

Step 1: All applicants complete an application form that includes an authorization permitting the nonprofit to conduct a background check, including criminal records, references, and verifying any information contained on the application. The application also contains a *truth clause*, which is a statement signed by the applicant, indicating that the applicant can immediately be eliminated from consideration in the hiring process or terminated from employment for providing false information during the hiring process.

Step 2: The nonprofit assigns one qualified staff member the job of first reviewing and verifying the factual information provided by applicants on their application forms and résumés—and then selecting which applicants to interview. By weeding out those applicants who don't meet minimum qualifications or whose factual information doesn't hang together, the nonprofit won't waste time interviewing someone who is simply not qualified to be hired. The staff person assigned to this task is responsible for contacting previous employers and seeking information to verify prior work history as well as contacting educational institutions to verify educational background, degrees, and certifications. The staff member who reviews minimum qualifications should use the same form or checklist for each applicant, noting what information has been verified: level of education, degrees, licenses, dates of employment with previous employers, and so forth. The staff member collecting this information should keep in mind that if at any point the review indicates that the applicant doesn't meet minimum qualifications, the applicant may be disqualified at that time.

Step 3: Only the applicants who meet minimum qualifications and whose factual background can be verified should be interviewed. During the interview the interviewer can further evaluate the degree to which the applicant's skills, demeanor and experience match the employer's requirements for the position. The interviewer may request or verify the list of references at this time. In some cases an applicant will provide additional factual information during an interview, which must be verified and recorded on the applicant's background check form.

Step 4: A copy of each form/checklist is maintained in an *application pending* file for each applicant until all verifications have been received. The staff member assigned to the fact verification task must follow up any requests for verification that aren't returned to the nonprofit.

If any discrepancy appears in the facts provided by the applicant, the nonprofit should either reject the applicant prior to spending the time and energy to interview the candidate, check additional records or references to resolve the discrepancies, or if warranted, contact the applicant again to explore missing information or discrepancies.

Remember:

❏ Obtain the candidate's written permission to check references.

❏ Always check references and verify information about education or past experience before making a final job offer.

❏ Follow up any discrepancies in information provided by the candidate during the hiring process. Investigate further as needed.

❏ Obtain as many references as feasible.

❏ Be skeptical of silence or evasiveness by someone providing a reference and commit to investigate further.

❏ Insist that the candidate provide relevant references—if none are provided, either disqualify the candidate or check references that haven't been provided by tracking down the applicant's most recent supervisors.

A Case in Point

An employee in a youth-serving nonprofit was accused of inappropriate conduct with a boy under his care. The nonprofit conducted a thorough investigation and didn't come up with any evidence of prior criminal records or inappropriate conduct. Later, when the same individual abused a child in another program in the community, the nonprofit was sued for negligence, but because the nonprofit had no knowledge of any actual wrongdoing (the investigation of the allegation was thorough and didn't uncover evidence of misconduct), the case against the nonprofit was dismissed.

If there had been evidence of prior inappropriate conduct, such as a prior conviction, it's possible that the court would have concluded that while the nonprofit didn't know about the misconduct, it *should have known*—resulting in a probable finding of liability on the basis of negligence by the nonprofit.

Screening for Past Criminal Conduct

Is it Legitimate to Reject an Applicant Due to Prior Criminal Activity?
Consideration of Convictions and Arrests in the Hiring Process

In April 2006 the Equal Employment Opportunity Commission (www.eeoc.gov) issued guidelines about race and sex discrimination that specifically address whether it's permissible for employers to ask about and consider past criminal activity during the recruitment process. (See EEOC Compliance Manual No. 915.003, issued 4/19/06, found at www.eeoc.gov/types/race.html.) The position of the federal government is that an employer may not exclude applicants based on arrests that didn't lead to conviction unless there is a business justification. To prove a *business justification* an employer must show that the applicant engaged in the conduct for which he or she was arrested, and that the conduct is both job-related and fairly recent. The EEOC notes, however, that, a business justification can rarely be demonstrated for blanket, across-the-board exclusions on the basis of arrest records.

State Laws: Thirty-six states allow employers to inquire about and make hiring decisions based on arrests that didn't lead to a conviction. Ten states—California, Hawaii, Illinois, Massachusetts, Michigan, New York, Ohio, Rhode Island, Utah, and Wisconsin—prohibit public and private employers and from using arrests that never led to conviction as the basis for rejecting an applicant for employment.

❏ For example, the Illinois Human Rights Act, which applies to employers with 15 or more employees, prohibits arrest-related inquiries, as well as an employer's use of an arrest as a basis for making any employment decision, whether hiring, discipline or termination. 775 ILCS 5/2-103(A). ✒

❏ Illinois requires all applications for employment to contain the following statement "Applicants aren't obligated to disclose sealed or expunged records of conviction or arrest." Illinois Criminal Identification Act, 20 ILCS 2630/3 ✒

Pennsylvania allows employers to ask about arrests that never led to conviction but prohibits employers from utilizing that information when making a hiring decision.

Arkansas, New Mexico and New Hampshire don't prohibit private employers from inquiring about or making decisions based on arrests that didn't lead to conviction, although public employers are prohibited from doing so.

In the guidelines issued on April 2006, the EEOC emphasizes that conviction, as well as arrest records, must be evaluated by prospective employers without regard to race or color, and that such records must be job-related and consistent with *business necessity*. When considering conviction records, the EEOC guidelines advise that three factors must be considered:

1. the nature and gravity of the offense(s);

2. the time that has passed since the conviction and/or completion of the sentence; and

3. the nature of the job held or sought.

Example: An employer may legitimately base a decision not to hire an applicant for a position in a day care center if the applicant's conviction was for a crime involving child abuse. However, it wouldn't be appropriate to automatically reject an applicant for a conviction 12 years ago involving failure to pay parking fines. In the latter case, the decision to reject the applicant based solely on the fact that he or she admitted to a past conviction could be considered discriminatory. If challenged, the employer would be required to defend the decision by showing that the applicant's failure to pay parking fines 12 years ago is closely related to a legitimate, job-related qualification for the day care position, or that there was another legitimate reason to reject the applicant.

In most states it's permissible to reject an applicant due to past criminal activity as long as there is a business reason for the rejection and a clear tie between a past criminal conviction the duties of the position. Know your specific state statute, and check your state's pre-employment inquiry guidelines for any limitations on questions about criminal records.

There is no question that potentially relevant information on individuals may be found in criminal history records, sex offender registries, child abuse registries, driving records, and through consumer reporting agencies. First, decide if the information from any of these sources is *necessary* for your applicant screening process. If your organization decides that record checks are necessary for some positions, you should conduct the record checks on all candidates for those positions. Checking criminal records on some but not all candidates for a specific position may be viewed as discriminatory or, at the very least, as negligent, because it will be hard to explain why an individual who had committed a crime wasn't screened in a manner that was consistent with the nonprofit's policies.

Some proponents of using criminal record checks assert that letting applicants know that a thorough background check, including a criminal record check will be run, will discourage individuals with disqualifying records from applying. Common sense supports this argument. Many people won't risk exposure, if they know that records exist that would disqualify them from service. Yet amazingly, reports continue to circulate about ex-offenders who have sought positions with nonprofits where they would have unsupervised access to children or other vulnerable persons.

The decision to conduct record checks should be based primarily upon the specific responsibilities of the position. If operating a motor vehicle isn't part of the position description, then why check driving records? If the position doesn't call for handling money or other organizational assets, then why conduct a credit history check? If the position won't expose the employee to vulnerable clients except in group contact under close supervision, are criminal history record checks for that position really necessary? New York law specifically advises that: "Employers shouldn't disqualify an applicant unless there is a direct relationship between the previous criminal offense and the specific employment sought, or if there is a question of safety or unreasonable risk to property, clients or the general public."

It's generally the nonprofit's choice whether to forgive and forget a prior conviction or to determine that the conviction disqualifies the applicant. This is a risk-balancing exercise. Each nonprofit needs to determine the level of screening required to protect the nonprofit and its vulnerable clients. Where no statute governs the situation, the nonprofit is left to make this difficult decision on its own. Ask: "*Is hiring this applicant going to create more of a risk than rejecting him/her because of the prior conviction?*" Documentation of the rational decision-making process showing the job-related reason for either rejecting, or accepting an applicant with a prior conviction, is essential.

Using official criminal, police, or credit records as screening tools may strengthen your position in litigation involving claims of negligent hiring. In contrast, an organization that never bothered to conduct a criminal history check is more likely to be held responsible for negligence, because it failed to do so. As the accessibility and affordability of record databases increases, it becomes more and more likely that juries will find nonprofits negligent for *not* conducting a background check that includes a review of criminal records.

Negligent Retention

Employers can be sued on the theory of *negligent retention* if it's shown that they should have terminated an employee who posed a risk of harm to clients or other employees. However, if an employer receives a complaint of inappropriate conduct, investigates the allegation and comes to a reasonable conclusion that the employee isn't posing a risk of harm, then retaining the employee isn't likely to result in liability. In a recent case in South Carolina a disabled client was abused by a bus driver. The plaintiff alleged that the social services agency was negligent in retaining the bus driver, who had previously grabbed a co-worker and tried to kiss her. That incident had been investigated by the nonprofit. At trial the court found that the prior incident with the co-worker, which had been investigated by the nonprofit, didn't necessarily put the nonprofit on notice that the plaintiff or others would be at risk. Therefore, the court found that the nonprofit's decision to retain the employee was *reasonable* and not negligent.

It should be noted that the employer in this case had to defend at trial the fact that it didn't terminate the employee. During the trial, the employer had to justify its actions with documentation that it had responded reasonably to a prior complaint about the employee's conduct and properly investigated the situation. Without a clear paper-trail of the nonprofit's response and investigation the court might not have found the nonprofit's conduct to be *reasonable*.

Misleading Résumés

Fifty percent of employment, education and/or credential reference checks revealed a difference of information between what the applicant provided and the source reported. (Source: ADP Eighth Annual Hiring Index.)

Sixty-one percent of human resource professionals surveyed said they find inaccuracies in résumés after carrying out background checks. (Source: SHRM Background Checks/Résumé Inaccuracies online survey, 2004.)

42.7 percent of résumés have significant inaccuracies. Example: The CEO of a national appliance store chain was forced to resign 12 years after being hired, because he had inflated his academic credentials on his résumé. His employer had conducted a background check at the time he was hired, but didn't verify his educational background. (Source: A 2005 survey conducted by Resumedoctor.com, a résumé consulting company in Burlington, VT.)

Consumer Reports: Using an Outside Source to Conduct Background Checks

Private vendors are becoming an increasingly common source for pre-employment screening. Most of these vendors are accessible through the Internet and offer a faster turn-around time than governmental agencies. Many offer a range of services including credentials verification, reference checks and criminal history record checks. Unlike reports issued by governmental agencies, the reports that these vendors generate are considered *consumer reports*, which are regulated by a federal law: The Fair Credit Reporting Act, 15 U.S.C. § 1681 et seq. (FCRA) and the fair consumer credit reporting laws of some states. These laws require employers to obtain written authorization for background checks and to provide written notice when an employer uses outside sources, such as credit bureaus, to collect background information on applicants or employees.

The FCRA requires employers to put applicants on notice that a consumer report will be sought, and used to evaluate their qualifications for employment. If an employer uses the report on an applicant or employee's background, (whether educational history, driving records, employment, credit history, or criminal history) to make a decision resulting in an adverse employment action (such as disqualifying an applicant or terminating an employee) the employer must inform the applicant of this fact in writing, and provide the applicant or employee with a copy of the report. The Web site of the Federal Trade Commission (FTC) (www.ftc.gov/bcp/conline/pubs/buspubs/credempl.htm) provides an outline of the requirements for employers using outside consumer credit agency reports. Key provisions appear below.

Key Provisions of the FCRA Amendments

Written Notice and Authorization

Before you can get a consumer report for employment purposes, you must notify the applicant in writing—in a document consisting solely of this notice—that a report may be used. You also must get the applicant's written authorization before you ask a consumer reporting agency (CRA) for the report.

The notice requirement under FCRA requires that employers provide a clear and conspicuous written disclosure to the applicant/employee *before* the consumer report is obtained, using a document that consists solely of the notice disclosure. A copy of the required notice can be downloaded from the FTC Web site: *A Summary of Your Rights Under the Fair Credit Reporting Act* (www.ftc.gov/os/statutes/2summary.htm or www.ftc.gov/bcp/conline/pubs/credit/fcrasummary.pdf).

Negative Reference Bolsters Retaliation Claim

The Tenth Circuit Court of Appeals held in *Hillig v. Rumsfeld*, that a negative job reference, when shown to materially harm the employee's future employment prospects, could constitute an adverse employment action sufficient to support liability for a claim of retaliation.

Hillig, who was a minority, had filed two EEO complaints for race discrimination at a prior employer. Both complaints were settled. She applied for a personnel clerk/assistant position and was told by an interviewer that she was a "perfect fit." A white female was awarded the position instead. An EEOC investigation revealed that the employer had received two negative references by supervisors with one providing very strong negative feedback including calling her a "(expletive) employee." The jury found that although the negative references weren't motivated by race bias they were made in retaliation for the prior EEO complaints. The jury awarded the plaintiff $25,000 on her retaliation claim.

Risk Management Tips

Consider establishing a policy indicating the nonprofit's intent to provide references for former employees and establishing consent as a condition of employment. Use an authorization form that releases the nonprofit from liability for providing references, and keep signed copies of the form in the nonprofit's personnel files.

Make certain that all staff understand whether their positions permit or prohibit them from giving references about former employees. Some employers may want to limit reference-giving to the human resources director. In other organizations senior managers may be permitted to give references. Any staff member permitted to give references should understand that it's never permissible to use inappropriate language in an oral or written reference.

> Several states have enacted their own version of fair consumer credit checking laws including California and New Jersey. Ask your employment attorney whether or not your nonprofit must comply with any state-specific obligations for compliance with these laws.

Adverse Action Procedures

If you rely on a consumer report as the basis for taking an adverse action—such as denying a job application, reassigning or terminating an employee, or denying a promotion—be aware that:

Step 1: Before you take the adverse action, you must give the individual a **pre-adverse action disclosure** that includes a copy of the individual's consumer report and a copy of *A Summary of Your Rights Under the Fair Credit Reporting Act*—a document prescribed by the Federal Trade Commission. The CRA that furnishes the individual's report will give you the summary of consumer rights.

Step 2: After you've taken an adverse action, you must give the individual notice—orally, in writing, or electronically—that the action has been taken in an **adverse action notice**. It must include:

❑ the name, address, and phone number of the CRA that supplied the report;

❑ a statement that the CRA that supplied the report didn't make the decision to take the adverse action and can't give specific reasons for it; and

❑ a notice of the individual's right to dispute the accuracy or completeness of any information the agency furnished, and his or her right to an additional free consumer report from the agency upon request within 60 days.

Source: FTC Web site: www.ftc.gov/bcp/conline/pubs/buspubs/credempl.htm

Checklist for Using Outside Vendors for Consumer Credit Reports

❑ Obtain prior written authorization from the applicant/employee to conduct the check.

❑ Give the applicant/employee written notice in the format prescribed by the FTC.

❑ Certify to the CRA that the previous steps have been followed, that the information being obtained won't be used in violation of any federal or state equal opportunity law or regulation, and that, if any adverse action is to be taken based on the consumer report, a copy of the report and a summary of the consumer's rights will be provided to the consumer.

❑ After reviewing the report received from the private vendor, an employer must maintain the confidentiality of the information by destroying the report received from the outside source.

❑ Before taking an adverse action, provide a copy of the report to the applicant/employee along with the summary of the consumer's rights.

❑ If the employer takes any adverse action against the applicant/employee, the employer must provide the applicant/employee with another written notice, an *adverse action notice*.

❑ Internal investigations that are conducted exclusively by the nonprofit's staff and that *don't utilize outside consumer reporting agencies or investigators* to obtain the information, *aren't* subject to FCRA.

Due to the complications that could arise from inadvertently triggering the FCRA provisions, it may be wise to defer checks by consumer reporting agencies until the end of the screening process. In this way, you can be pretty sure that an applicant meets all other requirements for employment pending the results of the record checks.

How to Use Information Received from Background Checks

Your nonprofit must decide how it will use information from record checks once you obtain it. Some states are very specific about an employer's obligations to destroy background information obtained from either the state police records or federal criminal records. As an example, New York requires employers to notify applicants in writing if a conviction record results in their rejection. You should question the significance of any information you receive. If there is adverse information, should it lead you to conclude that the behavior will be repeated? Recognize that the records discussed in this chapter may have limited usefulness as predictors of future behavior.

When Is Checking Criminal Histories Essential?

From a risk management perspective, it's most appropriate to conduct a criminal history records check on any applicant for a position with job duties involving unsupervised work with vulnerable clients. Many nonprofits can't afford to conduct criminal records checks on all applicants due to the time and expense involved. Yet, some states require nonprofits to conduct criminal history checks for certain types of employment. The summary below shows which states require criminal background checks in what situations.

State Law Requirements for Background Checks

The state laws noted here are subject to constant review and revision in state legislatures. This summary should therefore be used for reference purposes, rather than as a definitive guide.

Alabama: Licensed child and adult care centers, and employers in agencies, schools, and health care facilities that serve children, the elderly and the disabled, are required to conduct a criminal record check on applicants whether paid or volunteers. Unlicensed child and adult care agencies are permitted to conduct a criminal records check on paid and volunteer staff. Code of Alabama Title 38, Chapter 13

Alaska: Nursing facilities are required to conduct criminal background checks on employees. Alaska Code, Title 18, Chapter 20, Section 302.

Arizona: Child care personnel must be fingerprinted and register with the Dept. of Public Health and Safety in order to work in day care centers. Criminal record checks are required for persons employed (and some volunteers) by home-based service providers, child-serving agencies, developmental disability contract providers, shelters for victims of domestic violence, and nursing and home health care agencies. Arizona law also makes it a felony when applicants and volunteers fail to notify schools, preschools, child care providers and youth organizations of any prior convictions of dangerous crimes. Ariz. Rev. Stat. Ann. Sections 13-3716 ; 36-594.01 ; 36-883.02.

Arkansas: In order to maintain child care licenses, all owners and operators of child care facilities must demonstrate that they applied to the Identification Bureau of the Department of Arkansas State Police for a nationwide criminal background records check on each employee. Ark. Stat. Ann. Section 20-78-602; criminal record checks are required for employees of: school districts and child care facilities Ark Code Sections 20-78-602; 6-17-411; employees or volunteers of child welfare agencies Arkansas Code Section: 9-28-409; Employees of ElderChoice providers Ark. Code Section 20-33-203. *Note:* Charities may register with the State Police in Arkansas to obtain criminal record check information, but first must pass a resolution by the board of directors defining what convictions will disqualify a volunteer from service with the organization. Ark Code Section 12-12-1605.

California: No employers are *required* to conduct background checks. With the exception of *health facilities*, employers aren't permitted to ask about prior arrests; all employers may request information during hiring about convictions (except convictions involving marijuana that are more than two years old). California Labor Code 432.7

Colorado: Employers may not inquire about arrest. Employers may only consider convictions within the prior seven years and when the candidate is expected to earn less than $75,000 annually. Colorado has its own Consumer Credit Reporting Act, Title 14 Col. Rev. Stat. that permits disclosure to employers of credit reports as long as the subject of the report has provided written consent.

Connecticut: State policy encourages hiring qualified applicants with criminal records. Employers are prohibited from denying employment to anyone solely on the basis of a prior criminal record if that record has been erased. Employers are also not permitted to discriminate in hiring by making inquiries about, or terminate someone because of past criminal records that have been erased. If an application form contains any question about criminal history, it must include the following notice: "The applicant isn't required to disclose the existence of any arrest, criminal charge or conviction, the records of which have been erased." Conn. Gen. Statutes. Chapter 557 Sec. 51-51i If a state agency rejects an applicant because of a criminal history, the agency is required to send a written explanation of a rejection for employment based on a past conviction—however, this requirement doesn't apply to private employers. Conn. Gen. Stat. 46a 79, 46a80.

Delaware: Residential child care providers and providers that are contractors with the Delaware Department of Services for Children, Youth and Their Families (teachers, child care workers, social workers etc.) are required to conduct criminal record checks on employees and volunteers. Delaware Code, Chapter 3, Title 31 Section 309. Pre-employment criminal record checks *as well as drug tests* are required of employees in nursing facilities (nursing homes), assisted living facilities, intermediate care facilities for persons with mental retardation, neighborhood group homes, family care homes, and rest residential facilities. Detailed regulations provide for the testing, confidential record keeping and disqualification of employees with certain past criminal records. See 16 Del.C. Ch. 11 §§1141 and 1142.

District of Columbia: The District of Columbia Code requires personnel working in various kinds of health care facilities to undergo criminal history record checks and prohibits individuals convicted of specified crimes from being employed in these facilities DC ST § 44-552. Other facilities and programs may be required by law or regulation to conduct criminal history record checks DC ST § 4-1501.03.

Q: May we automatically disqualify an applicant due to a felony conviction?

A: The EEOC takes the position that it's impermissible to reject an applicant simply due to the existence of a past conviction. In some states, applicants for certain such positions as health care or child care workers must be disqualified for employment if they've been convicted of a violent crime, a drug-related offense, or a crime involving dishonesty, either because the applicant won't be able to get a license from the state, or because a state law mandates that an applicant with such a conviction isn't qualified for the position. In states where there is no regulation in this area, the answer should depend on the job duties of the position sought, and the particular crime committed by the applicant. Is a conviction for shoplifting 20 years ago relevant to a lifeguard position today? To a bookkeeping job?

Florida: The 2006 Florida Statutes Chapter 435 establishes two levels of screening for individuals employed by institutions caring for the developmentally disabled, or mentally ill, as well as other state-licensed facilities including schools and child care facilities. The statutes also set out the offenses for which an individual required to be screened will be deemed unfit and permit sharing of information gained under this Chapter with other employers.

Georgia: Employees in state licensed day care facilities must pass a records check conducted by the state in order to retain employment. [Ga. Code Ann. Section 49-5-69]

Hawaii: An employer may inquire about and consider an individual's criminal conviction record concerning hiring, termination, or the terms, conditions, or privileges of employment; provided that the conviction record bears a rational relationship to the duties and responsibilities of the position. Inquiry into and consideration of conviction records for prospective employees shall take place only after the prospective employee has received a conditional offer of employment but this restriction does not apply to employers who are expressly permitted to inquire into an individual's criminal history for employment purposes pursuant to any federal or state law.

Illinois: Child serving organizations may require, as a condition of employment, or volunteer services, that applicants and current employees sign a statement under penalty of perjury indicating whether they've ever been convicted of an offense involving intentional infliction of injury on a child, sexual abuse of a child or child abduction. See Ill. Rev. Stat. 820 Section 820 ILCS 210; Employers may not ask about an arrest or criminal history record that has been expunged or sealed, but employers are specifically permitted to use information about convictions. See Ill. Rev. Stat. 775 Section 775 ILCS 5/2-103 Illinois Human Rights Act.

Indiana: The Indiana Code permits the use of criminal history record information in the screening of employees and volunteers. There are some positions such as school teachers and child care workers who are required to undergo criminal history record checks.

Kentucky: An employer may request from the Justice Cabinet or the Administrative Office of the Courts, or both, records of all available convictions involving any felony offense, any misdemeanor committed within the five (5) years immediately preceding the application, of a person who applies for employment or volunteers for a position in which he or she would have supervisory or disciplinary power over a minor. Each child-care center must request all conviction information for any applicant for employment from the Justice Cabinet or the Administrative Office of the Courts prior to employing the applicant.

Maryland: Maryland law requires several kinds of programs for children to conduct criminal history record checks. Child care centers, schools, recreation centers and camps are among the services required to conduct criminal history record checks. See Md. Family Code § 5-561.

Missouri: A person, business, or organization that provides care, placement, or educational services for children, the elderly, or persons with disabilities as patients or residents, including a business or organization that licenses or certifies others to provide care or placement services, may obtain a Missouri criminal record review of a provider from the highway patrol by furnishing information on forms and in the manner approved by the highway patrol. See Missouri Revised Statutes §43.540.

New Jersey: Licensed child care facilities, day care centers and schools under the supervision of the Department of Education shall not employ or contract for services any worker in direct contact with children unless the employer has first conducted a criminal background check through the Division of Youth and Family Services or Department of Education. A separate statute requires employers in health care facilities serving the infirm elderly, including elder day care facilities, to conduct criminal background checks on all applicants for employment and makes it unlawful to employ an individual if the record check reveals certain criminal conduct. See N.J.S.A. 26: 2H-82 to 87; 45:11-24.3 to 24.9; 53:1-20.9a; 30:5B-6.1 to 6.9.

Ohio: Chartered private schools must conduct criminal record checks on applicants for employment in positions involving the care, custody, or control of a child. See Ohio Code Ann. Sections 3319.39. Since 1993, the Ohio General Assembly has passed several state laws requiring background checks for certain occupations including individuals who work with children, those who work with the elderly, and insurance agents.

Oregon: An organization may request from the Oregon State Police Open Records Section a criminal records check for purposes of evaluating the fitness of a subject individual as an employee, contractor or volunteer. The requesting organization must provide the individual's fingerprints to access state and federal criminal records. The organization requesting the records check must provide the OSP Open Records Section the criteria used for making a fitness determination. See OR Rev. Statutes § 181.5. Some positions require a criminal history record check such as school nurses, personnel administrators, and teachers must undergo a criminal background check for violations involving the use, sale, or possession of controlled substances, sexual conduct, theft, or a crime of violence. See OR Rev. Statutes § 342.227.

Rhode Island: Criminal record checks are required for positions involving the supervision of minors, or routine contact with children without the presence of supervisors, or for positions in residential care and assisted living facilities. See R.I. Gen. Laws Sections 16-48.1-2, 1-5; 23-17.4.30. In addition, any person seeking employment in a facility which is or is required to be licensed or registered with the department of health if that employment involves routine contact with a patient or resident without the presence of other employees, shall undergo a criminal background check. See General Laws of Rhode Island § 23-17.7.1-17. ✎

Texas: Texas laws require some positions such as school employees to obtain criminal history record checks. It also permits school districts to obtain criminal history record information on volunteers in the school. See Texas Education Code § 22-082, § 22-083, § 22-084. Standards for youth camps require staff to have criminal history records. See Texas Health and Safety Code § 141.009. ✎

Utah: In 2006, Utah enact several changes to its screening requirements for individuals with direct access to children or vulnerable adults. Employers and volunteers whose work requires direct access to children or vulnerable adults are required to undergo criminal history record checks as a condition of licensing. Individuals who have not lived in the State for five years must undergo a FBI record check. See Utah Code §62A-2-120.

Virginia: Virginia law only requires criminal background checks for public school district employees only. See Va. Code §22.1-296.1, 296.2. However, a law enacted in 2006 places a lifetime prohibition for any adult convicted of specified offenses from working as an employee or volunteer on school property. This could have ramifications for organizations that use school facilities for conducting programs. See Va. Code. § 18.2-370.4. ✎

Washington: There are several sections of the Washington Code that relate to criminal history record checks. One section of the law requiring criminal background checks pertains to public school district employees only. See Wash. Rev. Code Section 28A.400.303. However, other sections of the Code require regulations be developed that ensure that employees in child care and health care facilities are screened for criminal backgrounds. See RCW 43.43.842. ✎

A criminal record check is only as good as the day the check is run. The next day the applicant could be convicted of a crime! Screening doesn't stop with a criminal background check. Screening involves a spectrum of watchfulness and constant supervision to ensure that the people your nonprofit hires are suitable for the position. Checking criminal history records is only one step in a comprehensive screening process. Checking references, verifying employment information, educational background and prior volunteer experience can be equally revealing.

A Case in Point

A supervisor was skeptical when a candidate for an open position in a mentoring program provided three nonwork-related references. The candidate, who had five years teaching experience in a public school, didn't list the principal or department head at the school as references. After checking the references provided by the applicant, the employer contacted the principal of the school, who revealed that the candidate resigned from his teaching position after being confronted with evidence that he used his classroom computer to peruse pornographic Web sites when students were present.

Should Your Nonprofit Have a Contract With the CEO?

It isn't uncommon, but certainly not *de riguer* for nonprofits to have employment contracts with their CEOs. In the 2000 *NonProfit Times* (*www.nptimes.com*) Salary Survey 30 percent of responding employers reported that their chief executive had an employment contract. Contracts can address issues such as starting salary and salary increases, performance bonuses, housing, cars, expense allowances and severance pay. The expansion of using contracts that contain severance clauses (promises to pay the CEO additional compensation upon separation) can be explained by the need to attract and retain a shrinking pool of qualified CEO-level nonprofit leaders, and the recognition that the turnover of volunteer boards can result in unanticipated termination of the CEO by a new or changed board of directors.

A contract can help articulate specific job duties or expectations for the CEO, with buy-in from the board that is aware of and agrees with the expectations for the CEO's performance. A contract that spells out fringe benefits—a travel allowance, cell phone or car lease, or professional development allowances—can actually protect the organization by articulating the business reason and the dollar ceiling for such expenditures, which could otherwise be challenged by the IRS as *excessive* compensation for the CEO. A contract can spell out that the CEO will receive a promised payment in the event of termination, and in return the board of directors is often assured a period of notice prior to the CEO's departure. Sometimes it takes a contract to attract and hire a sought-after CEO. When drafted by an attorney skilled in employment matters, a contract can be a useful recruitment and supervision tool.

The downside of an employment contract is that if the board of directors isn't aware of the consequences, there will surely be damages to pay to the CEO if the contract is breached. The last thing any nonprofit could wish in the wake of a CEO departure is a breach of contract suit. Once signed, the contract carries the weight of legal commitment, which future boards of directors must appreciate and respect. Another potential downside to an employment contract, especially a longer-term one, is that the contract may tend to freeze the board into a static relationship with the CEO, rather than support a dynamic relationship with the ability to change as the organization inevitably changes. If a contract is used, it should be for a short term and reviewed every few years, to ensure that the terms of the contract, specifically the articulation of the CEO's performance, are consistent with the organization's strategic planning and fiscal realities.

Hiring Checklist

1. Review the Applicant's File

❏ Did the applicant sign an acknowledgment providing that 1) the nonprofit has authority to contact previous employers and conduct a thorough background check? 2) the applicant acknowledges the 'at will' nature of the employment? 3) if hired the applicant will abide by policies of the organization?

❏ Are there gaps in employment history that require an explanation by the applicant?

❏ Compare the application to the résumé, if submitted. Are the two documents consistent?

❏ Did the applicant write a cover letter? If so, is the letter grammatical and professional in appearance and appropriate in style?

❏ Look at work experience and volunteer history. Does the applicant's experience have any direct bearing on the qualifications for the open position? Note in your own records if the experience of each applicant is or isn't applicable.

❏ Look at the references provided by the applicant. Are the references professional or personal? If the applicant provides only personal references, you will need to follow up with the applicant to get contact information for professional/volunteer or work related references. If none are provided, consider tracking down and contacting the references the applicant should have provided (for example, prior supervisors).

❏ If the applicant will be subject to a criminal history records check, determine applicant's state of residence and how long the applicant has lived there. (If the applicant has recently moved to the area, it may be necessary to get criminal history background information from another state.)

❏ If the nonprofit is using an outside consumer reporting agency for background checking, is the proper Fair Credit Reporting Act Notice being provided to applicants? Does the nonprofit maintain a record of the signed notice in each applicant's file?

2. Conduct Interviews

❏ Prepare a script of questions that will be asked of each candidate for the open position. Is every single question job-related?

❏ Provide the applicant with a written job description.

❏ Explain the essential functions of the position as reflected on the job description, and ask if the applicant is able to perform all the job duties as described.

❏ Don't be afraid of silence. Ask open ended-questions and let the applicant fill the silence instead of the interviewer. Don't answer your own questions or *rescue* the applicant. The interviewer should listen more than talk.

❏ The interviewer shouldn't get side-tracked by personal comments such as, "Oh, is that a photo of your children?" In such a case, respond "Yes" or "No," without asking about the interviewee's family, marriage, child care arrangements or children's school/schedules which can be interpreted as discriminatory.

❏ Control the interview. If the applicant strays off topic, steer him or her firmly back.

❏ Don't promise the applicant anything. In closing, comment as positively as you can without making any commitments and give yourself time to consider and compare all the applicants for the position.

❏ Be clear about the next steps in the process. Tell the applicant when you expect to be making a decision and what needs to happen in the interim. Manage the applicant's expectations fairly.

❏ After the interview, the interviewer should date and document in an applicant interview file, as precisely as possible, facts provided by the candidate regarding past employment or other facts that can be checked through references. Also note factual observations with respect to job-related experience, skills or background. *Don't* document observations about personality or appearance. Keep notes in a special file, not on the résumé, application or cover letter.

3. Check References

❏ Verify educational credentials, especially that dates and sources of education, degrees conferred, licenses and certifications are accurate. Are certifications current?

❏ If the applicant will be driving as part of the applicant's duties, order a copy of the applicant's motor vehicle record.

❏ If the applicant or a background check indicates that the applicant has been convicted of a crime, go back to the applicant for supplemental information so that you can determine:

> (a) the number, nature, and circumstances of the criminal conviction(s);
>
> (b) the relationship of the crime(s) to the nature of employment;
>
> (c) how long ago the conviction(s) occurred; and
>
> (d) the applicant's efforts at rehabilitation.

❏ If applicable, check your state's sex offender registry records.

❏ Ask applicants who have been active in military duty to supply a copy of their DD-214 certificate of release from active duty.

❏ If the applicant would be working with accounts receivable or fund-raising proceeds as part of his or her job duties, consider a consumer credit check.

❏ Contact the references listed and send a copy of the written reference authorization signed by the applicant; request a candid response to whether the previous employer would have any reservations recommending the applicant for the position of (XYZ).

❏ Ascertain, if possible: 1) the reason(s) why the applicant left his or her previous job; 2) whether the applicant's former employer was satisfied by the applicant's performance; 3) was the applicant productive? 4) did the applicant work well with others? 5) did the applicant have any difficulty with punctuality? professionalism? 6) was the applicant professional in how she or he left the previous job? 7) would the previous employer rehire the applicant? 8) were there any disciplinary or performance problems?

4. *Document the Hiring Decision*

❏ Document whether the applicant is qualified for the position, and if so, how the applicant compares to other applicants. Is she or he the best qualified among all the other applicants?

❏ Does the applicant meet all the minimum educational qualifications for the position?

❏ Does the applicant meet all the minimum certification or licensing requirements?

❏ Were there any inconsistencies on the application, résumé or during the interview? Does the applicant demonstrate a commitment to the organization's mission?

❏ Does the applicant appear motivated? Honest?

❏ Were this applicant's references unqualified in their support for the applicant?

❏ Did the applicant's driving and/or criminal record check reveal a clean record?

❏ Does the applicant's previous work or volunteer experience indicate a set of skills or specialization that meets or exceeds the requirements for the position?

❏ If qualified, is hiring the applicant indicated in order to meet goals of diversifying the workplace?

In Chapter 3, we will explore risks to be aware of, and risk management policies important for nonprofits to implement when crafting employee handbooks.

Chapter 3   Employee Handbooks

Written workplace policies and procedures that are legally current and easy to follow are as important as adequate insurance. Policies that are clearly communicated to staff and consistently applied serve to safeguard against improvised solutions that can result in a lawsuit. Written policies are the starting point for ensuring that personnel dilemmas are resolved consistently and fairly. Moreover, several federal laws and many state laws require that workplaces distribute or post certain written policies. Up-to-date, legally sound, personnel policies are so significant that many insurance companies, funders and potential board members look to a nonprofit's personnel policies as an indication of security—or risk. Accordingly, to ensure that the nonprofit's policies reflect existing law and activity, a careful review of the nonprofit's employee manual (or handbook) should be scheduled at on a regular basis, no less frequently than every three years, or as needed when major changes occur at the workplace.

Usually, the chief staff executive (executive director or CEO) starts the process of revising or drafting policies by designating someone to lead the project. In large nonprofits, the project manager may be the organization's human resources director, or another member of the management team. In a very small or start-up nonprofit, a board member may be in charge. In some cases, an existing personnel committee may assume responsibility for drafting or revising personnel policies. It's the board of directors' responsibility to ultimately approve revised policies. Since state law will affect which policies are required and the individual nonprofit's culture will determine other policies, using a commercially available software package of personnel policy templates is only a beginning. It's important to have not only the committee's input but also a resource, such as an expert in local employment law, to provide specific state-law guidance. Many nonprofits have great success inviting professionals who work in the human resource departments of local corporations to become volunteers on the nonprofit's personnel committee. Including staff members on the committee ensures that the policies will address the practical problems that emerge through day-to-day management of the nonprofit.

The first step in revising or drafting personnel policies is to focus on overall organizational goals. In the context of the organization's short- and long-range goals, what's the primary objective of personnel policies in such areas as: recruitment, retention, supervision, compensation and benefits? For instance, is the nonprofit having trouble retaining key employees? Are salaries and benefits competitive in the marketplace? If not, what policies could be implemented to attract and retain top level staff? Is there a problem with absenteeism at the workplace? What policies will enforce expectations for time worked? Philosophically, does the nonprofit favor providing incentives for strong attendance instead of punishment for poor attendance? Should the workplace policies bend over backwards to be family-friendly, or does the workplace need an infusion of *corporate* style expectations to be taken more seriously by staff? Is there a middle ground?

Employee Manual Tips

❑ The first page after the cover page should set forth the disclaimer that employment is *at-will* and that the policies aren't intended as a contract, and that the employer has the discretion to revise the policies at any time, without notice to employees.

❑ Revised policies are intended to supersede previous policies, but don't take this for granted! This fact needs to be explicitly stated in the disclaimer.

❑ A table of contents or an index makes it easier for employees to find the sections that they're seeking.

❑ Make sure all new employees receive a copy of personnel policies in printed form and are aware of where the digital copy may be accessed. If you only point out to an employee where the policies may be found on the network server, there will be no way to prove that the employee *received* a copy of the policies.

❑ Make sure to *date* the current copy of employment policies so that when the nonprofit decides to revise the policies there will be a clear record of what policies were approved on what dates(s).

❑ Employee handbooks don't have to contain all operating procedures, such as emergency building evacuation procedures, or all details of benefits that may change from time to time. The personnel policies should refer to the summary plan descriptions of benefit plans, and communicate where an employee can obtain more information.

❑ It's never appropriate to copy and use another organization's policy manual wholesale—every organization has its own culture and values and a template set of policies probably won't have been reviewed by legal counsel, familiar with the laws specific to your nonprofit.

❑ Remember, if the nonprofit receives funding from a municipal, county, state or federal agency, there may be a special set of requirements that must be included in written policies to qualify as a government contractor or grantee.

Whatever changes are made, from revising how vacation time is calculated to reinforcing that employment is at will, a nonprofit employer should always communicate the changes to employees well before they're implemented. In some cases it makes sense to make changes effective in the following fiscal year, after announcing the changes well in advance. Any time rights or benefits are taken away the nonprofit should notify supervisors first, via a revised policy statement, then notify each employee by memorandum, and follow that up by distributing a copy of the revised, updated employee manual. Employees should each sign an acknowledgment that they received the updated manual, that they understand that the new manual takes the place of the former manual, and that they accept the terms of the newly revised policies.

In some cases, courts have found that additional consideration, such as a salary adjustment or increase in benefits, is required for employee handbook revisions to be effective. (In **Connecticut** an employer's attempt to change its right to terminate employees from a *just cause* standard to *at-will* status without additional consideration wasn't permitted; in **Illinois**, because the employer hadn't reserved the right to make changes to its handbook in the future, the court found that the employer was required to provide additional compensation to its employees prior to unilaterally changing the policies.) The general rule is that employees should be notified that the employee manual is changing, and the notification should be made in advance of the actual changes. This helps management monitor the staff's reaction to the proposed changes and address any disagreement early in the process. Usually when employees understand the financial or administrative business justification for the policy or practice, they're supportive of the changes, but it's better to have the opportunity to change their minds than to fend off criticism after the policy is changed, apparently to their detriment.

Courts in a number of states have said that employees must know exactly what provisions the employer altered. For example, in a **South Carolina** case, *Fleming v. Borden* (1994), the South Carolina Supreme Court held that employers may not amend their handbooks without making sure that employees have notice of every change. To assure that employees are aware of changes to personnel polices and don't challenge the nonprofit's right to make revisions:

❏ Post notices or circulate memos that explain the proposed revision(s). Issue the changed handbook well before its effective date for a *staff review period*.

❏ State on the front page of the handbook that it's effective on a specific date and that as of the effective date, the newly revised manual will replace previous versions.

❏ Ensure that all employees sign the acknowledgment (meaning that they've read the changes and understood them) and place the acknowledgment form in each employee's personnel files.

State Laws Requiring Posting of Certain Policies

The state laws noted here are subject to periodic review and revision by state legislatures. This summary should therefore be used for reference purposes, rather than as a definitive guide.

No federal or state law requires employers to produce or circulate an employee handbook, but several states specifically require or give employers the option of distributing notices of certain policies in an employee handbook format and require certain policies to be posted:

California: Employers must distribute to all employees an information sheet regarding sexual harassment. Cal. Gov't. Code Section 12950, ⬛ as well as a general poster on discrimination that's prohibited at the workplace. ⬛ The information can be incorporated in an employee manual that's distributed to all employees. (State law also requires that employers publicly post a discrimination poster issued by the California Fair Employment and Housing Commission that includes information regarding sexual harassment, including the recent requirement that supervisors receive training.) Employers must also include in their written policies a description of the "illness and injury prevention program" that all employers are required to implement in California. See Cal. Lab. Code Section 6401.7. ✐

Florida: Employers must post in conspicuous places on the premises a notice concerning all the protections of the Florida Civil Rights Act, including its anti-discrimination provisions, as well as unemployment benefits, workers' compensation benefits, and any toxic or hazardous substances that may be present in the workplace. All of the foregoing can be included in an employee manual that's distributed to all employees, in addition to the required posters.

Louisiana: Employers must post a copy of certain labor laws including: Fair Employment and Age Discrimination laws, Minor Labor Laws, Notice of Compliance to Employees re: workers' compensation and unemployment insurance, a notice that out-of-state motor vehicles must be registered within 30 days in Louisiana, notification of the prohibition of discrimination against individuals with the Sickle Cell Trait and smoking policies.

New York: Employers must notify employees in writing of, *or publicly post*, their policies on sick leave, vacation, personal leave, holidays and hours of work. See N.Y. Labor Law Section 195(5). ✐ This requirement can also be satisfied by giving each employee this notice upon hiring.

State Law Considerations Concerning Employment-at-Will and Employee Handbooks

The state laws and court cases summarized here are subject to constant review and revision in courts and state legislatures. This summary should therefore be used for reference purposes, rather than as a definitive guide.

Alabama: An explicit disclaimer will prevent a handbook from being a contract of employment. Oral promises of employment are recognized.

Alaska: Personnel policies may modify at-will employment relationships. The Alaska Supreme Court has held that when an employer represents to an employee that he [or she] will have a job so long as he [or she] is performing his [or her] duties, the employment is no longer "at will." *Eales v. Tanana Valley Medical-Surgical Group, Inc.* 663 P.2nd 958 (Alaska 1983); An employer's promise made in employee handbooks to discharge only for cause is enforceable in a breach of contract action by an employee. *Parker v. Mat-Su Council on Prevention of Alcoholism and Drug Abuse*, 813 P. 2d 665 (Alaska 1991); When an employee is promised a job and takes action in reliance on the offer, he [or she] may have a claim of promissory estoppel. *Glover v. Sager*, 667 P 2d 1198 (Alaska 1983); The Supreme Court has held that all contracts, including employment contracts, include an implied covenant of good faith and fair dealing. See *Mitford v. de La Sala*, 666 P 2d 1000 (Alaska 1983).

Arizona: Personnel policies may create a contract absent a clear disclaimer. Employers can't change a stated policy in a handbook unless the employees acknowledge agreement.

Arkansas: Handbooks aren't likely to be found to be contracts. "At-will" employees have no right to recover for alleged wrongful discharge. Oral contracts aren't recognized. However, employees who are hired for a definite term and are discharged before that term "without just cause" may bring a wrongful discharge action against their employer.

California: Personnel policies may create a contract absent a clear disclaimer. Oral contracts are recognized. However, under Cal. Lab. Code Section 2922, the general rule is that employment is terminable "at-will" by either party in the absence of an employment contract for a definite period. Employees may be terminated for any reason not expressly prohibited by federal, state or local law.

Colorado: Colorado is an employment-at-will state; absent an explicit contract to the contrary, every employment relationship is presumed to be "at-will," but disclaimers are still favored. See *Jones v. Stevinson's Golden Ford,* 36 P. 3d 129, 132 (Colo. App 2001).

Connecticut: Personnel policies may create a contract absent a clear disclaimer. Oral promises of employment are recognized. Public policy exceptions to terminations of "at-will" employees are recognized.

Delaware: Delaware is an employment-at-will state, but numerous exceptions exist: Employee manuals can create implied contracts and a consistent course of dealing (past practice) can create a binding obligation even in the face of a handbook disclaimer. Express promises by employers may modify the "at-will" status. Courts have recognized arguments of detrimental reliance and promissory estoppel by terminated employees. *Lord v. Souder*, 748 A. 2d 393, 398 (Del. 2000). Delaware courts have also recognized the implied covenant of good faith and fair dealing in employment relationships. See *E. I. Dupont de Nemours & Co. v. Pressman*, 679 A. 2d. 436 (Del. 1996). Oral promises aren't a contract without underlying written contractual language.

District of Columbia: Employment relationships of indefinite unspecified duration are "at will" and terminable by either employee or employer with or without cause. *Littell v. Evening Star Newspaper*, 120 F. 2d 36, 37 (DC Cir. 1941); Only evidence of clearly expressed contractual intent overcomes the "at-will" presumption. *Choate v. TRW, Inc.* 14 F. 3d 74 (D.C. Cir. 1994). Personnel policies may create a contract absent a clear disclaimer. Oral promises of employment are recognized.

Florida: If there is evidence that both parties intended to be bound, a personnel manual can be a binding contract, but generally Florida is an employment-at-will state.

Georgia: Georgia is a strong "employment-at-will" state. In the absence of a contract, employees may not base an action for wrongful discharge on the provisions of an employee handbook. Personnel policies aren't a contract of employment.

Hawaii: Personnel policies can be enforceable as a contract if the employer has circulated them and intends that employees rely on them.

Idaho: Idaho is an "at-will" state and unless contractually limited, employers or employees can end the employment relationship with or without cause or prior notice. Courts look for evidence that the handbook provisions were intended to be binding, and otherwise won't find that they're a contract.

Illinois: The Supreme Court of Illinois has held that employers can be contractually bound to follow provisions in handbooks or other policy statements if three essentials of contract formation are present: (i) the handbook or policy provision language must contain a promise clear enough for the employee to believe that an offer has been made; (ii) the statement must be communicated in such a way that he employee is aware of its contents and reasonably believes it to be an offer; (iii) employees must accept the offer by beginning or continuing to work after learning of the provision. See *Dulduleo v. St. Mary of Nazareth Hospital Center*, 115 Ill 2d. 482, 505 N.E. 2d 314 (1987).

Indiana: Personnel policy manuals are generally not a contract of employment, however, if an employee is made a promise and given independent consideration, the promise can be binding. Binding promises can be created by provisions in a handbook that suggest that termination is only for cause.

Iowa: Personnel policy manuals are generally not a contract of employment but the Iowa Supreme Court has recognized two exceptions: (i) employee handbooks that specifically limit termination except under certain conditions or for cause, *Phipps v. IASD Health Services Corp.*, 558 N.W.2d 198, 202 (Iowa 1997); (ii) employers may not terminate an employee in violation of public policy. See *Springer v. Weeks & Leo Co.*, 429 N.W. 2d 558, 560 (Iowa 1998).

Kansas: Personnel policy manuals may create a contract, absent a clear disclaimer, if there is evidence both parties intended to be bound.

Kentucky: Kentucky is an "at-will" state, but a discharge will be wrongful if it's contrary to a fundamental and well-defined public policy as evidenced by existing law, statutory or constitutional provision. See *Grzyb v. Evans*, 700 S. W. 2d 399 (Ky 1985). Personnel policy manuals may create a contract absent a clear disclaimer.

Louisiana: Personnel policy manuals may create a contract absent a clear disclaimer.

Maine: Generally a contract of employment for an indefinite time is "terminable at the will of either party" unless there is an employment contract that clearly and expressly restricts the right of an employer to discharge an employee. See *Taliento v. Portland West Neighborhood Planning Council*, 1997 ME 194, Section 9, 705 A 2d 696, 699 (Me. 1997).

Maryland: Maryland recognizes implied contracts so personnel policy manuals may create a contract absent a "clear and unequivocal" disclaimer. Maryland also recognizes an exception to employment "at will" for terminations in violation of public policy. Maryland doesn't recognize an implied covenant of good faith and fair dealing.

Massachusetts: State courts have been reluctant to hold personnel policy manuals to be binding contracts.

Michigan: Michigan is a strong employment "at-will" state, however, personnel policy manuals may create a contract, if the language states that discharge will only be for cause. Applications for employment may expressly disclaim contractual nature of personnel policies.

Minnesota: Personnel policy manuals may create a contract to discharge only for cause, where the handbook has been distributed to employees, and its provisions are definite, and it constituted an offer accepted by the employee by his or her continued service. Otherwise, the employment relationship is terminable at the will of either party. Minnesota recognizes an exception to employment "at-will" for reasons that contravene a clear mandate of public policy. See *Anderson-Johanningmeier v. Mid-Minnesota Women's Center, Inc.* 637 N.W.2d 270, 273 (Minn. 2002).

Mississippi: Employers may be bound by the progressive discipline procedures set forth in a handbook, however, an express "at-will" disclaimer will defeat a cause of action for breach of contract.

Missouri: Missouri courts have been reluctant to find that handbooks are binding contracts.

Montana: Montana is **not** an employment-at-will state. Employers must have good cause, defined as reasonable job-related grounds, to discharge employees based solely on failure to satisfactorily perform the job. See the *Montana Wrongful Discharge From Employment Act.* Mont. Code Ann. Section 39-2-904 and 39-2-903(5). Oral promises may establish contractual obligations.

Nebraska: Employers may be bound by the progressive discipline or grievance procedures set forth in a handbook, however, an express "at-will" disclaimer will defeat a cause of action for breach of contract, as will language that the procedures are guidelines rather than rules. Nebraska recognizes the implied contract theory and the public policy exception to employment-at-will.

Nevada: Personnel policy manuals may create a contract, absent a clear disclaimer. Nevada recognizes the public policy exception to employment-at-will.

New Hampshire: Personnel policy manuals may create a contract, absent a clear disclaimer. The general rule is that unless an employee is hired for a specific term, the employer may terminate the employee for any reason or no reason.

New Jersey: Personnel policy manuals may create a contract, absent a clear disclaimer. Disclaimers must be prominent, in bold face type, and in "plain English" in order to be enforceable. Oral promises are recognized. New Jersey also recognizes the public policy exception.

New Mexico: Personnel policy manuals may create a contract, absent a clear disclaimer but the provisions of the manual must be sufficiently definite in order to constitute a contract.

New York: Stated procedures in a personnel policy manual aren't considered to alter the status of an "at-will" employee, but statements in a manual may be binding if both parties agree to be bound.

North Carolina: Personnel policy manual, distributed to employees, doesn't necessarily alter the "at-will" status of employees, unless there are provisions that state that discharge will only be for cause. North Carolina recognizes the public policy exception to employment-at-will.

North Dakota: North Dakota is at at-will state by law: N.D.C.C. Section 34-03-01, however, the presumption of "at-will" employment *may* be overcome by statements in a manual. Where a handbook contains a clear and prominent disclaimer, employment remains "at-will."

Ohio: Ohio courts will examine all facts and circumstances to determine if a there was agreement created by a handbook that limits the right of the employer to discharge the employee.

Oklahoma: An employment manual doesn't by itself create a contract of employment, but an employer may be bound by stated policies if the employee forgoes other employment in reliance on policies in a handbook.

Oregon: Oral promises of lifetime employment will be upheld. Personnel policy manuals will be considered part of an employment contract. Where a policy states that employees won't be dismissed without "just cause," the meaning of "just cause" is subject to the court's review.

Pennsylvania: Personnel policies in a manual that's widely distributed may be considered an employment contract if there is evidence that both parties intended to be bound by its terms.

Rhode Island: When the term of employment is uncertain, "at-will" employment is presumed.

South Carolina: South Carolina is an "at-will" state, but recognizes the implied contract exception, so a handbook without a disclaimer and any language that implies a promise of termination only for cause can be considered a contract. Disclaimers must be underlined, in bold lettering, and prominently placed on the first page of the handbook and signed by the employee.

South Dakota: Employers may be bound by the progressive discipline or grievance procedures set forth in a handbook, however, an express "at-will" disclaimer will defeat a cause of action for breach of contract, as will language that the procedures are guidelines rather than rules. Employees hired for a stated annual salary are presumed to have been hired for one year.

Tennessee: Personnel policy manuals may create a binding contract absent a clear disclaimer.

Texas: Absent a specific agreement otherwise, the application for employment and policy manuals don't create a contract limiting an employer's right to terminate an employee "at-will." A personnel manual may be binding when both parties agree to be bound.

Utah: Where the term of employment is for an indefinite duration, employees have no cause of action for wrongful termination or for breach of contract. Oral promises of employment for a specific duration *can't* alter employment "at-will" status.

Vermont: Employment relationships are "at-will" *to the extent they aren't modified by contract.* Personnel policy manuals may be binding, if both the employee and employer specifically agree to be bound.

Virginia: "At-will" status of employment is presumed, however, provisions in a personnel policy manual may negate this presumption if a specific duration of employment is inferred or specified. Virginia recognizes the public policy exception to employment-at-will.

Washington: An employer may unilaterally change its handbook, however, the employees must receive reasonable notice before the changes are effective. Employers that promise specific treatment in handbooks will be bound by the language in the handbook. Washington recognizes the public policy exception to employment-at-will.

West Virginia: A personnel policy manual may create a contract, absent a clear disclaimer.

Wisconsin: A personnel policy manual may be binding when both parties agree to be bound.

Wyoming: A personnel policy manual may be an enforceable contract if the employee relied on its terms and had an expectation that the procedures would be followed. Disclaimers must be prominent, in bold face type, and in "plain English" in order to be enforceable.

The next section, Chapter 4, addresses the careful tightrope of providing competitive and legally appropriate compensation and benefits without stretching the resources of a nonprofit beyond its means.

Chapter 4 — Providing Appropriate Compensation and Benefits

The compensation and benefits area creates significant risk, making the nonprofit vulnerable where it hurts the most; trying to treat employees well. Even if the best possible candidates are hired, they may not stick around long enough to make an impact if the nonprofit can't offer a competitive salary and compensation/benefits package. The practical challenges of offering attractive compensation and benefits are compounded by the legal pitfalls of benefits administration. Unwittingly a nonprofit can increase its legal liabilities by designing compensation/benefits policies that either *don't comply* with the law or that make the nonprofit vulnerable to legal action. In this chapter, we explore best practices in benefits administration in response to state and federal law mandates and expose practices that can create legal risks, if not thoughtfully administered.

The Balancing Act: Reasonable Compensation

A generous compensation plan is critical to attract and retain good employees. Yet, when compensation is too high, the public and key stakeholders of an organization may lose faith in the nonprofit, and legal liability may be triggered. When compensation is too low, morale may be low and turnover high. In an effort to counterbalance the traditionally lower salaries offered in the nonprofit sector, and to attract and retain qualified staff, many organizations try to offer generous employee benefits.

The demographic reality post-2000 is that there is a growing shortage of CEO/executive director level employees to lead the nation's nonprofit organizations. Consequently, competition for the *best and the brightest* is sure to turn up the pressure on nonprofits to offer generous compensation packages, including fringe benefits. However, strategies to attract and retain have to be balanced by the restrictions on nonprofits as public benefit corporations. In the post-Enron era, there is an almost fervent public and regulatory focus on the nonprofit sector's accountability to mission and transparency in compensation practices. As a result of recent revisions to the IRS Form 990, electronic filing of annual reports with the IRS, and the ease of viewing a nonprofit's 990 on www.Guidestar.org, it's much easier to find out compensation levels of nonprofit executives and trustees, as well as former employees and trustees. Compensation is now also a focus of IRS enforcement proceedings to investigate nonprofit compensation practices that result in self-dealing, *private benefit* or *excess compensation*. Consequently, as a risk management step, all nonprofit managers should review compensation practices to ensure that attractive but reasonable compensation and benefit incentives are offered to reward employees, and also that a transparent review of all compensation practices occurs on a regular basis, reinforced by the nonprofit organization's written policies.

> IRS Form 990 is available for public inspection in accordance with U.S. Treasury regulations. With the exception of houses of worship, nonprofits that have yearly gross receipts of $25,000 must report their revenue and expenses annually to the IRS using this form. The IRS Form 990 requires nonprofits to list the annual compensation of the five highest paid employees and independent contractors, (those paid more than $50,000) and to report compensation to board members, *past* board members and *former* employees.

Caution! Compensation Practices Can Result in Penalties and Excise Taxes

Essentially, all compensation provided by the nonprofit must be reasonable and not excessive. Internal Revenue Code Section 4958 imposes an excise tax on *excess benefit transactions* between a disqualified person[7] and a tax-exempt organization. The disqualified person who benefits from an excess benefit transaction is liable for the excise tax. The nonprofit and board members who approved the transaction resulting in the excess benefit may also be liable for excise taxes, known as *intermediate sanctions.* The penalties can be significant: up to 25 percent of the excess, or as much as 200 per cent if the violation isn't abated, with fines of up to $20,000 for board members who knowingly approve excessive compensation practices.

---

7 Disqualified persons are generally the officers and directors of the nonprofit. The IRS defines disqualified persons as any person who is in a position to "exercise substantial influence" over the affairs of the tax-exempt organization. Family members and entities controlled by disqualified persons are also "disqualified persons." See IRC Section 4958.

Excessive Compensation and Private Benefit

While few nonprofits would conclude that they pay their staff *too much*, it's in fact incumbent on every nonprofit and every board to carefully evaluate and document compensation levels and the decision making process that results in compensation to staff, consultants, outside service providers (vendors) and to board members, where applicable. A private benefit transaction could result from a nonprofit entering into a contract with a vendor, such as a cleaning company, to provide services to the nonprofit. If the nonprofit pays more than market rate for the services, the transaction will result in private benefit. If the owner of the cleaning company also happens to be a board member of the nonprofit, the transaction will result in *private inurement* which is viewed by the IRS as a prohibited transaction.[8] To steer clear of penalties imposed by the IRS for private benefit or private inurement, all nonprofits should go through an annual exercise of evaluating whether compensation provided to consultants, vendors, staff and especially to board members, if applicable, is justified both by the value of services provided to the nonprofit and by the *going market rate* for similar services. This exercise requires the nonprofit to review comparable compensation data. *Comparable* data is that from similar organizations providing similar services, in a similar geographic area, and could include data from for-profit organizations, as well as from nonprofits. In practical terms, the IRS regulations require that every nonprofit: 1) regularly examines comparative compensation data from similar nonprofits, 2) specifically approves the compensation packages of top managers, and 3) carefully considers whether compensation arrangements are appropriate whenever the nonprofit pays for services from outside workers.

The Importance of Documentation

It's also critical to document that a nonprofit went through a process to determine that the compensation paid to anyone: consultants, vendors, employees—is reasonable. It's even more important to document compensation decisions relating to disqualified persons. Compensation to disqualified persons will **automatically** be considered excessive and subject the person who receives it to a 25% excise tax *unless* the board of the nonprofit documents the compensation decision in a timely manner and demonstrates that its decision-making process was reasonable. A "timely manner" is satisfied if the nonprofit reports the compensation on Form 990, on Form W-2 or 1099, or if the executive who received the compensation reports the benefit on his or her Form 1040. Perks such as cell phone use paid for by the nonprofit, personal components of business travel, personal use of employer-owned property, such as computers, club memberships and the like are all considered by the IRS to be "compensation" that must be reported. See IRC Section 4958 (www.irs.gov/pub/irs-tege/eotopice04.pdf). The IRS will presume that a compensation arrangement is valid as long *as the nonprofit can show that:*

(a)   the arrangement was approved by the nonprofit's board or a committee of the board composed entirely of individuals who don't have a conflict of interest with respect to the transaction,

(b)   the board or a committee of the board obtained and relied on appropriate comparative salary data prior to making its decision, and

(c)   the board or committee adequately documented the basis for its decision at the time it was made.

Minutes of a board meeting during which compensation was reviewed can be sufficient documentation if all the elements listed above are reflected in the minutes. The IRS doesn't require that nonprofits use expensive means to compare salary data; documentation of a phone call to another nonprofit, or that a review of another organization's IRS 990 was conducted is sufficient.

Obtaining Comparable Compensation Data

Comparative salary data is available commercially for a fee, but don't overlook more immediate sources, such as national nonprofit sector publications, United Way affiliates and statewide nonprofit associations, which are all starting to keep annual salary data. The board of directors should devote at least one meeting per year to evaluation and approval of top managers' compensation packages. The minutes of the board meeting should reflect that comparative compensation data was used.

8 Nonprofits that engage in private inurement can lose their tax-exempt status. Private inurement occurs when a disqualified person (which could be a board member, a senior staff member, or even a major donor) receives a financial benefit that's excessive—either more than market rates would command, or more beneficial to the disqualified person than to the nonprofit.

Note: Any nonprofit and its board of directors can be shielded from the stiff IRS penalties if the board reasonably relies on the written opinion of an outside expert, such as an attorney or accountant, who provides credible information that the compensation package or specific transaction in question doesn't constitute prohibited self-dealing or excess benefit.

As nonprofits offer more sophisticated compensation and benefit packages, liability risks escalate. The employee benefit area is highly regulated. As soon as a nonprofit offers a pension plan or 401K, a cafeteria plan, or a group health insurance plan, a series of federal laws is detonated: ERISA (Employee Retirement Income Security Act), ✎ governs pensions and deferred compensation; COBRA (Consolidated Omnibus Budget Reconciliation Act), ✎ and HIPAA (Health Insurance Portability and Accountability Act) ✎ govern group health insurance coverage. These complicated laws require special legal guidance. The intricate and constantly changing regulations of these laws are beyond the scope of this chapter. If your organization offers any type of deferred compensation, pension or group health plan, be sure to ask for frequent updates on legal requirements from your accountant and group health insurance carrier, as well as from your nonprofit's legal advisor.

Compensation and Pay Practices

Employees need to know details about their wage payments, such as what withholdings are automatically taken out of paychecks.[9] When an employee is hired, whether on an hourly or salaried basis, the employee's total compensation package (all economic benefits which accompany the position) should be identified. Most states have language such as the following from Maryland that requires employers to provide newly hired employees with a written statement of wages and payroll practices:

> "…An employer shall give to each employee at the time of hiring, notice of the rate of pay of the employee; and the regular paydays that the employer sets; for each pay period, a statement of the gross earnings of the employee and deductions from those gross earnings; and at least one (1) pay period in advance, notice of any change in a payday or wage." See Md. Code Ann. Lab & Employ. Sect. 3-504.

Even if not required by state law, this is prudent practice. Check your state's wage and hour regulations for specific state requirements.

Paydays and Paychecks

All states have specific laws regulating how frequently employees must receive paychecks. The Department of Labor's Web site provides a comprehensive chart (www.dol.gov/esa/programs/whd/state/payday.htm) showing the requirements in all 50 states. State wage payment guidelines specify when wages must be paid and how they're to be paid, such as by mail or at the place of employment. Some states permit wages to be paid less frequently than weekly, but it isn't automatic. (Examples: In New York, where manual workers normally must be paid every seven days, a special regulation permits nonprofits to pay manual workers in semi-monthly pay periods; in Connecticut, where weekly paychecks are the norm, a nonprofit needs a special waiver from the state's Department of Labor to pay employees less frequently.) All nonprofits should be familiar with individual state regulations. Copies of the state wage and hour regulations may be obtained by contacting your state's department of labor, wage and hour division or the equivalent governmental unit.

Deductions from Paychecks

It generally is illegal to withhold from an employee's paycheck anything other than social security, income tax and state insurance payments without the employee's prior written authorization. Most states have a specific wage regulation that restates this general rule. Example: In Indiana ✎ no deduction may be made from an employee's paycheck without written authorization of the employee, signed by the employer, with the provision that the employee may revoke the authorization at any time.

Q: Can a nonprofit's board of directors ever be personally responsible for payment of wages to the nonprofit's employees?

A: Generally not. If the nonprofit is incorporated, there is limited liability, meaning that the debts of the nonprofit, such as salary to its staff, remain the debts of the corporation. However, the IRS takes the position that in the event that the nonprofit fails to withhold payroll taxes, such as social security, the IRS can seek the required back-taxes from the board members *personally*. Federal and state law may differ on this point.

❏ In Colorado corporate officers are **not** personally liable for a corporation's unpaid wages to its employees under the Colorado Wage Claim Act. *Leonard v. McMorris*, No. 01SA380 (CO. February 3, 2003).

❏ The Massachusetts Wage Act (MGL c. 149, § 148) defines an "employer" as including "the president and treasurer of a corporation and any officers or agents having the management of such corporation" (which certainly would include volunteer board members who are officers of the nonprofit). Consequently, in Massachusetts board members could be liable for unpaid wages or back taxes under state wage claims.

---

9 Nonprofits must withhold federal social security payments (FICA) and state and local unemployment compensation and disability insurance payments, as required by state laws. However, tax-exempt charitable organizations are exempt from withholding federal unemployment taxes (FUTA) from employee wages.

Wage Garnishment

Title III of the Consumer Credit Protection Act (CCPA) 41 U.S.C. § 1671 ⬤ protects employees from discharge by their employers because their wages have been garnished, and it limits the amount of an employee's earnings that may be garnished in any one week. Federal law provides generally that not more than 25 percent of an employee's disposable income may be garnished. When an employer receives an official notice ordering the garnishment of wages, the nonprofit must comply with the order, although there are limits to the amount that should be taken from each paycheck. The employer should first contact the employee involved. Maintaining confidentiality and sensitivity to the employee's situation should be a given. A good approach is to meet with the employee and together call the IRS or state office that sent the order to clarify the practical impact of the garnishment. The U.S. Department of Labor Web site offers a fact sheet (www.dol.gov/esa/regs/compliance/whd/whdfs30.htm) that provides employers with guidance on this topic.

Practical Concerns With Paychecks and Compensation Practices

There are several practical issues pertaining to payroll administration that every nonprofit should address in its personnel policies to avoid disputes with employees over the very sensitive issue of paychecks. Issues to address include procedures for distributing paychecks when the regular payday falls on a holiday or a nonwork day, and whether payroll advances are permitted. Many state laws specify that if a regular payday falls on a nonwork day, such as a holiday, the payday will be the preceding day. Employees should be clearly informed that it's their responsibility to keep the employer current with address and name changes that might affect payroll practices. Because employees are so vigilant about any impact on their paycheck (Wouldn't you be?), this is an area where the nonprofit needs to pay extra attention not to violate state wage payment regulations or fail to meet the employee's expectations. Nowhere is this truer than at separation of employment. Many states have specific regulations that require employers to pay departing employees within a specific time period post termination. Address in the employee handbook whether or not departing employees receive compensation in their final paycheck for vacation time that they didn't use, or that was carried over (if applicable) from previous years. State law may govern the vacation time issue; whether carry-over is permitted or compensated upon termination is generally up to the nonprofit's discretion as described in personnel policies. If this issue is **not** addressed in personnel policies the nonprofit will be vulnerable to challenges by disgruntled employees who disagree how their vacation pay is handled in their final paycheck.

Many states are exploring ways to use new technologies for wage payment. Most states specifically permit direct deposit of wages into employee bank accounts, if they get advance written permission from the employee.

❏ Virginia now permits employers to pay wages by crediting prepaid debit cards or card accounts from which the employee is able to withdraw or transfer funds, as long as the employer has made full disclosure of any fees and as long as the employee has consented to such method of payment.

❏ Employers in Delaware are able to furnish pay statements electronically to employees, as long as the statements provide what is required by state law, and as long as the statements are in a format that permits the employee to maintain the statements.

❏ Employers in Minnesota may make payroll deposits using payroll card accounts.

Salary Administration Plan

Salary administration is a term referring to the guidelines that the nonprofit follows to determine reasonable compensation for staff, as well as to review the equity/fairness impact to ensure that there is no actual or apparent discrimination in the compensation of similarly situated employees. The risk management purpose of a salary administration plan is to monitor compensation to ensure that necessary adjustments are made, both to keep the nonprofit competitive in the marketplace, and to ensure compliance with the Equal Pay Act, Title VII, and state anti-discrimination laws.

Generally the responsibility for reviewing the overall salary administration planning function of the nonprofit belongs to the CEO and senior staff, with final approval of the annual budget by the board of directors. The nonprofit's policies should include a statement (which may be part of an affirmative action plan document) that compensation won't be affected by any non job-related characteristics. In some nonprofits salary adjustments will only be cost-of-living adjustments. In others, merit increases are the norm. Components of a salary administration plan should include:

❏ updating job descriptions periodically;

❏ reviewing comparative salary data in the nonprofit sector;

❏ performing salary reviews of all positions periodically to ensure that staff in the same or similar positions are treated equitably and that the compensation for a particular position is appropriate for the market value of services provided;

❏ drafting procedures for determining adjustments to compensation (some nonprofits will assign an upward limit to the potential percentage increase for various positions, or define a range of percentage increases that may be achieved if increases are based on merit);

❏ reviewing the procedures used to approve compensation adjustments;

❏ monitoring performance evaluations to ensure they occur regularly and support the compensation adjustments given to staff;

❏ if applicable, drafting a policy defining the criteria for awarding bonuses.

Note: It's important to emphasize in a written policy describing bonuses that they aren't automatic, but rather awarded at the discretion of the nonprofit depending upon the realities of the nonprofit's financial situation.

SAMPLE--

Bonus Policy

Bonus payments at year-end may be made at the discretion of [Name of Nonprofit] in recognition of the role a staff member has played in the conscientious and effective delivery of quality service. Bonuses aren't to be viewed as automatic annual fringe benefits, but are determined on a year-to-year basis, depending upon the financial status of the nonprofit at the time, and the merit of the particular employee's performance. To be eligible for a bonus an employee must have completed one full year of full-time service, and be employed by the organization at the time the bonus is issued.

Salary Adjustments

It's important to articulate in writing the basis for any salary adjustments. Nonprofit employee manuals often state that compensation levels are approved by the board members in connection with the budget approval process and that annual increases will be *made at the discretion of the board of directors*. If a nonprofit has a practice of awarding salary adjustments to reflect a cost-of-living increase, (COLA) increases may be provided to all employees, regardless of performance. This practice can be risky. If a poor performer receives a *raise*—no matter how small—the tendency of a jury is to interpret the increase as a signal of satisfaction with the employee's performance. This gives ammunition to an employee terminated for poor performance to argue that his raise proves that his employer was satisfied with his performance. Instead, freeze the salary of any employee performing at a marginal level. This should send a clear signal that either performance must improve, or the employee should look elsewhere for employment.

Final Pay

It's common for a nonprofit to face an unexpected conflict with a recently departed employee over the subject of the payment of accrued paid leave. Policies should articulate exactly what is owed to employees upon termination of employment. If paid leave is accrued throughout the year, when an employee is separated from employment in the middle of the year, the employee will expect to receive unused, but accrued, paid leave in his or her final paycheck unless the personnel handbook says otherwise. Nonprofits need to be clear about the process of accrual and whether or not employees whose employment is terminated are eligible for accrued unused paid leave.

Some states require that final paychecks be given out within hours, days, or immediately upon an employee's separation from employment. Stiff penalties can be imposed for failing to pay terminated employees in a timely manner. Not every state has a special regulation addressing termination pay. The general rule is that wages for time worked must be provided to an employee who is terminated or resigns at the next regularly scheduled payday.

State Laws Governing Final Pay Practices

The state laws noted here are subject to constant review and revision in state legislatures. This summary should therefore be used for reference purposes, rather than as a definitive guide

The following states have specific laws that govern when the final paycheck should by paid to an employee upon separation of employment, and governing carry-over and the pay out of vacation and sick leave upon termination of employment. Employers are permitted to have a use-it or lose-it policy unless the summary below provides otherwise.

Alabama: No statute

Alaska: If an employee is fired: within three days at the usual place and agreed upon location; If the employee quits: next regular pay day, at least three days after the employee gives notice. See Alaska Stat. §§ 23.05.140 et seq.

Arizona: If an employee is fired: within three days or the next regular pay period, whichever is sooner. If an employee resigns: the next regular payday; Employers that have a policy or practice of paying employees for vacation or sick days upon separation of employment must treat those days as if they were regular work days when wages are earned. See Ariz. Rev. Stat. Ann. § 23-350, 353.

Arkansas: If an employee quits: within seven days. See Ark. Stat. Ann. 11-4-405.

California: If an employee is fired: immediately upon termination. Final pay includes "vested vacation." If an employee quits: within 72 hours, unless they provided 72 hours notice, in which case final pay is due at the time of resignation. Employers in California can't require employees to keep their wages confidential or discipline an employee for disclosing the amount of his or her wages. Cal. Labor Code §§ 201, 202(a), 227.3. All vested paid vacation time provided by the employer's policy that hasn't been used upon termination of employment must be paid to the employee as wages at the employee's final rate of pay. Sick time, however, doesn't need to be paid upon termination of employment, unless the employer has a policy to the contrary.

Colorado: If an employee is fired: immediately upon termination. If an employee quits: the next regular payday. Colo. Rev. Stat. § 8-4-109. Accrued but unused vacation and/or sick days are wages under the Wage Claim Act and are due and payable upon separation of employment. Co. Rev. Stat. § 8-4-101(8)(a)(111) ; employers may have policies stating that unused vacation time doesn't carry forward into the next accrual period.

Connecticut: If an employee is fired: paid in full the next business day. If an employee resigns: next regular payday; Employers are required to pay earned vacation and/or sick days upon separation if they've a policy or contract to that effect. See Conn. Gen. Stat. §§ 31-71(c), 76k.

Delaware: Upon separation, whether termination or resignation: the next regular pay day; employers must pay all vacation and sick pay within 30 days of when it's due. See 19 Del. Code Ann. §§ 1103, 1009.

District of Columbia: If an employee is fired: the next work day. If an employee quits: the next regular payday or seven days from resignation, whichever is sooner. D.C. Code Ann. § 32-1303. No statute addresses payout of vacation and sick time, but according to the D.C. Court of Appeals, leave time is in the form of compensation and once vested is owed. In the absence of a policy to the contrary, such compensation is owed upon separation of employment. No law addresses carry-over. See *Jones v. District Parking Management Co.* DC App. 268 A. 2d. 860. (1970).

Florida: No statute

Georgia: No statute

Hawaii: If an employee is fired: immediately or the next day, if necessary. If an employee quits: the next regular payday, or immediately if the employee gives one pay period's advance notice of resignation. Haw. Rev. Stat. §§ 388-2, 3. Employers are required to pay earned vacation and/or sick days upon separation of employment if they've a policy or an employment contract that requires it; carry-over permitted. See *Casumpang c. ILWU Local 142*, No. 24508 (HI. Sup. Ct., October 18, 2005).

Idaho: If employee is fired: next payday or within 10 days, whichever is sooner. If employee makes a written request for earlier payment, within 48 hours of receiving the request. If employee quits: next payday or within 10 days, whichever is sooner. If the employee makes a written request for earlier payment, within 48 hours of receiving the request. Idaho Code §§ 45-608. No obligation to pay earned vacation or sick pay unless there is a contract or policy otherwise. See Idaho Code. § 67-5335.

Illinois: Separated employees should be paid full pay at separation where possible; but if not, no later than the next regular payday. Final pay must include earned vacation; If policies or employment contracts provide for paid vacation, the earned, unused potion must be paid to employees at their final rate of pay upon separation of employment. Employers may cap vacation or require employees to use it by a certain date provided a reasonable opportunity to use their earned time is given. See 820 Ill Comp. Stat. 115/5. Also, Ill. Admin. Code § 56-300.520.

Indiana: Employees who are fired must be paid the next regular payday for the pay period in which the firing took place. Employees who quit may be paid the next regular payday. Ind. Code Ann. § 22-2-9-2 ; 22-2-5-1 ; paid vacation and similar time off accrues throughout the year, pro rata, and employees are entitled to payment for unused, accrued vacation pay upon separation unless a clear employment policy provides otherwise. Employers who don't want vacation pay to accrue until the completion of the year or who don't want to pay terminated employees for accrued, unused vacation pay must formulate clear, written policies and ensure all employees are aware of the policy.

Iowa: Upon separation, whether discharge or resignation, employees must be paid by the next regular payday. Iowa Code §§ 91A.2 and 91A. 4 ; Wages include compensation owed to employees for vacation, sick and severance pay due to employees under a contract or policy. If vacations are due under an agreement or policy establishing pro rata vacation accrual, the increment must be in proportion to the fraction of the year that the employee was actually employed.

Kansas: Upon separation, whether discharge or resignation, employees must be paid by the next regular payday; Wages include earned vacation and/or sick pay pursuant to an employment contract. Once vacation or sick pay is earned, it can't be forfeited. Employers may define vacation or sick policies in such a way that the right to payment or vacation and sick time isn't earned until certain conditions are met. See Kan. Stat. Ann. § 44-313, 315.

Kentucky: Upon separation, whether discharge or resignation, employees must be paid not later than the next normal payday or 14 days after dismissal/resignation; Upon separation, employers must pay any vested vacation and other pay agreed to by the employer or provided in established policy. See Ky. Rev. Stat §§ 337.010(1)(c), 337.055 and 337.990(3).

Louisiana: Upon separation, whether discharge or resignation, employees may be paid by the next regular payday but no later than 15 days following the date of dismissal, whichever occurs first; Unused vacation is part of wages due employees upon separation. Payment for sick leave isn't required; Policies that provide for the forfeiture of unused vacation e.g., for quitting or discharge for cause, aren't permitted. See La. Rev. Stat. Ann. 23:631 and 632.

Maine: Upon separation, whether discharge or resignation, employees must be paid within a reasonable time after demand; defined as the next regular pay day after the employee's separation, or not more than two weeks after demand for payment. Payment of earned vacation and/or sick leave is subject to individual employer policies. See Me. Rev. Stat. tit. 26 § 626-A.

Maryland: Final pay must be paid on or before the date on which the employee would have been paid, but for the termination. Md. Lab. & Emp. Code Ann. § 3-505 ; No statute governs payment of vacation or sick leave upon separation; Employer's policy will prevail, assuming the policy was communicated to the employee in advance.

Massachusetts: If fired: immediately upon discharge. If the employee quits: on the next regular payday or on the following Saturday if there is no regular payday for that employee. Vacation or holiday pay reflected in oral or written agreements must be included in final pay. Employers must pay separating employees for earned but unused vacation if personnel policies so provide. No similar requirement for sick leave. See Mass. Gen. L. Ch. 149 §§ 148, 150A,159. ✎

Michigan: Upon separation, whether discharge or resignation, employees must be paid not later than the next normal payday. Payment for vacation or other fringe benefits may not be withheld from final pay without a written agreement signed by the employee. Mich. Comp. Laws. Ann. §§. 408.474, 408.475 ✎ ; no statue governing payment of vacation/sick upon separation. Employer policy will prevail.

Minnesota: If an employee is discharged: must be paid immediately, or "on demand" or within 24 hours of demand. If an employee quits: if payday is less than five days after last day of work, employer may pay on the following payday or 20 days after last day of work, whichever is earlier.; contractual employees who give at least five days notice must be paid within 24 hours of quitting; Employers must pay earned vacation time under the terms of any agreement including an employee handbook. See Minn. Stat. §§181.14, 181.74. ✎

Note: In Minnesota ✎, an employer must give a truthful reason why an employee was terminated, if requested in writing by the employee. Request must be made in writing by the employee within 15 working days of termination. The employer has 10 working days from receipt of the request to give a truthful reason in writing for the termination.

Mississippi: No statute governing when final paycheck must be provided to employees; No requirement that employers pay earned vacation and sick pay unless they've agreed to do so.

Missouri: Discharged employees must receive pay on the day of discharge. Final pay should include vacation pay. Mo. Rev. Stat. §§ 290. 110 ✎ ; The "earning" of vacation and sick time is treated as a contractual matter and determined by any agreement between the parties.

Montana: If employee is discharged for cause or "laid off:" must be paid immediately upon separation unless an employer's written policy states otherwise. Otherwise, wages are due to employees by the next regular payday, or within 15 days of separation, whichever is first. Mont. Code Ann. §§ 39-3-205 ✎ ; Once vacation pay has been earned it's considered wages and due in the same manner as regular wages.

Nebraska: Upon separation, whether discharge or resignation, employees must receive wages at the next regular payday or within two weeks of separation date, whichever is sooner; Vacation pay that's fully accrued and earned is wages under the Nebraska Wage Collection Act. Neb. Rev. Stat. therefore once earned, there is no forfeiture. Sick pay isn't required to be paid once earned. See §§ 48-1228 to 1232. ✎

Nevada: If an employee is fired: due immediately; If an employee quits: by the next regular payday or seven days after termination, whichever is earlier. Nev. Rev. Stat. §§ 608.030, 608.040 ✎ ; No statute on whether vacation/sick is paid upon separation.

New Hampshire: If employee is fired: within 72 hours of discharge; employees who provide notice of resignation must be paid on the next regular payday, or within 72 hours if the employee gives one pay period's notice. N.H. Code Admin. R. §§ 803.02 (e) ✎ ; Employers must pay employees unused compensatory time upon separation of employment. Employers may not have a policy requiring employees to use compensatory time within a certain period. See N.H. Rev. Stat. Annot. 275:43.

New Jersey: Upon separation, whether discharge or resignation: employees must be paid at the next regular payday. Employers aren't required to pay vacation/sick upon separation N.J. Stat. Ann. §§ 34:11-4.3 ✎ ; Whether an employer has a policy of "use it or lose it" is a matter of contract law. See *Chrin v. Cambridge Hydrodynamics, Inc. No.* A-3610-02T5 (App. Div. Dec. 30, 2003).

New Mexico: If an employee is fired: immediately upon discharge but may be paid within five days of discharge. N.M. Stat. Ann. Section 50-4-4 ✎ ; If an employee quits: next regularly scheduled payday. See N.M. Stat. Ann. § 50-4-5. ✎

New York: Upon separation, whether discharge or resignation: not later than the regular payday for the pay period in which the termination occurred. Unused vacation must be included. N.Y. Lab. Law §§ 191 and 198-c ✎ ; Employers aren't required to pay earned vacation/sick upon separation of employment if their policy notifies employees that they forfeit earned vacation pay upon termination of employment. *Note:* New York also requires that employers provide terminated employees, a written notice of specifying the date of their termination from employment, and the "exact date of cancellation of benefits within five days of termination". See N.Y. Lab. Code. ✎

North Carolina: Upon separation, whether discharge or resignation: next regular pay day; Employers are required to provide advance written notice in their policies and procedures of the basis for forfeiture of vacation time upon separation. See N.C. Gen. Stat. §§ 95.25.7, 25.12 and 25.13. ✎

North Dakota: If employee is fired: next regular payday. If employee quits: next regular payday. N.D. Cent. Code § 34-14-02 ✎ ; employers are required to pay all earned vacation and sick time upon separation of employment. Employer policies may not provide otherwise, but employers are permitted to have policies that require employees to "use it or lose it" by a date certain. Employees have to be given a reasonable opportunity to use the time and employers must demonstrate that employees had notice of the policy. See N.D. Admin. Code § 46-02-07-02. ✎

Ohio: Upon separation, whether discharge or resignation: first of the month for wages earned in the first half of prior month; 15th of the month for wages earned in second half of prior month. Ohio Rev. Code Ann. § 4113.15 ; no statute governs a private employer's obligations re: vacation/sick leave upon separation of employment.

Oklahoma: Upon separation, whether discharge or resignation: next regular pay period for which work was performed; earned but unused vacation and sick leave are payable upon separation of employment only if the payment is (i) agreed upon or (ii) provided by established policy. See Okla. Stat. Ann. Title 40 §§ 165.1.4 and 165.3.

Oregon: If an employee is discharged or separation occurs through mutual agreement, final pay is due the close of business the day after separation; due immediately if employee has given 48 hours' notice. Without notice, within five days or the next payday, whichever occurs first; Whether employers have to pay vacation/sick leave will be governed by the employer's policy and established practice. See Ore. Rev. Stat. § 652.140.

Pennsylvania: No statute governs final pay or payment of earned but unused vacation/sick leave.

Rhode Island: Upon separation, whether discharge or resignation: next regular pay period for which work was performed; When an employee has completed one year of service the employee must be paid for earned but unused vacation. See R.I. Gen. Laws §§ 28-14-4(a) and (b).

South Carolina: Upon separation, whether discharge or resignation: paid within 48 hours of separation or by the next regular payday, but in no case longer than 30 days from separation. S.C. Code 41-10-50; No statute governs payout of vacation/sick leave, but employers must follow established policy. Vacation and sick pay are considered "wages" so generally they're paid out upon separation of employment.

South Dakota: Upon separation, whether discharge or resignation, employees must be paid the next pay day or as soon as the employee returns the employer's property; No statute governs payout of vacation or sick leave but employers must follow their policies. See S.D. Codified Laws §§ 60-11-10 and 60-11-11.

Tennessee: Upon separation, whether discharge or resignation: paid in full no later than the next regular pay day following the date of dismissal or voluntary leaving, or 21 days following the date of discharge or voluntary leaving, whichever occurs last. Unpaid vacation must be included in final pay; Employers with at least five (5) employees must include vacation pay or compensatory time owed to employees in the final paycheck, if the nonprofit's policy so provides. See Tenn. Code. Ann. § 50-2-103.

Texas: If employee is fired: within six days. If employee quits: next payday. See Texas Code Ann., Labor § 61.014.

Utah: If employee is fired: within 24 hours. If employee quits: next regular payday; Payment of vacation/sick leave is required only if required by contract or policy of the employer. See Utah Code Ann. §§ 34-28-1, 28-2(4) and 28-5.

Vermont: If employee is fired: within 72 hours of termination. If employee quits: by the next regular payday; Employers are only required to pay earned vacation and/or sick leave upon separation if an agreement or policy so provides. See 21 Vt. Stat. Ann. §§ 342(c) and 345a.

Virginia: Upon separation, whether discharge or resignation: next scheduled payday. Va. Code § 40.1-29 ; no statute governs whether an employer must include earned vacation or sick leave in final pay.

Washington: Upon separation, whether discharge or resignation: next pay period. Wash. Rev. Code § 49.48.010; there is no statutory right to earned vacation or sick leave upon separation. In fact, a court found that an employee who has accrued vacation time as a result of his own decision to forego vacation, isn't entitled to vacation pay upon termination unless there was a contract or policy to the contrary. See Walters Center Electric. Inc. 8 Wa. App. 322 (1973). Employers should have a policy that clearly states whether employees are entitled to cash in lieu of time off for vacation or sick time otherwise the payment of unused fringe benefits may be owed them upon separation of employment. See *Teamsters Local 117 v. Northwest Beverages, Inc.* 95 Wa. App. 767 (1999).

West Virginia: If employee is fired: within 72 hours. If employee quits: immediately if employee has given one pay period's notice; otherwise, next regular payday; Employers must pay any accrued fringe benefits upon separation, if the employer's policy so provides. The W. Va. Supreme Court has held that the terms of employment concerning payment of unused fringe benefits "must be express." W. Va. Code § 21-5-1 et seq. See *Meadows v. Walmart Stores, Inc.* 207 W. Va. 203, 530 S. E. 2nd 676 (1999).

Wisconsin: If employee is fired: next payday or within one month, whichever is earlier. If termination is due to merger, relocation, or liquidation of business, within 24 hours. If employee quits: next payday; Employers are required to pay earned vacation and/or sick leave upon separation unless there is a policy to the contrary. See Wis. Stat. Ann. § 109.03.

Wyoming: Upon separation, whether discharge or resignation: within five business days; Earned and unused vacation must be paid within five (5) working days of separation. Employers may provide that unused sick days won't be paid upon termination of employment. See Wyo. Stat. Ann. §§ 27-4-104 and Wyo. Stat. 27-4-501(a)(iii).

Note that Wyoming, unlike most other states, permits the employer to offset in the final paycheck any debt to the employer incurred by the employee during employment.

Caution! Special rules may apply when a nonprofit is shutting its doors, and terminating many employees

The federal Worker Adjustment and Retraining Notification Act, 29 USC § 2101 et seq. (The WARN Act) (*www.dol.gov/compliance/laws/comp-warn.htm*) requires employers of more than 100 employees to provide at least 60 days notice prior to closing a site where 50 or more employees will lose their employment during a period of 30 days. The WARN Act doesn't require severance pay. However, several states have their own WARN Acts, and Maine's law includes a severance pay provision.

The state laws noted here are subject to periodic review and revision by state legislatures. This summary should therefore be used for reference purposes, rather than as a definitive guide.

Maine has an unusual severance pay law: If a place of employment shuts down operations or moves its operations, all employees are entitled to severance pay of at least one week's pay per year of service. The severance is in addition to final wages earned and is to be paid in the regular course of final payroll payments. See Me. Rev. Stat. Title 26 Ch 7, § 625-B.

Other states that have *plant closing* laws similar to the federal WARN statute are:

California: The provisions of the California WARN Act are parallel to federal law. See Cal. Lab. Code § 1400 et seq.

District of Columbia: Nursing homes and community residence facilities should, to the extent possible, give employees 90 days advance written notice before the voluntary closing of a facility that will affect the employment of more than 10 percent of the residents. The notice must contain the proposed date of closing, and the reasons for closing. Written notice that a facility's license is being restricted, suspended or revoked, or not renewed or that it's losing its Medicare or Medicaid certification must be given to employees within 30 calendar days. See D.C. § 44-1003.11.

Hawaii: Employers that are party to a sale, transfer of assets, merger or business transaction that employs, at any time in the preceding 12-month period, 50+ employees are covered by the Hawaii Dislocated Workers Act. The act requires employers to give 60 days' written notice of a "closing" to affected employees and to the state. In some cases the employer will also have to pay a dislocated workers allowance to discharged employees for a four-week period after the closing. In order for a "closing" to occur, three events must occur: 1) a sale, transfer, merger or other business takeover transaction; 2) a permanent shutting down of all operations; and 3) an actual or potential layoff or termination of employees. See Chapter 394 B, Hawaii Rev. Stat.

Illinois: Any employer with 75+ employees must notify workers of a mass layoff, relocation or employment loss. Notice must also be given to the state. See 820 ILCS 65/1 et seq. and 30 LICS 760/15.

Maine:

Maryland: The State of Maryland provides voluntary guidelines to assist employers mitigate the impact on employees as a result of a reduction in operations. See Md. Code Ann., Lab. & Empl. §§ 11-301(c), 302, 303 and 304.

Massachusetts: Employers with 50+ employees must notify the state "promptly" of the closing of operations or partial closing. Employers must also arrange with insurers to maintain health coverage for employees and their dependents for 90 days after a closing or partial closing. See Mass. Gen. L. c. 151A § 71B.

Minnesota: Employers with obligations under the federal WARN Act must also notify the state the names, addresses and occupations of affected employees. See Minn. Stat. Annot. § 116L.976.

New Hampshire: All employers with at least one employee for at least 20 calendar weeks, or with gross wages of $1,500+ who plan to lay off 25 or more individuals in the same calendar week, for seven days or longer, are required to file a mass layoff notice with the State. See New Hampshire Rev. Stat. Annot. 282-A:45-a.

New Jersey: New Jersey has adopted the federal WARN Act, therefore employers with 100+ employees are required to give employees 60 days' advance notice of a closing or mass layoff. See N.J.A.C. 1240-1.1-1.2.

Ohio: Employers that plan to separate 50+ employees because of lack of work must give notice to the state of the date(s) of separation and approximately how many individuals will be affected. The notice must be furnished at least three (3) working days before the date of the first layoff or separation. See Ohio Rev. Code § 4141.28.

South Carolina: If employees are required to give notice prior to separation (resignation), employers must give employees the same amount of notice of a closing of operations. See S.C. Code Ann. § 41-1-40.

Tennessee: Employers with 50 but not more than 99 employees must notify employees of reduction in operations and notify the state. There isn't a time requirement for the notice. "Reduction" is defined as a closing or partial closing affecting 50+ employees for more than three (3) months. See Tenn. Code Ann. §§ 50-1-601 through 50-1-604.

Wisconsin: Employers with 50+ employees must provide at least 60 days' advance written notice of a mass layoff that will affect 25+ employees, and must post a notice in a conspicuous place informing employees of their rights. Notice must also be given to the state. See Wis. Stat. § 109.07.

Regulation of Hours of Work, Minimum Wage and Overtime Payments

The Fair Labor Standards Act of 1938 (FLSA) (www.dol.gov/compliance/laws/comp-flsa.htm) (29 USC § 201 et seq. ⬤ ; 29 CFR Parts 510 to 794 (www.dol.gov/dol/allcfr/ESA/Title_29/Chapter_V.htm) and state wage and hour laws establish standards for minimum wages, overtime pay, recordkeeping, child labor and also define which workers are independent contractors as opposed to employees. Each state exercises regulatory oversight for wage payment and child labor in that state. State regulations of hours of work, child labor, minimum wage, and overtime are available on the Internet, as well as in booklets that can be obtained, free of charge, from the appropriate state agency.

Minimum Wage and Wages for Overtime

The minimum wage established by the federal government as of 2006 is $5.15 an hour. Each state may also establish a minimum wage. (Most states' minimum wages mirror or exceed $5.15 at present.)[10] A nonprofit organization is covered by the Fair Labor Standards Act (FLSA), if it's "engaged in interstate commerce" **and** if it has a total dollar "volume of business" of $500,000. While almost every nonprofit organization can be said to be engaged in interstate commerce, not every organization will meet the threshold dollar amount of the *business volume* test.[11] Consequently, the FLSA may not apply to your organization. However, **state laws will apply**, that most often mirror the federal law, with some exceptions.

Both federal and state wage and hour laws require that all employees (with minor exceptions for student workers and individuals whose earning or productive capacities for the work to be performed are impaired by physical or mental disabilities, including those related to age or injury) receive a **statutory minimum wage** for all work performed—and that employees *who aren't otherwise exempt*—receive **premium pay** for each hour worked in excess of what the applicable law has determined to constitute **overtime.** The federal law defines overtime as time worked in excess of 40 hours in a single work week. State laws can be quite different. Nonprofits need to know first whether the federal FLSA applies to their workplace in order to determine the applicability of the overtime rules. Second, nonprofits need to define who at their workplace is entitled to overtime.

Premium Pay Required for Overtime Worked

The FLSA requires employers to pay employees not less than 1.5 times their regular rates of pay for all hours worked in excess of 40 in a workweek, unless the employees are otherwise exempt. If a nonprofit organization isn't subject to the FLSA, then it's important to be familiar with the applicable state wage and hour regulations. When an organization is covered by federal law and the applicable state law is more stringent, the state law should be followed. (When an organization isn't covered by federal law, the state law governs.)

Determining Which Employees Are Exempt From Overtime

The FLSA and state DOL wage and hour regulations define which positions are exempt from being paid overtime. If the position doesn't meet the criteria for exempt employees set forth in wage and hour regulations, the position must be classified as nonexempt (hourly). The FLSA was amended in April 2004 in an attempt to clarify the classification of exempt employees. The DOL final regulations amending the FLSA can be found at the DOL's Web site: www.dol.gov/esa/regs/fedreg/final/2004009016.htm.

Summary of FLSA Definitions of Exempt Categories

Executive: An employee whose (i) primary duty is "management of the enterprise;" (ii) and who customarily and regularly directs the work of two or more other employees; and (iii) has authority to hire or fire other employees[12] or whose suggestions and recommendations as to hiring, firing, advancement, promotion or other change of status of other employees are given particular weight.

> Examples of *management* include: interviewing, selecting, and training employees; setting and adjusting pay and work hours; appraising employee productivity and efficiency; handling employee complaints and grievances; disciplining employees; and planning and apportioning work among employees; planning and controlling the budget.

Administrative: An employee (i) whose primary duty is the performance of office or nonmanual work directly related to the management or general business operations of the employer; and (ii) whose job includes the exercise of discretion and independent judgment with respect to matters of significance.[13]

---

10 The Web site of the federal Department of Labor maintains an interactive map showing each state's minimum wage at *www.dol.gov/esa/minwage/america.htm.*

11 The following employers are covered by the FLSA regardless of their dollar volume of business: hospitals; institutions primarily engaged in the care of the sick, aged, mentally ill, or disabled who reside on the premises; schools for children who are mentally, or physically disabled or gifted; preschools, elementary, and secondary schools and institutions of higher education; and federal, state, and local government agencies.

12 The exempt executive need not have authority to make the ultimate decision, which may rest with the board of directors.

13 Factors include, but are not limited to:
• Whether the employee has authority to formulate, affect, interpret, or implement management policies or operating practices
• Whether the employee carries out major assignments in conducting the operations of the business
• Whether the employee performs work that affects business operations to a substantial degree, even if the employee's assignments are related to operation of a particular segment of the business

Every employer subject to the Fair Labor Standards Act's minimum wage provisions must post, and keep conspicuously posted, a notice explaining the act in a conspicuous place in all of their establishments. The posting can be obtained from the DOL at the following Web site: www.dol.gov/esa/regs/compliance/posters/flsa.htm.

Small Nonprofits Be Aware!

If the nonprofit's operations are small, with a budget of less than $500,000, state law will apply. The nonprofit needs to know whether state law defines overtime as something other than 40 hours worked in a single week. State wage regulations, if applicable, will also define which workers are exempt from overtime.

Examples: In *Alaska*, overtime isn't required for workplaces with fewer than four employees. In *Maryland*, after 48 hours worked in a week, premium pay is owed to residential employees of institutions primarily engaged in the care of the sick, aged or mentally ill. In *Kentucky*, premium pay must be paid for the seventh day of work for those employees who regularly work seven days a week. In *Minnesota*, premium pay must be paid after 48 hours of work in a single week. In *Montana*, premium pay must be paid for any work over eight (8) hours a day, unless the employee and employer have mutually negotiated to work four 10-hour days in a work week.

Note: Discretion and independent judgment *doesn't* include: (i) applying well-established techniques, procedures or specific standards described in manuals or other sources; (ii) clerical or secretarial work; (iii) recording or tabulating data or performing mechanical, repetitive, recurrent or routine work, such as data entry.

Professional: An employee whose primary duty is the performance of work requiring advanced knowledge in a field of science or learning that's customarily acquired by a **prolonged course** of specialized intellectual instruction. (The *professional* classification requires **more** than a high school level education). Specialized academic training is a prerequisite for being considered a professional; best evidence that an employee meets this requirement is possession of the appropriate academic degree. Example: teachers with teaching degrees or certifications are exempt; teachers' aides who don't have the same academic qualifications are nonexempt.

Other exempt categories that may apply to a nonprofit employer

Creative artists, dancers, actors, journalists, and specialized information technology professionals and *highly compensated employees.*

Highly Compensated Employees Are Exempt When They:

❏ Earn total annual compensation of at least $100,000;

❏ Earn at least $455 per week, paid on a salary or fee basis;

❏ Perform office or nonmanual work; and

❏ Customarily and regularly perform any one or more of the exempt duties identified in the standard tests for the executive, administrative or professional exemptions.

Independent Contractors: Proceed With Caution

Most nonprofits engage a range of independent contractors and consultants who bring specialized skills and training that supplement the talent of the nonprofit's paid and volunteer workforce. Common arrangements with independent contractors may include short-term assignments, such as the delivery of board development training, and a long-term or an ongoing relationship whereby a contractor provides weekly counseling or psychiatric services to service recipients. Although the use of independent contractors is common in the nonprofit sector, the proper engagement and classification of contractors presents a continuing challenge for nonprofit leaders. Nonprofits that hire independent contractors or consultants must be certain that these independent workers have been properly classified, and aren't, in the eyes of U.S. Department of Labor regulators, actually employees of the nonprofit. Upon determining that the nonprofit has mistakenly labeled employees as *contractors*, the DOL may hold the nonprofit responsible for back overtime, if applicable, as well as tax withholdings, employer contributions and potential penalties. Misclassifying employees as independent contractors is one of the most common mistakes that result in a nonprofit's liability for DOL penalties.

There are a number of reasons for the continuing confusion about the proper classification of independent contractors. First, there is no single source of authority that a nonprofit may consult and rely on. Three regulatory sources offer guidance: the federal Internal Revenue Service, the federal Department of Labor, and the various state departments of labor. Second, many nonprofit leaders gravitate to the use/designation of independent contractors due to the associated simplicity of paying a flat fee or hourly fee for service.

The IRS has developed a 20-factor test that it uses to investigate contractor status. Different states may weigh some of the factors differently, but the 20-factor test is a good starting point to review whether or not the workers that your nonprofit treats as independent contractors are properly classified. Most states have their own definitions of independent contractor status, and the state department of labor can audit a workplace independently of the federal DOL; thus it's wise to check both the IRS 20-factor checklist and your particular state definitions. In Massachusetts, for example, to be classified as an *independent contractor*, an individual must 1) be free from control and direction in the execution of his or her job; 2) perform a service outside the usual course of business of the employer; and 3) routinely work in an independently established trade, occupation, profession or business. The IRS factors are far more detailed.

Employee/Independent Contractor 20 Factor Test

In the chart below we have depicted the IRS 20-Factor Test in an easy-to-use format that will allow you to quickly distinguish the characteristics of employees versus independent contractors. Remember, it's not what you call a worker that matters, it's what they do and how they service your organization that counts in making the proper classification.

	Employees	Independent Contractors
1. Instructions	Employees comply with instructions about when, where, and how work is to be performed.	Contractors set their own hours and do the job in their own way.
2. Training	Employees are trained to perform services in a particular way. They're required to take correspondence courses and attend meetings. Other methods also indicate that the employer wants the services performed in a particular way.	Contractors use their own methods and receive no training from the purchaser of their services.
3. Integration	Services of an employee are merged into the business. Success and continuation of the business depends upon these services. The employer coordinates work with that of others.	The success and continuation of the business aren't dependent on services provided by a contractor.
4. Services Rendered Personally	An employee doesn't engage other people to do the work.	Contractors are able to assign their own workers to do the job.
5. Hiring, Supervising, Paying	An employee hires, supervises and pays workers at the direction of the employer for example, acts as foreman or representative of the employer).	Contractors hire, supervise and pay the other workers as the result of a contract. A contractor agrees to provide materials and labor and is responsible for the results.
6. Continuing Relationship	An employee continues to work for the same person year after year.	Contractors are hired to do one job. There is no continuous relationship.
7. Set Hours of Work	An employee's hours and days are set by the employer.	Contractors are masters of their own time.
8. Full Time Required	An employee normally works full time for an employer.	Contractors are free to work when and for whom they choose.
9. Doing Work on Employer's Premises	Employees work on the premises of an employer; or on a route, or at a site, designated by the employer.	Contractors work off-site (not on an employer's premises) and use their own offices, desks, and telephones.
10. Order or Sequence Set	An employee performs services in the order or sequence set by the employer.	Services are performed at a contractor's own pace.
11. Oral or Written Reports	Employees are required to submit regular oral or written reports to the employer.	Contractors submit no reports other than invoices and perhaps progress reports.
12. Payment by Hour, Week, Month	Employees are paid by the employer in regular amounts at stated intervals.	A contractor is paid by the job on a straight commission, or hourly or a flat fee.
13. Payment of Business and/or Travel Expenses	The employer pays employees' business and/or travel expenses.	Contractors take care of their own expenses and are accountable only to themselves for expenses.
14. Furnishing of Tools, Materials	An employer furnishes tools, materials, etc.	Contractors furnish their own tools, etc.
15. Significant Investment	An employee has no significant investment in the facilities used to perform services.	A contractor has a real, essential and significant investment.
16. Realization of Profit or Loss	An employee can't realize a profit or loss by making good or bad decisions.	Contractors can realize a profit or suffer a loss as a result of their services or decisions.

	Employees	Independent Contractors
17. Working for More Than One Firm at a Time	An employee usually works for one employer at a time.	An independent contractor works for a number of persons or firms at the same time.
18. Making Services Available to the General Public	An employee doesn't make services available to the general public.	Contractors have their own offices and assistants. They hold business licenses, are listed in business directories, maintain business telephones, and otherwise generally make their services available to the public.
19. Right to Fire	An employee can be discharged at any time.	Contractors can't be fired so long as product results meet contract specifications.
20. Right to Quit	Employees can quit their jobs at any time without incurring liability.	Contractors agree to complete a specific job and are responsible for satisfactory completion; or they're legally obligated to pay damages, generally by the terms of their contract for services.

Risks for Violation of the FLSA or State Wage and Hour Laws

When a violation of wage and hour laws occurs it's often because the employer did not classify a worker correctly, resulting in underpayment of wages, and underpayment of the employer and employee contributions that are withheld from wages (example: failure to contribute state unemployment and temporary disability insurance, and failure to contribution or withhold social security at the federal level). Consequently, often when an employer has to settle a score with the DOL, there is a large and unexpected bill to pay to the government.

Penalties: There are generally also penalties to pay for violation of state or federal laws. Penalties for violations of the FLSA include criminal prosecution for willful violations, carrying fines up to $10,000. A subsequent conviction can result in imprisonment. Employers who willfully or repeatedly violate the minimum wage or overtime pay requirements are subject to civil money penalties of up to $1,000 per violation. Violations of state law will carry separate penalties. If the violation isn't willful, the employer should try to negotiate with the state or federal DOL to eliminate or substantially reduce the employer's liability for penalties. Insurance policies won't cover penalties for violation of laws.

Checklist for Recognizing When Overtime Is Required

1. Know the classification of your employees. Job descriptions should define whether the position is *exempt* or *nonexempt*.

2. Know what categories of workers are nonexempt in your state. Generally those workers who are paid hourly and whose work is primarily either physical/manual or clerical in nature or directed by others, and whose job doesn't require any advanced educational background, are defined as nonexempt.

3. Nonexempt workers must be paid premium pay (1.5 times their regular hourly wage) for overtime. Generally any time worked in excess of 40 hours in a single work week entitles nonexempt workers to premium pay. There are some significant exceptions in various states. Know whether the federal law or your state law applies. (Whichever law is most favorable to the employee will govern.)

4. Nonexempt employees must be paid for every hour worked. Since the reward for working overtime is premium pay, nonexempt hourly workers may not be given any other reward for overtime, such as compensatory time off—unless the time off is within the same week as the extra time worked.

5. The use of compensatory time by a nonexempt worker is permissible when the nonexempt worker takes the compensatory time off in the same work week as the extra time worked (so that the total time worked in one week doesn't reach the overtime threshold).

6. When a nonexempt worker works more than his or her regularly scheduled work week, but not more than the statutory threshold for overtime, the employee only needs to be paid *straight time* (regular hourly wages) for the extra hours worked.

Overtime and Compensatory Time

There is still much misunderstanding about the correct use of compensatory time off, commonly called comp time. Nonprofit employers continue to inaccurately link *overtime* (time worked in excess of a regularly scheduled work week that's defined by federal and state law) with eligibility for comp time. Check your employee handbook. Is comp time mentioned? In a nutshell, it's a violation of federal wage and hour regulations to award comp time instead of premium pay to nonexempt staff for working overtime, unless the comp time off is the equivalent of, and in the same week as the extra time worked. To add to the confusion, some state laws refer to *compensatory time* (usually for public employees) and various states have their own definition of *overtime*. Consequently, this is an area where nonprofit managers are well-advised to know whether the FLSA applies to their nonprofit, and if not, become very familiar with their individual state's wage and hour laws.

A Word About Compensatory Time Off

There is no legal requirement under state or federal law to pay exempt salaried staff (professional, administrative, and executive staff) premium pay (overtime) to compensate them for extra time worked. It shouldn't be a surprise that exempt staff are expected to work as long as it takes to accomplish their work. While the nonprofit may have specific expectations about the time during the day that an exempt worker is at the office, or the number of hours worked on a regular basis during the week, there should be no salary deductions if fewer than normal hours are worked and no premium pay for overtime.

Nevertheless, many nonprofits wish to reward employees for efforts above and beyond the call of duty by giving them time off which is typically called *compensatory time off*, or *comp time*.

The correct way to use compensatory time off for exempt staff is to simply permit them flexibility to take time off, at a convenient time for all involved, as a reward for their extra hard work. The time off should be scheduled and approved by the exempt staff's supervisor, to be taken during the current pay period. It's generally not appropriate to permit exempt employees to save comp time and use it in the distant future. Generally when that happens, the exempt employee will mentally, if not in writing, keep track of extra time worked in hourly increments and actually take compensatory time off hour for hour for the extra time worked. If this occurs on a regular basis the nonprofit is considered by the U.S. Department of Labor to be treating the exempt employee as if he or she were an hourly worker, thereby risking a finding that all exempt workers reporting to the same supervisor are misclassified as exempt, when they should really be nonexempt. The result is that the nonprofit would be liable for overtime payments for that employee (and other employees in the same job category who report to the same manager), as well as back taxes and employer contributions for all the affected employees, plus penalties.

Special State Law Overtime Rules

The state laws noted here are subject to constant review and revision in state legislatures. This summary should therefore be used for reference purposes, rather than as a definitive guide.

The following states have unusual regulations pertaining to overtime (OT) and compensatory time off:

Alaska: OT is defined as more than 40 hours a week **or** more than 8 hours a day; OT requirements don't apply to employers with fewer than 3 employees. See Alaska Stat. Sect. 23.10.060. See also: *Alaska Employer Handbook.*

> ### Danger Zone! Don't Treat an Exempt Employee as a Nonexempt Employee
>
> It invites trouble to misclassify employees or to classify them one way but treat them inconsistently with their classification. Consequently, it can be risky to treat exempt workers as if they were nonexempt (hourly) by requiring them to fill out time sheets that track their hours of work or by docking their pay in ways that the DOL considers to be inconsistent with exempt worker treatment.
>
> Make sure there is a difference between exempt staffs' time records and hourly staffs' time records: Hourly workers record their hours worked for their employer, in total. Exempt workers only keep track of the total hours worked on behalf of a particular grant. Example: Sally worked from 9 am to 12 pm on Tuesday for Nonprofit X. Sally is nonexempt. She took lunch and then worked from 1 pm to 5 pm for Nonprofit X. Sally marked on her time sheet that she worked 3 hours in the morning and 4 hours in the afternoon, for a total of 7 hours. Some of those hours were credited on a separate time sheet or Excel spreadsheet on her computer as being hours during which she was accomplishing tasks to further the goals of Grant ABC, administered by Nonprofit X.
>
> On the other hand Tom, who is exempt, worked however many hours he worked all week for Nonprofit X. During that time he spent 25 hours accomplishing tasks to further the goals of Grant XYZ. While he didn't write down his total work hours each day or for the week, he did record on a special excel spreadsheet the hours he worked (and the actual dates, if applicable) on tasks associated with Grant ABC.

Arizona: Employers *may* provide compensatory time off hour for hour for the extra time worked in lieu of compensation, at the discretion of the employer. This only applies when the employer is **not** covered by the FLSA. See Arizona Rev. Stat. Title 23, Article 9, 23-391.

California: Compensatory time off in lieu of overtime compensation was abolished in 2002. OT defined as over 8 hours in a day; 40 hours a week. Workers who work in excess of 12 hours in a single day must be paid 2x their regular rate of pay. Through mutual agreement a 10-hour work day within a 40 hour workweek may be arranged and no premium pay will be owed for the 10-hour day. See CA Labor Code Section 510, 511.

Florida: OT defined as over 10 hours per day for manual workers.

Idaho: Employers and employees are free to agree on work hours that will be compensated and those that will be OT. See Idaho Stat. Title 44-1203.

Kansas: OT defined as time worked over 46 hours per week. See Kan. Stat. Ann. Sect. 44-1204.

Kentucky: OT must be paid to employees working seven days in any work week, for the time worked on the seventh day. Ky. Rev. Stat. Ann. 337. 050. Under state law, OT is **not** applicable to employees who work in private, nonprofit residential facilities licensed by the Cabinet for Health and Family Services to serve abused and neglected children, or as in-home companions for the mentally ill, sick, elderly or infirm. Note that state exceptions for OT only apply when the workplace isn't subject to the FLSA.

Maryland: OT is work over 40 hours in a seven (7) day work week. See Maryland Guide to Wage Payment Standards.

Michigan: OT is defined as over 10 hours in a single day. See Mich. Comp. Laws Annot. § 408.401.

Minnesota: OT defined as over 48 hours per week. See Minn. Stat. Ann. Sect. 177.25.

Nebraska: OT wages can be claimed under the Nebraska Wage Payment and Collection Act only if those overtime wages were previously agreed to by the employer and the employee. Nonetheless, even in the absence of a previous agreement concerning overtime compensation, compensation for overtime can be claimed under the federal Fair Labor Standards Act for hours worked in excess of 40 during a given week. *Freeman v. Central States Health & Life Co.*, 2 Neb. App. 803, 515 N.W.2d 131 (1994). Neb. Rev. Stat. Section 48-1229; Compensatory time off or premium pay may be granted at the discretion of the supervisor for nonexempt employees when they're required to work over 40 hours in a workweek if their usual workweek is 40 hours. See Neb. Rev. Stat. Section 81-117.01, 02.

Nevada: OT is defined as hours worked over 40 hours in a work week, and over 8 hours in one day unless by mutual agreement the employee works a scheduled 10 hours per day for 4 days during the week. See Nev. Rev. Stat. 608.018.

Rhode Island: Employees working on Sundays or holidays must be paid 1.5 times regular rate of pay. See R.I. Gen. Stat. Title 25, Ch. 25-3.

Overtime Nuances Governed by State Wage Regulations

If your nonprofit **isn't** covered by the FLSA, then state law governing overtime applies. Consequently, if an employee works 45 hours a week, but no more than 9 in any day, in a state where overtime is defined as working over 10 hours in a single day, the employee should be paid straight time for all hours worked that week even though the total is over 40 hours.

The Center recommends verifying procedures for calculating the overtime rate with your state DOL wage and hour authorities for any of the following situations:

❑ When an employee works two distinct jobs for the nonprofit, it's possible that the total number of hours worked per week will exceed the state OT threshold or the federal 40 hour threshold. If both jobs are nonexempt jobs, the total hours worked must be considered. If the jobs are at different rates of pay, usually the job the employee was working when he surpassed 40 hours is the rate of pay used for OT calculations.

❑ Sometimes one employee will actually be employed by a nonprofit in two distinct capacities. If the employee works one job as an exempt employee, and one job as a nonexempt employee, then generally only the hours worked as a nonexempt employee are considered for OT purposes.

❑ When an employee is required to remain *on-call* to meet the needs of the nonprofit, the *on-call* time could be considered *work* time for purposes of calculating OT and for wage payment. Check the rules in your state for on-call time. Generally if an employee is free to go about her or his business with a beeper or cell phone, without restrictions on where she is or what she is doing, she isn't working and doesn't have to be paid for the on-call time.

❑ When employees sleep in a residential facility where they're employed, special rules apply to determine what portion of their sleeping time, if any, is work time and should be compensated. While state laws may differ, the FLSA permits employers to exclude up to 8 hours from work time when shifts are exactly 24 consecutive hours. To permit a sleep-time exclusion requires that there be an *agreement* with the employee. An employee who takes a job which has a sleep-time exclusion in place will be deemed to have *agreed* to it. There must also be adequate sleeping facilities, and the employee must normally have the opportunity to obtain 5 hours of sleep. The 5 hours need not be consecutive. If an employee doesn't have the opportunity to get at least 5 hours of sleep, no sleep-time exclusion is permitted. Any time during the sleep period when an employee wakes up to attend to clients and is actually performing work must be counted as compensable work time.

Regulation of Meal and Rest Breaks

Most states wage and hour laws, as well as state child labor laws, govern whether and how long of a meal or rest break must be provided to workers. Care should be taken with youth volunteers and young paid staff whose work hours are governed by child labor laws. Some state laws specify that the meal or rest periods are unpaid, but generally they're paid. Check your state's wage and hour regulations for specifics.

State Laws Governing Minimum Meal Periods and Paid Rest Breaks[14]

Note: Federal regulations require that breaks shorter than 20 minutes be paid. With that exception, the rest and meal periods noted below **need not be paid**, unless otherwise noted.

The state laws noted here are subject to constant review and revision in state legislatures. This summary should therefore be used for reference purposes, rather than as a definitive guide.

Alaska: Volunteers who are minors (under 18) are entitled to a break of at least 30 minutes during the course of the work shift if they're scheduled to work for six or more consecutive hours. See Alaska 23.10.350(c).

California: Every nonexempt employee working more than 5 hours a day is required to have at least 30 minutes for a meal break; except if the total hours worked in a day is less than 6 hours, then the meal break may be waived by mutual consent of the employer and employee; Employees working more than 10 hours a day are entitled to a second meal break of 30 minutes; except if the total hours worked in a day is no more than 12 hours, the second meal period may be waived by mutual consent. Also every nonexempt worker is entitled to a rest period (based on a 10-minute period for every four hours worked) insofar as practicable, in the middle of the work period, unless the employee's total work time is less than 3.25 hours. See CA Labor Code § 512(a) .

Colorado: Employers are required to give a meal period of 30 minutes if an employee works for 5 or more hours. If the nature of the work doesn't allow for uninterrupted meal periods, the employee must be permitted to consume an *on-duty* meal while performing job duties, which is paid work time. Every employer is required to provide a rest period in the middle of each 4-hour work period. A compensated 10-min rest period every four hours is permitted. See Colorado Minimum Wage Order Number 22.

Connecticut: Employees working more than 7.5 hours are entitled to a meal break of at least 30 consecutive minutes after the first two hours, and before the final two hours of work. Employers are exempt from the requirement if (i) requiring compliance would be adverse to public safety, (ii) the duties of the position may only be performed by one employee, (iii) the employer employs fewer than 5 employees on a shift at a single place of business, and (iv) the continuous nature of the operation requires employees to be available to respond to urgent conditions and employees are compensated for break and meal periods. See Conn. Stat. § 31-51ii.

Delaware: Employees working at least 7.5 hours are entitled to an unpaid meal break of at least 30 minutes, after the first two hours and before the last two hours of work. See Del. Stat. Tit. 19 § 707.

Florida: No state law governs meal or rest breaks for adults. Volunteers who are minors (under 18) must be provided with a 30-minute break for every 4 hour period worked.

Loss of Exemption Through Improper Docking

In general, exempt employees **may not be *docked* less than a full day's compensation**. There are seven specific exceptions for situations when a full day's pay may be deducted from an exempt worker's pay.

The seven exceptions from the no pay-docking rule are:

1. Absence from work for one or more full days for personal reasons, other than sickness or disability (when the employee isn't using an excused day: a personal day or a vacation day);

2. Absence from work for one or more full days due to sickness or disability, if deductions are made under a bona fide plan, policy or practice of providing wage replacement benefits for these types of absences;

3. Penalties imposed in good faith for violating safety rules of *major significance*;

4. Unpaid disciplinary suspension of one or more full days imposed in good faith for violations of workplace conduct rules;

5. Unpaid leave taken pursuant to the Family and Medical Leave Act;

6. To offset any amounts received as payment for jury fees, witness fees, or military pay; or

7. Proportionate part of an employee's full salary may be paid for time actually worked in the first and last weeks of employment.

Improper deductions include:

❑ Deduction for a partial-day absence to attend a parent-teacher conference;

❑ Deduction of a day of pay because the employer was closed due to inclement weather;

❑ Deduction of three days of pay because the employee was absent from work for jury duty, rather than merely offsetting any amount received as payment for the jury duty, if that's the employer's policy (Many employers permit employees to keep the small amount they receive for jury service.);

❑ Deduction for a two-day absence due to a minor illness when the employer doesn't provide wage replacement benefits for such absences.

Note: The practice of making improper deductions from salary **will result in the loss of the exemption** for the *entire time period* during which the improper deductions were made, and for **all employees** in the same job classifications or who are working for the same managers responsible for the actual improper deductions. Isolated or inadvertent improper deductions won't result in the loss of exempt status *if the employer makes an immediate correction by reimbursing the employee.*

---

14 If a state isn't listed, there is no special law governing this issue.

Hawaii: No state law governs meal or rest breaks for adults. Minors age 14–16 must be provided with at least 30 minutes for a rest or lunch period for every five hours worked.

Illinois: Employees working at least 7.5 continuous hours are entitled to at least a 20-minute meal break, beginning no later than five hours after the start of the work period. The law doesn't apply to employees who monitor individuals with disabilities and who are required to be on call during an entire eight-hour period. Full time employees (over 20 hours weekly) must be permitted at least 24 consecutive hours of rest in every work week. See Ill. Comp. Stat. Ch. 820 § 140/2,3.

Iowa: Any minor under age 16 employed or volunteering for more than 5 hours a day must be provided with an "intermission" of not less than 30 minutes. See Iowa Code § 92.7.

Kentucky: A meal period ("lunch period") must be provided to employees in the middle of their work shift, but no sooner than 3 nor more than 5 hours after the start of their shift. Ky. Rev. Stat. § 337.355; In addition to the lunch period, a 10-minute rest period must be provided to employees for every 4 hours they work. See Ky. Rev. Stat. 337.365.

Louisiana: Any minor who works five hours must be provided with a 30-minute meal break. See La. Rev. Stat. Ann. § 23:213.

Maine: Employers with 3+ employees are required to provide employees working six consecutive hours to 30 consecutive minutes for a rest/meal break. See Me. Rev. Stat. Ann. 26 § 601.

Massachusetts: Employees working six consecutive hours are entitled to at least 30 consecutive minutes of rest/meal break. Employees can voluntarily waive their meal break (written waivers are recommended) but must be paid for all hours worked. State law doesn't require a rest break, but as a practical matter many employers provide a 10 to 15-minute break. See Ma. Gen. L. 149 § 100.

Michigan: A minor (under 18) who works at least five hours of continuous work must receive at least at 30-minute meal/rest period M L C 409.112.

Minnesota: Each employee working four consecutive hours of work is entitled to adequate time to visit the restroom. Employees working longer than four consecutive hours are entitled to "sufficient time to eat a meal" (unpaid). See Minn. Stat. Ann. § 177.253; Minn. Stat. Ann. § 177.254.

Montana: Employers aren't required to provide a rest or a meal break but if an employee takes a break of 30 minutes or less the time must be paid. In order for a meal break to be unpaid, the employee must be completely relieved of any duties and the break must be longer than 30 minutes. See Mont. Admin. R. 24.16.1006.

Nevada: Employees working a continuous eight-hour shift must be given a 30-minute meal period. Employees working more than 3.25 hours must be provided a 10-minute rest period, provided "wherever practicable," preferably in the middle of each work period at the rate of 10 minutes of rest for each four hours of work. Rest periods are paid and time worked. An employee can waive rest and meal periods, however, written waivers are recommended. See Nev. Rev. Stat. 608.019. See also Nevada Admin. Code, § 608.145.

New Hampshire: Employees working more than five consecutive hours must be permitted at least 30-minutes for a meal, unless it's feasible for the employee to eat during performance of his work and the employer permits the employee to do so. If employees work during meal periods they must be paid. See N.H. Rev. Stat. Annot. § 275:30-a.

New Jersey: No requirements for rest/meal periods for adults; Minors (under 18) who work for more than 5 continuous hours must be provided with a break of at least 30-minutes for lunch. Breaks of less than 30-minutes are unpaid. See N.J.S.A. § 34:2-21.4.

New York: Employees who work shifts longer than 6 hours that extend over the noon meal period are entitled to a 30-minute lunch break. Employees who start their work before 11 am and end after 7 pm are entitled to an additional meal period of at least 20 minutes between 5 pm and 7 pm. See N.Y. Stat. Tit. 1 Article 5 § 162.2.

North Dakota: Employees must be provided a 30-minute meal period for five or more consecutive hours of work or when two or more employees are on duty. See AC Art. 46-02-07-02(5).

Oklahoma: Minors working more than five hours must be provided with a 30-minute cumulative rest period, and minors under age 16 must be permitted a 60-minute cumulative rest period for each eight consecutive hours worked. See Okla. Stat. Title 40 § 75.

Oregon: Employees must be provided with a paid rest period of not less than 10-minutes for every segment of four hours worked. This rest period is separate from and in addition to a required meal period, of not less than 30 minutes for employees working six or more hours. Employees are generally relieved of work duties and the meal period is generally unpaid. Employees who perform any tasks during the meal period must be paid. Oregon Admin. Rules 839-20-050 ; Minors are entitled to a 15-minute rest period for every four hour period of work. Minors are also entitled to a 30-minute meal period beginning no longer than 5 hours after the employee starts work. Fourteen and 15 year olds must be relieved of all work duties during lunch. Sixteen and 17 year olds may work through the meal period if they're paid and business conditions require it. See Oregon Admin. Rules 839-021-0072.

Pennsylvania: Minors working for more than five continuous hours must be provided with a lunch period of at least 30 minutes. Breaks under 30 minutes must be paid. See 43 Pennsylvania Statutes § 46.

Tennessee: Employers must provide an unpaid rest/meal break of at least 30-minutes for those employees working for six or more consecutive hours. Exception for employees in workplace environments that, by their nature. provide ample opportunity for rest or breaks. TN Stat. § 50-2-103(h) ; A similar provision impacts minors, but without the exception for workplaces providing an opportunity for rest periods.

Utah: There is no requirement that employers provide adults with rest/meal periods. If an employer chooses to provide a meal period, the break should be paid, unless it lasts at least 30 minutes and the employee is completely relieved of any work duties. Minors are entitled to a meal period of at least 30 minutes within the first five hours of their work day. The meal period must be paid unless the minor is relieved of all duties. Minors are also entitled to a 10-minute break during every four hour period, and no minor may work longer than 3 hours without a break. See Utah Admin. Code Rule R610-1-2; R610-2-3.

Vermont: Employers are required to provide reasonable breaks for meals and rest. See 21 Vermont Stat. Ann. § 304.

Virginia: Effective July 1, 2005, Virginia has **repealed** its Day of Rest law, which had required all employers to provide all employees with one 24-hour rest period each week and allowed non-managerial employees in many industries to chose Saturday or Sunday as their day of rest. Minors under age 16 must be allowed a 30-minute meal break for every five hours of continuous work. See Va. Code 40.1-80.1B.

Washington: Nonexempt employees who work five consecutive hours are entitled to at least 30-minutes for a meal period that should commence no less than two hours nor more than five hours from the beginning of the work period. Meal periods are paid if the employee is required to remain "on duty" on the premises or at a prescribed worksite. Employees can't be required to work more than five consecutive hours without a meal period. If an employee is working three or more hours of overtime, a break of at least 30-minutes prior to or during the period of overtime is required. Non-exempt employees working three or more consecutive hours must be provided with a rest period of at least 10 minutes for each four hour period of work, except where the nature of the work permits employees to take intermittent breaks the equivalent of the required rest period. See Wash. Admin. Code 296-126-092.

West Virginia: Employees working six or more consecutive hours must be provided with at least 20 minutes for meals unless the employee can eat while working or is provided necessary breaks. WV Stat. § 21-3-10a ; Minors under age 16 working for more than five consecutive hours must be provided with a 30-minutes meal break. See W. Va. Code § 21-6-7(a)(7).

Wisconsin: Employers are recommended to provide employees with at least 30-minutes for each meal period, reasonably close to the usual meal period time, or near the middle of a shift. Shifts of six consecutive work hours should be avoided. Employers must pay employees for meal periods that are less than 30-minutes during which the employee is required to provide any work duties. *Note:* In contrast to federal Fair Labor Standard Act requirements, employers are required to maintain daily time records *for exempt,* as well as nonexempt employees, noting the times meal periods begin and end. See Wis. Admin. Code § DWD 274.02 and § DWD 272.11.

The next section, Chapter 5, focuses on fringe benefits—the package that can make or break a hiring deal and retain or lose a valued employee to a new position elsewhere.

Q: Must workers be paid during their meal break?

A: Generally not. A business isn't required to pay for meal periods if workers are free from any duties for their entire meal period.

However, nonexempt workers must be paid during their meal break when:

❏ They're required (or allowed) to remain on duty, actively working.

❏ They're required to be on-call at the business premises or designated worksite and available to return to duty even if they aren't in fact called back to duty.

❏ They're called back to duty during their meal period even though they normally aren't on call during the meal period.

Chapter 5

Fringe Benefits for Nonprofit Employees

The perception, whether real or fictional, is that employment in the nonprofit sector doesn't pay well, but offers good benefits. The reality is that innovative benefits are extremely important not only in the nonprofit sector, but throughout the U.S. workplace, especially as the workforce ages and the labor market tightens. Studies reveal that while employees expect to be fairly compensated, they place great store in benefits that increase the quantity and quality of their leisure time. Effective recruitment and retention continue to be a major concern. In 2005, nearly a quarter of the U.S. workforce changed jobs. Nonprofits and for-profits alike attempt to offer generous benefits with an eye towards recruiting, retaining and rewarding the best employees.

In 2005 MetLife conducted a national study of employee benefit trends. The following emerged:

❑ Almost 40 percent of employees said that benefits offered at their job are the reason they stay with their employers.

❑ 31 percent of employees said that the benefits offered by their current employer played a major role in their decision to select their current job.

❑ The cost of health care insurance was cited as the most significant benefit-related concern; therefore employers who pay a large share of health care costs and offer sound health insurance plans are most desirable.

❑ The majority of employees cited the "overall quality of co-worker and/or customer relationships" as their top criteria when trying to decide whether to join or stay with their current employer.

❑ The opportunity for a "good work/life balance" emerged as the second most important criteria for selecting or staying with their employer.

❑ "Working for an organization whose purpose/mission I agree with" was the third most important reason cited for selecting or staying with an employer.

❑ "Opportunities for financial advancement, skill building and professional growth" were also important criteria.

The study also revealed that among the benefits most appreciated by employees are: telecommuting (allowing employees to work from home or from a location remote from a central office), health insurance paid by the employer, and flexible hours (the latter two benefits are more prevalent in smaller workplaces with fewer than 50 employees, while telecommuting is more prevalent in larger workplaces). One of the fastest growing benefit trends is the use of the Internet for enrollment, information, claims filing and online education on such topics as health issues and financial planning.

Maintaining employee satisfaction means giving employees what they need to grow: personalized feedback on their performance, professional development opportunities; time to re-energize away from work; and little perks that make their jobs easier—even fun—and reinforce that they're being treated fairly. Selecting the right employee benefit package can ensure that such positive factors are in place. However, inequity in the application of benefits can result in serious dissatisfaction. The introduction of any new benefits should be carefully considered and reviewed to ensure that employees have a fair opportunity to take advantage of the benefit.

Who's Entitled to Benefits?

Each nonprofit is entitled to determine what benefits to offer which staff members, with one caveat: what is offered to one employee must be offered to all other similarly situated employees in order to avoid charges of discrimination. For example, a nonprofit could decide that part-time staff aren't entitled to personal days, but full-time staff are, or that part-time staff receive vacation leave on a reduced or *pro rata* basis compared to full-time staff. These choices are legal. However, the same nonprofit shouldn't offer two weeks paid *new parent leave* to female employees, but only three days paid new parent leave to male employees. Eligibility for benefits should be clearly spelled out in employee manuals to manage expectations and clarify who is entitled to which benefits.

Domestic Partner Benefits

While there is no mandate to do so, many employers are extending health insurance, flexible spending accounts and other benefits to domestic partners of employees. For example, an employer may expand the definition of *immediate family* to include domestic partners, which may impact bereavement leave policies, and sick leave or family leave. Federal law permits employers to extend COBRA and FMLA benefits to domestic partners, at the employer's discretion. As of 2006, 49 percent of Fortune 500 companies reportedly offer domestic partner benefits, compared to only 25 percent in 2000. (*Source: Human Rights Campaign Foundation, "Domestic Partner Benefits, Employer Trends and Benefits Equivalency for the GLBT Family," March 2006*). As of August 2006, eight states recognize the legal union of domestic partners, which requires insurance companies in those states to make insurance products available for domestic partners. A 2000 study by the Society for Human Resource Management showed slightly more employers extended benefits to opposite sex partners than to same-sex partners. Whether to extend benefits to domestic partners of employees is a matter for the nonprofit to determine and is subject to negotiation with insurance carriers.

Employees Need to Know About Their Benefits

Whatever benefits are offered, it's important to communicate to staff early and often all the details. Employee benefits are only as valuable as the employees' perception of them. Clear communication about each employee's benefit package is critical. During the recruitment interview, describe the fringe benefits available to employees. At orientation, give each new employee a summary sheet outlining his or her benefits. Distributing an annual employee benefit summary statement that itemizes the dollar value of each benefit is an example of the type of communication that, with very little extra time or effort, can increase the staff's appreciation for their benefits. It's becoming more common to redesign internal communication pieces to include easy-to-read written materials and multimedia presentations on employee benefits. The presentations can be delivered via a notebook computer during new staff orientation to communicate workplace policies and describe employee benefits.

Reinventing Employee Benefits

In addition to the usual menu of vacation, sick and personal days, nonprofits are increasingly using additional benefits to add value to employees' compensation packages. These additions include retirement plans and long-term disability insurance. Other types of benefits that are considered innovative are the expansion of health insurance to include dependents and nontraditional family members, flex-time, reimbursement for tuition or professional development activities related to the employee's job, a notebook computer for work-at-home flexibility, parking paid by the nonprofit in urban areas, cell phone reimbursement, and travel/mileage expense reimbursement for employees who do extensive work-related driving. Many other little perks can be used to reward, motivate and thank your staff—discount coupons for a local florist or car wash, on-site massages, balloons or flowers sent to the employee's home to congratulate a special effort, recognizing an employee of the month, and sending cards on the anniversary date of employment, or employees' birthdays. These acknowledgements of individual employees can go along way towards making them feel valued in the workplace.

Some organizations tie the nonprofit's mission to employee benefits: a land conservation organization makes a cabin in the woods available to staff for a getaway weekend. It isn't necessarily a fatter paycheck that keeps employees in their jobs; often recognition for a job well done and a supportive atmosphere is just as effective as a raise. Benefits that enhance an employee's time spent with family, or that provide special opportunities not found in typical corporate America are likely to continue to be the hallmarks of the nonprofit sector in the 21st century.

The Cost of Employee Benefits

The cost of benefits really has two perspectives: the cost to the employer, and the cost to the employee because of taxable income. Benefits such as car allowances, meals or lodging, if not offered primarily for the benefit of the nonprofit, result in taxable income to the employee and may be seen as personal benefits to certain staff rather than in furtherance of the nonprofit's mission. The nonprofit employer should be aware that certain benefits—even those that the nonprofit doesn't consider part of the employee's *salary*—are considered part of the employee's overall compensation package and not only will trigger the employee's liability for income taxes but may be reported on the nonprofit's annual return to the IRS (Form 990) as additional compensation to employees.

Recruitment Bonuses

A small number of nonprofits have found that offering a recruitment bonus to candidates for a top-level position often makes the difference between losing and landing a prime candidate. These recruitment bonuses might consist of just moving expenses, or a lump sum payment (typically between 5 to 15 percent of base salary) in addition to moving expenses, to be paid during the first months of employment or upon formal acceptance of the position. Such payments are usually governed by the terms of a contract for employment stating that the bonus payment is contingent upon the candidate's acceptance of the position and continued employment for a certain period. A contractual agreement is prudent in this case, because unless language prevents it, the candidate might accept the position and the bonus, but resign a few months later. Consequently, recruitment bonuses may serve as a lure, but are only effective if the nonprofit simultaneously protects its own interests. Documentation of the bonus is critical in light of the concern over penalties for excess compensation.

Annual Bonuses

Monetary bonuses are increasingly a common component of nonprofit executives' compensation packages. Surveys indicate that bonuses are more common for top staff leaders in civic associations and cultural organizations than in educational or human services organizations. When bonuses are used, they're most often offered to reward exceptional performance in higher level staff positions, such as executive directors, development directors[15], program managers, and chief financial officers. Bonuses are generally given as a percentage of annual salary and linked to the nonprofit's performance and financial health. When bonuses are offered it's *imperative to document the formula used to calculate the bonus amount*. This documentation is critical in the event that other employees who either didn't receive a bonus, or received lesser amounts, allege that the bonus policy is discriminatory.

❏ Employers must ensure that bonuses are awarded in a nondiscriminatory manner. Employees in a protected class who receive a lower bonus, or no bonus, can challenge the bonuses as discriminatory. Employers must therefore be prepared to justify the awards of bonuses with legitimate, job-related, nondiscriminatory reasons.

❏ The nonprofit must never penalize someone on military or FMLA leave by withholding a bonus during their leave.

❏ Bonuses shouldn't be paid to nonexempt employees in lieu of overtime payments.

❏ Bonuses are taxable income to the recipient and in many states considered *earned* wages, therefore, if awarded, bonuses can't be forfeited upon termination of employment.

Performance/Merit Bonuses: Some smaller nonprofits fortunate enough to have funds left over at year-end use bonuses to reward employees and recognize outstanding performance. Boards perceive bonus pay to be an effective tool to motivate and reward strong performance. Bonuses also answer the concern among many nonprofit boards that providing a bonus is better for the organization's long-term financial health. A bonus in the current year may be perceived as more fiscally prudent than implementing an increase in salary levels that will impact the nonprofit in future years.

Incentive Bonuses: Bonuses for staff, who have made it through a particularly tough year, especially a year when no salary increases are possible, are a welcome gesture of appreciation that may help rebuild morale. Small bonuses can also be used as incentives for staff in numerous ways to motivate performance. Incentive bonuses could include offering an *attendance bonus* (given to those with perfect attendance), *longevity bonus* (to reward employees after a certain number of years with the nonprofit) and *safety awards* or *suggestion awards*, (given to recognize an inventive idea shared by an employee that the nonprofit adopted).

Other Benefits

Flexible Work Schedule

Offering staff the ability to adjust their hours to meet their personal needs, while at the same time meeting the needs of the nonprofit, is a benefit that many people identify as a hallmark of the nonprofit sector. Nevertheless, flexible work hours may not be possible in every nonprofit or for every staff member. When there are some employees who are able to flex their hours and some who aren't, morale may suffer unless the reasons for granting or not granting flex time are transparent, and based on legitimate business needs of the nonprofit. Inequity creates inherent risk at the workplace. Risk management means evaluating the risk and determining steps that balance risk and reward for the nonprofit. Each nonprofit will have its own strategy for achieving the proper balance. That stated, flexible time is one of the most coveted benefits in today's workplace.

---

15 It's in violation of The Code of Ethical Principles and Standards of Professional Practice ⬢ adopted by the Association of Fundraising Professionals in 2004 for fundraising professionals to accept compensation that's a percentage of funds raised. See *www.afpnet.org*. Consequently, a performance-based bonus for development officers shouldn't be determined as a percentage of funds raised, although successful performance may be a factor in the decision to award a bonus.

Cafeteria Plans

Cafeteria plans permit employees to channel earned income into an account from which pre-tax dollars are deducted to pay for certain expenses, generally group health insurance, child and dependent care, and other uninsured medical expenses. Cafeteria plans save money for both employees and employers, since no FICA, Medicare or state unemployment taxes are paid on the amounts redirected by the employee towards the various premiums or payments. Such plans should be established with guidance from legal counsel.

Housing and Meals

Providing housing support is a trend that may be growing in certain parts of the country.[16] Housing support may be in the form of assisting an employee with mortgage applications, or actually paying points or broker fees on the employee's behalf, or providing employees with housing at no or low cost. Care needs to be taken that the nonprofit doesn't engage in any transactions that the IRS would consider to result in private benefit or excess compensation. Educational and human service organizations may provide job-related housing when 24-hour supervision and on-site living are a critical part of an employee's job duties. Housing and meals are a tax-free benefit to employees, as long as the housing and meals are provided on the premises of the nonprofit and are primarily for the convenience of the nonprofit. The nonprofit should document such benefits with a written policy, emphasizing the benefit to the nonprofit and, if applicable, stating that housing/meals are a condition of employment.

> **Caution: Reimbursement May Be Required**
>
> In California, wage and hour laws require employers to reimburse employees who use their own equipment or incur expenses in connection with their work. Cal. Lab. Code 2802 requires employers to "….indemnify his or her employee for all necessary expenditures or losses incurred by the employee in direct consequence of the discharge of his or her duties…." This regulation is viewed as requiring employers to reimburse employees for vehicle use. The IRS mileage reimbursement rate is presumptively a reasonable reimbursement rate. Visit *www.irs.gov* and use the search term "mileage" to verify the current rate.

Sabbaticals

A few nonprofits offer paid sabbaticals or offer their senior staff the opportunity to apply for fellowships that will pay for the executive to take a sabbatical for professional development purposes. Eligibility for an unpaid leave of absence after a defined tenure with the nonprofit can also be offered as a benefit to retain valuable employees.

Cell Phone, Auto Leasing and Travel Allowances

Perks that can be seen as personal in nature are perhaps the most suspect to the public and regulators, who are cynically attuned to the abuses exposed in recent years in the media as a result of certain CEO's of prominent national organizations who traveled first class, drove fancy cars, entertained lavishly and spent freely on a charity's corporate credit card. Whenever a nonprofit extends spending allowances to staff for benefits that could also be personal in nature, it behooves the nonprofit to set reasonable spending limits and require documentation of all expenses, with prior approval required for large dollar expenditures over a specified amount.

Commuting and Parking Subsidy

Employers may provide a tax-free payment to employees up to an amount capped by the tax code per month for train or bus ticket fees, or for parking fees, as long as the subsidy is made available to each similarly situated employee so that illegal discrimination isn't an issue.

Club Memberships

Memberships in eating clubs are fairly common among cultural organizations, educational institutions and foundations, particularly in the Midwest. Club memberships are sometimes donated by the clubs themselves in exchange for being listed on a nonprofit's donor list. Memberships can be justified as an expense that benefits the nonprofit's mission if used by senior staffers for meetings with donors. However, as with housing subsidies, travel allowances, cell phone and auto allowances, care should be taken to document the legitimate business reasons for the nonprofit to extend these benefits to an employee.

Educational Assistance

There are special tax code provisions for tax-free tuition reimbursement up to a specific level, periodically defined by the tax code. The tax-free benefits of educational reimbursement policies are only applicable for employees—not spouses or dependents. The nonprofit may define eligibility criteria, as long as it doesn't discriminate in favor of highly compensated employees.

---

16 This benefit is more common on the East and West coasts of the USA and for larger nonprofits. A survey conducted by the *Chronicle of Philanthropy* found that housing benefits were most common in New York City.

Employee Assistance Programs (EAPs)

EAPS are more common in larger nonprofits that contract with a vendor to make it possible to provide mental health counseling and other forms of assistance for employees when warranted, such as when the employee has revealed that she or he is addicted to alcohol or drugs, requires financial advice or has been the victim of sexual harassment. The value of such counseling is tax-free to the employee up to certain limits. Care should be taken to make assistance available to similarly situated employees to avoid claims of discrimination among employees. Assisting employees in times of crisis can be seen as a worthwhile risk management strategy, because employees who are under severe stress at the workplace aren't generally productive and indeed can be quite destructive if they don't receive assistance through a crisis.

Loans

Nonprofits should absolutely not make loans to board members and officers because of the inherent conflict of interest that is created in lending money to someone in a position to direct the actions of the organization. Loans to nonprofit executives are not prudent for the same reason. Some organizations insist that they are unable to attract and retain employees without offering assistance in the form of loans, such as for housing. While special compensation arrangements in the form of a loan might greatly enhance an employee's ability to work for a nonprofit, being indebted to the nonprofit employer might place untenable pressure on the employment relationship, especially if the employee is separated from employment prior to paying off the loan. Where loans are offered to employees, it is incumbent upon the nonprofit to obtain expert legal assistance so that compensation in the form of a loan is reported properly and to ensure that loan documents are drafted consistently with lending laws in the applicable state(s) and with terms that are fair both to the employee and to the nonprofit.

Health Insurance

Group health insurance plans are regulated by a growing number of federal laws. Increasingly it's in a nonprofit's best interests to strive to offer the broadest and best coverage for staff. A premium-only plan allows employees to make any required contributions for their health insurance on a pre-tax basis, which also saves the nonprofit from FICA and Medicare contributions.

Generally the insurance policy will dictate which employees are eligible to participate in the group policy. Some policies define eligibility in terms of hours worked per week, making some part-time employees ineligible for participation in health insurance plans. Remember that reduction of work hours, whether due to termination of employment or a change from full time to part time status or for any other reason, can cause employees to become ineligible for insurance. When that occurs, the nonprofit is required to notify the employee of his or her ineligibility for health benefits under the plan, and of the employee's right (and dependents' rights) to continuation benefits pursuant to COBRA (applicable to workplaces with 20 employees) or the mirroring state law (for smaller nonprofits.)

Life Insurance/Disability Insurance

Some nonprofits provide life and disability insurance policies (completely paid by the nonprofit) to employees during their employment. The nonprofit may determine at its discretion which categories of employees are eligible. Alternatively, the nonprofit can negotiate with an insurance provider to make a group policy available to all employees at their own cost, but at a more competitive rate than might be otherwise available. A policy with a death benefit in excess of $50,000 must be included in an employee's income and is subject to FICA and Medicare taxes. For this reason, most employers offer a policy for a death benefit of $50,000 or less.

Pension Plans

Pension plans are governed by a federal law, the Employee Retirement Income Security Act (ERISA). Pension contributions are made on an annual basis by the nonprofit and the employee, who contribute to a trust for the benefit of all participating employees. Eligibility for participation is governed by ERISA: when a pension plan is available at a workplace, *all employees working over 20 hours must be eligible for participation in the plan*. Pension plans should be set up by employee benefits and tax specialists, because they're highly regulated and violation of administration rules carries penalties.

Tax Deferred Retirement Plans—403(b) Annuity Plans and 401(k) Plans

403(b) Plans

A nonprofit may consider the use of a 403(b) plan as another way to provide employees with tax-deferred income. Such plans are tax-deferred retirement plans available to 501(c)(3) nonprofits and public schools. Under these plans, both employee and employer contributions may be made, earnings are accrued, and taxes are deferred until the participant begins to withdraw the account balances. A 403(b) annuity may be voluntary only, with no employer contributions and practically no employer involvement, or the employer may actively sponsor the plan. Employees may contribute annually up to a certain amount, capped by the tax code. Such plans should be set up by employee benefits and tax specialists. Violating applicable regulations may cause a contribution to be taxed as gross wages in the offending year.

401(k) Plans

In 1996, federal regulations were changed to permit tax-exempt organizations to sponsor 401(k) plans. The 403(b) plans aren't available to 501(c)(4) and 501(c)(6) tax-exempt organizations, but 401(k) plans are. Unlike a 403(b) plan, in a 401(k) plan there is a waiting period before employees can begin making contributions. There are other differences between 403(b) and 401(k) plans that a service acting as plan administrator can best describe. Whichever plan structure is selected, the formation and monitoring of a plan should be outsourced to a benefits expert.

Severance Pay

A few nonprofit employers offer an automatic severance payment of several weeks' compensation to staff who are separated from employment due to the elimination of their position, a termination forced by economic circumstances, or similar reasons not having to do with performance or unsatisfactory conduct. Severance policies themselves aren't governed by any particular federal or state law, but their implementation will be scrutinized for fairness and nondiscriminatory application.

Caution: Severance Pay May Be Risky

In the opinion of the authors, severance payments that aren't paid in accordance with a policy should rarely if ever be offered as an enticement to an employee to resign or retire absent a special Termination Agreement and Release, which is a legal agreement that offers compensation to the employee in return for the employee's waiver and release of all legal claims against the employer. Releases should be drawn up by a lawyer familiar with the Older Workers Benefits Protection Act (OWBPA).

Time-Off Benefits—Vacation, Sick Days and Personal Leave

Paid time off is the apex of employee benefits. No state mandates that any private nonprofit employer provide paid sick, personal, holiday or vacation leave benefits—however, it's considered standard to provide governmental holidays off as paid leave, as well as a certain number of paid sick days and vacation leave. Many nonprofits also provide for personal leave, which is paid time off to be used at the discretion of the employee, as long as it isn't inconvenient for the nonprofit. Offering two weeks vacation and 10 to12 sick days per calendar year is most common. Since no state law requires employers to give workers paid vacation, sick leave or personal days, the number of days of paid leave offered, and the determination of which employees are eligible for paid leave are entirely at the discretion of the nonprofit.

Most employers consider the employee's length of service when determining eligibility for paid time off, which results in longer service employees enjoying more paid vacation time on an annual basis. Many nonprofit boards wonder whether they're too generous with paid time off, others wonder whether their policy is generous enough. The answer can only be gleaned by comparing your practices to similar nonprofits in your area, by gauging the satisfaction of your staff, and analyzing their use of paid leave. For instance, if employees tend to use up their paid sick leave within the first few months of the fiscal year, perhaps the nonprofit isn't being realistic enough about the likelihood of illness among staff members.

Alternatively, perhaps employees don't feel motivated to come to work, and therefore find any excuse to call in *sick*, knowing that they've a sufficient number of paid sick days for their use.

It's important is determine the nonprofit's philosophy concerning paid time off. What is the purpose of vacation? Is it to provide your staff with an emotional and mental respite from the workplace—rest, rejuvenation and relaxation? If so, when employees use *vacation* days for their own illness, they're robbing themselves of a significant employee benefit. The misuse of vacation leave may signal that the nonprofit doesn't offer an adequate number of paid sick days, or that the employee has difficulty with time management or misunderstands the nonprofit's policy on paid leave. Abuse of paid leave may signal a need to re-engineer the benefits offered or recommunicate the philosophy behind the policies. In some cases it's necessary to discipline or even terminate staff who continue to abuse paid leave after being put on notice that their use of paid leave isn't consistent with the nonprofit's policies.

Vacation Carry-Over

The practice of *carrying over* unused vacation time creates a liability on the nonprofit's books. Accrued but unused vacation appears as a liability on the Statement of Financial Position (balance sheet) as *vacation payable*, which can be a hefty number, if the nonprofit has a large staff and a generous vacation policy. For nonprofits with ongoing or periodic cash-flow challenges, the vacation payable liability may present a practical problem, too. If this is a concern, the organization should consider adopting a policy that prohibits or places a limit on vacation carry-over.

Before approving a policy permitting carry-over, make sure that there is a sound reason for it. Generally vacation is most useful when it provides employees with paid time off to recharge their batteries. Consequently, a carry-over policy may not be consistent with the goal of giving employees time off in a way that will increase their productivity. However, many nonprofit executives are unable to use the time allotted to them annually. For them, accumulated vacation time can serve as a cushion of income that they will be entitled to post-separation, if the nonprofit's policies will pay out the carry-over upon termination. Payout upon termination may be determined by state law. Carry-over doesn't have to be automatic. Policy language can state that carry-over will be permitted only at the discretion of the employee's supervisor. If that policy is followed, be sure to require *written* authorization from a supervisor or the executive director for carry-over and be sure that, as with all benefits, there is oversight to ensure that vacation carry-over isn't being subjectively approved for some employees but not others.

Time Banks

One innovative way to provide for paid leave without dictating its use by staff is to give employees a *bank* of paid leave into which they deposit earned time and deduct it as needed, for whatever use. Employees can even donate their earned but unused paid leave to the *joint bank account*, for use by their colleagues or themselves in an emergency. Note however, that if there is no differentiation between vacation/personal/sick leave collected in a time bank, it's most likely that whatever is in an employee's bank must be paid to employees upon separation of employment in states that regard accrued vacation as compensation owed to employees upon separation of employment.

Holiday Leave

Almost every employer designates certain days during the year, generally national holidays, which are given to the staff as paid days off. The particular days that will be recognized as paid holidays vary from nonprofit to nonprofit. Since many nonprofits provide vital community services on national holidays, it isn't uncommon to find a nonprofit whose doors are open on a national holiday, when other commercial establishments are closed. Many nonprofits give staff a floating holiday that can be used for religious holidays when the nonprofit isn't closed for business.

Care should be taken, however, to comply with specific state laws (for instance in Maine no commercial businesses are supposed to be open on Memorial Day, Independence Day, Labor Day, Thanksgiving Day or Christmas Day.) Nonprofits that interact with state or federal government agencies will usually elect to recognize government holidays as either days when the nonprofit is closed or less fully staffed than regular days. When a national holiday falls on a weekend, employees who weren't scheduled to work that day generally don't get paid for that holiday, but may receive paid time off the preceding Friday or subsequent Monday. Personnel policies should address the nonprofit's practices in this regard.

It's customary to notify staff in writing of their entitlement to holiday leave by distributing a list of the dates during the upcoming calendar year that will be considered holidays. Employers are free to determine that only full-time and regular (as opposed to part-time and temporary) employees are eligible for paid holiday leave.

Holiday Policy Tips

Holiday policies typically identify 1) the number of days off for which the staff is paid but not expected to come to work, 2) whether any *floating* holidays are given during the year, and 3) whether premium pay will be offered to staff requested to work on a holiday when the nonprofit is otherwise *closed*. Paying a staff member overtime or a special bonus for working on a holiday is only appropriate if the employee is classified as nonexempt or where required by state law.

If any staff member requests to take a different day off as a holiday because of his or her religion, this request should be honored—unless it creates an undue hardship on the employer—because of the legal obligation to accommodate religious beliefs. Always consider the request carefully, and if there is no major administrative or financial impact, honor the employee's request. The legal mandate requires employers to make a reasonable accommodation for the individual who is requesting a different day off because of a religious belief. The employee requesting the special day off may be asked to make up the time on another day. If the nonprofit determines that the request can't be honored, as a risk management measure the decision-maker should document the analysis in writing, and be prepared to defend the decision on the grounds that the complying with the request would have created an *undue hardship*.

Vacation Leave

No state law requires employers to provide vacation leave to employees, but virtually all employers do. Most nonprofits provide vacation leave based on the tenure of the staff member. Three to four weeks of paid vacation time seems to be the upper limit for the majority of nonprofit employees (and for-profit employees) nationally. Part-time staff may be entitled to less vacation leave on a pro rata basis of a full-time staff member's entitlement to leave. There is no obligation to provide paid vacation leave to part-time or temporary employees. The thorniest issue surrounding vacation leave is whether or not employees are entitled to vacation pay upon separation of employment. Generally this issue will be governed by the written policy of the nonprofit that has been developed after carefully considering applicable state law.

Vacation Policy Tips

In addition to describing eligibility and the number of days of vacation to which staff are entitled, written vacation policies should always state that vacation will be granted upon written approval at the discretion of the nonprofit, after a written request has been submitted well in advance of the requested time off. Since it may not be possible to honor all requests, vacation leave may be approved on a first-come basis, or on the basis of seniority with the nonprofit. Written policies and requiring requests and approvals in writing is crucial. Written policies should also clarify whether vacation leave that's unused by year's end may be carried over into the next year. When employees are discharged, it's common for them to dispute the amount of their final paycheck, often disagreeing with their former employer about how many vacation days they were entitled to, accrued, used or carried over. The nonprofit's policy and records of requests/approvals can serve as an important, irrefutable defense to a former employee's claim that he or she is owed more vacation than was included in her final paycheck.

Vacation—Earned or Not?

Some nonprofits permit employees to take their entire vacation up-front, as long as it's requested for a convenient time. Others require employees to *earn* time off by working a certain number of days before being eligible to use their earned vacation. The latter system is generally referred to as a *vacation accrual* policy. The accrual method has advantages. In the *up-front* system, an employee may take all her or his vacation in January and then resign in February. When an employee has taken more vacation than she or he was entitled to, the nonprofit should only withhold the vacation from the final paycheck if the nonprofit has articulated a policy of doing so, and has written authorization from the employee beforehand.

Under an accrual system, only the earned number of vacation days will be owed to separating employees, if the nonprofit's policy so provides. In some states, vacation is considered compensation to be paid at termination (for example, California, Illinois, Massachusetts, Michigan, Missouri, New Jersey, New York and Tennessee). In those states, the nonprofit's policies should clearly state that only earned but unused vacation will be included in final pay. Therefore, in these states, the final paycheck of separating employees must include earned but unused vacation pay, in accordance with the nonprofit's policies.

Holidays Within Vacation Periods

To clarify that a holiday during a vacation period neither adds to nor subtracts from an employee's entitlement to vacation, many nonprofits include a written statement in their vacation policy such as: "In the event a holiday observed by this nonprofit falls during a period of vacation, the holiday will be paid as a normal holiday and won't be charged against the employee's vacation leave entitlement."

Vacation and Newly Hired Staff

A newly-hired employee working during his or her *introductory*, or *work test* period is generally not entitled to take vacation. A separate issue to consider is whether the new hire accrues vacation leave during the work test period. It seems harsh to deny newly hired staff the opportunity to earn vacation during their work test period, especially if they continue on as a productive staff member, although there is no legal impediment to such a policy.

Vacation Leave and Leaves of Absence Tips

If the nonprofit permits employees to take personal or administrative leave, such as sabbaticals, it's helpful to identify in writing whether the employee must use up all available vacation leave prior to, or during the any other leave period. Mandatory use of vacation during unpaid leave should be articulated in a written policy and communicated to employees at the beginning of any leave period, to avoid any surprises for the on-leave employee and to preserve the nonprofit's legal right to require its use during a leave period. If applicable, the nonprofit's employee manual should also include the written policy that employees don't earn vacation leave during a leave of absence.

Sick Leave

Most nonprofits pay their staff for a certain number of days of sick leave to compensate staff for a short period of illness or injury. Longer illnesses are addressed by family and medical leave policies, and by short and long term disability insurance. Most often sick leave is treated as a use-it-or-lose-it benefit, with policies clearly stating that unused sick leave won't be carried over into the next year, and that no compensation will be provided for unused sick leave. Some employers will compensate employees for unused sick days as a reward for healthy employees, but that can also be seen as a penalty to employees who are sick through no fault of their own. It's a sound practice, especially in New York and Michigan, to have a written policy addressing whether unused sick leave will be compensated or not, because sick leave could arguably be considered a benefit owed to employees pursuant to an oral or written contract. Sick day carry-over is more common in small workplaces (under 50 employees) where no state or federal family leave laws apply. Carry-over permits employers to maintain up to a prescribed number, usually no more than 30 days, of paid sick leave for use in the event they become seriously ill, and are out of work for a period of time. Note that sick leave carry-over policies inherently require the nonprofit to maintain the job of the employee out on sick leave until all sick leave has been exhausted.

Sick Leave Policy Tips

The written sick leave policy should clearly describe the process for notifying the employer of an illness or injury that prevents the employee from coming to work. It's helpful to remind staff through the written policy that abuse of the sick leave policy (such as calling in sick when the employee is actually doing something else that day) is grounds for termination.

Sick leave policies normally address:

❏ eligibility requirements;

❏ the process for notifying the employer that the employee will be out sick;

❏ the number of sick days to which an employee is entitled on an annual basis;

❏ whether sick leave may be taken during the introductory work test period;

❏ whether sick leave accrues during the introductory period;

❏ whether unused sick leave is compensated upon termination of employment or at the end of the fiscal year; and

❏ whether sick leave is carried over at the end of the year and, if so, whether there is a maximum number of days which may be carried over.

Fitness to Return to Work After Sick Leave

In many nonprofit workplaces, especially those serving children, employees are required to produce a medical certification prior to an employee's return from a sick leave lasting several days or as a result of a contagious condition. The medical certification should provide clearance for the employee to return to work, by stating that the employee who was out sick is able to meet job requirements and won't pose a threat of illness to others upon his return.

Note: If the workplace is a covered employer for purposes of FMLA, employers should require an employee to produce a medical certification for any short absence from work due to illness lasting three or more days, in order to assess whether that short period of absence should properly be designated as family and medical leave under federal law.

The Challenge of the Chronically Absent Employee

Watch Out!
Remember, an employee will be eligible for family and medical leave under the federal Family and Medical Leave Act if: 1) there are 50+ employees on the payroll, 2) the employee has worked for a year, serving 1,250+ hours, 3) the employee has missed three days of work, and 4) is under the continuing care of a physician for a serious health condition. Prior to firing any employee who has been *out sick* for an extended time, review whether the employee was entitled to family and medical leave. If so, it would be a violation of the FMLA to terminate the employee without first designating the employee's absence as FMLA leave, and permitting the employee up to 12 weeks of unpaid leave, with medical benefits maintained as if the employee were coming to work every day. The leave time runs from the employee's first day of missed work. It's up to the employer to designate the time off work as FMLA leave, or a parallel leave available under the applicable state family/medical leave law.

Certainly one of the biggest challenges any manager faces is the challenge of the undependable employee. It's helpful for legal defense purposes and when counseling employees to focus on the concept of *dependabili*ty rather than *excessive absenteeism*. The phrase, *excessive absenteeism*, calls for a subjective opinion: are three, or five, or 25 missed days "excessive"? If the nonprofit gives an employee 12 sick days, is taking all 12 sick days "excessive absenteeism"? Not according to the nonprofit's policy. In contrast, focusing on dependability conveys the message that the employee has failed to meet the minimum expectations of the nonprofit because the nonprofit can't depend on the employee to show up for work.

If an employee calls in sick but isn't eligible for sick leave, the resulting day off from work is an *unexcused absence*. (*Unexcused* is used to describe the absence because no policy of the nonprofit excuses the absence.) Employees shouldn't be paid for unexcused absences, because they're a violation of policy. Directly after an unexcused absence, a performance counseling session should be scheduled to remind the employee of the basic expectation that he or she come to work and the consequences of any further unexcused absences.

Review with the employee the nonprofit's policy on paid leave and the employee's record of absenteeism. Discuss the issue of dependability with the employee. Clearly articulate the consequences of unexcused absences: warn the employee that subsequent unexcused absences will result in discipline, and that his job is at risk. Meanwhile consider whether or not there are barriers to this employee's ability to come to work. Does he or she lack motivation? Transportation? Child care? Ask the employee what needs to happen in order for him or her to get to work. Enlist the employee's ownership into becoming a more dependable employee and finding the solution to absenteeism problems.

In cases where an employee has been warned about lack of dependability, and the employer has checked to make sure that the absence isn't covered by the federal FMLA, an employer is justified in terminating an employee for any subsequent unexcused absences and may, in some cases argue that the employee's violation of attendance policies renders the employee ineligible for unemployment compensation.

Note: A law passed in Georgia in 2005 requires employers who are terminating an employee for excessive absenteeism to provide advance written notice to employees that unemployment benefits may be denied because of a violation of the employer's attendance policy.

Job Abandonment

In extreme cases, where the employee doesn't show up for work, doesn't contact the nonprofit, and has no accrued leave time available, the nonprofit should notify the employee of his or her termination and articulate the reason for the termination as *job abandonment.*

Using Sick Leave to Care for a Family Member

At the employer's discretion, the sick leave policy may state that sick leave can be used for time off to care for an immediate family member or a relative who isn't an immediate family member. This provision is most often used by smaller nonprofits (under 50 employees) that aren't covered by the federal or applicable state's family leave law.

Use of Accrued Sick Leave During Other Leaves

In some states, employers may **not** require employees to use their accrued paid sick leave during any period of disability leave, including family and medical leave. If permitted under state law, the policy of requiring employees to use accrued sick leave prior to, or simultaneously with, other leaves of absence must be in writing, and the employee must be notified of the policy prior to the commencement of the employee's other leave.

Personal Days

In an effort to give employees the benefit they cherish most—time off—some nonprofits allow their staff paid personal days which are used for something other than the employee's own illness or vacation. Up to three days annually is the usual number of personal days available, depending on an employee's tenure with the nonprofit.

Exempt employees have a more flexible workday, since they're usually not bound by specific work hours. Most nonprofits find that exempt employees have no need for personal days since they may leave work to conduct personal business, as long as they've made arrangements with their supervisor to do so, and make up the work at another time. Part-time staff are typically not granted personal days.

Personal day policies should spell out whether or not:

❑ newly hired employees are eligible for personal days during the introductory work test period;

❑ eligibility is dependent on the number of years employed;

❑ unused personal days may be carried over or compensated;

❑ personal days are available in half days or only full days; and

❑ personal days may be taken by part-time as well as full-time staff.

In the next section, Chapter 6, leaves of absence, whether due to medical needs, military service or other issues will be discussed.

Chapter 6

Leaves of Absence

When an employee is *out on leave*, whether due to a work-related injury, the employee's own disability, a family member's illness, or some other reason, it's incumbent upon the nonprofit to determine how long the employee can permissibly remain out of work and still return to work, and also to communicate to the employee his or her rights and obligations while on leave. Not all employees will be entitled to a leave of absence. Some employees will only have the time that's available to them based on their unused sick leave. On the other hand, some nonprofits, because of their size or state law requirements will be obligated to provide employees with unpaid leave that may include job protection and maintenance of health insurance benefits. In addition to these laws or as a supplement to them, most nonprofits have their own personnel policies that address leaves of absence for various reasons. Knowing what laws and policies apply and whether or not a particular employee is eligible for a leave of absence is key to avoiding the risk of violating state and federal laws or personnel policies that govern leaves of absence.

What Laws Govern Leaves of Absence?

The Family and Medical Leave Act (FMLA) (www.dol.gov/esa/regs/statutes/whd/fmla.htm) applies to employers with 50 or more employees (full and/or part time) working either in one workplace or within 75 miles of one another. The FMLA requires employers to provide an unpaid leave of absence of up to 12 weeks with job protection and maintenance of health insurance and other benefits. Employees are eligible for FMLA leave after they've worked at least 1,250 hours (full time) and have been employed for a full year. Comprehensive information about compliance with the FMLA may be found at the U.S. Department of Labor (DOL) Web site: www.dol.gov/esa/whd/fmla/index.htm. Twelve states have passed family leave laws that are similar to the federal FMLA. Many of the state laws apply to workplaces with fewer than 50 employees.

State FMLA Laws May Apply

To date, 12 states have their own version of the FMLA that applies to private nonprofit employers. **California** ✎ (applies to employers with 50+ employees; employees eligible if they've worked for more than one year; provides up to 12 weeks of leave; more generous than federal law regarding pregnancy benefits); **Connecticut** ✎ (applies to employers with 75 or more employees; provides up to 16 weeks of leave in a 24 month period); **District of Columbia** ✎ (applies to employers with 20+ employees; eligible employees are those who have worked for at least a year without a break in service, 1000+ hours; provides for up to 16 weeks unpaid leave during a 24 month period for care of seriously ill family member, or birth of a child or placement of child with employee; more expansive definition of "family member" than federal law); **Hawaii** ✎ (applies to workplaces with 100+ employees; provides leave to care for parent-in-laws; doesn't apply to employee's own serious health condition); **Maine** ✎ (applies to employers with 15+ employees; provides 10 weeks leave in a 2 year period); **Minnesota** ✎ (applies to employers with 21+ employees; provides for birth and adoption leave only); **New Jersey** ✎ (applies to employers with 50+ employees; provides for up to 12 weeks leave, but not for the employee's own serious health condition); **Oregon** ✎ (applies to employers with 25+ employees; provides up to 12 week leave and 12 weeks additional leave for childbirth); **Rhode Island** ✎ (applies to employers with 50+ employees; provides 13 weeks leave in two consecutive calendar years); **Vermont** ✎ (applies to employers with 10+ employees; provides for 12 weeks plus additional time off for child health care emergencies); **Washington** ✎ (applies to employers with 100+ employees; FMLA is in addition to the 12 weeks provided by the state law for child birth or illness during pregnancy); and **Wisconsin** ✎ (applies to employers with 50+ employees; provides for no more than 8 weeks).

For states that have their own Family Leave Acts, the U.S. Department of Labor has prepared a helpful guide that compares the federal requirements with various states' requirements. State specific charts are available at the DOL Web site: *www.dol.gov/esa/programs/whd/state/fmla/index.htm.*

Providing Leave as an Accommodation for an Employee With a Disability

Even when a nonprofit isn't covered by the FMLA/state family leave laws, or when an individual employee isn't eligible under these laws for leave, the nonprofit may still be required to provide a leave of absence to an employee as a *reasonable accommodation* for a disability. The Americans with Disabilities Act (ADA) (www.dol.gov/odep/pubs/misc/summada.htm)

Leaves of Absence: Developing a Policy for Your Nonprofit

Even if your nonprofit isn't covered by state federal family leave laws, the nonprofit needs its own policy on leaves of absence to address situations when employees are out of work. Many nonprofits are so small that the federal FMLA or state laws that provide leave for family care or medical purposes don't apply, or individual employees may not be eligible because they've only worked for a short period of time. Therefore it's incumbent upon the nonprofit to develop a policy that will provide guidance when workers face situations that require them to be out of work. A nonprofit's own policy needs to address how long the employee can be out of work, whether benefits, such as health insurance, will be maintained during the period of leave, and whether the employee will be reinstated to his or her former position after the leave of absence. Many nonprofits that aren't obligated to maintain an employee's position use language such as the following to address an employee's return to work after a leave of absence:

"[Name of Nonprofit] will make every effort to reinstate employees to their former positions after a leave of absence, however, reinstatement and job assignments are at the discretion of [Name of Nonprofit]."

Various state laws require employers to provide unpaid leave to employees in certain circumstances and prohibit employers from retaliating against employees for exercising their rights to such leave:

❏ Military leave

❏ Witness leave

❏ Jury Duty leave

❏ Crime Victim leave

❏ Leave for adoptive parents

❏ New parent leave

❏ Leave for attendance at school activities or to take children to doctors' appointments

❏ Leave to attend doctors' appointments with elderly relatives

❏ Leave for organ or blood marrow donors

---

applies to workplaces with 15 or more employees, but many state laws that prohibit discrimination on the basis of disability apply to workplaces with fewer employees. The ADA and state laws require employers to make reasonable accommodations for qualified individuals with a disability. A leave of absence is often the appropriate accommodation. The ADA and state laws governing disability discrimination don't prescribe how long a leave is required—the employer needs to determine on a case-by-case basis, what is *reasonable* under the circumstances.

It's critical to know whether your nonprofit is covered by either the federal FMLA or the ADA, or a mirroring state law. Later in this section, we provide a framework to help you determine whether an employee is owed a leave of absence under which laws. First, it's important to recognize that in addition to state and federal *family leave* laws, there are other laws that provide employees with a leave of absence, and job protection during that leave.

Other Reasons for a Leave of Absence

There are various other reasons why an employee might need a leave of absence. State and federal laws apply when employees who serve in the military or the reserves are called to training or active duty during employment. Additional state laws may govern an employer's obligation to provide a leave of absence for an employee to serve as a juror or a witness, or for other reasons. These laws require that employees are provided with an unpaid leave of absence and prohibit employers from retaliating against employees who take a leave of absence for reasons protected by law.

Most nonprofits make provisions in their policies for special leaves of absence for bereavement or attendance at funerals of family members, and some provide special unpaid leaves for educational or professional development purposes, or provide for a special leave at the nonprofit's discretion (often called *administrative leave*), which can be used for disciplinary purposes during an investigation of wrongdoing. Whatever the leave, the nonprofit needs to manage the employee's expectations about the right to return to work, the length of time of the leave and the impact of the leave on the employee's other benefits.

State Temporary Disability and Workers' Compensation Laws

State laws governing workers' compensation and temporary disability insurance payments provide compensation (income replacement) when workers are unable to work due to work-related illness and injury or as a result of a nonwork-related temporary disability **but** these laws govern compensation only and don't provide any job security, or ensure that the employee's health insurance benefits will be maintained during the time the employee is out of work.

It's a common misconception that when an employee is out of work, *on workers' comp* or *on disability*, that the employee may *not* be terminated. Actually, these insurance protections don't promise job security. It certainly would be a violation of law to fire an employee *in retaliation* for filing a workers' compensation claim, or *in retaliation* for filing a claim for disability; however, if the termination is for another reason, such as the employee was provided with a leave of absence but didn't return to work when the leave was exhausted, or is no longer able to perform the essential functions of the job, a termination will be lawful.

Caution is advised any time adverse action is taken against an employee who has filed a claim for disability or workers' compensation. It's basic risk management wisdom to ensure that the documentation of the action clearly shows that the reason for the action was based on the business needs of the nonprofit, not motivated by retaliation against the employee for exercising their rights to workers' compensation or disability insurance benefits.

How to Comply With Various Leave Laws

The single most important issue for nonprofits to address when managing leaves of absence is whether the leave qualifies the employee for family leave under state or federal law, or whether there is another law or policy that applies. A common mistake made by many employers is to permit an employee to be out of work (whether due to a temporary disability or a work-related injury qualifying the employee for workers' compensation) and not designate the leave as family leave, even though the employee qualifies for family leave. It's the *nonprofit's responsibility* (not the employee's choice) to determine whether any requested leave qualifies the employee for either federal or state *family leave* (or both federal and state leave simultaneously.) It's to the employee's benefit to be covered by family leave since family leave protects the employee's job for a certain period of time. It's also to the *nonprofit's* benefit to start the clock running on family leave, because designating the start of family leave provides the nonprofit with certainty about how long the employee's job must be maintained. If the nonprofit doesn't designate an employee's leave as family leave, the nonprofit risks violating leave laws and confusing the employee about what his or her rights to reinstatement are. A confused and disappointed employee is more likely to be upset when told that his job is no longer available, than one who realized early on that he would be given a limited time period of leave with job protection.

The Federal Family and Medical Leave (FMLA)

The Family and Medical Leave Act of 1993 (FMLA) extends significant rights to employees who are eligible: FMLA leave gives employees protection of their health benefits during a leave of absence and the right to re-instatement after exhausting their family leave. The FMLA requires employers with 50 or more employees (either full or part time) to give eligible employees up to 12 weeks of unpaid leave when the employee or an immediate family member has a *serious health condition* or needs leave to care for a newborn child, an adopted child, or a child who has been placed with the employee for foster care. *Immediate family member* is defined as a child, spouse, or parent.[17] During the 12 weeks of leave the employer must maintain the employee's health insurance and other benefits as if the employee were still actively at work, and must preserve the employee's position so that the employee can be returned to the same, or to a *substantially similar* position at the end of the leave. If the employee fails to return to work at the exhaustion of family leave, there is no obligation to maintain the employee's employment.

There are two exceptions to the requirement to restore employees to their position or to an equivalent position at the conclusion of family leave. Reinstatement isn't required if the nonprofit experiences some event, such as the loss of a grant that paid the salary of the employee on leave, or a general downsizing during the leave, which would have resulted in the employee losing his or her job had he or she not been on leave. Secondly, key employees (highly paid, salaried) don't have to be reinstated if doing so would cause the nonprofit substantial and grievous economic harm. The employer must notify the employee in writing of his or her status as a key employee, indicate the reasons for denying job restoration, and provide the employee a reasonable opportunity to return to work.

Employers may not use an employee's FMLA leave as a negative factor in performance ratings, salary adjustments, or promotions, and may not treat an employee adversely in any way because he or she exercised the right to take FMLA leave. This means that a supervisor can't deny an employee a raise because she or he wasn't there part of the year. Employers also may not terminate an employee who is out on leave for an FMLA qualifying condition. Violations of the FMLA or state family/medical leave laws usually arise when an employee is terminated after an absence from work for a health-related reason without ever being provided with the formal benefits of job-protected leave. The result is that the employee is entitled to bring an action for wrongful termination against the employer, based on a violation of the FMLA/state family leave law. Violations result in damages and penalties and can also entitle the employee to reinstatement.

Notification Requirements Under the FMLA

Both the employee and the employer must comply with FMLA notice requirements. The FMLA requires employees who have a foreseeable need for leave to inform their employers at least 30 days in advance of the requested leave period. (Some state laws permit shorter notification periods.) If the employee doesn't give proper notice for a foreseeable type of leave, the employer may delay the commencement of the employee's leave until the appropriate notice period has passed. If the reason for the leave is unforeseeable, the employee is supposed to give as much notice as possible and the employer may not penalize the employee for not giving advance notice.

When the employer learns that the employee is requesting leave, the employer must determine whether the requested leave should be designated as family leave, or some other type of leave, and inform the employee *in writing*, whether the requested leave will count as an approved leave of absence. It's in the nonprofit's best interest to identify any requested leave early on as either approved leave for a definite period of time or not. Without clear approval of a leave of absence for a specific time period, the result is usually that the employee is absent on some sort of ill-defined, vague *leave* for a considerable period of time, and it will be unclear whether the employee can be replaced, even if the nonprofit needs to fill

---

17 An employer may extend the definition to include parents-in-law or extended family members.

> Not all workplaces are covered by the FMLA, and not all employees will qualify. If a nonprofit's own policies state: "We will follow the federal FMLA" then the nonprofit will be required to comply with all the regulations that accompany the FMLA.

> Even if an employee never asks for a particular leave of absence, the employee may still be entitled to the protections offered by the federal law under the FMLA, a state law or the nonprofit's own policies. Court cases have concluded that an employee's request for family leave doesn't require any magic words or even require that the employee utter the phrase, *family leave*. It's the employer's responsibility to determine whether an employee is eligible for a leave of absence and to tell him so as soon as the management of the nonprofit becomes aware that an employee requires a leave of absence. If an employee is out of work *on leave* and the nonprofit isn't sure whether or not the employee in fact is eligible for a leave of absence, the most prudent step is to initially designate the employee's leave as family leave or some permitted leave, and then verify the employee's eligibility. If the employee doesn't cooperate, or it turns out that the employee isn't eligible for a leave of absence, then the nonprofit should inform the employee of that fact, and often termination will be appropriate unless the employee is able to return to work.

the position. Additionally, there will be no certainty as to whether it's permissible to terminate the employee because the employee was never officially notified of his or her rights to a specific leave. Termination of an employee without officially designating an employee's leave of absence as family leave will expose the nonprofit to liability for violation of state leave laws or the federal FMLA, if they apply. Therefore, as soon as the nonprofit realizes that the leave of absence qualifies the employee for FMLA or state family leave, the nonprofit should designate the leave as family leave, dating from the time the employee was first out of work. Retroactive designation is permitted. Often state and federal family leave will run concurrently. Similarly, if a state family leave law or the FMLA doesn't apply, it's incumbent on the nonprofit to designate the employee's time out of work as either approved leave or not, so that both the employee and the nonprofit will have clarity as to the employee's rights to return to work and benefits during the leave of absence.

As soon as the supervisor realizes that an employee is *out on leave* or management is aware of an employee's need for a leave of absence, the analysis of eligibility for leave should begin and prompt notification to the employee of the employee's rights to leave should follow. An employer must first determine whether the employee is eligible under the federal or a state law, or under the nonprofit's own leave policies; or whether the employee is disqualified from leave because of various reasons, such as 1) she or he has previously exhausted entitlement to family leave in the preceding months; 2) the employee's reason for leave isn't a covered reason under the applicable law or policy; 3) the employee failed to provide the nonprofit with sufficient proof of the reason for leave; or 4) the employee failed to provide the requisite notice of a need for leave.

A Framework for Decision-Making

Step 1: Determining Eligibility for Leave

When trying to determine whether an employee is eligible for a leave of absence, the first issue is whether the nonprofit is covered by the federal or state family leave law, or both simultaneously. Federal law covers nonprofits with at least 50 employees on the payroll for each of 20 or more weeks during the current or preceding calendar year, as long as the employees work within a 75 mile radius of the employer's primary work site(s). A detailed explanation of which employers are covered under the federal FMLA is available at the following DOL Web site: www.dol.gov/dol/allcfr/ESA/Title_29/Part_825/29CFR825.104.htm.

If the FMLA doesn't apply, evaluate whether the ADA requires a leave of absence as an accommodation: Does the employee have a disability that requires accommodation through a leave?

If neither the FMLA or the ADA applies, is there a leave of absence defined by a state law that this employee would be eligible for? Is there any other policy of the nonprofit that would afford this employee a leave of absence, requiring the nonprofit to keep his or her job open for a specific length of time, or require reinstatement of the employee at the conclusion of the leave?

If none of the above is applicable, then there is no particular roadmap for this employee's leave. The nonprofit is free to implement a leave policy that balances the employee's personal needs with the business needs of the nonprofit. Document the decision, and remember that similarly situated employees should be treated equitably. Any policy that's created ad hoc will be viewed as a precedent for future treatment of similarly situated employees.

Step 2: Is the Employee Eligible?

If the FMLA, a state family leave law, or the nonprofit's own leave policy applies, the next step is to determine whether the particular employee needing leave is eligible under the laws/policy. A detailed explanation of eligibility under the FMLA is available at the following DOL Web site: www.dol.gov/dol/allcfr/ESA/Title_29/Part_825/29CFR825.110.htm.

For an employee to be eligible for FMLA leave, the employee must have worked for the nonprofit for more than 1,250 hours in the previous 12 months. The 12 months need not be consecutive, but the hours of service requirement applies to the 12 months immediately preceding the requested leave. As a result, the FMLA doesn't cover part-time or seasonal employees who work fewer than 1,250 hours in the year prior to the leave request.

Some state laws base eligibility on a different number of hours worked, or permit leave within a different number of months, such as 12 weeks of leave within 24 months.

If the employee isn't eligible under federal FMLA or state family leave law, perhaps the employee is eligible under the nonprofit's own leave policy. A nonprofit's own policies on leaves of absence may define eligibility differently.

Step 3: The Reason for Leave Must Be Covered by Family Leave or Other Leave Laws

The FMLA provides for leave in cases of childbirth, adoption, or placement of a foster child with an employee. Family leave is also available where either the employee, or an immediate family member, has: 1) a *serious health condition* 2) which prevents the employee or the immediate family member from going to work (or from going to school) for three or more days; as long as 3) the employee or family member is under the continuing care of a physician or medical health professional.

State family leave laws are generally similar to the federal law, but may differ slightly. A nonprofit that isn't covered by the federal or state family leave laws is free to determine its own criteria for eligibility. Know your nonprofit's policies!

The nonprofit may require the employee requesting leave to provide documentation that the reason for the leave is a reason that qualifies for leave. Documentation should definitely be required when an employee requests leave because of a medical condition, to verify that the illness or injury qualifies as a serious enough condition to merit a leave of absence. The employer may make the employee's entitlement to leave contingent upon receiving a certification of the employee's condition from the employee's doctor. Such a certification is required for FMLA eligibility.

As defined by the FMLA, a *serious health condition* is one which involves continuing treatment by a physician and which causes any period of incapacity for more than three calendar days to attend work or school, or to perform other daily activities. Chronic health problems, especially those that require continuing treatment, such as liver failure, diabetes, cancer, and other health conditions, such as at-risk pregnancies that may involve long-term incapacity, also qualify as serious health conditions under the FMLA.

A nonprofit that isn't covered by the FMLA or similar state family leave laws may define health conditions that make an employee eligible for a leave of absence differently.

Medical Certification of a Serious Health Condition

The determination of whether an employee has a *serious health condition* for eligibility for federal FMLA shouldn't be made by the nonprofit. To determine whether a serious medical condition exists, the nonprofit must review a written certification from a health care provider that describes the serious health condition. The U.S. Department of Labor has designed a form for this purpose that the nonprofit may customize. See DOL Form WH-380, ☜ which is an optional form that may be used to obtain a medical certification from a health care provider.

The certification should be maintained in confidential files, separate from other employee personnel records. It's up to the employer to give the employee the certification form and then for the employee to take the form to his or her health care provider and request that the physician fill it out.

The employee is required to provide the employer with the certification within 15 days of the employee's request for leave. However, often the employee and the health care provider aren't able to return the certification for review by the nonprofit in a timely manner. In such cases, the nonprofit should *temporarily* designate the leave as family leave until such time as the nonprofit can review the health care provider's certification. If the employee fails to provide a health care certification of a serious health condition, the nonprofit isn't required to designate the leave as family leave, and instead can treat the leave in any way consistent with other leave provisions or policies of the nonprofit. The basic rule is that for an employee to benefit from the protections of the FMLA, the employee must comply with the act's requirements—and vice versa for the nonprofit.

Step 4: Informing the Employee of the Right to a Leave of Absence

When an employer realizes that an employee is out of work for a reason that qualifies the employee for a leave of absence, or when an employee requests a leave of absence, the following should be addressed in writing to the employee:

1. A designation of whether the leave will qualify as FMLA leave, or state family leave or both; or some other leave available under the nonprofits' own policies, (if not, why not) and the starting and ending dates for the permissible leave.

2. If applicable under the nonprofit's own policies or if the leave is federal FMLA, a request that the employee provide the nonprofit with a Certification of a Serious Health Condition from a medical health care provider within 15 days. Inform the employee that until the certification is received, the leave will be deemed to qualify as family/medical leave,

but that if the certification isn't received or a finding of serious health condition isn't supported by the certification, the leave will be recharacterized or denied, as appropriate.

3. Inform the employee about any requirements during the leave of absence and prior to his or her return to work, such as 1) the requirement to contact the nonprofit during leave to provide information about the expected return date, 2) to provide a *fitness for work* certification prior to returning to work; and 3) the requirement to notify the nonprofit in advance when the employee desires to return to work.

4. Communicate the nonprofit's policy concerning accrued paid leave, such as whether the employee will be required, or has the choice, to use accrued paid leave simultaneously with family/medical leave.

5. Communicate the employee's responsibility for health-care premium payments during the period of leave, if applicable. Inform the employee of potential liability for health care premium payments paid on his or her behalf by the nonprofit during the employee's leave, if the employee fails to return to work after his or her leave.

6. Inform the employee of his or her right to be restored to the same or an equivalent position as long as the employee returns to work when his or her leave has been exhausted (provide return date). If reinstatement to the same position isn't required by law, inform the employee of the nonprofit's policy on reinstatement, such as: "every effort will be made to restore you to your previous position, however, reinstatement to the same or an equivalent position is at the nonprofit's discretion."

7. Inform the employee that if she or he fails to return to work at the expiration of leave, the nonprofit will treat the failure to return as a resignation.

Notice Required by Employers Covered by the FMLA

If an employer provides all employees with an employee handbook that describes the employer's policies regarding leave, wages, attendance and similar matters, the handbook must incorporate information on FMLA rights and responsibilities and the employer's policies regarding FMLA. See FMLA Regulations, 29 CFR Part 825.301(a) (*www.dol.gov/dol/allcfr/ESA/Title_29/Part_825/29CFR825.301.htm*).

When an employee is eligible for FMLA, regulations require that the employer provide the employee with written notice of his or her rights under the FMLA (and applicable state law). DOL Form WH-381 (*www.dol.gov/esa/forms/whd/WH-381.pdf*) is an optional form that an employer may use for this purpose. The employer may customize the form but must make sure to include the following:

1. Whether the leave will be counted against the employee's FMLA leave entitlement;

2. Requirements for furnishing a *medical certification* (Form WH-380) for a serious health condition and the consequences for failing to do so;

3. The employee's right to substitute paid leave and whether the employer will require the substitution of paid leave;

4. Requirements for making any health benefit premium payments; consequences for failing to make timely payments; and, circumstances under which coverage might lapse;

5. Requirements to submit a fitness-for-duty certificate to be restored to employment;

6. Whether the employee is a key employee (and if so, that reinstatement may not be automatic);

7. The employee's right to reinstatement when the leave is completed; and

8. The employee's potential liability if the employer makes the employee's health insurance premium payments while the employee is on unpaid FMLA leave if the employee fails to return to work.

Form DOL WH-381 should be provided to the employee within a reasonable time after the employee gives notice of the need for FMLA leave (or the employer learns of the employee's need for leave) or within one or two business days, if feasible.

Frequently Asked Questions About Leaves of Absence Policies

Responses to frequently asked questions about the FMLA may be found on the following DOL Web site: www.dol.gov/elaws/esa/fmla/faq.asp.

How Much Leave Does the Employee Get?

The federal law gives employees 12 weeks of unpaid leave, generally to be taken in a continuous period of leave. State family leave laws or the nonprofit's own personnel policies may provide a more or less generous leave period. Typically employees taking leave due to the birth or placement of a newborn can take their leave at any time during the first year post-birth/adoption. To the extent that state laws are more beneficial to the employee, they will control (for example, the District of Columbia, which provides for up to 16 weeks of leave.)

Can an Employee Ever Be Entitled to More Than 12 Weeks of FMLA Leave?

There are generally three circumstances under which an employee may be entitled to more than 12 weeks of family leave: First, when the state law is more generous than the federal law. For example, this is true in the District of Columbia which provides 16 weeks for family leave, and in Alaska which provides 18 weeks. Second, a nonprofit may have a more generous leave policy. Third, an applicable state law might entitle an employee to family leave for reasons different than the federal law, and the employee may therefore qualify for leave under both laws independently. For example: an employee could potentially be entitled to 12 weeks of leave to address his or her own serious health condition under the FMLA, and subsequently be entitled to an additional leave period later in the year to take care of an immediate family member. Such scenarios make it critical to define in writing for the employee the reason for leave eligibility each time an employee requests leave or is out of work for a qualifying reason.

Can an Employee Take Leave on a Reduced Schedule or Intermittently?

Intermittent leave is leave that gives the employee a few hours off here and there on a schedule as the employee requires. Taking leave on a reduced leave or intermittent basis doesn't reduce the total amount of time available to the employee for the leave. For instance, taking leave on a *reduced leave schedule* would be a leave schedule that reduces the number of required working days per work week, or hours per work day required of an employee, such as a three-day workweek, working only mornings. There is no limit to the size of an increment of leave when an employee is on a reduced leave or intermittent leave schedule. The nonprofit can limit the increments to the shortest size time period which the nonprofit's timekeeping and payroll system permits. In some cases the employer may require the employee to temporarily transfer to another position that's better suited to intermittent leave or a reduced leave schedule. The alternative position should have equivalent pay and benefits and closely approximate the equivalent duties of the employee's regular position.

Under the FMLA, employees are entitled to leave on a reduced schedule or intermittent basis in two situations: 1) After the birth/adoption/placement of a child, if both the employee and employer agree, and 2) as of right, for the care of a parent, child or spouse with a serious health condition, or for the employee's own serious health condition.

For nonprofits that aren't covered by the FMLA, either state law or the nonprofit's own leave policy should be reviewed to address this issue.

Can Reinstatement Ever Be Denied?

If the employee doesn't return to work at the end of the leave period, the employer has no obligation to reinstate the employee. The employer may terminate the employee, as long as the employer has followed all the requirements of the FMLA/state law (or the nonprofit's own leave policy). These requirements might include giving the employee appropriate notice of the employee's obligations prior to, and during, leave. The FMLA gives employees no greater rights than if they were continuously employed. Therefore, if the employee's position would have been eliminated due to a reorganization that occurred during the employee's leave period, then termination of the employee won't violate the FMLA. Similarly, if the employee was hired for a specific task or discrete project, the employer has no obligation to restore the employee if the task has been completed or the project is over. A nonprofit's policies on leaves of absence should spell out this point to manage all expectations fairly. A nonprofit may also deny leave or reinstatement to any employee who fails to provide a medical certification of a serious health condition, or a certification of fitness for return to work, as long as the nonprofit has given the employee notice that such certifications are required.

Are There Any Exceptions to the Right to Reinstatement?

Generally an employee returning from FMLA/state family leave is entitled to be restored to his or her former position, or to an equivalent position with equivalent benefits, compensation, and other terms and conditions of employment. There is an exception to this general rule under the FMLA and some state laws: a nonprofit doesn't have to restore a *key employee* (defined as among the highest paid 10 percent of the staff) if to do so would cause *grievous economic injury* to the nonprofit's operations, as long as the nonprofit informs the employee of the decision to deny reinstatement when the nonprofit decides that such injury will occur. Key employees are otherwise entitled to the same benefits as other employees who are eligible for family leave. It's the nonprofit's burden to determine and prove that economic hardship would result from reinstating a key employee. The standard set by the U.S. Department of Labor is high. *Grievous economic injury* means that reinstatement of a key employee would threaten the economic viability of the nonprofit's operations, or cause long-term economic injury. An explanation of the rights of *key employees* is available at the following Web site of the DOL: www.dol.gov/dol/allcfr/esa/Title_29/Part_825/29CFR825.219.htm.

Special Exception for Teachers

Another exception to the reinstatement requirement is narrowly confined to teachers. See 29 CFR 825.600 et seq. (*www.washingtonwatchdog.org/documents/cfr/title29/part825.html#825.600*). A private elementary or secondary school may require an *instructional employee* to delay a return from leave until a natural break in the academic year. *Instructional employees* are those whose principal function is to teach and instruct students in a class or individual setting. Athletic coaches, driving instructors, and special education assistants are instructional employees. (There are also special rules pertaining to a school's right to limit leave requests for intermittent or reduced leave schedules when the requested leave of an instructional employee covers more than 20 percent of the total number of working days during the leave of absence.)

Prudent Record Keeping

The FMLA requires employers to document their compliance with the FMLA by making and maintaining records that demonstrate compliance with the FMLA for at least three years. Whether or not a nonprofit is covered by the FMLA, it's wise to keep careful records of employees' eligibility, requests, and any denials of requests for leaves of absence. Employers should maintain a file, separate from the employee's regular personnel file, where documentation pertaining to leaves of absence is maintained. This file would contain all memos about requests for leave, all correspondence between the employee and nonprofit about leaves of absence, and any memos that describe the nonprofit's determination as to eligibility or ineligibility. See FMLA Regulations, 29 CFR 825.500.

The records aren't required to be in any special format. Generally the nonprofit's regular payroll and personnel records will suffice. The records must show who was on the payroll when, and the dates that any employee took a leave. For compliance with the FMLA, the leave must be specifically designated as *FMLA leave* in the nonprofit's records. Copies of the nonprofit's FMLA policy and notices sent to employees regarding their rights and obligations concerning leave must be maintained, too. Medical certifications should be maintained separately from regular personnel records, in confidential files along with all other medical information on employees, in compliance with the ADA.

Coordination of Family Leave With Sick Leave and Other Leave Policies

When family/medical leave is unpaid, employees may try to find a way to receive income during any period of unpaid leave. When an employee qualifies for workers' compensation, or state temporary disability payments, the employee will be on unpaid status from the nonprofit but will receive benefits from the state for a period of time. Alternatively the employee may use his or her accrued paid leave during any period of family leave or other unpaid leave of absence if the nonprofit's policies so permit. (The FMLA specifically permits employers to have a policy allowing employees to simultaneously use accrued paid leave with FMLA leave.) Some state laws specifically permit use of accrued paid leave during family leave. It's helpful to clarify this option for staff by having a written policy permitting employees to use their accrued paid leave during any period of unpaid leave. (A caveat: when the employee is receiving income replacement from the state, such as workers' compensation or state disability benefits, compensation from the employer will generally disqualify the employee from receiving his/her full allowance of disability or workers' compensation payments.)

There is an important distinction between *permitting* an employee (upon the employee's request) to use accrued paid leave during family/medical leave and *requiring* the employee to do so. Employers may only require employees to substitute accrued paid personal and vacation leave if the nonprofit has a policy in place that requires employees to use their accrued leave prior to, or simultaneously with, any other leave of absence (such as a disability leave). Many employers prefer such a *required use* policy because it prevents the unexpected result of employees reaching the end of their leave time and then making an additional request for vacation or personal leave, disrupting staffing plans.

The FMLA also permits substitution of accrued paid *sick* time simultaneously with FMLA leave, however, some state family leave laws don't permit substitution of paid sick leave. Therefore, check your state's family leave law before permitting or requiring employees to use accrued *sick* leave simultaneously with FMLA leave.

What Happens at the End of Family Leave?

An employer needs some advance notice of when an employee plans to return to work. It's perfectly acceptable for a nonprofit to have a provision in its leave policies that requires employees to contact the nonprofit during their leaves with advance notice of their anticipated return to work. The U.S. Department of Labor regulations specifically provide that an employee may not be required to take more family leave than is needed, and that the employee may return to work earlier than the expiration of his or her FMLA leave, provided that the employee on leave gives the employer reasonable notice, which is defined as at least two business days.

Employers not covered by the FMLA or an equivalent state law are free to require more than two business days' notice. If the employee doesn't return to work at the conclusion of the designated leave, the employer has no obligation to continue to employ the employee. Watch out for the possible requirement to accommodate an employee with an extended leave. In cases where an employee has been out on family/medical leave for his or her own serious health condition, the condition could be a disability that would require the employer to make a reasonable accommodation. The employer may be obligated to consider whether an accommodation is feasible. In some cases extending the leave of absence is an appropriate accommodation. When an employee doesn't return to work, the last day of the employee's family/medical leave is the triggering event for COBRA eligibility, requiring the nonprofit to provide adequate notice of the right to benefit continuation pursuant to COBRA regulations. For smaller workplaces (COBRA only applies to employers with 20 or more employees) there are usually parallel notice obligations under state law requiring employers to notify employees of a triggering event causing the employee to cease being eligible for group insurance benefits.

> The FMLA regulations go into detail on all of these subjects. The regulations are explained on the DOL Web site: www.dol.gov/dol/allcfr/ESA/Title_29/Part_825/toc.htm.

Prior to returning to work at the conclusion of a leave of absence for the employee's own health condition, employees should be required to present a *fitness for work* certification from the employee's physician. This certification will help determine whether there are any restrictions due to the employee's own health which may impact the employee's performance at work, and whether the employee can indeed perform the essential functions of her position upon her return from leave. A policy requiring a fitness for work certification is a prudent policy for all employees returning from any type of leave of absence.

Communicating With the Employee Who Is on Family Leave

It's essential to keep in communication with employees on leave so the nonprofit can plan for staffing needs at the expiration of leave. An employer may require that an employee regularly contact the nonprofit during the employee's leave, to keep the nonprofit informed about his or her intentions to return to work. If any employee gives an unequivocal notice of the intent not to return after the expiration of leave, all rights to the designated leave cease. (In other words, the nonprofit doesn't have to maintain the employee's health benefits, or keep the employee's position open. Such notice would also be a triggering event for COBRA.) Sometimes an employee will express to the employer that she or he is *not sure* whether she or he will be returning to work at the end of a leave absence. This isn't sufficient for the nonprofit to terminate the employee's leave or its protections. A follow-up with the employee is essential and the nonprofit should assume that the employee intends to return, unless the employee communicates otherwise.

Payment and Recovery of Health Benefit Premiums

Depending on the terms of the particular leave of absence, the nonprofit may have to pay for whatever portion of health insurance premiums the nonprofit would normally pay if the employee were actively working. Consequently, it's important to make arrangements for employees out on leave to pay their portion of premiums and to tell them it's their responsibility to do so. If employees normally pay a portion of their premiums, and the employee on leave fails to make a payment after 30 days, the employer is no longer obligated to maintain the employee's insurance. However, clear, advance notice is wise any time benefits will be terminated, and under the FMLA, the nonprofit is required to restore that employee's coverage upon return to active employment at the end of FMLA leave, without any qualification requirements.

If an employee fails to return after FMLA leave for a reason other than the continuation, recurrence, or onset of a serious health condition, either affecting the employee or an immediate family member, the nonprofit is entitled to recover any health insurance premiums paid on behalf of the employee during the FMLA leave. Several states permit the employer to require employees on leave to place premium payments in escrow accounts until their return from leave. Once the employee returns to work the escrow payments are returned to the employee. If the employee doesn't return to work at the end of the family leave, the escrow account is used to reimburse the employer for previously paid health insurance premiums. The nonprofit isn't able to recover premiums paid during any portion of the FMLA leave for which the employee was compensated, such as when the employee was receiving compensation due from accrued vacation leave simultaneously with FMLA leave.

FMLA Compliance Reminder!

The FMLA requires reinstatement to the same or an equivalent position:

❏ Upon return to work at the end of FMLA leave, the employee is entitled to be returned to the same position the employee held when leave commenced, or to an equivalent position with equivalent benefits, pay, and other terms and conditions of employment.

❏ If the employee is unable to perform an essential function of the position because of a physical or mental condition, including the continuation of a serious health condition, the employee has no right to restoration to another position under the FMLA. *However, the employer's obligations may be governed by the Americans with Disabilities Act (ADA).*

❏ *Note the following exceptions to the FMLA requirement to reinstate an employee after leave:* If the employee is a *key employee* reinstatement may not be automatic; also when something happens that would have caused the termination of the employee whether or not she or he were on a leave of absence, reinstatement isn't automatic.

FMLA Best Practices and Risk Management Strategies

1. Know which laws (FMLA, state family leave, ADA, state disability laws, or the employee's own leave policies) apply in the current situation.

2. Include written policies in any employee handbook that identify what leaves employees at the nonprofit are entitled to take advantage of, and the eligibility requirements and key provisions of each.

3. Train supervisors on the policies and train supervisors to recognize when employees are eligible for leave and to document all requests and eligibility for leave.

4. Identify each time an employee is *out of work*, whether she or he is eligible for what kind of leave of absence.

5. Communicate with the employee on leave: The nonprofit should document in writing to the employee on leave:

   ❏ the date that his or her leave started.

   ❏ the date it ends, and

   ❏ that if the employee fails to return to work at the conclusion of the leave the nonprofit will have no obligation to maintain his or her employment.

   ❏ whether the employee has obligations to communicate with the employer during the leave of absence about his or her expected return to work date. (The FMLA specifically permits the employer to require that the employee provide periodic reports during FMLA leave regarding the employee's status and intent to return to work.)

   ❏ what obligations the employee has in connection with health insurance coverage, such as premium payments, that normally would be taken care of through payroll deductions.

   ❏ whether the nonprofit will require the employee to provide a *Fitness to Return to Work* certification from a health care provider.

6. Require employees who are on leave or seeking leave due to a serious health condition to provide verification of the health condition with written notice from a health care provider.

   DOL Form WH-380 ✎ is an optional form that may be used to obtain a medical certification from a health care provider.

7. Require a Fitness to Return to Work certification from the employee's medical health professional. This policy must be uniformly applied to all employees returning from leave for their own serious health condition. See FMLA regulations Section 104 (a)(4). ✎

8. If there are major policy changes at the workplace while the employee is on leave, send the employee documentation of such changes and obtain proof of delivery.

Basic Risk Management Strategies to Reduce Liability for Violation of Leaves of Absence Laws

❏ **Preparation:** Know in advance that leaves of absence raise a host of issues and try to address those issues through written policies, before you discover than an employee is *out on leave*.

❏ **Documentation:** The FMLA documentation requirements provide guidance for best practices: Document: 1) whenever requests for leave and accommodations are considered and discussed with an employee; 2) an employee's eligibility for leave, outlining his or her rights and obligations to comply with the nonprofit's leave policies. If the nonprofit has an employee manual, include policies that address leaves of absence. When adverse decisions are made affecting an employee who is on leave, document why the action is necessary from a business perspective.

❏ **Consistency:** Be consistent in how leaves of absence are administered. Inconsistent treatment feels unfair! A feeling of being treated unfairly is the basis of almost all employment litigation.

❏ **Compassionate communication:** Verbally inform the employee(s) as soon as possible whether the employee's reason for being out of work is covered by any special leave of absence policy of the nonprofit or state or federal law or a combination thereof. When an employee is distracted by health or family concerns, the employee won't be searching through an employee manual for policy guidance. Provide the employee with a carefully worded letter telling him or her exactly when the leave starts, when it ends and what his or her responsibilities are during the leave of absence. Be especially clear about how the leave impacts the employee's right to reinstatement and to receive benefits, such as insurance.

❑ **Remain receptive to complaints and concerns.** When an employee is out of work for health or family reasons, the employee will be especially sensitive to the loss of a job or of benefits. If the employer nonprofit makes a decision that's unpopular with the employee and his family, be receptive to the concerns. Try to answer questions and resolve concerns early, rather than holding your breath to see if a lawsuit is filed.

❑ **Don't retaliate (or appear to retaliate!)** Taking an adverse employment action against an employee *because* she or he requested family leave is prohibited as a violation of the FMLA and of many state's public policies. When an adverse action, such as a termination, is necessary, protect the nonprofit with adequate documentation of the reason for the action, emphasizing the business needs of the nonprofit that justify the action.

❑ **Follow closely any internal policies and procedures in the organization's handbook.** Before taking any significant step that will negatively impact an employee's situation, always consult your organization's personnel policies or employee handbook to determine whether the situation is covered. If so, *follow your established procedures*. If the procedures really don't make sense for the situation at hand, consult with legal counsel.

❑ **Consult with legal counsel, experienced in employment matters.** Leaves of absence and compliance with the ADA can get very complicated. In advance of a crisis, identify legal resources in your community where you can receive advice from an employment lawyer; ideally one who has worked with other clients in the nonprofit sector.

Synopsis of State Family Leave Laws and Special Leave Laws

The state laws noted here are subject to constant review and revision in state legislatures. This summary should therefore be used for reference purposes, rather than as a definitive guide.

Alabama: Leave for female employees for childbirth, pregnancy and related conditions should be provided on the same terms given to other employees with temporary disabilities.

Alaska: Leave for female employees for childbirth, pregnancy and related conditions should be provided on the same terms given to other employees with temporary disabilities.

Arizona: Leave for female employees for childbirth, pregnancy and related conditions should be provided on the same terms given to other employees with temporary disabilities.

Special Rules for Crime Victims: The Arizona Crime Victims Leave Act requires employers to allow employees who are crime victims or the immediate family member of a crime victim who is killed or incapacitated to attend proceedings relating to the prosecution of the criminal. Employers may not retaliate or discipline employees for taking time off and the employee's seniority must be preserved. The leave doesn't have to be paid; employees may use their accrued paid vacation or sick time. Employees must provide documentation of the need for leave. Employers must maintain records on the leave in a separate confidential file. See A.R.S. § 13-4439. ✑

Arkansas: Family leave applies to public school teachers only: The Teachers Minimum Sick Pay Law guarantees minimum periods of leave. Teachers injured by an assault or other criminal act committed against them in the course of their employment are granted leave with full pay for up to one year. Ark. Code Annot. §§ 21-4-201 through 205 . School employees: The School Employees Minimum Sick Pay Act guarantees minimum periods of leave similar to the Teacher's act. See Ark. Code Annot. §§ 6-17-1301. ✑

Special rules for organ and bone marrow donors: Employers must provide unpaid leave to allow employees to serve as organ donors or bone marrow donors. See Ark. Code Annot. § 11-3-205.

California: The state law applies to employers with 50 or more employees; types of leave allowed are consistent the federal FMLA. Employees must have worked for more than a year to be eligible. Any employer who provides sick leave must allow employees to

Danger! *Don't* wait for the employee to ask for a particular leave and don't assume that the type of leave the employee requests is the correct leave for the situation. As soon as the nonprofit realizes that that an employee is *out on leave*, the nonprofit needs to identify what types of leave apply and identify the rights and obligations of both employer and employee.

Tip: If the employee is eligible, it's in the employee's and the nonprofit's best interests to assign the time *out on leave* as protected leave (such as FMLA) because:

❑ The employee's job will be protected for the entire time that the employee is on family and medical leave, if the leave is either state or federal leave or job protection is an aspect of the nonprofit's policy on family/medical leave.

❑ The nonprofit will have *certainty* as to **when** it's possible to terminate an employee (at the conclusion of leave period, if the employee doesn't return to work).

Postings Required!

The FMLA and several states, including the following, require that a notice be posted at the workplace explaining employee's rights to family leave: Alaska (*www.dol.gov/esa/regs/ compliance/posters/fmla.htm*), California, Colorado (*www.coworkforce.com/LAB/ Posting%20Requirements.pdf*), District of Columbia (*www.ohr.dc.gov/ohr/site/ default.asp*), Massachusetts (maternity leave); New Jersey, North Dakota, Washington, and Wisconsin.

use up to six months' worth of accrued leave to care for an ill child, parent, spouse or domestic partner. In cases of pregnancy, childbirth or related conditions, employees at workplaces with five or more employees (except nonprofit religious associations) are entitled to at least four months unpaid leave for employee's own disability due to pregnancy, childbirth or a related condition under the California Fair Employment and Housing Act. (Note that this is a rare instance when the state law, the California Family Rights Act, doesn't run concurrently with the FMLA) Pregnant employees are entitled to up to four months pregnancy disability leave under the Fair Employment and Housing Act (which is concurrent with the FMLA for the employee's own serious health condition), which may be followed by a 12-week California Family Rights Act leave to enable the new parent to take care of the child; If both parents are employed with the nonprofit, the employer may limit the aggregate leave to a total of 12 weeks, and nonprofits may deny leave to any employee if the leave is to take care of a child, but the child's other parent is unemployed or on family leave. Employers may refuse to reinstate *key* employees if hardship would result, provided that the employer gives the employee prior notice of intent to deny reinstatement; Employers aren't required to compensate employees during leave. Paid time off (accrued leave, vacation) may be used along with family leave, but accrued sick leave may only be used if the family leave is for the employee's own illness. See Cal. Gov't Code § 12945.2; Labor Code § 233.

Special Rule for School Visits: All employers must provide time off for parents to meet with teachers or school administrators. Employees must give employer reasonable notice before taking time off. Employer may not discriminate or retaliate against employees. Employers with 25 or more employees that grant any type of unpaid leave must provide unpaid leave time up to 40 hours per child for time off to participate in an activity at a child's school. However, employees must provide reasonable notice and may either use existing paid leave (vacation, personal and compensatory time off) or may take unpaid leave. See Cal Lab Code § 230.7, 230.8.

Colorado: There are no state law provisions for family leave affecting private employers, however, the Civil Rights Commission has ruled that pregnancy-related disabilities should be treated the same as other temporary disabilities [Rules 80.1-80.11], and there is a statute which requires employers to give the same leave to adopting parents as provided to biological parents (except for adoptions by the spouse of the custodial parent). See Colo. Rev. Stat. Ann. § 19-5-211.

Connecticut: Employers with at least three employees are required to give any female employee in pregnancy, childbirth or related situations, the same leave, benefits and rights to reinstatement as a temporarily disabled employee would receive. In instances of the employee's own illness, or the birth, adoption, or illness of a child, parent, or spouse (or civil-union spouse), employers with at least 75 employees must provide up to 16 weeks of leave in a 24-month period. Eligible employees are those that have worked at least 12 months and 1000 hours in the 12-months preceding the first day of leave. [*Note:* This is more generous than the federal FMLA 12-week leave.] Reinstatement is required. The leave doesn't have to be paid and the employer doesn't have to maintain the employee's health benefits at the employer's expense. No exemption for key employees. See Conn. Gen. Stat. Ann. § 31-51kk et seq.

Special rules to permit employees to serve in public office: Employers with 25+ employees must provide leave for employees to serve full time in state or municipal offices, for no more than two consecutive terms. See Conn Gen. Stat. Ann. § 31-51L

Delaware: Leave for female employees for childbirth, pregnancy and related conditions should be provided on the same terms given to other employees with temporary disabilities.

District of Columbia: Employers with 20+ employees are required to grant employees up to 16 weeks of family and medical leave during any 24-month period and must preserve benefits and provide reinstatement at the conclusion of the leave. Leave may be used for the employee's own serious health condition, or the serious health condition of a family member, the birth of a child, placement of a child with the employee for adoption or foster care, or placement of a sick child with the employee when the employee assumes parental responsibilities. The District of Columbia's law includes domestic partners who live together and share a *"committed relationship"* as *"family members."* To be eligible for leave employees must have worked at least 1,000 hours during the 12-month period immediately preceding the request for leave. During leave, benefits must be maintained and seniority preserved. Employees may substitute accrued paid leave but it's counted against the total of 16 weeks of available leave. Employers must post a notice explaining the state law. Failure to post can result in $100 fines for each day of noncompliance. There are exceptions to the state law: employers with fewer than 50 employees need not reinstate salaried employees who are among the five highest paid staff members, and employers with 50 or more employees need not reinstate salaried employees who are among the top 10 percent wage earners, provided that the employer gives notice to the employee, and can show that economic injury would result due to reinstatement. Intermittent leave is permitted with some limitations. The employer may limit the total leave taken by two employees who work for the employer to a total of 16 weeks in 24 months, and restrict simultaneous leave to a total of four weeks. See D.C. Code Ann. § 36-1302 [check also DC Code § 32-501, 502 and 503.]

Leave for Parental Attendance at School Events: All employers must give employees a total of 24 hours of unpaid leave (unless the employee opts to use paid leave) to attend a school-related event. Immediate and extended family members are eligible (natural parents, aunts, uncles, grandparents, their spouses and guardians). Whenever possible the employee must give 10 days notice to the employer of the requested leave. The posting requirement applies to this provision as well as to family and medical leave. See D.C. Code Ann. § 36-1601 et seq.

Florida: Leave for female employees for childbirth, pregnancy and related conditions should be provided on the same terms given to other employees with temporary disabilities.

Georgia: Leave for female employees for childbirth, pregnancy and related conditions should be provided on the same terms given to other employees with temporary disabilities.

Hawaii: Employers with 100+ employees are required to give employees who have worked for six months up to four weeks of unpaid leave. The employer must reinstate the employee and preserve benefits. Reasons for leave include birth or adoption of a child, or the serious health condition of a child, parent or spouse. "Parent" is defined more broadly than under federal law. There is no provision for leave due to the employee's own illness. However, if leave is needed due to the employee's pregnancy, childbirth or related conditions, then all employers (even those with fewer than 100 employees) must provide a reasonable period of leave, as determined by the employee's physician, given on the same terms as any leave provided to any other temporarily disabled employee. See Haw. Rev. Stat. Ann. § 398-1 et seq.

Idaho: Leave for female employees for childbirth, pregnancy and related conditions should be provided on the same terms given to other employees with temporary disabilities.

Illinois: State law provides leave to female employees for childbirth, pregnancy and related conditions. Employers with at least 15 employees must provide leave to female employees for the birth, pregnancy and related conditions on the same terms as would be available for any temporarily disabled employee. See 56 Ill. Admin. Code § 5210 (1985).

Special Leave for Victims of Domestic Violence: Employers with at least 50 employees must permit victims of domestic violence or employees with someone in their household who is a victim, up to 12 weeks unpaid leave. The employee must provide up to 48 hours advance notice when practicable. Employees may substitute any accrued paid leave. Employers may not retaliate against anyone for exercising rights to leave. See Illinois Victim's Economic Security Act, 820 ILCS 180/1 et seq.

Special Leave for School Visits: Employers with 50+ employees must provide up to eight hours of unpaid *school visitation* leave to employees who have worked for six consecutive months of service. Leave is limited to four hours in one day. Employees must submit written requests in advance and the employer may refuse the request if the employee's leave would result in more than 5 percent of the staff being absent. Employee must exhaust all accrued paid leave (vacation, personal and compensatory leave) before eligibility for school visit leave. Employers must make a good faith effort to let employees flex their schedules to make up the work. See 820 ILCS 147/10, 147/15 and 147/20.

Indiana: Leave for female employees for childbirth, pregnancy and related conditions should be provided on the same terms given to other employees with temporary disabilities.

Iowa: Employers with at least four employees must treat pregnancy, childbirth and related conditions the same as any temporary disability, providing the employee up to eight weeks of disability leave, and maintaining benefits during the leave. See Iowa Stat. Ann. § 216.6.

Special Leave to Serve in Public Office: Employers with at least 20 employees must provide unpaid leave without loss of benefits earned to employees who are elected to public office (municipal, county, state or federal) or unpaid leave to attend board meetings if an employee is appointed to a state board (without loss of credited benefits). Employers aren't required to pay health or other benefits during leave. See Iowa Code §§ 55.1.

Kansas: State regulations affecting all employers require that pregnancy, childbirth and related conditions be treated the same as any temporary disability, Upon return to work within a reasonable time, reinstatement to the same or an equivalent position is required. There are no other state law provisions governing family and medical leave. See KS ADC § 21-32-6.

Kentucky: State law provides leave to female employees for childbirth, pregnancy and related conditions. Employers with eight employees must treat pregnancy, childbirth and related conditions the same as any temporary disability and give the employee up to eight weeks of disability leave, and maintain benefits during the leave. All employers must provide up to six weeks for employees who adopt a child under the age of seven. Reinstatement rights, while not stated in the law, may be implied. See Ky. Rev. Stat. § 337.015 (1995).

Special Rules for Emergency Responders: Employers may not discipline or retaliate against employees who are late or who miss work because they're responding to emergencies as volunteer firefighters, rescue squad members, emergency medical technicians, etc. See Ky. Rev. Stat. § 337.100 (Page 871 of the pdf).

Louisiana: Employers with 26+ employees are covered by Louisiana's state law governing pregnancy, childbirth and related conditions, which requires employers to give female employees up to six weeks disability leave for normal pregnancy and childbirth or up to four months of disability leave with accrued vacation leave for pregnancy, childbirth and related conditions. Reinstatement is required at the end of leave. Employers may impose reasonable notice requirements on employees, such as leave commencement and duration. Employees may apply accrued vacation leave toward the leave period. The treatment of benefits for female employees on disability leave must be the same as for any other employee on temporary disability leave. See La. Rev. Stat. Ann. § 23: 342 (1998).

Special Rules for Bone Marrow Donors: Employers with more than 20 employees must give bone marrow donors paid leave of up to 40 hours annually. See La. Rev. Stat. Ann. § 40:1299.124.

Special Rules for School or Day Care Center Visits: Employers may give employees up to 16 hours of unpaid leave during any 12-month period to visit their children's school or day care, upon reasonable notice given to the employer, as long as the conferences or activities can't reasonably be scheduled during non-working hours. Employees may use accrued paid vacation or other leave in lieu of unpaid school visitation leave. See La. Rev. Stat. Ann. § 23:1015.2

Maine: All employers must give female employees temporary leave for childbirth, pregnancy and related conditions on the same terms given to other employees with temporary disabilities. Additionally, employers with 25+ employees must give any employee with 12 months of consecutive service up to 10 weeks of unpaid family leave for the employee's own serious health condition, or that of a child, parent or spouse, as well as the birth, or adoption of a child. Reinstatement is required but may be denied under some business hardship conditions. Benefits must be maintained (at the employee's expense) and the employee may use accrued paid leave in place of any or all of the family leave. Except in medical emergencies, employees must give 30 days' notice of intent to use leave. There is a posting requirement to notify employees of the state law. See Me. Rev. Stat. Ann. tit. 26 § 844 ; tit 5 Section 4572-A (1989).

Maryland: Employers who grant leave with pay for employees following the birth of a child must give the same leave with pay to employees when a child is placed with them for adoption. See Md. Code Ann. Lab & Empl § 3-802.

Special Rules for Leave for Emergency Responders: Employers may not discharge or retaliate against an employee for participation in any activity (such as civil air patrol, volunteer firefighter etc) as a response to an emergency declared by the governor when the employee provides written documentation that participation was required. See Md. Code Ann., Lab. & Empl. § 3-703.

Massachusetts: The Massachusetts Maternity Leave Law doesn't apply to social clubs, fraternal organizations or to corporations *not organized for private profit,* consequently, nonprofits are exempt. Massachusetts has no other family leave law, however, the Massachusetts Small Necessities Leave Act applies to all employers covered under the federal FMLA and provides employees with 24 hours unpaid leave in a 12-month period to attend a child's routine medical and dental appointments, school activities; the act also provides for leave so that employees may attend elderly (over age 60) relatives' routine medical and dental appointments or other appointments relating to the employee's own care. Eligibility for such leave is the same as the FMLA (1,250 hours and one year of service). The employee is required to provide seven days' notice of the anticipated date of leave, unless necessity for leave isn't foreseeable, in which case the employee is expected to provide as much notice as possible. See Mass. Gen. L.c. 149 § 52D.

Michigan: All employers must give female employees temporary leave for childbirth, pregnancy and related conditions on the same terms given to other employees with temporary disabilities. There are no other state family and medical leave provisions affecting private employers. See Michigan Directive to State Contracts, Civil Rights Commission, § 11, para. G.5 (1978).

Minnesota: Minnesota's Parenting Leave Act provides that employers with 21+ employees in one location are required to provide employees up to six weeks of leave for the birth or adoption of a child. Reinstatement to same or comparable position is required except in cases of layoff. All benefits must be maintained during leave. Employers may require employees to apply any employer-provided paid leave towards the six weeks of unpaid childbirth or adoption leave. Employees may use sick leave for leave due to the injury or illness of a child. See Minn. Stat. Ann. Sections 181.940-944. M.S.A. §§ 181.940 et seq.

Special Rules for School Visits: Minnesota law also requires all employers to give employees who work 20+ hours a week, up to 16 hours of unpaid leave during any 12-month period to attend school conferences or activities that can't be scheduled during nonworking hours. Employees may use accrued paid leave. See M.S.A. § 181.9412.

Special Rules for Bone Marrow Donation: Employers with 20+ employees must grant leave without pay to employees who work 20+ hours weekly, up to 40 hours. See M.S.A. Section 181.945, and 181.9455.

Special Rules for Employees Seeking Restraining Orders: Employers must provide *reasonable* time off to employees who need to obtain a restraining order due to harassment or domestic violence. See M.S.A. § 518B.01.

Mississippi: Leave for female employees for childbirth, pregnancy and related conditions should be provided on the same terms given to other employees with temporary disabilities.

Missouri: The Missouri Commission on Human Rights regulations provide that it's a violation of law to terminate a temporarily disabled employee due to the unavailability of leave if doing so has a disparate impact on employees as a result of gender. Consequently, employers in Missouri should treat female employees who are pregnant or who have given birth the same as any other employee with a temporary disability. There are no other state family or special leave provisions affecting private employers. See 8 CSR § 60-3.040.16 B (Page 6).

Montana: The Montana Maternity Leave Act makes it unlawful to discharge a woman due to pregnancy or refuse to grant her reasonable leave, or deny disability benefits or require her to take mandatory leave. All employers must give female employees temporary (unpaid) leave for childbirth, pregnancy and related conditions on the same terms given to other employees with temporary disabilities. Reinstatement to the original job or to a position with equivalent pay, and accumulated benefits is required except when changed circumstances make reinstatement impossible or unreasonable. Employers can apply accumulated paid disability or leave benefits towards the pregnancy leave. Adoption isn't covered. See Mont. Code Ann. §§ 49-2-310 and 311 (1997).

Nebraska: Leave for female employees for childbirth, pregnancy and related conditions should be provided on the same terms given to other employees with temporary disabilities.

Bone Marrow Donors: Employers are encouraged to grant paid leaves of absence to employees who are bone marrow donors.

Nevada: Leave for female employees for childbirth, pregnancy and related conditions should be provided on the same terms given to other employees with temporary disabilities.

Special Rules for School Visits: Employers must provide unpaid leave for employees to attend conferences requested by a school administrator during work hours, or for responding to a notice of an emergency involving a child during work hours. See Nev. Rev. Stat. § 392.920.

New Hampshire: Employers must permit female employees to take leave for pregnancy-related reasons or post childbirth in the same manner as any other employee with a temporary disability. When the employee is physically able to return to work, her original job or a comparable position must be made available unless business necessity makes it impossible or unreasonable. For all other purposes, including benefits, pregnancy, childbirth and related conditions must be considered temporary disabilities, and an affected female employee must be treated in the same manner as any other employee. There are no other state law provisions for family or special leaves affecting private employers. See N.H. Rev. Stat. Ann. 354-A:7, VI.

New Jersey: The state Family Leave Act is very similar to federal law except that it doesn't cover an employee's own serious health condition. Covered employers (those with 50 or more employees, at least one of which is in New Jersey) must grant up to 12 weeks of unpaid leave in a 24-month period to eligible employees for the serious health condition of an immediate family member, or the birth, adoption, or placement of a child in foster care with an employee. Employees must have worked one year and at least 1,000 hours of service to be eligible for leave. Reinstatement is required; however, leave may be denied if it would create an economic hardship. Also, key employees, (defined as the top 7 or 5 percent highest paid employees) may be denied leave. Employers that deny leave must give prior notice, or allow the employee to return from leave for 10 days. Employees may not *moonlight* while on leave. There is a posting requirement. Employers aren't required to maintain health benefits unless the leave is taken under federal law simultaneously. *Note:* State family leave doesn't begin until temporary disability post-pregnancy ends but federal family leave can run concurrently with state temporary disability. See N.J. Stat. Ann. § 34:11B.

New Mexico: Leave for female employees for childbirth, pregnancy and related conditions should be provided on the same terms given to other employees with temporary disabilities.

New York: Anti-discrimination laws in New York that apply to all employers provide that employers must treat pregnancy, childbirth and related issues the same as any other temporary disability; natural birth and adoption must be treated the same. The law provides that all employers must provide the same leave to employees who take a leave of absence for the birth of a child, adoption, or commencement of parent-child relationship. The law doesn't provide leave for care of a seriously ill family member or the employee's own serious health condition. The leave may be unpaid. No maximum or minimum length is provided by law, as long as the leave is the same for adoptive or birth parents. The law doesn't require employers to maintain health benefits or reinstate employees after leave. There are no notification requirements but employers may adopt policies requiring notice. See N.Y. Lab. Law § 201-c.

Special Rules for Bone Marrow Donors: Employers with 20+ employees are required to provide up to 24 hours of leave to female employee bone marrow donors who work an average of 20 or more hours per week. Reinstatement and benefits are to be provided on the same terms as for other temporarily disabled employees. See N.Y. Labor Law §§ 202a and 202-b.

North Carolina: *Special Rules for School Visits:* All employers must give any employee with parental responsibilities up to four hours leave in any 12-month period for school-related activities. Employers may require employees to submit a written request two days prior to the leave, and to supply written verification from the school of the employee's participation in the school activity. See N.C. Gen. Stat. § 95-28.3.

North Dakota: Leave for female employees for childbirth, pregnancy and related conditions should be provided on the same terms given to other employees with temporary disabilities.

Ohio: Leave for female employees for childbirth, pregnancy and related conditions should be provided on the same terms given to other employees with temporary disabilities.

Special Rules for Volunteer Firefighters/EMTs: Employers may not discharge or discipline employees who miss work or are absent because they're responding to emergencies. Employers may charge the employee's missed work against regular pay. See Ohio Rev. Code § 4113.41.

Oklahoma: Leave for female employees for childbirth, pregnancy and related conditions should be provided on the same terms given to other employees with temporary disabilities.

Oregon: The Oregon Family Leave Act applies to employers with 25+ employees. Up to 12 weeks of unpaid leave must be provided for care of a child with a nonserious health condition, as well as for the adoption, birth, illness of a child, foster child, parent-in-law, or spouse, or for the employee's own illness. (Note that the Oregon law defines "family member" more broadly than the federal law). An additional 12 weeks is available to female employees with any illness, injury or condition related to pregnancy or childbirth that disables them from performing any job duties or for an employee using the leave for his or her sick child. Eligible employees are those with 25 hours or more each week for the 180 days immediately preceding the leave request. Employers can require employees to give up to 30 days notice and may reduce the employee's leave by three weeks for failure to give timely notice. There are exceptions to the notice requirement in cases of unexpected premature birth, illness or injury, or condition that requires home care. Employers don't have to maintain the employee's health benefits during leave. Employers must reinstate the employee upon return from leave to the same or an equivalent position and restore benefits unless the employee's job would have been "renamed or reclassified" had the employee not been on leave, in which case the employer must restore the employee to "any available equivalent" position. Leave to take care of a newborn or newly adopted child must take place within 12 months of the birth/placement. If both spouses work for the same employer the employer may deny concurrent leave except when one spouse is needed to care for the other, or one spouse has a serious health condition and the other is needed to care for a child who also has a serious health condition. Employers need not give leave when there is another family member available to care for a child requiring home care. Employees may use paid accrued vacation time during family leave time. Accrued sick leave may be used in addition but only for leave to care for an infant or child under the age of 18 years who is newly adopted or placed in foster care, or an adopted child or foster care child is over 18 years but incapable of self-care. There is a posting notice and penalties for noncompliance. See Or. Rev. Stat. § 659A.150 et seq.

Special Rules for Employees to Attend Criminal Proceedings: Unless providing unpaid leave would present an undue hardship, employers with 6+ employees are required to provide leave to employees who are crime victims and have worked more than 25 hours per week in the 180 days before the leave. See ORS 659A.190(4) and 659A.192.

Pennsylvania: State law provides leave to female employees for childbirth, pregnancy and related conditions. Employers with four or more employees must give female employees temporary leave for childbirth, pregnancy and related conditions on the same terms given to other employees with temporary disabilities. Leave for child care must also be available to male employees. See Human Relations Commission Pregnancy Guidelines, (1975).

Rhode Island: The Rhode Island Parental and Family Leave applies to all employers and provides leave for pregnancy and birth, adoption, or serious illness of a child, parent, parent-in-law, spouse or of the employee him/herself. Employees who have worked for the same employer for 12 consecutive months are eligible for up to 13 consecutive work weeks of unpaid or paid leave (depending on the employer's policies) in a 24 month period. Reinstatement is required and health benefits must be maintained on the same terms as for active employees. There is no allowance for intermittent leave or for an exception for key employees. The employer may require the employee to place payment for premiums in escrow during leave but must refund the money upon the employee's return to work. A posting notice is required and serious penalties may be imposed for violations. See R.I. Gen. Laws § 28-48.

Special Leave for School Visits: Employees who have worked for 12 consecutive months for their employer are entitled to up to 10 hours of leave for school conferences, or any school related activities for their child(ren). The leave is unpaid but the employee may substitute paid vacation or any other appropriate leave. Employers must provide 24 hours notice of leave and make reasonable efforts to schedule the leave so as not to disrupt the employer's operations. See R.I. Gen. Laws § 28-48-12.

South Carolina: Leave for female employees for childbirth, pregnancy and related conditions should be provided on the same terms given to other employees with temporary disabilities.

Special Rules for Bone Marrow Donors: All employers with 20+ employees at one site must give female bone marrow donor-employees a leave of absence consistent with temporary disability.

South Dakota: Leave for female employees for childbirth, pregnancy and related conditions should be provided on the same terms given to other employees with temporary disabilities.

Tennessee: Employers with 100+ full-time employees must provide up to four months of leave to employees who have been employed by the same employer for at least 12 consecutive months as a full-time employee for the birth or adoption of a child. Reinstatement is required. The leave may be paid or unpaid, depending on the employer's policy. An employer doesn't have to cover the costs of benefits while an employee is on maternity leave unless it does so for all employees on leaves of absence. See Tenn. Code Ann. § 4-21-408 (1991).

Texas: Leave for female employees for childbirth, pregnancy and related conditions should be provided on the same terms given to other employees with temporary disabilities.

Utah: Leave for female employees for childbirth, pregnancy and related conditions should be provided on the same terms given to other employees with temporary disabilities. State law specifically prohibits employers with 15+ employees to discriminate on the basis of pregnancy, childbirth or pregnancy-related conditions. See Utah Code § 34A-5-106(1).

Vermont: The Vermont Parental and Family Leave Act provides that employers with 10+ employees must provide up to 12 weeks of unpaid parental leave (for childbirth or adoption) and that employers with 15+ employees must provide up to 12 weeks of unpaid leave for an employee's own serious illness or the illness of a child, spouse, parent or parent-in-law. Eligible employees are those who have been employed continuously for one year and at least 30 hours per week. Employees may apply up to six weeks' accrued paid sick or vacation leave toward family leave. All employment benefits continue during leave. Reinstatement is required unless the employee would have been laid off for reasons unrelated to the leave. The employer may only refuse to reinstate if it notifies the employee with reasonable notice of its intent to hire a permanent replacement and the employee performed unique services and hiring a replacement was the only way to prevent grievous economic injury. The employer may require the employee to pay the cost of benefits during leave. A posting notice is required. See 21 V.S.A. § 470 et.seq.

Special Short-Term Leave: In addition to the leave described above, a short-term leave of up to four hours in any 30-day period is available, not to exceed 24 hours in any 12-month period. The leave may be taken (i) to participate in pre-school or school activities (ii) to accompany a sick child, stepchild, foster child, parent, spouse, civil union partner, parent-in-law or parent of a civil-union partner to routine medical appointments or (iii) other appointments for professional services related to their care and well-being or (iv) to respond to medical emergencies involving an employee's child, stepchild, foster child, parent, spouse, civil union partner, parent-in-law or parent of a civil union partner. See Vt. Stat. Ann. tit. 21, §§ 471 and 472.

Virginia: Leave for female employees for childbirth, pregnancy and related conditions should be provided on the same terms given to other employees with temporary disabilities.

Washington: The Washington Family Leave Act requires that all employers permit employees to use their choice of sick or other paid leave to care for 1) a child with a health condition that requires treatment or supervision or 2) a spouse, parent, parent-in-law, or grandparent of the employee who has a serious health condition or an emergency condition. See Wash. Rev. Code §§ 49.12.270 and 49.12.265.

Special Leave for Pregnancy Related Conditions: Additionally, all employers must provide female employees with a leave of absence for the period in which she is sick or temporarily disabled because of pregnancy or childbirth-related conditions. The terms and conditions of the leave may be determined by the employer's policies governing temporary disabilities. Illness or disabilities caused by or contributed to pregnancy, miscarriage, abortion and childbirth or recovery therefrom must be treated as a temporary disability under any sick leave plan or temporary disability plan. See Wash. Rev. Code § 49.78.030.

West Virginia: Leave for female employees for childbirth, pregnancy and related conditions should be provided on the same terms given to other employees with temporary disabilities.

Wisconsin: The Wisconsin Family and Medical Leave Act, which applies to employers with at least 50 employees, provides for up to eight weeks of family leave and two weeks of medical leave in a 12-month period, defined as a calendar year beginning January 2. Family leave can be used for the birth of a child or the placement of a child with an employee for adoption and for caring for an employee's child, spouse, or parent with a serious health condition. The law provides for intermittent leave. Employees must give the employer advance notice. Employers may require certification of the reason for leave from a physician. Employees may substitute accrued paid leave for any portion or all of family leave, but employers can't require employees to substitute accrued leave unless the employer's policy provides that requiring substituted leave can only be applied so that the result is "no more restrictive" than the leave provided by state law. The employer must maintain health benefits on the same terms as if the employee were in active employment, but may require the employees on leave to deposit money in an escrow account to pay for the eight weeks of health care premiums. The employer must refund the money when the employee ends employment within 30 days after the end of leave. Reinstatement is required except when it's impossible due to business necessity. There is no key employee exception for reinstatement. A posting of notice to employees is required. Employers with at least 25 employees must also post a notice explaining their own policies on family and medical leave, if applicable. See Wis. Stat. Ann. § 103.10.

Wyoming: Leave for female employees for childbirth, pregnancy and related conditions should be provided on the same terms given to other employees with temporary disabilities.

Jury Leave—Witness Leave

Nonprofits should establish a policy on jury and witness duty in order to ensure compliance with federal and state laws and to advise employees of their right to paid or unpaid leave for serving as a juror or a witness. Federal law and many state laws specify that it's unlawful to "discharge, threaten to discharge, intimidate, or coerce" employees who have been called to jury service, therefore, employers should check their state law before drafting personnel policies relating to jury leave. Even where there is no specific state law addressing jury service or witness leave, employees can successfully claim that it's in violation of public policy not to pay them during their jury or witness duty, on the basis that their employer is taking adverse action against them for exercising their duty as citizens. Retaliation could also include failing to credit an employee serving on a jury for sick, vacation or other accrued benefits. Violations of state laws pertaining to jury service can result in fines, compensatory and punitive damages, back wages, and in some cases imprisonment.

Jury Leave Policy Tips

❑ Policies on jury service should specify that employees called to report to jury duty or to serve as a witness must alert their employer in a timely fashion, and provide proof of such service in order to be eligible for wages.

❑ To avoid claims of retaliation, employees serving on a jury should be treated just as any other employee on a leave of absence, following the nonprofit's own policies on leave of absence. Thus, employees serving on a jury are entitled to health insurance and other benefits to the same extent as any other employee out on leave. Most state laws require that benefits remain intact during jury service.

The most critical issue to address is whether employees will be paid for the duration of their jury service. Most nonprofits have policies that provide for wages during jury leave for at least some portion of the jury service. Many nonprofits choose to pay the difference between their employee's regular wages and the small amount provided to jurors as a daily wage. Others decide that permitting the employee to keep their payment from the court is important. Employers concerned about paying employees for protracted jury service should include language in their jury leave policy such as: "Employees on jury leave will be paid full wages for up to [two weeks] of jury service but no longer." However, in certain states, nonprofit employers don't have that option: Alabama, Arkansas, Colorado, Connecticut, Louisiana, Massachusetts, Nebraska, New York, Tennessee, and West Virginia require employers to maintain an employee's regular wages during jury duty, with certain limitations. Requirements for paying employees for jury service, and other idiosyncratic policies having to do with jury leave, are summarized in the next section.

A new area of leave has developed in the past decade: Leave for victims of a crime that permits an employee leave from work without pay to attend court proceedings, serve as a witness or go to court to obtain a temporary restraining order against an attacker. Typically these crime victim leave laws prohibit discharge or retaliation against employees who need a leave from work to attend court proceeding relating to the crime that resulted in their injury. Where applicable, individual state crime victim leaves are noted in the next section.

Jury and Witness Leave Laws/Crime Victim Leave

The state laws noted here are subject to constant review and revision in state legislatures. This summary should therefore be used for reference purposes, rather than as a definitive guide.

Note: Unless otherwise mentioned below, there is no requirement that jury or witness leave be paid.

Alabama: *Jury Service:* Employees must be excused from work and are entitled to their "usual compensation" when called for jury service, but employers aren't entitled to subtract the fee the employee receives for jury service. Employees can't be required to use their accrued vacation, or sick leave during jury leave. As long as the employee reports for work at his next regular work time after being dismissed from jury duty, the employer may not take any adverse action. Employers with five or fewer employees are protected from having more than one employee serve on a jury at the same time. See Ala. Code § 12-16-8.

Witness Leave: No law.

Crime Victim Leave: Allows victims of a crime to respond to a subpoena and testify in criminal proceedings or participate in reasonable preparation for a criminal proceeding. See Ala. Code § 15-23-81. ✒

Alaska: *Jury Service:* Employers may not threaten, penalize or discharge employees who are called to serve on a jury or as a witness when the employee was a crime victim. Time off doesn't need to be paid. An employee can bring a civil action against an employer for damages. See Alaska Stat. § 09.20.037; 12-61-017. ✒

Witness Leave: No law applicable to private employees.

Crime Victim Leave: Allows victims of a crime to respond to subpoena and to attend court proceedings to give testimony. See Alaska Stat. § 12.61-017. ☞

Arizona: *Jury Service:* Employees must be given leave and may not be retaliated against for jury duty. The jury leave doesn't have to be paid. Employees can't lose seniority or other benefits because of jury service and may not be required to use accrued sick or vacation time. The law requires the court to reschedule or postpone jury service for employers with five or fewer employees if another employee is serving as a juror at the same time. See Ariz. Rev. Stat. § 21-236. ☞

Witness Leave: When the employer has 50+ employees, witness leave is required for employees who are crime victims. See A.R.S. § 23-1501. ☞

Crime Victim Leave: Requires employers to give leave, which may be paid; employee can elect to use accrued paid leave. See Ariz. Rev. Stat. § 13-4439 ☞ (for criminal offenses) and Ariz. Rev. Stat. § 8-420 (specifically for juvenile offenses). ☞

Arkansas: *Jury Service:* Employees can't be discharged, lose sick leave or vacation time or be penalized due to their service on a jury. Employees are entitled to full compensation in addition to any fees received for time spent on jury service. Employees can't lose their vacation time, sick leave or suffer any retaliation as a result of jury service See Ark. Code § 16-31-106 ☞ and § 21-4-213; ☞ or witness duty. See Ark Code § 21-4-213 ☞ .

Witness Leave: No law applicable to private employees. *Crime Victim Leave:* An employer may not discharge or discipline a victim or a representative of a victim for participation at the request of a prosecuting attorney's request in preparation for a criminal proceeding or attendance at a criminal justice proceeding if attendance is reasonably necessary to protect the interest of the victim. See Ark. Rev. Stat. § 16-90-1105. ☞

California: *Jury Service:* Employees must give their employers reasonable notice of their summons for jury service. Employees can't be discharged or discriminated against for being called to jury service. See Cal. Labor Code § 230 ☞ or service as a witness; See Cal. Gov't Code § 9414. ☞

Witness Leave: Employees called to appear in court as a witness may not be discharged or discriminated against, provided they provide their employer with reasonable notice. It's a misdemeanor (criminal offense) to harass an employee for serving as a witness. See Cal. Gov't Code § 9414. ☞

Colorado: *Jury Service:* Employers may not take adverse action against employees who take time off work to serve on a jury. Employer must pay wages up to $50 per day for the first three days of service for employees serving as grand jurors or trial jurors. Employees can sue for back pay and attorney's fees. See Colo. Rev. Stat. §§ 13-71-126 ☞ and 13-71-134(1). ☞

Witness and Crime Victim Leave: Laws pertaining to lawful conduct outside work would be violated by discharging or retaliating against an employee for testifying during nonworking hours; Employers may not discharge or discipline any victim of a crime or family member of a crime victim for honoring a subpoena to testify in a criminal proceeding or for participating in the preparation of a criminal proceeding. See Colo. Rev. Stat. §§ 24-34-402.5 ☞ and 24-4.1-303(8). ☞

Connecticut: *Jury Service:* It's unlawful for employers to discharge, threaten or otherwise coerce employees who receive a summons or serve on a jury. Employers must pay full-time employees (those working 30 or more hours per week) regular wages for the first five days of jury duty, except for days when the employee wouldn't have earned regular wages. Employees may sue for back wages and attorneys fees, and violators may be fined or imprisoned. See Conn. Gen. Stat. §§ 51-247 ☞ and 247a. ☞

Witness and Crime Victim Leave: Employers may not discriminate against an employee for responding to a subpoena and appearing as a witness in a criminal case. Crime victims can't be discriminated against for attending court proceedings and participating in police investigations relating to the crime against them. See Conn. Gen. Stat. § 54-85b. ☞

Delaware: *Jury Service:* It's unlawful to threaten, discharge, intimidate or coerce an employee who receives a summons or serves on a jury. Employers may be fined $500. Employees may also bring a civil action for reinstatement, back wages and reasonable attorney's fees. See Del. Code. Ann. Tit. 10 § 4515(c). ☞

Crime Victim Leave: Employers can't prohibit a crime victim from taking leave to respond to a subpoena, participate in trial preparation or attend trial proceedings as reasonably necessary to protect the victim's interests. See Del. Code Ann. Tit. 11 § 9409. ☞

District of Columbia: *Jury Service:* Employers can't discharge, threaten, intimidate, or coerce any employee who receives summons or serves on a jury or attends court as a prospective juror. For jury service of five days or less, petit or grand jurors employed full time by employers with 10+ employees are entitled to their usual compensation less the fee received for jury service. Violators are guilty of a criminal offense. Discharged employees may recover lost wages and other damages and seek reinstatement. See D.C. Code § 11-1913(a), (b) ☞ and D.C. Code § 15-718. ☞

Witness Leave: Employers may not threaten, discharge or otherwise coerce employees because they receive or respond to a summons to serve as a witness. See D.C. Code § 11-1913(a),(b) and (c).

Florida: *Jury Service:* Employees can't be discharged or threatened with discharge because of jury service. Employees may recover compensatory and punitive damages as well as attorney's fees. See Fla. Stat. § 40.271.

Witness and Crime Victim Leave: Employers may not discharge employees who need a leave to testify in response to a subpoena. See Fla. Stat. Ann. § 92.57.

Georgia: *Jury Service:* Employers may not discharge, discipline, threaten or otherwise punish employees because they're absent to attend a court proceeding in answer to a subpoena, summons for jury service or other court order. The law protecting employees serving on a jury doesn't protect employees charged with a crime; the employer may require an employee to give reasonable notice of the expected absence or delay in reporting to work. Employees may recover actual damages and reasonable attorney's fees. See Ga. Code Ann. § 34-1-3.

Witness and Crime Victim Leave: Employers may not discharge, discipline, or otherwise penalize employees who are absent to attend a judicial proceeding in response to a subpoena, summons for jury duty or other court order or process. Employers may require employees to provide "reasonable notice" to be eligible for leave. It's a criminal offense in Georgia to threaten or interfere with a witness with the intent to deter the witness from testifying freely. See Ga. Code Ann. § 34-1-3 and § 16-10-93.

Hawaii: *Jury Service:* No state law specifically grants employees leave for jury duty, but employers may not discharge or coerce employees for serving as jurors, responding to a summons or attending court for prospective jury service. Employees may bring a civil suit for lost wages and reinstatement. Continued compensation during jury service is only required for state employees. See Haw. Rev. Stat. § 612-25.

Witness and Crime Victim Leave: Employers may not discharge or coerce employees for serving as a witness, responding to a subpoena or participating in a court proceeding as a victim of a crime. See Haw. Rev. Stat. § 621-10.5.

Idaho: *Jury Service:* Employers are prohibited from discharging an employee for taking jury service leave. Employers may be fined $300. Employees may bring a civil action for three times the amount of lost wages, reinstatement and attorney's fees. See Idaho Code § 2-218.

Witness Leave: There is no specific law governing witness leave.

Illinois: *Jury Service:* Employees must be given time off, and may not be discharged for "taking time off for jury service as long as the employee gave reasonable notice" (defined as providing a copy of the jury summons within 10 days of the date the summons was issued to their employer). Employers aren't required to pay the employee for time off to serve as a juror, but employees are entitled to insurance and other benefits of employment during jury service. Employers may not threaten, discharge, discipline or coerce employees called for jury service. Employees may bring a civil action for lost wages, benefits, reinstatement and attorney's fees. See 705 ILCS 305/4.1 and ILCS 310/10.1.

Witness Leave: Employees may not discharge, threaten or otherwise punish employees who are witnesses to a crime because of time lost resulting form being subpoenaed to appear at a criminal proceeding. State law also prohibits discrimination or harassment against individuals who attend, participate in, or prepare for criminal or civil court proceedings relating to domestic or sexual violence in which an employee is a victim and has requested leave. See 725 ILCS 5/115-18 and 820 ILCS 180/30.

Indiana: *Jury Service:* Employers may not knowingly discharge, threaten, or deprive an employee of employment opportunities who has been called for jury service. Violators are subject to imprisonment and a $1,000 fine. See Ind. Code § 35-44-3-10.

Witness and Crime Victim Leave: Employers may not discharge an employee for taking leave to respond to a subpoena. See Ind. Code § 35-44-3-11.1.

Iowa: *Jury Service:* Employers may not discharge or threaten an employee who receives a notice to report for jury service, serves as a juror or attends court for prospective juror service. Employees discharged in violation of the provision may bring a civil action for lost wages, reinstatement and attorney's fees. See Iowa Code § 607A.45.

Witness and Crime Victim Leave: Employers must permit victims to serve as a witness in criminal cases. Employees may recover attorneys' fees and court costs if an employer violates this law. See Iowa Code § 915.23.

Kansas: *Jury Service:* Employers may not discharge or threaten to discharge a "permanent" employee because of jury service. Employees may bring a civil action for lost wages, benefits, other actual damages, reinstatement and attorney's fees. See Kan. Stat. Ann. § 60-514.

Kentucky: *Jury Service:* Employers may not discharge, threaten or coerce employees because of jury service, responding to a summons or attending court as a prospective juror. See Ky. Rev. Stat. § 43.173.

Witness Leave: Employers may not discharge employees for taking time off to appear in any local, state or federal court or administrative hearing. Employees must give notice before taking time off and they must present documentation of their need to serve. See KRS § 337.415.

Louisiana: *Jury Service:* Employers are required to provide a one day leave of absence at full pay and without reduction of any benefits such as vacation or sick leave. Employers may not threaten or discharge or take any adverse action against employees for jury service. Employees may bring a civil action for lost wages, benefits, and reinstatement. Violators may be fined $100–$1,000. See La. Rev. Stat. Ch. 23 § 965.

Witness Leave: Leave isn't required, but employers are prohibited from discharging, discriminating, or retaliating against employees because they testify or furnish any information in any investigation or proceeding relative to the enforcement of any state labor laws. See La. Rev. Stat. Ann. Louisiana 23:964.

Maine: *Jury Service:* Employers can't deprive an employee of employment, or threaten or coerce an employee with respect to loss of employment due to jury service. Employers must maintain an employee's group health insurance coverage while the employee is absent for jury duty. Violators may be fined $500 and imprisoned. Employees may bring a civil action for lost wages, reinstatement, and attorney's fees. See Me. Rev. Stat. Ch. 14 § 1218.

Witness Leave: No law.

Crime Victim Leave: All employers must allow leave to victims of violence to prepare for and attend court proceedings, to receive medical treatment or to attend to the medical treatment of their child, parent, or spouse, or to obtain services to remedy a crisis caused by domestic violence. See 26 M.R.S.A. § 850.

Maryland: *Jury Service:* Employers can't discharge an employee solely because of time lost as a result of responding to a summons or attending court as a juror. Violators may be fined up to $1,000. See Md. Code Ann.,. Cts & Jud Proc. § 8-105 , and 8-401.

Witness and Crime Victim Leave: Employers can't discharge employees solely because they lose time while responding to a subpoena requiring service as a witness. See Md. Code Ann.,. Cts & Jud Proc. § 9-205.

Massachusetts: *Jury Service:* Retaliation is prohibited against employees because of jury service. Employers must pay for the first three days of jury service. No retaliation: Mass. Gen. L. c. 234A § 61 ; Payment: Mass. Gen. L. c 234A § 48. No discharge: Mass. Gen. L. c. 268 § 14A.

Witness and Crime Victim Leave: Crime victims or witnesses who notify their employer may not be discharged or penalized for serving as a witness, responding to a subpoena or attending court proceedings. See Mass. Gen. Laws. Ch. 258B § 3(1) and 268 § 14B.

Michigan: *Jury Service:* Employers can't discharge employees because they're called for jury duty. Employers also may not require employees serving on jury duty to work additional hours to make up for time lost during jury service. Violators may be held in contempt of court. See Mich. Comp. Laws 600.1348.

Witness and Crime Victim Leave: Employers may not discipline or discharge crime victims or a victim's representative for responding to a subpoena or attending a court proceeding at the request of a prosecuting attorney. See Mich. Comp. Laws § 780.762.

Minnesota: *Jury Service:* Employers are prohibited from threatening, coercing or discharging employees because of jury service. See M.S.A. § 593.50.

Witness Leave: Employers are prohibited from discharging, disciplining or threatening to discharge victims or witnesses because they've been subpoenaed or requested by a prosecutor to attend court. See M.S.A. § 611A.036.

Crime Victim Leave: Employers must give "reasonable" time off to employees to attend court proceedings if the employee, his or her spouse or next of kin was a victim of a "heinous crime." See M.S.A. § 611A.036.

Mississippi: *Jury Service:* It's unlawful to threaten or intimidate employees concerning jury service or attempt to persuade anyone to avoid jury service. Violators may be held in contempt of court. See Miss. Code Ann. § 13-5-23.

Witness and Crime Victim Leave: Employers must permit employees to respond to a subpoena or participate in reasonable preparations for a court proceeding. See Miss. Code Ann. §99-43-45.

Missouri: *Jury Service:* Employers may not discharge, discipline, threaten or subject an employee to any adverse action because of jury service. Discharged employees may bring a civil action for lost wages, other damages and reinstatement, and attorney's fees. See Mo. Rev. Stat. § 494.460(2).

Witness or Crime Victim Leave: Employers must permit a victim or an employee who is a member of the victim's family to respond to a subpoena or participate in preparation for a criminal proceeding. See Rev. Stat. Mo. § 595.209(1)(14).

Montana: *Jury Service:* No laws applicable to private employers.

Witness and Crime Victim Leave: Employers must permit victims or employees who are a member of a victim's family to participate in preparations for or attendance at a criminal proceeding.

Nebraska: *Jury Service:* Employers may not discharge, **reduce pay**, or retaliate against employees because of absence from work due to jury service. Employers may reduce wages by the amount paid by the court for jury service. See Neb. Rev. Stat. § 25-1640.

Witness Leave: No law.

Nevada: *Jury Service:* Employers can't discharge or threaten to discharge an employee for jury service. Discharged employees may bring a civil action against their employers for lost wages and benefits, reinstatement, up to $50,000 in punitive damages and attorney's fees. Employees must give their jury summons to their employer at least one day prior to the day their jury service is to start. See Nev. Rev. Stat. § 6.190.

Witness and Crime Victim Leave: Employees must be permitted to take leave to attend judicial or administrative proceedings in which they're a witness or have received a subpoena to appear as a witness. See Nev. Rev. Stat. § 50.070.

New Hampshire: *Jury Service:* Employers may not threaten, coerce or deprive an employee of employment because of jury service. Violators may be held in contempt of court. Discharged employees may bring a civil action for lost wages and reinstatement. See N.H. Rev. Stat. § 500-A:14.

Witness Leave: No law.

New Jersey: *Jury Service:* Employers must allow employees leave to serve on juries and can't discharge or otherwise discriminate against employees due to jury service. See N.J.S.A. § 2B 20-17.

Witness Leave: The NJ Conscientious Employee Protection Act protects employees from retaliation for testifying as a witness concerning any violation of law. See N.J.S.A. § 34:19-3.

New Mexico: *Jury Service:* Employers may not discharge, threaten, or coerce employees due to jury service. Employers can't require employees to use accrued paid leave during jury service. See N.M. Stat. § 38-5-18, § 38-5-19.

Witness Leave: No law.

New York: *Jury Service:* Employees who notify their employer in advance can't be fired or otherwise penalized for jury service. Employers with 10 or more employees must pay the first $40 of an employee's daily wages for the first three days of jury service. See N.Y. Jud. Law § 519.

Witness Leave: Employees can't be discharged for being witnesses in criminal matters if the employee is a victim or acting pursuant to a subpoena. Employers may pay employees during witness leave and may request verification of an employee's need for time off for service as a witness. See N.Y. Penal Code § 215.14.

North Carolina: *Jury Service:* Employers can't discharge or demote employees because of their jury service. Violators must reinstate employees to their former positions and may be liable for other damages. See N.C. Gen. Stat. § 9-32.

Witness Leave: No specific law, however, discharge of an employee for serving as a witness would likely be considered a violation of public policy.

North Dakota: *Jury Service:* Employers can't discharge, threaten or coerce employees due to jury service. Violators will be fined $500 and/or jailed up to 30 days. Employees who are discharged may bring a civil action for reinstatement, up to 6 weeks' back pay and attorney's fees. See N.D. Cent. Code § 27-09.1-17.

Witness or Crime Victim Leave: Employers may not retaliate or discharge employees who take leave to give testimony pursuant to a subpoena. See N.D. Cent. Code. § 27-09.1-17.

Ohio: *Jury Service:* Employers can't discharge or threaten to discharge an employee due to jury service if the employee gives the employer reasonable notice before beginning jury duty. Employers may not require or request employees to use accrued paid leave. Violators will be held in contempt of court. See Ohio Rev. Code § 2313.18.

Witness and Crime Victim Leave: Employers must grant leave and may not take adverse action against employees because they serve as a witness in criminal, grand jury, delinquency hearings or because they assist prosecutors in preparing criminal cases. See Ohio Rev. Code §§ 2151.121.1, 2930.18, 2939.12.1, and 2945.451.

Oklahoma: *Jury Service:* Employers can't discharge employees for serving on a jury. Employees may elect to use accrued paid leave, but employers may not require them to do so. Violations are misdemeanors, punishable by fines up to $5,000. Discharged employees may bring a civil action for actual damages, mental anguish and lost earnings (past and future). See Okla. Stat. Ch. 38, §34, 35.

Witness Leave: No law

Oregon: *Jury Service:* Employers must grant leave and can't discharge or intimidate employees due to jury service. If the employee is exempt, the employer has to pay the entire week's salary if the employee performs any work during the week. Discharged employees may bring a civil action for reinstatement and back pay. Violators are subject to fines up to $500. See Ore. Rev. Stat. § 10.090.

Witness Leave: Employers may not penalize or retaliate against employees who are subpoenaed to testify at court proceedings. *Dunwoody v. Handskill Corp.* See 185 Or. App. 605, 60 P 3d 1135 (Or. App. 2003).

Pennsylvania: *Jury Service:* Employers can't discharge or deprive an employee of any seniority or fringe benefits due to jury service. Employers in a "service industry" with fewer than 15 employees are exempt. Discharged employees can bring a civil action for back wages, benefits, reinstatement and attorney's fees. See Pa. Consol. Stat. Ch 42. § 4563.1.

Crime Victim Leave: Employers are prohibited from discharging or penalizing employees who are crime victims or family members of crime victims who take leave to be witnesses. See 18 Pa. Code § Ch 4957.

Rhode Island: *Jury Service:* Employers can't discharge or otherwise discriminate against employees due to jury service. Employees can't suffer any loss of position, wage increases, promotion opportunities, or any other compensation related benefit due to jury service. Violators are guilty of a misdemeanor and may be sued for an injunction and damages. See R.I. Gen. Laws § 9-9-28.

Crime Victim Leave: Employees who need to go to court for proceedings pertaining to the crime or to seek protective orders may not be discharged or retaliated against. See R.I. Gen. Laws § 12-28-10, § 12-28-13.

South Carolina: *Jury Service:* Employers may not discharge or demote an employee for jury service or for complying with a subpoena. Discharged employees may bring a civil action for one year's wages or the annual difference in salary before and after demotion. See S.C. Code Ann. § 41-1-70.

Witness Leave: Employers may not discharge or demote an employee for complying with a subpoena. See S.C. Code Ann. § 41-1-70.

South Dakota: *Jury Service:* Employers can't suspend, or discharge an employee due to jury service. Violations are misdemeanors. Employees returning to work after jury service are entitled to reinstatement at the same rate of pay, same job, same status and seniority. Temporary leaves of absence for jury service may be with or without pay at the employer's discretion. See S.D. Codified laws §§ 16-13-41.1, 2.

Witness Leave: The Supreme Court of South Dakota has held that it's a violation of public policy to terminate an employee who responds to a subpoena to attend a court proceeding. See *Niesent v. Homestake Mining Co.*, 505 NW 2d 781 (S.D. 1993).

Tennessee: *Jury Service:* Employers with five or more employees must excuse employees for jury service for as long as their service is required, as long as the employee shows the jury summons to their supervisor the first day after receiving it. To be entitled to time off, the employee's responsibility for jury service must exceed three hours for each day of leave requested. Leave may be paid, minus payment for serving as a juror, but employers aren't required to pay employees for more time than was actually spent serving on the jury and traveling to serve on the jury. It's unlawful to discharge or discriminate against an employee due to jury service if the employee has provided the required notice. The state law doesn't apply to employees who have been on their job less than six months. See Tenn. Code §§ 22-4-108.

Witness Leave: No law.

Texas: *Jury Service:* Employers may not discharge a "permanent" employee due to jury service. Employees must be returned to their job after jury service "unless the employer's circumstances have so changed as to make re-employment impossible or unreasonable." Temporary workers aren't protected. Employees must give actual notice of intent to return to work as soon as practical after release from jury service. Employees may not be required to use accrued leave. See Tex. Code Ann. § 22-4-108.

Witness Leave: Employers may not discharge, discipline or penalize employees who comply with a valid subpoena to appear in a civil or criminal or any other proceeding. Employees who are discharged may seek reinstatement. See Labor Code § 52.051.

Utah: *Jury Service:* Employers can't discharge, coerce, or threaten to discharge an employee because of jury service. Employers aren't permitted to require employees to use regular leave time for jury service. Violators are guilty of criminal contempt and can be fined $500 and/or imprisoned up to 6 months. Discharged employees may bring a civil action for reinstatement, lost wages, and reasonable attorney's fees. See Utah Code § 78-4-21.

Witness and Crime Victim Leave: Employers may not discharge or otherwise coerce employees who attend depositions or hearings in response to a subpoena. See Utah Code § 78-11-26.

Vermont: *Jury Service:* Employers can't discharge or penalize employees called for jury service or to serve as a witness before any tribunal under oath. Employees must be permitted to accumulate employee benefits but don't have to be compensated. Violators may be fined $200. See Vt. Stat. Ch. 21 § 499(a).

Witness and Crime Victim Leave: Employers can't discharge, or penalize employees in any manner regarding benefits as a result of absences due to serving as a witness. The protection extends to crime victims, a victim's family member or a victim's representative. See 21 Vt. Stat. Ann. § 499(b). Also 13 Vt. Stat. Ann. § 5313.

Virginia: *Jury Service:* Employers can't discharge or adversely affect any employee receiving a summons or serving as a juror. Employees may not be forced to use sick or vacation time. Employees who appear for four or more hours in court can't be required to work after 5 pm. Employees must give employers reasonable notice of summons. See Va. Code § 18,2-465.1.

Witness and Crime Victim Leave: Employees who are summoned or subpoenaed to appear in court can't be discharged or have any adverse action taken against them and can't be required to use sick or vacation time. Defendants in criminal cases aren't entitled to leave and aren't protected. Employees must give employer reasonable notice. See Va. Code 18.2-465.1.

Washington: *Jury Service:* Employers must give sufficient leaves of absence to employees called for jury service and can't discharge, threaten, coerce, harass or deny promotions due to jury service. Employer may deduct any pay provided for jury service. Intentional violations will subject the employer to criminal charges. Discharged employees may bring a civil action for reinstatement, damages and reasonable attorney's fees. See Wash. Rev. Code § 2.36.165 and Washington Admin Code § 356-18-120.

Witness Leave: No law.

West Virginia: *Jury Service:* Employers can't discharge, threaten, or **reduce the pay** of an employee due to jury service. Employees don't have to be paid for time they're actually absent for jury service. The court can order reinstatement, back pay and attorney's fees. Violators are guilty of civil contempt and subject to fines $100–$1,000 and/or 60 days in jail. See W. Va. Code Sections 53-3-1, 61-5-25a.

Witness Leave: No law.

Wisconsin: *Jury Service:* Employers must grant leave for jury service for the duration of the employee's jury service. Employers must consider the time spent on jury service for purposes of seniority and pay advancement. Employers may not use the employee's absence for jury service as a basis for discharge or discipline. Discharged employees may bring an action for back pay and employer may be fined $200. See Wis. Stat. Ann. § 756.255.

Witness Leave: Employers may not discharge and must allow employees who have been subpoenaed leave to testify in an action or proceeding pertaining to a crime.

Crime Victim Leave: Employees subpoenaed to testify as a result of a crime in which they were a victim, or involving an incident that occurred during the course of their work, **must be paid for the time lost from work**. Employees must notify their employers the first business day after receiving the summons/subpoena. The employer may not decrease or withhold pay due to time lost resulting from compliance with the subpoena. See Wis. Stat. §103.87.

Wyoming: *Jury Service:* Employers can't discharge, threaten to discharge, intimidate, or coerce employees due to jury service. Employees must be reinstated without loss of seniority or benefits. Courts can grant "appropriate relief" including reinstatement. Employees may bring a civil action for reinstatement, punitive damages, costs and attorney's fees. See Wyo. Stat. § 1-11-401.

Witness and Crime Victim Leave: Victims or witnesses responding to a subpoena can't suffer any change in terms of employment solely as a result of responding to a subpoena. See Wyo. Sta. §1-40-209.

Voting Leave

Even though most polls are open before and after traditional working hours, care should be taken to accommodate employees whose working hours make it difficult to get to the polls. A little more than half the states require employers to give employees time off to vote, with some states specifying that the voting leave must be paid. Discharging an employee who refused to vote would be a violation of public policy in many states. A few states require employers to post a notice at the workplace explaining employees' rights to time off to vote. In the absence of applicable voting leave laws, employers aren't required to give employees paid time off to vote. However, if your state has a *time off to vote* statute, you should consider a written policy to ensure compliance. The policy should address:

❏ how much time off will be given (two hours is the norm, but the policy could provide that two hours is the maximum and that employees shouldn't take more time off than is needed to cast their vote);

❏ whether the time off is paid;

❏ whether the time off policy applies for all elections, or only national/state elections;

❏ whether employees are required to give the nonprofit notice of the need for time off in advance; and

❏ whether the time off is confined to a certain time of day, such as: "Time off to vote will be provided to employees on voting days at the (beginning)/(end) of the workday."

Time Off to Vote Laws[18]

The state laws noted here are subject to constant review and revision in state legislatures. This summary should therefore be used for reference purposes, rather than as a definitive guide.

The following states have laws addressing voting leave:

Alaska: Employees who don't have two consecutive hours of nonwork time while polls are open may take enough paid leave to vote in state elections. See Alaska Stat. 15.15.100.

Arizona: Employers are required to provide time off if there are fewer than three consecutive hours between when the polls open/close and the beginning/end of the employee's workday. The time off must be paid if the employee would otherwise be working. Employees must provide advance notice to their employer of the need for time off in order to be protected by the state law. Arizona's law applies to primary and general elections. See Ariz. Rev. Stat. § 16-402.

Arkansas: Employers must schedule the work hours of employees on election days to provide employees with sufficient time off to vote. The law applies to all elections. See Ark. Code Annot. § 7-1-102.

California: Employees are entitled to take up to two hours without loss of pay to vote if they don't otherwise have sufficient time outside of working hours. Employers may provide that the time off is at the end of the workday and must be requested in advance. Employers must post a conspicuous notice of employees' right to take time off not less than 10 days prior to the election. See Cal. Elec. Code §§ 14000 and 14001.

Colorado: Employees are entitled to take up to two hours without loss of pay to vote during the period the polls are open. The law isn't applicable to employees who have sufficient time outside of working hours to vote. See Co. Rev. Stat. § 1-7-102 and 31-10-603.

Florida: Employers are prohibited from discharging or threatening employees who vote in state or local elections or who refuse to vote. Employees are required to provide their employer with reasonable notice of their need for time off to vote. See Florida Stat. Ann. §104.081.

Georgia: Employers are required to grant employees up to two hours to vote if the employee is otherwise unable to vote during nonworking time. Employers may specify the hours an employee may use. The time off doesn't have to be paid. Employees must provide advance notice to their employer of the need to take time off to vote. See O. C. G. A. § 21-2-404.

Hawaii: Employees are entitled to time off to vote up to two hours (excluding lunch or rest periods) between the opening and closing of the polls if they otherwise are unable to vote during nonworking hours. See Hawaii Rev. Stat. § 11-95.

Idaho: Employers aren't required to grant time off to employees to vote, but it's unlawful to threaten discharge to influence an employee's vote. See Idaho Code §18-2319.

Illinois: Employers must provide up to two hours off for an employee to vote if the employee requests the time off in advance. Employers may specify the hours when the employee may be absent. Employees are prohibited from imposing any penalty on employees who take time off to vote. See 10 ILCS 5/7-42 and 10 ILCS 5/15-15.

Iowa: Employers must provide employees with time off to vote with no pay deduction if the employee doesn't have three consecutive hours off work while the polls are open. Employers may require that employees submit a request in writing in advance and the employer may specify the hours when the employee may be absent. See Iowa Code § 49-109.

Kansas: Employers must provide employees with up to two hours to vote with no pay deduction. Employers may specify the hours when the employee may be absent. Employers may not require the employee to use any of his or her regular meal period. See Kansas Stat. Ann. § 25-418.

Kentucky: Employers must provide employees with at least four hours to either vote or cast an absentee ballot. Employees who are election officers must be given the entire day off to attend training or to serve as an election officer. Employees must request time off in advance and employers may specify the hours when the employee may be absent. Employees may not be penalized from taking reasonable time off to vote unless they fail to vote under circumstances that didn't prevent them from voting. State law doesn't specify whether the time off is paid or unpaid. See Ky. Rev. Stat. §§ 118.035 ; Ky. Const. §148.

Maryland: Employers must give employees up to two hours off if the employee is otherwise unable to vote during nonworking hours. The law applies to all elections. No wage deduction is permitted if employee demonstrates proof of voting. See Md. Code Elect. Law §10-315.

18 If a state isn't listed, there is no specific provision on time off to vote.

Massachusetts: The voting leave law in Massachusetts only applies to mercantile, manufacturing and mechanical workplaces. See Mass. Gen. L. c. 149 § 178.

Michigan: No law specifies that an employer must provide time off for employees to vote, but it's a misdemeanor to threaten to discharge or discharge an employee "for the purpose of influencing" the employee's vote. See MCL 168.931.

Minnesota: Employees may be absent in the morning to vote. Employees must also be given time off to serve as election judges, although their pay may be reduced by the amount they receive for serving as an election judge. Employees must provide a certificate demonstrating the hours to be served and their compensation for serving as an election judge and must provide their employer with 20 days notice of the need for time off. See M. Stat. Ann. § 204C.04 ; (election judge) M. Stat. Ann. § 204B.19.5.

Missouri: Employees must be given three consecutive hours off, unless the polls are open three consecutive hours outside of working hours. Employers may require that employees provide advance notice of the need for time off and may specify the hours that the employee may be absent. The law applies to all elections. No wage deductions provided employees actually vote. See Rev. Stat. Mo. § 115.639.

Nebraska: Employers must give employees up to two hours off if the employee doesn't have two hours of continuous off-duty time while the polls are open. The time off must be with pay if the employee provided advance notice of the need for time off. Employers may specify the hours when the employee may be absent. See Neb. Rev. Stat. § 32-922.

Nevada: Employers must provide time off if it's impractical for the employee to vote during nonworking hours. "Sufficient time" is one hour if polls are up to two miles from place of employment, and two hours for two to 10 miles; and three hours for over 10 miles. The law applies to all elections. The employee must provide advance notice of the need for leave. Wage deductions prohibited. Nev. Rev. Stat. 293.463.

New Mexico: Employers should give employees two hours off unless the employee's workday begins more than two hours after polls open or ends more than three hours before the polls close. Employers must pay hourly employees for time off to vote. The law applies to all elections, including elections of Indian nations, tribes or pueblos. Employers may specify the hours when the employee may be absent. See New Mexico Stat. Ann. § 1-12-42.

New York: Employers must provide up to two hours of paid leave for employees to vote unless the employee has four consecutive hours outside of work time when the polls are open. Employees are required to notify their employer no less than two and no more than 10 working day before an election of their need for time off. Employers must post the state law's requirements. The time off law applies only to primaries, and local elections. The employer can specify that the time off must be either at the beginning or end of the work day. See N.Y. Election Law §§ 3-110 and 17-118.

North Dakota: State law encourages employers to provide time off to vote if they can't vote during nonworking time, but such policies aren't required. See N.D.C.C. § 16.1-01-02.1.

Ohio: Employers may not interfere with, discriminate, or retaliate against employees for taking a reasonable amount of time off to vote, but the time off doesn't have to be paid. See Ohio Rev. Code §§ 3599.05.

Oklahoma: Employers must give employees up to two paid hours off to vote. Wages can't be docked if the employee shows proof of voting. The law isn't applicable to employees who begin work three hours or more after the polls open or end work three hours before polls close. The day before the election employees must notify employers of their request to take time off. The law applies to all, except school board, elections. See Okla. Stat. Title 26 § 7-101.

South Dakota: Employers must give employees time off only if the employee doesn't have two consecutive nonworking hours to vote. The law applies to all elections. Wage deductions prohibited. Employers may specify the hours the employee can be absent from work. See SDCL 12-3-5.

Tennessee: Employers must give employees up to three hours off unless the employee has three consecutive nonworking hours in which to vote. Employees must provide advance notice before noon the day before the election. The employer may specify the hours that the employee may be absent. The law applies to state, county, and local elections and primaries. It's illegal for employees to accept wages for time off to vote if they don't vote. See Tenn. Code Annot. § 2-1-106.

Texas: Employers are prohibited from knowingly refusing to permit an employee leave to vote if the employee doesn't have two consecutive nonworking hours during which to vote; employers are also prohibited from subjecting an employee or threatening to subject employees to a penalty for taking time to vote. The law applies to all elections. Wage deductions aren't permitted. See Election Code § 276.004.

Utah: Employers must give employees two hours off to vote unless the employee has at least three hours during nonworking hours to vote. No wage deductions may be made except hourly paid employees. The employee must request the time off in advance. Employers may specify the hours the employee is absent from work. The law applies to general elections. See Utah Code § 20A-3-103.

Virginia: There is no law concerning time off to vote but employers must provide unpaid leave for an employee to serve as an "officer of election." Such employees may not be discharged or retaliated against for taking time off as needed to serve provided that the employee gives reasonable notice of the need for time off. See Va. Code. 24.2-118.1. ✎

Washington: Employers must give employees two hours off unless the employee has two consecutive nonworking hours (not including meal breaks). The law applies to general, primary, and special elections. Wage deductions prohibited. See Wash. Rev. Code § 49.28.120. ✎

West Virginia: Employers must give employees up to three hours of paid leave and may not reduce wages unless the employee has three or more hours off between the opening/closing of the polls and the beginning/end of work. Employees must request time off in writing at least three days before the election. The law applies to all elections. See W. Va. Code § 3-1-42. ✎

Wisconsin: Employers must give employees three hours off to vote if they request the time off in advance, but the employer doesn't have to pay the employee for the time off. Employers may specify the hours the employee may be absent from work. The law applies to all elections. See Wis. Stat. § 6.76. ✎

Wyoming: Employees are entitled to an hour (other than a meal period) off provided they vote. The employer may specify the time the employee is absent from work. The law applies to general and primary elections, or special election to fill a vacancy in Congress. No wage deduction provided employee shows proof of voting. See Wyo Stat. § 22-2-111. ✎

Bereavement Leave

Recognizing that the death of a family member triggers family obligations and may make employees too grief-stricken to work, most nonprofits provide paid time off in the event of the death of an immediate family member of an employee. Since this is an emotional time in an employee's life, it's best to have a clearly written policy in advance, ready and waiting so that the nonprofit doesn't have to invent the policy as the employee is packing bags to attend a funeral.

There are no state laws that govern how many days' bereavement leave an employer must give to employees or whether the time off is paid or not. Employers generally offer a few days of paid leave (three days is usual) but in many cases the employee may be the primary executor of an estate and require more days off than the policy permits, so permitting employees to use vacation leave or even sick leave in conjunction with bereavement leave can be a tremendous help.

Bereavement Leave Policy Tips

Policies generally address whether the leave is paid or unpaid, the definition of *family member*, the number of days of leave, and whether vacation or other accrued time off may be used to extend bereavement leave. If the policy doesn't define *family member*, employees legitimately may expect leave for persons they consider to be family members, such as domestic partners and even close family friends who have served as surrogate family members. When the policy is unclear, it generally does more harm than good to deny leave, but care should be taken to make the same leave available to all similarly situated employees, to avoid claims of favoritism or discrimination.

Military Leave

Federal law prohibits discrimination against employees on the basis of military status. The federal Uniformed Services Employment and Reemployment Rights Act (USERRA) 38 U.S.C. Section 4301 ✎ prohibits workplace discrimination against individuals because of their service in the Armed Forces, the Reserves, the National Guard or other uniformed services. USERRA also requires that all employers provide an unpaid leave of absence to employees who are members of, or applying to be members of the military. To qualify for military leave under USERRA, the employee must provide advance notice to his or her employer. An overview of USERRA ✎ may be found on the U.S. Department of Labor's Web site.

USERRA generally requires all employers to grant up to five years of unpaid leave to employees who are members of, or apply for membership in, the armed forces. In 2006 the provisions of USERRA were extended to cover first responders for Homeland Security disasters. Employers must continue benefits, such as health insurance, at the employee's expense. To qualify for reinstatement, the employee must reapply for employment within the deadlines specified in USERRA.

USERRA requires that the employer promote the employee upon reinstatement if a promotion would have occurred had the employee not been on leave, and must reinstate the employee to an equivalent position or one that most closely approximates the employee's original job. USERRA also requires that employees be given credit for any months and hours of service the employee would have been employed but for his or her military service when determining eligibility for FMLA leave. A special memo was recently issued by the DOL providing guidance for employers on this topic: www.dol.gov/esa/whd/fmla/userra.htm.

Further protection is offered for employees returning from active duty because they may not be discharged from employment *for one year following their return to work*. Reservists who are ordered to active duty for training for not less than 12 consecutive months may not be discharged without cause for six months following their return.

State Military Leave Laws

State military leave laws generally mirror USERRA's requirements, including the anti-discrimination and retaliation provisions, but many expand or supplement an employer's obligations considerably. Notably, the Illinois Family Military Leave Act, provides leave for family members of servicemen during the deployment period. In states that don't have a specific military leave law, but where military status is a protected category for employment discrimination purposes, it could be argued that it's a discriminatory practice to deny unpaid leave to an employee seeking a reasonable period of leave to participate in military service. Many state laws require employers to offer short-term military leave *with full pay* (as few as 17 days in some states) but most merely require that the employer provide an unpaid leave with re-employment rights. Some laws specifically require the employer to maintain the employee's benefits during the leave. A common paid leave period is two weeks, which is the duration of most reservists' training. Benefits should be continued for employees during short leaves because employees returning from leave must be offered at least the same benefits they enjoyed when they left. Employers should treat benefits during the military leave the same way they treat benefits during other types of employer-granted leave.

Military Leave Policy Tips

Policies generally:

❏ define which employees are eligible;

❏ define the amount of leave permitted;

❏ define whether benefits and salary continues through leave;

❏ define reinstatement rights and the time within which the employee must apply for reinstatement;

❏ address the employer's obligation to offer an appropriate substitute position if the employee isn't able to conduct his or her previous job;

❏ define the employee's obligation to notify the employer about the need for military leave; and

❏ define whether employees are required to show their military orders or that the employee satisfactorily completed service.

State Military Leave Laws[19]

The state laws noted here are subject to constant review and revision in state legislatures. This summary should therefore be used for reference purposes, rather than as a definitive guide.

In many cases the federal USERRA provides greater rights than individual state laws addressing military leave. Employers should follow whichever law, state or federal, provides the most protection to the employee.

California: California law broadly prohibits discrimination or any adverse employment actions, such as failure to promote, against members of the armed forces, which includes the California National Guard. The California military leave statute is more generous than USERRA, because it provides that an employee returning from military leave of any length is protected from termination except for "cause" for one year. See Cal. Mil. & Vet. Code § 394.

Georgia: Employers must grant up to six months leave during any four-year period for employees to attend any service school. See O.C.G.A. §§ 38-2-279.

Hawaii: Employers are required to provide employees who are members of the National Guard leave while they're engaged in the performance of ordered service and while going to and returning from service. The leave doesn't have to be paid. Upon return, the employee must be reinstated, if still qualified, to the same position or a position of like seniority, status and pay. See Hawaii Rev. Stat. 121-43.

Illinois: Employees and new hires who have enlisted in the U.S. Armed Forces or state militia training or who are ordered to active duty must be granted a leave of absence. Those who receive an honorable discharge or have evidence of satisfactory completion of service are entitled to be restored to the same or an equivalent position unless reinstatement is impossible because of the employer's

---

19 If a state isn't listed, there is no specific provision on military leave.

changed circumstances. Employees must reapply within 90 days of discharge or within one year after hospitalization following military discharge. See 330 ILCS 60/1 et seq. ; 20 ILCS 1805.

Additionally, employers with 50+ employees are required to grant spouses and parents of military personnel up to 30 days' unpaid leave during the time that federal or state deployment orders are in effect. Employees with between 15-50 employees must provide up to 15 days of unpaid military leave. See Illinois Family Military Leave Act (2005), 820 ILCS 151/1.

Indiana: Employers must provide employees who are members of the Indiana National Guard, or retired naval, air, or ground forces of the U.S. military, leave equal to the number of days that the member is called to active duty. The military leave is in addition to the employee's vacation leave. See I.C. § 10-16-7-1.

Iowa: Employers must provide unpaid leave to members of the National Guard or reserves to perform active duty or training. Employers are required to restore the employee to the employee's former or to a similar position. The leave must not impact the employee's vacation, sick leave, or other benefits. Temporary employees aren't protected by the law. See Iowa Code § 29A-43.

Kansas: Employers must provide employees called to active duty in the state's armed forces (National Guard, Air National Guard) temporary leave provided that the employee gives advance notice. While on leave employees are eligible for any benefits that the employer provides to other employees on leaves of absence. Employees must be restored to their former positions with no lost of status, benefits, or seniority provided they report within 72 hours from their release from military service. Employees are protected from discharge for one year from re-employment. See Kansas Stat. Annot. 48-517.

Kentucky: Employers must provide employees who are members of the National Guard unpaid leave to perform active duty or training. Employees must be returned to their former jobs with the same seniority, status, pay and other rights, as if they hadn't been on leave. Kentucky law prohibits discrimination on the basis of military status. See Ky. Stat. Rev. §§ 38.238, 38.250, 38,460. 38.990.

Louisiana: The Louisiana Military Service Relief Act is parallel to the USERRA, however, it provides that reinstated employees can't be discharged from work without cause for one year after reinstatement. See La. Rev. Stat. Ann. § 29:38 et seq.

Maine: Employers must provide leave for employees who are members of the National Guard or reserves. On return, employers must reinstate employees if they're still qualified to perform the duties of their former positions or to a position with the same salary, seniority, status and other benefits. Employers must permit employees on military leave to continue participating in health insurance plans at the employee's expense. See 26 M.R.S.A. § 811(2) and (3).

Maryland: Maryland has adopted the USERRA as state law applicable to members of the Maryland Army National Guard and Maryland Air National Guard, when ordered to military duty, regardless of the length of service. See Md. Code Ann. Publ. Safety § 13-701.

Massachusetts: Employers must provide leave for reserve military training for up to 17 days per calendar year. Employers are required to reinstate the employee to the same or a similar position with the same status, pay, and seniority and other benefits. The leave can be paid or unpaid according to the employer's policy. See Mass. Gen. L. c. 149 §§ 52A.

Michigan: Employers must provide leave to employees for military service and must reinstate employees without loss of pay, status, or seniority, if the employee applies within 15 days following discharge from military service. Employees aren't eligible for reinstatement if the have been in the service for 5+ years (with several exceptions noted in the law). See MCL 32.274. et seq.

Minnesota: Employers are prohibited from hindering or preventing any person from performing military service by threatening discharge. See M.S.A. §192.34.

Mississippi: Employers may not deprive any former U.S. armed services member or current reserve member of employment or discriminate in any condition based on military leave. Re-employment is required for employees who complete their duty or training a long as they're still qualified, and were discharged or released under honorable conditions. See Miss. Code Ann. §§ 33-1-15 and 33-1-19.

Montana: The Montana Military Service Employment Rights Act (2005) provides that any person ordered to federally funded military duty is entitled to all the protections under federal law (USERRA). The act also prohibits employers from denying employment, re-employment, reinstatement, or any other employment benefits to a person because of military status, or potential membership in the state militia. See Mont. Code Ann. § 10-1-101.

New Jersey: Employers must provide leave for military duty and must reinstate employees who reapply within 90 days from release from military service, regardless of the amount of time of the military service, unless the employer's circumstances have changed making it unreasonable to do so. Full-time employees who enter temporary military service of up to three months must be reinstated if they apply for re-employment within 10 days of release from their military service; reinstatement includes restoration of all seniority and benefits as if the employee hadn't been on leave. Employees may only be discharged for "cause" for up to one year after re-employment.

New Mexico: Employees, other than temporary workers, who leave their jobs to enter the U.S. Armed Forces, National Guard or any organized reserve, are entitled to reinstatement if they serve on active duty and are discharged or released from active duty honorably. Employees must make an application for re-employment within 90 days of release. Employers must restore employees to the positions previously held, or to positions with like seniority, status, and pay unless the employer's circumstances have so changed as to make it impossible or unreasonable to do so. Employees on leave are entitled to participate in insurance and other benefits as if they weren't on leave, and may not be discharged without cause for one year after re-employment. See New Mexico Stat. Ann. § 28-15-1et seq.

New York: Employers are prohibited from discharging employees for taking military leave. Employees (other than temporary positions) on active duty must be re-employed as long as they received a certificate of completion of military service and the employee is still qualified to perform the job and applied for re-employment within 90 days of the end of service. Employees taking leave for drill or annual training or instruction must be re-employed if they apply for re-employment within 10 days of the end of service, and if on leave for initial or full-time training, within 60 days. Leave doesn't have to be paid. See N.Y. Military Law §§ 317 and 318.

Ohio: Ohio law provides merely that: "The determination of reinstatement and re-employment rights of …permanent private employees in the uniformed services must be made in accordance with the federal Uniformed Services Employment and Reemployment Rights Act of 1994," with the addition that criminal punishment is possible for violations. Ohio extends its protections to the Ohio National Guard. See Ohio Rev. Code §§ 5903.01.

Oklahoma: The state has adopted the USERRA as state law and specifically made it applicable to the Oklahoma National Guard. See Okla. Stat. Title 44 § 71, 208.

Oregon: Employers must provide leave to employees called to active duty with the Oregon National Guard or other state militia, including the militia of other states. See ORS 399.230.

Rhode Island: The Employment Rights of Members of Armed Forces is parallel to the USERRA but also extends rights to members of the National Guard in Rhode Island. If an employee misses work because of National Guard training activities, the time missed can't affect vacation leave, sick leave of eligibility for bonuses or other benefits. See R.I. Gen. Laws §§ 30-11-2 to 30-11-6, 30-21-1 et seq.

Texas: Employers must provide leave to employees who are members of the state military forces when they're called to authorized training or duty and must return the employees to the same employment without loss of accrued time, or any benefits of employment, unless the employer's circumstances have changed and re-employment is impossible or unreasonable. Employers may require written notice of the employee's intent to return to work but may not delay re-employment by demanding documentation that isn't readily available at the time the notice is given. See Government Code § 431.006(a)(b).

Utah: Employers must provide members of the U.S. Military reserves to up to five years if they're called to active duty or to training. After release, employees are entitled to return to work with the same seniority, status, pay and vacation they would have had if they hadn't been on leave. See Utah Code § 39-1-36.

Vermont: Employers must provide reserve or National Guard members with at least 15 days leave within one calendar year, with or without pay, for active duty or military training unless their position with the employer was temporary. Leave is without loss of seniority, status, pay or benefits. Employees who provide 30 days notice to their employer of the date of their departure and intended return to work are required to be re-employed, if qualified. Reinstatement must be to the same or a similar position with the same status, pay and benefits. See 21 Vt. Stat. Annot. § 491.

Virginia: Employers are required to provide leave to members of the National Guard and other state forces with or without pay, when ordered to active duty. Employees may not be forced to exhaust vacation leave or other accrued benefits.

Washington: Washington residents who voluntarily leave employment to enter active duty or training in the Washington National Guard or the U.S. armed forces, (or leave employment to determine physical fitness qualifications for such service) must be re-employed promptly upon discharge from the service if they provide timely notice to the employer and as long as the employer's circumstances haven't so changed as to make it impossible, unreasonable, or against public interest to do so. Employees must receive an honorable discharge or other proof of satisfactory completion of their service and reapply to their employer within 90 days of their date of separation or release from training or service. See Wash. Rev. Code § 73.16.035.

Wisconsin: Wisconsin's Fair Employment Act prohibits discrimination against individuals on the basis of their membership in the National Guard, state defense forces or any reserve component of the United States or Wisconsin. See Wis. Stat. § 45.50.

In the next section, Chapter 7, we examine an employer's obligation to treat employers fairly in the disciplinary process and risk management strategies to avoid legal liability as a result of terminating an employee.

Chapter 7 Discipline and Termination

The Fundamental Fairness Formula

Most employees in the nonprofit sector have an altruistic outlook and expect their employer to share it. This same outlook can cause a nonprofit employee to call a lawyer when the person perceives that the nonprofit has failed to follow the law, or has treated him or her unfairly. The expectation of fairness may be higher in the nonprofit sector than in the for-profit sector, where employees often take for granted that their employers are more focused on the bottom line than on the needs of employees. In contrast, employees of nonprofits are used to mission-based organizations, which exist to benefit the public good and not to line the pockets of shareholders or executives. Consequently, employees at nonprofits expect to be *taken care of* by their employers, just as their employers takes care of those who benefit from their charitable missions. As a result, nonprofit employees have few qualms about holding their employers accountable for what they perceive to be unfair treatment.

Fairness, or lack of it, can make a big difference in a legal action. When an employer treats an employee unfairly, courts and juries tend to find some way to hold the employer responsible. However, if the employer can demonstrate, through documentation, that it had legitimate business reasons for its actions, and treated the employee fairly throughout, there is less likelihood that liability will result.

There is a very simple formula that every nonprofit should follow to ensure that employees are being treated fairly. We call this formula the Fundamental Fairness Formula. Adhering to this formula embodies the essence of "taking the high road" with respect to your employment practices. The formula should be used prior to taking any adverse employment action (termination, demotion, discipline, suspension, or a disciplinary salary free) towards an employee. The formula reduces the risk that an employee will find the nonprofit's actions unfair. Additionally, insurance carriers, judges and juries will find that if the formula has been followed, the nonprofit has treated employees fairly and acted legally.[20] The formula should be used by all nonprofits as a risk management strategy and by supervisors as a guide for documenting their disciplinary decisions.

What Is the Fundamental Fairness Formula?

The formula is five-step method to self-check that an employee is being treated fairly, whether at an initial stage of discipline or when termination is recommended for performance reasons. (The formula isn't appropriate in instances where conduct is so damaging that termination is warranted, or in the case of economically necessitated downsizing, or the elimination of a position for administrative reasons, all of which are discussed later in this section.)

In a nutshell, the formula consists of the following steps:

❏ Notice of performance expectations and consequences

❏ Performance counseling

❏ Opportunity to correct

❏ Consistency with internal policies and procedures

❏ Objective review by someone other than the decision-maker

1. **Notice of expectations and consequences**—The first step is to provide an employee with notice of the expectations surrounding the issue at hand, be it absenteeism, wearing unprofessional clothing, or making insensitive remarks to a co-worker. Promptly schedule a performance counseling session with the employee to express concerns about the employee's performance. The objective of the performance counseling session is to remind the employee about the

---

20 The Fundamental Fairness Formula will also demonstrate that the nonprofit hasn't discriminated illegally against an employee who was adversely affected by the nonprofit's actions. Cases interpreting an employer's obligations under Title VII requires an employer to demonstrate that its actions were based on legitimate business needs, rather than motivated by illegal discrimination. Following this formula helps fulfill the employer's burden of proof.

nonprofit's expectations and explain how the employee failed to meet these expectations. If the issue is addressed in the personnel policy manual, open it to the policy and go over the policy with the employee.

The second aspect of this step is to put the employee on notice of the consequences should the employee fail to meet the nonprofit's expectations in the future. The supervisor should explain in direct terms that if the employee doesn't improve his or her performance, or cease the conduct in question, the employee risks appropriate discipline, such as a salary freeze, suspension or termination. Notice of consequences is important, because it takes the element of surprise out of discipline. Nearly every experienced supervisor has worked with someone who was clueless about the seriousness of his or her deficiencies, and who never considered that failure to correct those deficiencies would subject him or her to dismissal. Make sure that the employee is *on notice* not only of the nonprofit's expectations and the employee's failure to meet those expectations, but also of the *consequences* of subsequent performance failings. It's sufficient to say: "If you don't correct this problem, your job will be at risk."

2. **Performance counseling**—The second step of the formula is the actual performance counseling session in which the notice occurs. In essence the notice given to the employee in a counseling session is the same as a written warning because subsequent to the meeting, the supervisor should document that the meeting occurred, and place the memorandum in the employee's file.

    A copy may be provided to the employee, or the employee may be told that a memo summarizing the session will be placed in her or his file.

    During the counseling session the supervisor's goals should be:

    ❑   to put the employee on notice of the nonprofit's expectations,

    ❑   to clarify how the employee's conduct or performance has fallen short of those expectations,

    ❑   to give the employee notice of the consequences should the employee continue to fail to meet the nonprofit's expectations, and

    ❑   to discuss with the employee what steps the employee should take, within what time frame, to meet the nonprofit's expectations.

    It's helpful for the supervisor to focus on what needs to be communicated to the employee by writing out ahead of time the goals of the performance counseling session, the points which the supervisor must make to communicate clearly that the employee hasn't met expectations (using specific examples), and what specific action steps will be required of the employee to bring his or her performance up to a level of satisfactory performance. The supervisor should determine ahead of time what an acceptable time frame would be for improvement. The supervisor's conference planning notes will make an effective outline to rely on when the supervisor meets with the employee.

    During the performance counseling session, the supervisor should take notes, summarizing the points made by both parties and the responses given. After the performance counseling session is over, the supervisor should turn those notes into a memorandum documenting that the performance counseling session occurred and what was covered. The employee should be asked to sign the memo, which should then be placed in the employee's file. As previously noted, a copy may also be given to the employee. The risk with this approach is that the memo may inadvertently be viewed by other staff, violating the employee's privacy expectations. If the employee wants to add something to the memo, he or she should be permitted to do so. If the employee refuses to sign the memo, the supervisor should simply make a note on the memo: "Shown to employee on (date). Employee refused to sign."

    If a counseled employee refuses to sign the memorandum, the supervisor should encourage the employee to add, in writing, anything else that she or he believes needs to be included in the memorandum to accurately memorialize the counseling session. Permitting the employee to do so is helpful for two reasons: first, having an opportunity to express disagreement diffuses some of the employee's anger and gives the employee a feeling of *due process*. Second, the employee's written statement can provide the employer with a window into the thinking of the employee, which can help the employer address the employee's concerns, if legitimate, and can provide a window into the thought process of a potential plaintiff. With the written statement in hand, the nonprofit can better anticipate what arguments the employee may make if the employee challenges any aspect of the disciplinary process.

3. **Opportunity to correct**—Giving the employee the opportunity to correct deficiencies is the third step of the Fundamental Fairness Formula. Judges and juries regard it as fundamentally unfair to discipline an employee when the employee has no idea that she or he isn't performing up to snuff. The general rule is that an employee should be

reminded about the expectations for performance and then given an opportunity to improve. If there is no improvement, the nonprofit has treated the employee fairly, because it has given the employee a second chance.

What constitutes a *reasonable time* to correct a deficiency will be different in every case. For some performance issues, such as using inappropriate language around clients or co-workers, immediate improvement is reasonable. The reasonable opportunity for improvement may simply be a warning: "Don't do it again. If you do, here are the consequences." In other cases, such as where an employee needs to improve a specific skill, it will be reasonable to give the employee more time to bring performance to a satisfactory level. Whatever the reasonable time period, the objective should be to put the employee on notice and give the employee a second chance, rather than summarily terminating him or her. This is an essential element of fundamental fairness. It's also a critical element in mounting a legal defense to the employer's subsequent action if it includes termination or discipline.

It's necessary to discuss with the employee the time period and what the employee must do during the improvement period to demonstrate satisfactory performance. The supervisor should consider this an opportunity to act more like a coach than a schoolteacher. Sometimes employee performance is lagging because the employee doesn't realize how critical certain job duties are in the overall scheme of services provided by the nonprofit. Sometimes the employee is simply not motivated because of reasons that aren't obvious to the supervisor. The counseling session is the opportunity to explore any obstacles to the employee's improved performance and to encourage the employee to take responsibility for his or her own success.

4. **Consistency with internal policies and procedures**—The fourth step of the formula is to check the nonprofit's own policies and procedures to make sure that the supervisor is following any progressive disciplinary steps described in the nonprofit's policy handbook. Such policies are in place to promote consistency. Consistency in disciplinary actions is crucial for the fair treatment of employees. It's important to make sure that the nonprofit's policies are followed and that similarly situated employees are treated similarly. Consequently, if in the past an employee was disciplined in a certain way for the same transgression as currently being reviewed, it would be best to follow precedent, unless there is a business-related reason to depart from it.

    Remember to document the rationale behind deviating from policy or past precedent as it occurs, so that if the nonprofit's actions are challenged, a concurrent account of the decision making will exist.

    At this point, if the employee continues to perform in an unsatisfactory manner through the end of the performance improvement period, or doesn't significantly improve, or makes it through the reasonable time period, but lapses at some time in the future, the nonprofit is in a safe position to invoke appropriate consequences, including termination of employment. Be sure to complete the final step of the Fundamental Fairness Formula before proceeding.

5. **Objective review**—The fifth step of the formula is to seek an objective review of the situation by a third party— someone who hasn't been emotionally involved in the decision-making process up to this point. An objective review guards against subjective motives dominating the evaluation or termination process. Often the supervisor involved in the particular situation doesn't know how similar situations in the past were resolved. Or the supervisor may see the precipitating incident as the last straw in a series of unacceptable, yet undocumented, actions by the employee. The objective review can help monitor the consistency of discipline throughout the nonprofit, as well as lend a second set of eyes to a situation which always carries a risk of liability. The objective reviewer, whether the nonprofit's legal counsel, the CEO, or even a personnel committee of the board, should ensure that the employee has been treated with fundamental fairness before adverse action is taken.

Fundamental Fairness Formula—Objective Review Checklist Before Taking Action

1. Failure to meet expectations:

❑   Can the decision maker articulate: 1) what expectations the employee failed to meet? 2) how the employee failed to meet those expectations? 3) the business need or job-relatedness of the expectation that the employee failed to meet? (for example, "the employee's unprofessional conduct has caused his supervisor to lose faith in his judgment.")

❑   Has the decision-maker documented 1) how the employee failed to meet the nonprofit's expectations? 2) that the employee was provided with notice of his or her failure to meet expectations? 3) that the employee was given notice of the consequences of failing to meet expectations? and has the decision-maker documented 4) that the employee was given a reasonable time to improve, and 5) that after a reasonable time period the employee's performance or conduct still did not meet expectations?

❑ Can the performance expectations or failure of this particular employee to meet expectations be tied to any of the organization's strategic goals? If so, it's helpful to underscore the business need or job-relatedness of the expectations for the employee's performance. Example: "Sally's failure to submit satisfactory case notes on her home visits with foster parents is jeopardizing the agency's ability to submit status reports to funders in a timely manner."

2. **Documentation—Has the nonprofit documented that notice was given to this particular employee of both expectations and consequences?**

❑ Is there a policy governing the issue in writing? If so, is it a written document that this employee received? Can the nonprofit prove that this particular employee received the policy in its most recent version?

❑ Is the documentation sufficient to show that the employee should have been on notice? Are there memos summarizing conversations with the employee? Are the memos dated? Do the dates make sense in terms of what you know about the situation? (In one instance an employer relied on a counseling memo dated prior to an employee's hire date—it turned out there were two employees with the same last name and the memo in the file pertained to the wrong employee).

❑ Even if the supervisor claims they occurred, did the supervisor document formal performance counseling sessions with this employee? (If not, it may be necessary to hold one final performance counseling session and give the employee one final opportunity to correct deficiencies.) Sometimes a supervisor will have his or her own memos or a datebook/calendar in which the supervisor recorded that she or he met with the employee. If the general subject matter of the discussion is noted on the calendar, that can be a *contemporaneous business record* sufficient to prove that the supervisor met with the employee and put the employee on notice.

3. **Reasonable opportunity to correct deficiencies—Has the nonprofit given the employee a reasonable time to correct the deficiency? To defeat a claim of unfair treatment, an employer must show that it gave an employee notice of deficiencies and an opportunity to correct those deficiencies, prior to taking adverse action against the employee.**

❑ A reasonable time period will be different in every case, depending on how easily the deficiency can be overcome.

❑ Not every situation will require a reasonable time to correct or a *waiting period.* For instance, when an employee threatens violence, that employee shouldn't be offered a *reasonable opportunity to correct* his conduct, but instead should be immediately suspended. After a *cooling off* period and an investigation, if warranted, a decision whether to terminate the employee can be made.

4. **Policies and Procedures—Have all internal procedures been followed?**

❑ Has the nonprofit followed its own procedures?

❑ Has the nonprofit followed its past practices from other, similar situations? If not, does the policy manual arguably give the nonprofit the discretion to make a different decision this time?

5. **Legal Compliance—Have all external laws been followed?**

❑ If the nonprofit is aware of the legal issues involved, did someone check to make sure that applicable state and federal laws are being followed?

❑ Has the nonprofit reviewed its past and proposed actions with an employment lawyer?

6. **Objective Review—Has the decision maker checked with an objective third party prior to making a final decision? Is there a clear business-related reason for the action to be taken?**

❑ An objective third party should play devil's advocate and ask questions as if he or she were a fact finder or investigator challenging the nonprofit's action. This dry run can uncover weaknesses in the nonprofit's position before any action that will have a negative impact on the employee occurs.

❑ Supervisory level staff who are about to make decisions adversely affecting an employee should automatically review the situation with the executive director/CEO who can serve as the third-party objective reviewer.

❑ If the decision maker is the executive director/CEO, he or she should seek the opinion of an objective third party. Board members, other top-level nonprofit executives, insurance agents, outside legal counsel, or a staff member at the Nonprofit Risk Management Center can serve as resources for a nonprofit that is facing a troublesome personnel issue. CEOs and boards shouldn't be shy about sharing their dilemmas with a discreet third party who 1) has a connection to the organization, and 2) appreciates the privacy issues involved.

Final Step—Has the nonprofit documented that all the steps outlined in the formula were followed?

A Nonprofit's Fundamental Obligation: Evaluating Performance and Addressing Substandard Performance

Evaluating performance is sound management and critical for the long-term health and prosperity of the nonprofit. In most cases, the nonprofit's staff members are among the organization's most valuable assets. Employees influence the public's perception of the nonprofit, provide services to clients, and may be responsible for the welfare of vulnerable individuals on a daily basis. When employees can see how their own work successfully supports the achievement of the nonprofit's goals, a more effective organization will result. Boards of directors should insist that supervisors are trained in effective performance counseling techniques, that the appraisal forms are regularly reviewed for ease of use and effectiveness, and that prudent personnel practices relating to supervision are followed.

The law considers employees and volunteers to be the nonprofit's *agents* while they're acting in accordance with the authority vested in them by the nonprofit. Consequently, when an employee or volunteer is out in the community representing a nonprofit and acts unprofessionally or causes injury to someone, that conduct is legally attributed to the nonprofit, unless the nonprofit can show that the conduct was unauthorized. (Additionally, the public attributes the unprofessional conduct of employees and volunteers to the nonprofit, putting the nonprofit's good will in the community in jeopardy.) When a nonprofit overlooks conduct that's unacceptable or dangerous, the nonprofit is increasing its overall risks. It's simply not acceptable for supervisors to condone conduct that doesn't reflect the nonprofit's standards of integrity. It should also be unacceptable in the nonprofit's culture to ignore the risks created when employees or volunteers perform at a substandard level. Tolerating substandard performance isn't respectful of the limited resources available to the nonprofit. Instead the behavior sends the message that inefficiency and ineffectiveness are good enough. When a nonprofit leader is reluctant to terminate an underperforming staff member, the result is that the nonprofit actually wastes its resources redoing the work of the poor performer. Keeping an employee employed because the nonprofit is afraid of a lawsuit isn't risk management—doing so actually increases the nonprofit's exposure on several levels. In the worst case, failing to adequately supervise an employee can result in a legal claim of *negligent supervision*. Additional risks include the harm to morale in an otherwise high performing work environment. Talented employees may become frustrated and disillusioned when they see management ignoring poor performance by a co-worker. Finally, the presence of a poor performer hinders the nonprofit's ability to achieve its mission, and represents poor stewardship of donor funds. For these reasons, all supervisors from senior administrators on down must take the obligation to monitor, evaluate and address the performance of their subordinates seriously.

A growing number of court cases involve the performance appraisal process as the principal determining factor in a judgment of damages against an employer. Typically the litigation is brought by someone fired or denied a promotion, who then claims to be the victim of race, sex or age discrimination. The employer defends itself by claiming that the plaintiff (employee) simply wasn't doing his or her job. The plaintiff easily rebuts the employer's case by showing that his or her performance appraisals never mentioned any concerns or disappointments with performance. Employers that can present strong performance appraisal documentation are in a good position to defend their actions, whereas those that don't have written support for their position most often face liability. Consequently, evaluating the performance of staff and documenting the process carefully is where the rubber meets the road in employment-related risk management. Most often, if there is a smoking gun in an employment action, performance appraisals (or the lack thereof) are the weapons of choice.

Effective Performance Counseling

An important component of evaluating a nonprofit's effectiveness is taking a close look at the effectiveness of employees. Performance counseling is critical to the success of the nonprofit's operations, yet it's a task which most supervisors approach with insecurity or let slip completely due to their own discomfort with the process. Supervisors often have the misleading impression that counseling is always negative. When performance counseling is viewed as job coaching, it's very positive. If supervisors are held accountable in their own performance evaluations for their skills as job coaches in motivating and counseling their subordinates, there is a higher percentage of follow through. Be prepared to provide supervisors with guidance in the art of performance counseling.

In order to follow the Fundamental Fairness Formula, supervisors must clearly communicate expectations of performance to the employees that report to them. Rarely are the concrete expectations of an employee's performance adequately expressed in written form. Job descriptions and employee handbooks address some aspects of performance goals, but it's up to supervisors to fill in the blanks and to do so clearly and promptly, whenever specific behaviors are seen. Notice of expectations requires regular communication throughout the work relationship about the policies and procedures in the employee handbook. Counseling should take the form of immediate recognition of positive or negative performance, periodic informal coaching, more formal performance counseling discussions on a regular basis, as well as the formal annual appraisal, often called an annual performance review. In addition to performance counseling when needed, every employee expects and deserves a formal written evaluation, usually completed annually that highlights the employee's strengths, as well as goals for improvement or growth.

Mission-based Evaluations

Each employee should understand how his or her job duties support the accomplishment of the nonprofit's mission. Annual performance reviews are appropriate forums to acknowledge and celebrate achievements that support the nonprofit's organizational goals and objectives. An employee who doesn't understand why it's important to collect data on donors won't be thrilled to come to work each day to enter numbers into a spreadsheet. In contrast, coming to work each day is far more exciting and motivating for employees when they understand the role they themselves play in the overall strategy of the nonprofit's growth. Performance appraisals that are primarily forward looking, (that is, highlighting the areas where an employee needs to improve to support the accomplishment of the nonprofit's goals) rather than reflective, (that is, focused on where an employee's performance fell short in the past) are most effective in motivating employees toward stronger performance.

1. *Self-Evaluation.* Mission-based performance appraisals start with a self-evaluation completed by the employee. The self-evaluation is an opportunity for the employee to reflect on accomplishments and challenges, and whether his or her past performance in a given time period has fallen below, met, or exceeded his or her own expectations. This assessment gives the employee ownership of the performance appraisal process. The self-appraisal process is also a good opportunity to explore whether the employee encountered any obstacles (internal or external to the nonprofit) that kept the employee from achieving her or his goals and explore what, if anything, supervisory staff can do to help the employee achieve future goals. The employee and supervisor should explore together what educational opportunities, relevant to the employee's professional development, could help improve her or his performance or skills. The employee should be asked to draft goals for his or her performance for the coming months that support the organization's overall goals for the same time period. The employee's own goals may not be as comprehensive as his or her supervisor believes necessary. Consequently, the employee's self-appraisal work should culminate in a statement of goals for the upcoming year that's jointly developed by the employee and his or her supervisor.

2. *Supervisor's Assessment.* After the self-appraisal, the next step is the supervisor's assessment of the employee's performance and accomplishments for the same time period. Taking into consideration all the comments on the employee's self-appraisal, the supervisor should respond to the same questions that were posed to the employee. If there is a disagreement between the employee's perception of his or her own performance and the supervisor's viewpoint, the disconnect can shape the discussion and expectations for performance that may require clarification.

The most insightful appraisal format is pure narrative because supervisors are then forced to describe the employee's performance and can't make the mistake of checking a box that doesn't apply. However, narrative responses are also legally risky, because a supervisor's comments might go off in a direction that's irrelevant and subjective. Most successful appraisal forms use a combination: short narrative responses to preselected performance criteria. Often there is a summary statement or rating, which is useful when a distinction based on performance is required between similarly situated employees. Consequently, the supervisor should make an overall assessment of whether the employee's performance fell below, met or exceeded expectations.

Performance appraisal software and human resources consultants are available to help customize appraisal forms. Customization is recommended over simply borrowing a format from another workplace. On the other hand, many nonprofits successfully borrow forms developed for another organization, and then customize those forms as they discover what works and what doesn't.

The best insurance against any pitfall in the performance appraisal process is the final step of the formula. The third-party objective review requires that each supervisor's supervisor review the evaluations before they're finalized. An objective review by an administrator one tier above the actual supervisory relationship can expose subjective comments or inconsistent rankings. The objective review is also an opportunity to evaluate how well the supervisors are conducting their roles as job coaches. For the objective third-party review to be effective, the nonprofit needs to work out a schedule for annual or six-month reviews that factors in time for an objective review and any revisions that might be required as a result.

Performance Appraisal Do's and Don'ts

Keep the following considerations in mind when conducting performance appraisals or training others:

1. *Don't fill in a box if it doesn't apply to the job or employee being reviewed.* Instead, write "not applicable."

2. *Avoid subjective comments that aren't job-related.* The number one mistake made by supervisors is to make a comment on the appraisal form that isn't job-related. Every remark, example or criticism must be job-related. Ensuring that evaluations are objective, rather than subjective, is the job of the third-party reviewer, but the format of the appraisal can help remind supervisors by prompting them to provide for specific job-related examples to support their conclusions.

3. *Never award undeserved high marks. It's a major mistake to overrate marginal performers.* Some supervisors, who don't have control over salary adjustments, may be concerned that if they give a subordinate a bad review, the employee won't get a very good raise. In other cases, a supervisor may be fearful that poor marks will cause an employee's performance to worsen. Consequently the nonprofit ends up with numerous cases of *grade inflation*, which is legally dangerous and deflates the employee's incentives for improving performance.

4. *Never give an employee whose performance is problematic a good raise or check a satisfactory or higher rating when the comments reflect performance concerns.* A positive ranking or a salary increase is logically inconsistent with the nonprofit dissatisfaction with the employee's performance. Sometimes salary adjustments are given to weaker performers in an attempt to be equitable, such as when cost-of-living salary adjustments are given to all staff. This is a mistake. An employee who isn't pulling his or her weight is a burden on the rest of the staff and shouldn't be rewarded. It sends a mixed message to other employees who are performing well. Rewarding a poor performer promotes a co-dependent relationship. The employer is enabling and encouraging behavior it doesn't want to promote. Employees don't necessarily have to receive a salary increase at the same time. When an employee's performance is poor, freeze his salary.

5. *Make sure the person completing the appraisal has personal experience supervising the employee, so that the comments on the appraisal reflect personal observation rather than rumor, reputation or hearsay.*

6. *It isn't advisable to make comments that give an excuse for the employee's failure to meet expectations.* Supplying excuses is like giving a plaintiff's (employee's) lawyer a hand grenade. Don't do it.

7. *Focus on employee behavior and actions, not on the employee's intent.* It's virtually impossible to prove that an employee isn't trying or has a poor attitude. Instead, the supervisor can state that an employee didn't succeed in meeting goals, or wasn't present at important meetings, or didn't contribute to the team's efforts to the same extent that other employees did.

8. *Remember that a change of supervisors may spell trouble.* Frequently employees feel unfairly treated when a previous supervisor was tolerant of certain conduct that a new supervisor believes is unacceptable. Culture shock results. The Fundamental Fairness Formula (notice of expectations, performance counseling and an opportunity to correct the performance failing in a reasonable timeframe) is especially important during the initial getting-to-know-you phase. The new supervisor has changed the expectations and the employee needs to know what the new expectations are and what the consequences will be.

Trends in Performance Evaluations

More and more nonprofits are moving to a merit-raise system that rewards strong performance with the possibility of a higher salary adjustment. This system provides an incentive for employees to improve performance. A merit-raise system also rewards strong performers, helping with the nonprofit's ability to retain the most effective employees. A common way to structure a merit-raise system is to create a salary scale that assigns a certain percentage or range of percentages for salary increases in each of several categories. Each employee is eligible for whatever percentage raise is appropriate, given the range for the salary earned by the employee and the nonprofit's financial situation. For example, *Unacceptable* would merit no increase. *Meets expectations* would merit a 1 percent to 3 percent increase; *Exceeds expectations* would be eligible to earn a 3.5percent to 4.5 percent increase, and *Greatly exceeds expectations* would be awarded a 5 percent + increase. The finance committee can determine the budget for salary and compensation for the coming year by looking at historic data on the number of employees in each salary and performance range.

The newest trend in performance evaluations is a multisource assessment, also known as the 360-degree evaluation. Each supervisor reviews the subordinate, who may also review him- or herself, and be reviewed by clients and co-workers. In turn, the subordinate provides comments on his or her supervisor's performance. An estimated 90 percent of Fortune 1000 companies use some form of multisource assessment. Usually the data on each supervisor is collected anonymously and bypasses the supervisor, going directly to the supervisor's supervisor for evaluation, to protect against real or perceived retaliation.

As supervisors and subordinates become more comfortable with the process, supervisors can directly review feedback from their own subordinates. In theory, the idea of a multisource system is supposed to provide the highest level of management with a good sense of the effectiveness of the organization's supervisory staff and to build a sense of collective accountability for the overall performance of the nonprofit. An existing culture of trust and honesty among staff helps this structure succeed. Implementing 360-degree evaluations can also foster a sense of ownership in the success of the nonprofit among all employees. Multisource assessments also help ferret out concerns that may be just under the surface and otherwise wouldn't come to light.

Discipline and Documentation

Disciplinary Options

When disciplining an employee, first follow whatever disciplinary procedures exist within the organization's own policies. Nonprofit personnel manuals often contain language that describes how and when disciplinary procedures will be invoked. Some nonprofits have policies that are called *progressive discipline* policies. If there are no established written procedures for disciplinary action, the supervisor (after following the Fundamental Fairness Formula, of course) is left to his or her own discretion concerning what discipline is appropriate. The most usual options for discipline (in order of seriousness) are: verbal and written warnings, salary freezes, demotion or transfer to a different position, final written warnings, one-time one-day paid suspension, (also known as decision-making leave or a day of commitment) unpaid suspensions, and discharge.

There is debate about the purpose and usefulness of unpaid suspensions as a tool to discipline an employee. Some authorities believe that giving an employee a taste of unemployment isn't sufficient motivation to improve performance, and only causes anger and resentment. Unpaid one-day suspensions may jeopardize the status of an exempt worker, unless the employee is being disciplined for a significant policy violation, such as a safety rule. However, unpaid suspensions are definitely appropriate in cases of wrongdoing by an employee when discharge, while not elected on the spot, is being considered. The suspension period gives the nonprofit time to investigate, confirm and document suspected wrongdoing and avoids making a decision to terminate in the heat of an emotional moment.

Paid suspensions are intended to invoke a sense of obligation and resolution to improve performance, and are generally used as a once-in-a-career benefit. A paid suspension can be considered an involuntary day of commitment, if used to make the employee more accountable for the improvement of his or her own performance. Since the employee is being paid, the employer is permitted to request homework, such as requiring the employee to provide a written statement upon return to work explaining how the employee plans to address the concerns that resulted in the suspension. The instructions might be:

> *"In addition to giving you a final written warning about _____, we are giving you a day off with pay so that you may rethink your commitment to our organization. The purpose of this paid suspension is to impress upon you the seriousness of your (misconduct) (inappropriate conduct) (actions). If you choose not to return to work the day after tomorrow, we will respect your decision and your employment will terminate effective close of business tomorrow. If you decide to return to work you will be required to submit a written action plan, outlining the concrete steps you will take to correct this problem. I specifically want you to address_____. You will need to present this written action plan to your supervisor first thing upon your return to work. This is a once-in-a-career benefit. If you decide to return to work, you will be expected to adhere to the action plan, if it's accepted by your supervisor. If your supervisor finds the action plan inadequate, or you fail to adhere to the action plan, your employment with us will be terminated."*

It's expected that employers will match appropriate discipline to the seriousness of the offense and also demonstrate consistent, equitable treatment of employees. Most managers would agree that a model employee with 20 years' experience, who violates a work rule, would probably not be treated in the same way as a short-term employee with a spotty work history. However, consistent application of discipline is the key to fairness. For instance, a supervisor may not be as inclined to discharge a bookkeeper found asleep on the job as someone responsible for the safety of young children found sleeping on the job. However, if the child-care worker is a minority and the bookkeeper isn't, the child care worker might win a lawsuit for wrongful discharge based on discrimination. The challenge for all employers is how to reconcile being consistent in the application of discipline, but still take into consideration the specific facts that tend to make each disciplinary incident unique.

Probation[21]

Probation is a period of time during which an employee's performance is subject to close scrutiny, because the employee has been told of dissatisfaction with his performance and of the need to improve within a specific time period. The probation period gives the employee the opportunity to correct deficiencies. If the employee's performance during the probation period shows that the employee will never meet the nonprofit's expectations, the nonprofit doesn't have to wait until the end of the

---

21 We believe that introductory work period or work-test period or simply, introductory period is a better phrase to describe the first few months of employment than probation, which implies that the employee has been the subject of a disciplinary action.

probationary period. It's often better to terminate employment than to prolong the relationship with an employee who is unproductive or counter-productive, because of the impact of the underperforming employee on the rest of the staff.

If the employee fails to meet expectations at any time after the probation period, his or her employment should be terminated. Unless the reason for the performance failing is completely separate from failings that led to the probation, the nonprofit doesn't have to start the counseling process all over again.

Evaluate these four criteria when determining the most appropriate level of discipline:

❏   the severity of the offense,

❏   the employee's past performance record,

❏   the employee's length of service with the nonprofit, and

❏   the nonprofit's past practice when dealing with this sort of situation.

Progressive Discipline

Progressive disciplinary procedures are those requiring that the first instance of a performance failure be treated as a warning, with successive occurrences resulting in more serious disciplinary measures. The goal of progressive discipline is to formally communicate problems to employees in a direct and timely manner to allow the employee to improve his or her performance. The clear legal advantage of progressive discipline is that it requires the nonprofit to follow the Fundamental Fairness Formula. The first warning in a progressive disciplinary system is the equivalent of notice to the employee of how the employee has failed to meet the nonprofit's expectations.

Progressive discipline is typically a series of increasingly serious disciplinary steps. The disciplinary progression might include the following: first offense = verbal warning (which is documented by the supervisor in the supervisor's file); second offense = written warning in the employee's file; third offense = final written warning or suspension pending discharge. However, **progressive discipline should never be rigidly applied**. The written policy language in the nonprofit's handbook should preserve the nonprofit's discretion to exercise flexibility in applying the warnings warranted under the circumstances. Then, if it seems more appropriate at first instance to suspend rather than warn an employee, the nonprofit isn't locked into any step of the progressive discipline policy.

Progressive discipline, if consistently applied and with flexibility for unusual cases, can be an effective risk management tool, because it affords some assurance of fundamental fairness. The downside of progressive disciplinary policies is that they can create contractual obligations, if not carefully drafted. In most states policy language can be binding on the nonprofit under the theory of implied contract. A pitfall of progressive discipline is that because the policy lists disciplinary steps in a certain order, it may appear to a supervisor (and the employee) that the only options are what is listed in the policy. Even with language that states that the disciplinary policy isn't a contract, employees will expect to be treated as described in the policy. Employees regard policies as promises. "Taking the high road" in employment practices requires an employer to live up to its promises, so make sure that progressive discipline policies are drafted to permit flexible application.

Choosing Appropriate Discipline

A challenge for any supervisor faced with the need to discipline an employee is determining what disciplinary action is appropriate in each instance. When is a written warning enough? A related issue is how the supervisor disciplines an employee for multiple performance failings. What if multiple concerns seem to be completely unrelated? Does the nonprofit discipline each separately? If supervisors can find a link between seemingly unrelated concerns, the nonprofit has a compelling case for determining that a more serious disciplinary action is warranted.

Linking separate incidents can be accomplished by realizing that there are essentially four basic types of performance concerns: 1) policy violations 2) performance failures (example: lack of skills, failure to meet deadlines, or other failures relating to expectations for the job's outcomes), 3) inappropriate or unprofessional conduct, and 4) lack of dependability (example: unexcused absences, or tardiness). Examine each performance concern. Does it fall into one of these four categories? If the employee is causing concerns on several fronts, do the performance issues fall into the same category? If so, a more serious disciplinary step may be warranted.

Finally, there is always the catch-all explanation that the nonprofit has "lost faith in the employee's professional judgment" or determined that the employee's performance will never meet the nonprofit's expectations.

Whatever action is taken, the nonprofit must document the reason for the discipline and what steps were taken to provide the employee with notice. Remember, many juries take the position, "If it's not in writing, it didn't happen."

Practical Tips for Effective Performance Counseling

1. *Planning for the Performance Counseling Session*

   When preparing for the conference with the employee, the supervisor should take notes and outline what he or she plans to tell the employee. Use the notes as a script for the conference. It breaks the ice if the supervisor first shares with the employee something positive that she or he appreciates about his or her performance. Follow with any concerns. Focus on the conduct or performance goals that are *expected* for this employee or any employee in the particular position at issue, and suggest a road map of concrete strategies the employee could undertake to get to where she or he needs to be. The supervisor should decide on an appropriate time frame to test whether this employee is capable of meeting his or her expectations on this issue. The supervisor should consider what he or she thinks an appropriate consequence would be. Termination? Demotion? Salary freeze? Trimming the areas of this employee's responsibility?

2. *The Performance Counseling Meeting*

   After sharing something positive and sharing specifics about his or her concerns and the expectations that he or she and the nonprofit have for the employee's performance, the supervisor should employ active listening techniques in response to the employee's comments. The supervisor should ask the employee to share what concrete steps the employee will take to meet the expectations expressed.

   After the employee finishes speaking, the supervisor should echo back to the employee to confirm the employee's commitment to change: "Ok, so this is what I heard you say. You said that you would try to take an earlier bus so that you will get to work about 20 minutes earlier and have time to get settled before your work day starts to be ready to work right at 9 am. Is that correct?" The supervisor should take notes as she or he is echoing back what the employee said. This will help the supervisor focus on what the employee said and will also assist the supervisor with documenting the counseling session. If the employee's suggestion isn't on target, the supervisor should suggest a different strategy and ask the employee if she or he would have any objection to trying that strategy. The supervisor should continue with the active listening technique until he or she and the employee are in agreement about the next steps for the employee to take. Also, the supervisor should try to find out whether there are any external obstacles that are preventing the employee from meeting the nonprofit's expectations. The supervisor should explore what strategies can be employed to help the employee meet goals or satisfy expectations. How can the supervisor help him or her? What time frame is needed? The supervisor shouldn't end the session without a clear picture of the steps the employee has committed to take and the timeframe agreed upon.

   The supervisor's last comments should be to tell the employee the consequences of not meeting the nonprofit's expectations: "If you aren't consistently ready to start work at 9 am, as demonstrated to us over the course of the next week, your job will be at risk."

3. *Documentation of the Performance Counseling Session*

   After meeting with the employee, the supervisor should draft a performance counseling memo, which will be placed in the employee's personnel file. The employee can sign it, although this isn't necessary. Since the memorandum summarizes what the employee discussed with the supervisor, the contents of the memorandum shouldn't be a surprise. Similarly, it shouldn't be a surprise to the employee if subsequently he or she is disciplined for failing to meet the expectations discussed in the meeting. The memorandum in his or her file should be sufficient documentation that the employee was on notice of the expectations, and was given a reasonable opportunity to meet those expectations. The memorandum will generally track the supervisor's planning notes prior to the performance counseling session unless some unanticipated issues were uncovered during the counseling session.

   Everyone expects employers to document everything. If the management staff isn't yet comfortable and consistent with documentation of performance concerns, this is a red flag for potential liability. If the Fundamental Fairness Formula is followed, there should be a clear outline for supervisors to follow as they draft their performance counseling memos, that highlights the business-related reason for any personnel action. This is important because a disgruntled employee's legal action against the nonprofit will often be based on the allegation that there was an illegal, unfair reason—not a legitimate business reason—for the action taken.

   Through documentation the rational and legitimate business needs for an action are preserved so that even someone who knows nothing about your mission, programs or staffing requirements, can understand that the action taken was appropriate. Remember: a jury of the nonprofit's peers will seldom include other nonprofit managers. Documentation has to be clear enough that someone wholly unfamiliar with the nonprofit's operations can understand management's thinking at the time it took disciplinary action against the employee.

In basic terms, firing an employee without prior counseling will flunk the fairness test. So will trying to prove that the supervisor gave the employee notice, without being able to prove that a counseling session ever took place. Consequently, documentation of all counseling sessions is critical. While a notation on the supervisor's calendar—"Met with Anne to discuss absenteeism"—is helpful to establish the date a counseling session occurred, it's not sufficient to prove what was said to Anne. An essential step is to prepare a post-conference memo that reviews the expectations and consequences and any time frames agreed upon for corrective action.

Documentation Pitfalls

Some final words about documentation. Employers should never put in writing any critical comments about an employee filing a workers' compensation claim, or taking medical leave or having a medical condition. Requests for medical leave, and all other medical information must be maintained in separate files from performance memos. Supervisors aren't permitted to take an employee's medical history into account when evaluating performance.

Second, don't create *secret files* on employees. Clever attorneys can discover the files and request copies. Fairness requires that employees be made aware of the nonprofit's criticisms of their performance. And the point, after all, of this counseling session is to bring concerns about performance to the attention of the employee with the goal of having him or her improve it.

Third, try to encourage a culture where written memoranda aren't threatening. Why not require supervisors to regularly write complimentary memoranda to their subordinates about duties well performed? Avoid the appearance that a paper trail is being created with respect to one employee by making it a practice to frequently document observations about all employees' performance.

Finally, keep in mind that if litigation develops, written warnings carry more weight than verbal ones. An employee might successfully argue that management didn't deem the concerns serious enough to put in writing.

The purpose of documentation is to preserve a current situation so that in the future, when those involved are no longer employed by the nonprofit, or have no memory of the situation, the memorandum in the file can serve as accurate institutional memory. Documentation of disciplinary actions and performance concerns should be written as if the person reading it has no familiarity with the nonprofit or the individuals involved. Never let stand handwritten notes that only the author can decipher; ask that such notes be typed before filing. Remember that documentation is written not only for the nonprofit, but also for a potential future audience of hostile adversaries, judge or jury.

Fundamental Fairness Formula—Self Test

1. **Business Needs**—Is there a job-related reason for the action?

   ❏ Has the decision maker articulated what the job-related or business need for the action is?

   ❏ Have you documented the business need or job relatedness of the action?

   ❏ Has the board of directors supported the business need for the action in any way, such as through written long-range plans or goals?

   ❏ Does the employee involved know the job-related reason for the action? If not, see next step.

2. **Notice of Expectations and Consequences**—Does the employee involved have notice of the nonprofit's expectations and the consequences that will occur should those expectations not be met?

   ❏ Nonprofits should establish expectations for an employee's performance, job duties and workplace policies, but those expectations must be communicated to the staff. Don't make the mistake of assuming that an employee knows what the nonprofit expects or what the business needs for certain actions are. It's up to the nonprofit to clearly communicate expectations and underlying rationale. Communication can be through written policies, memos, or posted notices.

   ❏ Notice can also be communicated in one-on-one counseling sessions with the employee(s), or staff meetings, training sessions, and during new employee orientation.

   ❏ Are the consequences of not meeting the nonprofit's expectations clear? For example, "If you violate the confidentiality policy, you may be terminated from employment." It may be obvious, but tell employees what will happen if they fail to perform to a level that meets expectations.

3. **Documentation**—Has the nonprofit documented that notice was given to this particular employee?

Tell the Truth

Don't label a separation something that it isn't. Why? *Because nonprofit organizations aren't supposed to lie.* (Characterizing a termination as one thing when it's really something else will be seen as deceitful.)

If you aren't sure what category of termination you are dealing with, just stick to the generic phrases: termination, or separation of employment.

Service Letter Laws

Several states have a law such as Minnesota's that requires employer's to provide written notice to an employee of the reason for termination either if the employee requests it, or automatically upon termination. Minnesota's law *www.revisor.leg.state.mn.us/stats/1 81/933.html* is typical:

"Notice required. An employee who has been involuntarily terminated may, within 15 working days following such termination, request in writing that the employer inform the employee of the reason for the termination. Within 10 working days following receipt of such request, an employer shall inform the terminated employee in writing of the truthful reason for the termination." Minn. Stat. Ann. Section 181.933

Other states with similar requirements include: California, Tennessee, and New York.

❏ Is there a policy governing the issue in writing? If so, is it a written document that this employee received? Can the nonprofit prove that this particular employee received the policy in its most recent version?

❏ Is the documentation adequate? If, for example, a supervisor warned an employee about lack of timeliness, did the supervisor write a memo summarizing the conversation? Is the memo dated? Signed? Does the memo reflect the date that the supervisor and employee met to discuss tardiness?

4. **Reasonable Opportunity to Correct the Situation**—If the issue pertains to an employee's unsatisfactory performance, has the nonprofit given the employee a reasonable time to correct the deficiency?

❏ In order to defeat a claim of unfair treatment, an employer must show that it gave an employee notice of deficiencies and an opportunity to correct those deficiencies, prior to taking adverse action against the employee.

❏ In situations of poor performance, judges and juries regard it as fundamentally unfair to discipline an employee without giving the employee a chance to improve. The general rule is that an employee should be reminded about the expectations for performance and then given an opportunity to improve. If there is no improvement, the nonprofit has treated the employee fairly because it has given the employee a second chance.

❏ A reasonable time period will be different in every case, depending on how easily the deficiency can be overcome.

❏ If, after a reasonable time, the employee has still not brought his or her performance up to a level which meets the nonprofit's expectations (or his or her supervisor's expectations), then the nonprofit can discharge the employee—after taking the last step of the Fundamental Fairness Formula: getting an objective review.

❏ Not every situation will require a *reasonable time to correct* or a *waiting period*. For instance, when an employee brings a loaded gun to work, that employee shouldn't be offered a reasonable opportunity to correct his or her conduct.

5. **Policies and Procedures**—Have all internal procedures been followed?

❏ Has the nonprofit followed its own procedures, both written and unwritten?

❏ Has the nonprofit followed its past practices? If not, does the manual permit departure from the guidelines set forth in the manual through a clear, prominent disclaimer that states that the handbook isn't a contract of employment?

6. **Legal Compliance**—Have all external laws been followed?

❏ If the nonprofit is aware of the legal issues involved, did someone check to make sure that applicable state and federal laws are being followed?

❏ Has the nonprofit reviewed its actions with employment counsel?

7. **Objective Review**—Has the decision maker checked with an objective third party prior to making a final decision?

❏ An objective third party is less likely to have an emotional investment in the issue at hand, and more likely to see any hidden discrimination or unfair treatment.

❏ An objective third party should be able to ask questions as if she or he were a fact finder or investigator challenging the nonprofit's action. This dry run can uncover weaknesses in the nonprofit's position before injury occurs to the employee.

❏ Supervisory level staff who are about to make decisions adversely affecting an employee should automatically review the situation with the CEO who can serve as the third-party objective reviewer.

❏ If the decision maker is the CEO, he or she should seek the opinion of an objective third-party. board members, other top-level nonprofit executives, insurance agents, outside legal counsel, or a staff member at the Nonprofit Risk Management Center can serve as resources for a nonprofit which is facing a troublesome personnel issue. CEOs and boards shouldn't be shy about sharing their dilemmas with a discreet third-party who 1) has a connection to the organization, and 2) appreciates the privacy issues involved.

Final Step—Has the nonprofit documented that all the steps outlined in the formula were followed?

Use this N.O.T.I.C.E. checklist to ensure that the *Fundamental Fairness Formula* has been followed.

❏ **Notice:** Did the employee have notice of expectations and consequences?

❏ **Objective review:** Can the supervisor explain the business-related reasons for the actions taken to the satisfaction of an objective, third-party reviewer?

❏ **Time to correct the deficiencies:** Was the employee given a reasonable time to correct deficiencies, or improve his or her conduct?

❏ **Inform the employee of the consequences that will follow if those goals aren't met.** *Document the counseling session.*

❏ **Counseling:** Did the employee receive counseling? Was the employee told that performance is inadequate, his or her job is at risk, and were the goals for the employee to meet the nonprofit's expectations discussed?

❏ **Examine the policies and procedures of the nonprofit.** Were all relevant procedures followed? If they weren't followed, why not? Is this documented?

Termination Checklist

❏ Is there any contractual language that limits the circumstances in which the nonprofit may terminate the employee?

❏ Are there any procedural requirements that the nonprofit needs to follow prior to termination that haven't yet been followed with this employee?

❏ Is there written documentation in the employee's file of the reason for dismissal or lay off?

❏ Are the business-related reasons for termination articulated in writing?

❏ How old is the employee? Did age play a factor in the decision to terminate?

❏ Does the employee have a disability? If so, has a reasonable accommodation been attempted?

❏ Who will replace the employee? Someone younger? Different sex? Different religion? Different sexual orientation? Different culture or nationality? Is there a pattern that could be described as discriminatory?

❏ Was the employee aware that termination was a possibility or was likely?

❏ Is there documentation of that awareness?

❏ If the discharge is based on failure to follow policy or violation of policy, can the nonprofit document that the employee was aware of the policy?

❏ Does the nonprofit have proof that the employee received the personnel manuals or policies that are relevant to his or her termination?

❏ Has the employee been given notice of deficiencies and a reasonable opportunity to correct them?

❏ Does this employee have any expectations, either because of promises made, or because of past practices of the nonprofit, that employment is assured for any specific length of time, or that terminated employees would receive any special treatment, such as severance pay?

❏ Has the nonprofit discharged or disciplined other employees for similar reasons? Was the treatment consistent with this employee's treatment?

❏ Has the employee recently filed a workers' compensation claim, or a sexual harassment complaint or any other complaint of illegal conduct?

❏ Is the employee a minority or in any protected category?

❏ What did the employee's most recent performance evaluation conclude about the employee's performance? Does the evaluation support termination?

Termination of Nonprofit Employees[22]

Whenever someone is separated from employment, there are emotional ramifications for both the individual who is separated and those who remain employed by the nonprofit. Consequently, it's shrewd risk management to conduct any termination of employment with great care and true compassion.

There are various names given to the event that results in a separation from employment. Each of these names or terms carries emotional baggage, because of semantic implications, which in turn can sabotage the termination from a legal perspective. It's important to know, and to properly label, what's really going on. For example, the following are terms that are used to describe separation from employment:

❏ *Termination* (also referred to as being *fired* or *let go*, with no particular implication as to the reason for the termination.)

❏ *Dismissal* (implies that the employee's performance or conduct was unsatisfactory.)

❏ *Retirement* (implies that the employee has voluntarily decided to cease being gainfully employed.)

❏ *Lay-off* (implies that employees are being put on unpaid leave status, but as soon as work is available they may be rehired: *Random House* dictionary definition: "…an interval of enforced unemployment.")

❏ *Reduction in force* (implies that more than one staff member is being terminated, but no particular implication as to the reason for the terminations; generally, **not** appropriate to use when an employee's performance was unsatisfactory.)

❏ *Reorganizing* (implies that positions are being eliminated and that reporting relationships are being restructured.)

❏ *Elimination of a position* (describes a situation where a particular position is being eliminated; no implication as to the reason, although generally not appropriate when the reason is poor performance.)

---

22 Volunteers, as well as employees, can be involuntarily terminated from service with a nonprofit. The same principles that are discussed in this section pertaining to paid staff are applicable to volunteers. However, a volunteer who is separated from service to a nonprofit organization is unlikely to have legal standing to bring a lawsuit under state or federal employment laws. Instead, the volunteer might bring a state court claim against the organization for "intentional infliction of emotional distress" or a similar tort claim. While the volunteer bringing such a lawsuit wouldn't be entitled to money damages for "lost wages," he or she might be able to recover a significant monetary award from the organization; certainly the organization would suffer from the experience of being named as a defendant in a lawsuit, regardless of any monetary damage award. An involuntarily separated volunteer might attempt to cause other difficulty for the nonprofit, such as harming the morale of remaining volunteers or generating negative publicity by a letter to the editor of the community paper.

❏ *Right-sizing* (implies that the organization was overstaffed to begin with, although this is really just a buzzword invented to put a positive spin on the concept of downsizing.)

❏ *Delayering* (implies that managers are being fired.)

Terminating an employee is the single most risky action a nonprofit can take. The vast majority of lawsuits filed against nonprofits and nonprofit board members are employment-related. The majority of these suits stem from a discharge action. Consequently, it's imperative to have a well-documented file prior to terminating the employment of any employee, regardless of the reason. Assume that every termination may result in a legal challenge.

Nevertheless, terminating an employee who isn't pulling his or her weight, or one who is unaware of basic job requirements or simply acting inappropriately, can be the best risk management step the nonprofit takes. Firing an employee is never easy, but sometimes it makes sense both legally and from a business standpoint. If the nonprofit has honored the Fundamental Fairness Formula, documentation should be in place to support the nonprofit's actions.

Certainly there are situations when putting an employee on notice and giving him or her an opportunity to improve isn't advisable. Some conduct justifies termination or suspension without an opportunity to improve. When an employee acts recklessly or dangerously, violates safety policies or exhibits aberrant behavior, it's advisable to take immediate action rather than to give the employee a second chance. In such cases, the recommendation to suspend the employee pending a termination decision should be put in writing as soon after the event as possible, explaining why suspension and termination thereafter was appropriate. The reason may seem clear today, but it probably won't six months from today.

Whether driven by poor performance, economics or some other reason, the decision to terminate a staff member is never easy. Discharging someone is an emotional challenge. Managers often cause greater exposure to liability than necessary by avoiding any confrontation in the process of discharging an employee. However, employees who aren't given a reason for their termination are quick to conclude that there was an illegal reason why they were terminated. By not communicating the reason, or not appearing confident and in control, the nonprofit can open itself to risks.

A Nonprofit's Right to Discharge an Employee

Most employees have an at-will relationship with their nonprofit employer. This means that they're hired at the will of the nonprofit, and that the employment relationship may be terminated either at their own will, or at the will of the nonprofit. The nonprofit employer of an at-will employee doesn't require specific cause to terminate the at-will worker's employment. Yet, some employment manuals specifically state that termination may only be *for cause*. In such cases, it's imperative that the nonprofit review the examples of cause listed in the manual and make sure that the reason for termination is among those on the list. Similarly, an employee working under the terms of a contract enjoys any protections or provisions detailed in the contract. Generally the contract addresses termination of employment, and it may or may not specify that cause is required for termination, or that upon termination there will be a penalty to the employer for early termination of the contract.

A *for cause* standard may be created by policy language that states that termination can only be for: "… (followed by a list of reasons). In such cases, the reason given by the nonprofit for the termination in its internal documentation and given outwardly to the employee must fit with the reasons in the manual. There are numerous other ways in which an at-will

A Case in Point

In 2003, an employee at Crown Motor Co., filed charges of harassment against Crown Motor. After Crown Motor launched its own internal investigation of the charge, Abbott, a co-worker of the complaining employee, identified himself as a witness to the alleged harassment. Several months later Abbott was discharged for what Crown Motor said was a legitimate business reason: insubordination. Abbott sued, claiming that his discharge was in retaliation for his willingness to be a witness in his co-worker's harassment case. To support his claim, Abbott offered statements made by management about "getting back at employees" who took action against the employer. He also alleged that his supervisor had told another employee that he had been fired because he "got involved in other people's business." Finally, Abbott claimed that he had been given a negative job reference by Crown Motor when he was looking for work post-termination. The Appeals Court found that Abbott had enough evidence to demonstrate that his employer may have been motivated by retaliation, despite its claim that it had legitimate business reasons to discharge Abbott.

Lessons From Real Life: How *Not* to Fire an Employee

Don't fire an employee on *Take Your Daughter to Work Day* when the daughter is present… or leave a message that an employee is fired on the home answering machine for the employee (and his or her family) to discover upon return from vacation… Don't escort a senior executive out of the office between two police officers in full view of rest of the staff… or fire an employee by moving his or her belongings into the hallway…

Housekeeping on the Way Out

Departing employees should be told that they no longer have access to networked computer systems or permission to access data that's owned by the nonprofit. Meanwhile, the nonprofit should take whatever steps are needed to deny former employees access to computer networks, unless there is an exceptional reason to continue a former employee's access to the nonprofit's computer files.

employment relationship can be altered. In one case, an oral promise of *due process* at the workplace created an obligation to hold a substantial review of an employee's performance prior to termination. Throughout the past decades the assumption of at-will employment has been steadily eroding. Consequently, it's more important than ever to follow the Fundamental Fairness Formula, which requires the nonprofit to check its internal policies and procedures and an objective review prior to terminating an employee.

Given the very risky nature of employee terminations, use extreme caution. If possible, never terminate an employee on the spot. If the employee's performance is unsatisfactory, termination should only occur after a reasonable opportunity for rehabilitation has been afforded the employee. If the employee's conduct is the decisive factor in the termination, make sure that the conduct is documented and that the employee either was, or should have been, on notice that the conduct was inappropriate. In cases of outrageous, dangerous, unprofessional or illegal conduct, when immediate termination seems the only judicious response, take a moment to consider whether it would make sense to initially suspend the employee, confirm that termination is appropriate and then terminate with the reasons documented and well thought out. The suspension/investigation period, however brief, will afford the nonprofit the opportunity to objectively re-evaluate the circumstances to be sure termination isn't creating a greater risk.

Just Do It

Retaining an employee who is a poor performer, or who should be terminated for other reasons, is as much of a risk as firing an employee; yet sometimes not firing someone can create a more destructive atmosphere. The labor market may be tight, and qualified replacements hard to find, but these obstacles shouldn't deter nonprofit managers from firing an employee whose continued employment is counter-productive for the nonprofit. In fact, continuing the employment of some employees may create more of a liability risk than a carefully managed termination. When already-stretched staff members have to make up for the ineffectiveness of an underperforming employee, morale problems are inevitable, and the longer a poor performer is permitted to linger, the more difficult it will be to defend a lawsuit later.

One of the most difficult cases to defend is that of the employee who wasn't fired when she or he should have been. The longer an employee is employed without any paper trail to demonstrate the nonprofit's disappointment, the more explosive the scenario when the employee is finally terminated. First of all, the employee has had no clue that her or his conduct or performance is unsatisfactory. Therefore termination is usually a surprise. With surprise comes anger and the likelihood that the terminated employee will telephone an attorney. Age discrimination is often a factor escalating the liability risk, since older workers may have had a longer tenure with the nonprofit, and therefore their substandard performance may have been ignored for a longer period of time. When a nonprofit has tolerated a poor performer over a long time, it isn't credible to a jury that poor performance is a legitimate reason for termination. The employee's attorney will have a great time with the employee's supervisor on the witness stand: "You mean this employee worked for you for seven years and never received a negative performance review until the week you fired her?"

Remember: fundamental fairness requires that employees have notice of the nonprofit's expectations, how their performance fails to meet those expectations, and a reasonable opportunity to correct their deficiencies. Without the notice, the fact-finder won't believe that the termination was legitimate. Consequently, instead of putting off documentation and discipline, just do it.

Proceed With Caution! Wrongful Termination Theories

The following theories are often used by plaintiffs to claim that their termination was illegal:

❏ Breach of contract (oral or written)

❏ Discrimination

❏ Intentional infliction of emotional distress

❏ Defamation

❏ Violation of FMLA (employee was fired when she should have been given family leave)

❏ Retaliation

❏ No good cause

❏ Violation of public policy

The Potential Plaintiff

What does the nonprofit do if it suspects that an employee it's planning to fire has consulted with an attorney? Sometimes an employee will make a flurry of requests, such as to see his personnel file, workplace policies or a copy of personnel evaluations. The employee may have seen the handwriting on the wall and consulted with an attorney. Don't do anything differently, other than consult with legal counsel. Don't deny access to personnel files, especially when those files may actually help the nonprofit. (The employee should know what's in his file anyway.) Don't give the employee any ammunition to claim that the nonprofit was *out to get* him or her. One of the worst things to do in such situations is to treat the employee in a way that could be interpreted as *retaliatory*. Don't terminate an employee who has filed a complaint of harassment or a workers' compensation claim without consulting legal counsel because both actions are a setup for a retaliation claim.

Avoiding Retaliation Claims

The number of charges filed with the EEOC claiming retaliation under Title VII doubled in the 10-year period between 1992 and 2002, making it the fastest growing category of claims. Retaliation claims amount to almost one-third of all charges filed with the EEOC each year. If an employee has complained of sexual or other illegal harassment, or has filed a workers' compensation claim, or has alleged or *blown the whistle* on some practice of the nonprofit that the employee believes is improper, termination of that employee could easily result in a retaliation claim. Make sure to involve legal counsel in such situations. Employees who have identified themselves as witnesses to harassment are similarly protected from retaliation. Each of these situations is particularly troublesome when the complaining employee is legitimately a poor performer. In such cases, consult with counsel, document all performance failings, and address the performance concerns while resolving the employee's grievance or complaint.

Communicating the Termination Decision

Don't fire an employee using remote control. Do it in person and be sensitive to the employee's privacy and pride. Two representatives of the nonprofit's management team should participate in the termination conference: one to talk, and one to take notes. The objective of the final conference with the employee is to clearly explain that employment is over, briefly reiterate the reason, and explain what the immediate consequences are for the employee in terms of final pay and benefits. The nonprofit needs to communicate whether the employee is expected to gather personal belongings and leave immediately, or will have more time to wind up affairs with the nonprofit.

In situations where the employee is violent or unstable, it may be simply too risky to meet with an employee to conduct a termination conference in person. In those cases, legal counsel should assist the nonprofit in drafting a termination letter. The termination letter should accurately describe the reasons for discharge and the final pay and other benefits to which the discharged employee may be entitled.

Final Pay

The nonprofit should tell the employee when the final paycheck will be delivered, if not immediately. All obligations owed to the employee, such as pay through the last date of active work and any vacation pay owed, should be prepared for the employee's departure date, and provided to the employee within the time period required by state law. In some states final pay is owed immediately upon termination or within 24-hours, and in others it isn't due until the next regularly scheduled paycheck. Know your state's requirements.

Note: it's never permissible to withhold a final paycheck as ransom for keys or other property of the employer. If the employee owes the nonprofit time (such as in cases where the employee took more vacation than she or he had accrued) the nonprofit may be permitted to offset whatever is owed against final pay, if the employee provides a written authorization. Remember that it's generally illegal to withhold anything from an employee's paycheck without the employee's prior written authorization.

"Why Was I Discharged?"

Many nonprofit managers wonder whether they must tell the employee the reason for his or her termination. Some state laws (Tennessee, New York, California and Minnesota) require employers to provide terminated employees with a written

> ### "We Were Trying to Be Kind, but She Didn't Get the Signal"
>
> An older worker who was a substandard performer had worked for a nonprofit for several years, but her performance had never been evaluated in writing. In her final year of employment her supervisor left the agency, leaving the CEO of the agency to evaluate her performance. The executive realized that the employee wasn't pulling her weight. Simultaneously, the nonprofit was re-evaluating the employee's entire department and the board decided to reorganize and hire a senior-level employee to take charge of the reorganized department. The executive met with the employee in an attempt to communicate his concerns with her performance, and told her that her department was going to be restructured, her job eliminated, someone hired for the senior staff position, but that a part-time position would be available for her. The CEO never terminated the employee, but the part-time position wasn't acceptable to her, so she resigned. She sued the agency for *forced resignation* and intentional infliction of emotional distress. The former employee is $40,000 richer and the agency is wiser. "We should have terminated her long ago…We were so gun-shy about her age that we didn't think we could fire her. Were we ever wrong."

notice of termination or statement of the reason for termination. Where there is no such requirement, it's still an important risk management step to articulate, in internal written documentation, and to the discharged employee, the job-related reason for termination. If the nonprofit's management can't articulate an objective job-related reason for the termination, this is a red light. Stop, reconsider the action, and contact a legal advisor to confirm the legality of the termination.

Plan for the Termination Meeting

Get to the point of the conference quickly and be direct. Like all difficult employee conferences, it's helpful to write out beforehand everything that should be communicated so that no omissions will be made. Then use the written document as a script for the conference and as an outline for the follow-up memorandum, which should be placed in the employee's personnel file. Some managers have found that termination conferences are easier if they rehearse using a tape recorder.

The job-related business reason for the termination should be explained to the employee as objectively and unemotionally as possible. Since what is said in the final conference is often used against the employer, watered down or long and meandering explanations for the termination will only get the nonprofit in trouble. Be direct and concise. The nonprofit's representatives may be empathetic, but shouldn't make any excuses or equivocate about the termination. Show respect for the employee, by allowing the employee to respond without interruption. One of the two nonprofit representatives should take careful notes on the employee's response. Should the employee become emotional, showing appropriate empathy is better than ignoring the employee, but no physical contact, not even a sympathetic arm around the shoulders, should occur. The nonprofit's representatives should avoid being drawn into an argument or discussion of the merits of the decision, and should cut off the meeting if anyone becomes overly emotional or if the discussion becomes heated. If the discussion ignites, the nonprofit representatives should close the conference, stating simply, "We regret that you feel this way, but this is [the nonprofit's] decision. We wish you well in the future."

Details, Details

Either at a subsequent exit interview or before the termination meeting concludes, the nonprofit representatives should review the impact of termination on the employee's group health insurance benefits, request the employee's computer password as well as the return of agency property, such as computer diskettes, keys, or credit cards. Another important issue to discuss may be the nonprofit's policy on confidentiality, reminding the departing employee that it wouldn't be professional to discuss confidential information about clients, or important data belonging to the nonprofit, such as donor lists. Two final issues to cover with the employee are the nonprofit's reference policy (how requests from prospective employers seeking employment history will be handled) and the impact of termination on the employee's ability to qualify for unemployment compensation. (Voluntary separations and terminations due to misconduct usually disqualify an employee from eligibility for unemployment compensation.)

Voluntary Separation of Employment

A *resignation* implies that the separation of employment was voluntary. Resignations, job abandonment and failure to return from an authorized leave of absence are *voluntary quits*. Employees who resign or quit are generally disqualified from later being able to complain that they were discharged, and are generally ineligible for unemployment compensation. Therefore, the characterization of *resignation* can have legal significance to protect the nonprofit from a lawsuit for wrongful discharge. Nevertheless, just because an employee has resigned doesn't automatically insulate the nonprofit from legal troubles. When an employee gives notice that he or she will be resigning from employment, often the resignation is verbal. To memorialize the resignation the nonprofit should draft a written acceptance of the resignation, acknowledging the termination date in the memorandum. This ensures that later, when most of the details are forgotten, there will be irrefutable evidence that the employee voluntarily tendered his or her resignation.

Constructive Discharge

There is a legal theory called *constructive discharge,* which holds that even when an employee resigns, the employee may bring suit for wrongful termination or seek unemployment compensation on the theory that the wrongful acts of the employer made the workplace so intolerable that the plaintiff had no choice but to resign from employment. This theory is often used by plaintiffs alleging harassment, or workplace discrimination, claiming that the harassment by co-workers or management was so awful that they resigned—but that their resignation should actually be characterized as a discharge.

Negotiated Resignations

There are times when an employee is given the choice between resigning and being terminated. This choice is often accompanied by a negotiated settlement agreement in which the employee is informed that he or she will be terminated, but that the nonprofit will permit the employee to resign, if that's his or her choice. Some employees will choose to resign as a way of preserving their dignity in the process of losing a job. Because the employer initiated the separation, the employee will probably be eligible for unemployment compensation. Whenever an employee resigns in these circumstances, the nonprofit should consider asking the employee to sign a *separation agreement and release*, which is a legal document in which the employee promises to resign from employment and also promises not to bring a legal action against the nonprofit in the future, in exchange for some additional compensation, such as a severance payment.

Notice of Separation

Many nonprofits have policies that describe employment as at-will and state specifically that "termination may be with, or without notice." In other workplaces, it's common for the employer to require employees to give notice and to provide staff with notice prior to termination. Notice periods vary from nonprofit to nonprofit, but generally employers like to be notified at least two weeks before an employee's last day of work. While this may be convenient for the nonprofit, there is really no way to require an employee to give the nonprofit notice of resignation. Deterrents such as a policy that states that employees who fail to give notice will have a record in their file that their termination was *not in good standing* are generally perceived as empty, spiteful threats. Nonprofits may not threaten to withhold pay if no notice is given, since most states require final pay to be distributed within a short period of time following the employee's last day worked. In some states (but not all), an employer may adopt a policy providing that an employee who resigns without giving notice automatically forfeits accrued, unused vacation pay. This practice is prohibited in many states, including California, Illinois, Massachusetts, Michigan, New Jersey, and New York. In recognition that most employers have little or no leverage to enforce notice requirements, many nonprofits have decided to word their notice policies as a *request* for notice, with a reminder that providing notice is an expectation of professional conduct. Some nonprofits state in their policies that employees who resign without notice aren't eligible for future employment.

It should be noted that requiring employees to give notice is usually accompanied by the parallel expectation that the nonprofit will give employees the same time period of notice prior to termination of employment. If the nonprofit doesn't want to be held to always having to give employees notice prior to termination, or a payment in lieu of notice, then the nonprofit shouldn't require employees to give notice prior to resignation. On the other hand, if the nonprofit has made a promise, whether in a personnel policy manual or elsewhere, that employees will be given a certain period of notice prior to being separated from employment, that time period must be honored. In extreme circumstances, the nonprofit could require that the employee stop work immediately in which case the nonprofit would pay the employee *wages in lieu of notice* for the duration of the notice period.

Resigning employees will sometimes request to work up to a certain date, or request vacation for a period of time after their final day in the office. Neither request must be honored. The nonprofit may instead inform the employee that his or her last day of employment will be the date specified, thereby ceasing payroll liability (tax withholdings and health insurance premiums) for that employee. Instead of being *on vacation* post-separation, the employee may either take vacation prior to leaving the workplace or receive a lump sum equal to earned but unused vacation, if state law requires it or the nonprofit's policies provide this benefit.

Continuation of Health Insurance Benefits: COBRA and Parallel State Laws

Since loss of benefits is often on the minds of employees while they're losing their jobs, it's important to inform all separating employees of their right to health insurance benefits continuation. Most employers are required by state and/or federal law to provide employees with written notice of the employee's right to continue participating in health insurance plans, after termination. Workplaces with more than 20 employees are subject to the federal COBRA requirements, requiring employers to notify employees, in writing, at the outset of employment about employees' eligibility to elect continuation of health care insurance at their own cost. See 29 C.F.R. 2590 (www.dol.gov/ebsa/regs/fedreg/final/2004011796.htm). COBRA regulations also require that employers provide a formal written notice to employees when a qualifying event, such as termination of employment or reduction of work hours occurs and that employees must notify their employer when certain qualifying events occur, such as a determination of disability.

The U.S. Department of Labor issued final rules in 2004 that describe the content of the notices that must be provided to employees, as well as the timing of the notice. Sample notices that comply with the final rules are provided on the DOL Web site.[23] The *election notice* that's required in conjunction with a termination should be sent certified mail so that the nonprofit can prove notice was sent. If a former employee never receives notice and is dropped from health insurance coverage, and then requires medical care post termination, the nonprofit will be responsible for the former employee's medical bills. Additionally, there are penalties for noncompliance with COBRA, of $100 per beneficiary, per day of noncompliance.

---

23 Employee election form and explanation: *www.dol.gov/ebsa/modelelectionnotice.doc* and Initial COBRA notice: *www.dol.gov/ebsa/modelgeneralnotice.doc*

Summary of the Final Rules on COBRA Compliance

❑ The initial COBRA notice must be provided to all employees no later than 90 days from the date on which the covered employee or spouse first becomes covered under the plan.

❑ **Single Notice.** A single notice addressed to a covered employee and covered spouse is usually sufficient as long as they reside at the same location. A separate notice to dependent children who share the residence with the employee or spouse isn't required.

Notice Requirements for Employers

❑ Employers' Notice to Administrator. The employer must provide, to the administrator, a qualifying event notice when the qualifying event is the employee's death, termination of employment (except termination for gross misconduct), reduction of hours, or Medicare entitlement of the covered employee. The notice must also contain the date of qualifying event. This notice must be provided not later than 30 days after the date of the qualifying event.

Notice Requirements for Covered Employees

❑ The covered employee/qualified beneficiary is required to notify the employer when certain events occur:

   ❑ Divorce or legal separation.

   ❑ Child no longer dependent under the terms of the plan.

   ❑ A second qualifying event occurs that entitles the qualified beneficiary to an extension of COBRA coverage.

   ❑ When the qualified beneficiary is determined to be disabled by the Social Security Administration (and/or determined to no longer be disabled by the Social Security Administration).

The plan must establish reasonable procedures for qualified beneficiaries to use when notifying the plan administrator. These procedures must be disclosed in the Summary Plan Description (SPD).

The qualified beneficiary must notify the plan administrator of these events no later than 60 days after whichever of the dates is latest:

❑ the date of the qualifying event.

❑ the date the qualified beneficiary loses coverage as a result of the qualifying event, or

❑ the date the qualified beneficiary is informed of their responsibility to provide the notice.

Employee Notice of Disability

Notice must be provided by the covered employee not later than 60 days after whichever of the dates is latest:

❑ the date of the determination of disability by the SSA.

❑ the date of the qualifying event.

❑ the date the qualified beneficiary loses coverage due to the qualifying event.

❑ the date the qualified beneficiary is informed by the plan, of the responsibility to provide such notice.

Many insurance plans or independent service providers will handle COBRA record keeping (which is extensive) and notices for the nonprofit, however, the nonprofit should require that the service send the nonprofit a copy of all employee notices, since ultimately the nonprofit is legally responsible for providing employees with notice.

COBRA also applies to insurance coverage for dependents of employees. Dependents who are covered by the nonprofit's health insurance plans should also receive a notice when a qualifying event occurs that makes them eligible for continuation benefits.

Most states have a similar notice requirement for benefits continuation which may apply to workplaces that aren't covered by COBRA (workplaces with fewer than 20 employees.)

State Laws Governing Continuation Coverage

The state laws noted here are subject to constant review and revision in state legislatures. This summary should therefore be used for reference purposes, rather than as a definitive guide.

Arkansas: Applies to all employers; continuation coverage can extend for 120 days. See Arkansas Code Annot. Section 23-86-114.

California: Applies to all employers; employers must notify employees within 15 days of termination of group coverage. See Cal. Health and Safety Code Sections 1373.62; 1373.6,1374.58 and Cal. Insur. Code Section 12671.

Colorado: Applies to all employers; employers must give employees notice within 10 days of termination of employee's right to continue existing coverage, the amount the employee must pay, how, when and where payment is to be made and that failure to make a timely payment will result in lack of coverage. Employees must notify employer within 30 days of termination of the intent to elect continuation coverage. See Colo. Rev. Stat. Sections 10-16-108 through 10-16-201.5 and 10-16-214 through 10-16-217.

District of Columbia: Applies to all employees not covered by COBRA; Employers must offer employees not eligible for COBRA the right to continue benefits under the employer's health insurance plan for three months, unless the employee was discharged for gross misconduct. See D.C. Code Section 32-732.

Florida: Applies to small workplaces; employees must be permitted to participate in continuation coverage for an additional 18 months (29 months if disabled). Employees have to apply for coverage within 63 days after termination in the group policy. See Fla. Stat. Ann. Sections: 627.6692 and 627.6675.

Georgia: Applies to all employers; individuals who participated in group health plans for at least six months are entitled to continuation coverage for the remaining portion of the policy month, as well as three additional policy months. See O.C.G.A. Sections 33-24-21.1 and 33-24-21.2.

Hawaii: Applies to all employers; employees are permitted continuation coverage when they're unable to earn wages because of hospitalization or sickness; Employers must pay the employer's portion of premiums for up to three months. See Chapter 393, Section 11, 13, and 15, Hawaii Rev. Stats.

Idaho: Applies to all employers offering major medical overage; employers must make a continuation policy available to employees without any underwriting criteria. See Idaho Code Section 41-2220.

Illinois: Applies to employers that provide major medical insurance coverage; requires employers to continue coverage for up to nine months. See 215 ILCA Sections 5/367 5/267e, and 5/367.2.

Indiana: Applies to small employers; employees who have been continuously covered under a health insurance plan for at least 90 days who lose coverage because of termination of employment, reduction in hours, marriage dissolution or attainment of the age specified in the plan, are entitled to continuation benefits and to receive a conversion policy, if requested. See Indiana Code Sections 27-8-15-31 and 27-8-15-31.1.

Iowa: Applies to all employers; requires continuation of benefits or conversion of a health insurance policy following temporary or permanent layoff; approved leave of absence (such as failing to return after FMLA leave) or termination of employment. See Iowa Code Chapter 509B.

Kansas: Insurance companies must provide continuation benefits for six months when employment is terminated for any reason. Unlike COBRA, which places the burden of continuation on the employer, Kansas law places the burden of notice of continuation rights on insurers. See Kansas Stat. Annot. 40-2209(i).

Kentucky: Insurance companies and self-insured employers have obligations to provide continuation coverage as long as the employee has already been insured for three months and payment is made within 31 days. Continuation coverage ends on the earlier of 1) 18 months after coverage would otherwise have ended; 2) when payments aren't made in a timely fashion, and 3) when the group policy ends and isn't replaced. See Ky. Rev. Stat. Section 304,18-110.

Louisiana: Applies to all employers with fewer than 20 employees; employees who would lose coverage because of termination of employment are entitled to continue coverage for themselves and dependents if they've been continuously insured for three months; coverage continues until the individual becomes eligible for other group coverage, or it the premium isn't paid or a covered HMO moves out of the service area. See La. Rev. Stat. Ann. Section 22:215.13.

Maine: Applies to all employers; where a group policy was issued prior to January 1996, employees who have been employed for at least three months under a group policy are entitled to conversion. See 24-A Maine Rev. Stat Annot. Section 2809-A.

Maryland: Applies to all employers; State law is in addition to COBRA's requirements; Employees and dependent spouses who would otherwise lose insurance due to termination are entitled to continuation coverage for up to 18 months; until they fail to make premium payments in a timely matter or until they become eligible for other coverage or are entitled to convert to an individual policy. See Md. Code Ann. Ins. Sections 15-409, 15-412 and 15-414.

Massachusetts: There is a *mini-COBRA* statute applicable to employers with two to 19 employees, as well as another state law for employers with 20+ employees; for employees participating in small employer plans may have continuation coverage for either 18 or 36 months, depending on the circumstances; employers have an obligation to provide notice to employees; Employees and their dependents covered under group plans who lose coverage due to layoff or death are allowed to continue coverage for up to 39 weeks. In no event may the period of continuation coverage be greater than the period of time the employee was covered under the plan. See Mass. Gen. L.c. 176J Section 9 and 175 Section 110G.

Michigan: Applies to all employers; employees who have been covered under a group policy for at least three months are entitled to elect to convert their policy to an individual policy upon termination of employment unless termination is for gross misconduct. Dependents are also eligible. See Mich. Code L. 500.3612 (2) and (5).

Minnesota: Applies to all employers; every group insurance policy must provide that employees who are involuntarily or voluntarily discharged or laid off may elect to continue coverage for up to 18 months or until the employee is covered under another plan, provided the new plan doesn't exclude any pre-existing conditions. Employees who elect continuation coverage are required to pay their former employer the cost of the continued coverage. **Employers must notify employees of their rights within 10 days of termination.** See Minn. Stat. Ann. Sections 62A.17, 62A.21, 62A.146, and 62E.16.

Mississippi: Applies to employers not covered by Cobra (workplaces with one to 19 employees); provides that employees who have been covered for at least three months immediately prior to termination must be entitled to continuation coverage. The employee must make a written election of continuation on a form furnished by the insurer and pay in advance the amount of contributions requested. See Miss. Code Ann. Section 83-9-51.

Missouri: Applies to employers not covered by COBRA (workplaces with one to 19 employees); terminated employees who were participating in group health insurance continuously for the preceding three months may continue coverage under a group policy for up to nine months. Employees are required to pay the premiums and may convert to an individual policy if certain conditions are met. See Rev. Stat. Mo. Sections 376.428, 376.892 and 376.397.

Montana: Applies to all employers; Group insurance covering disability and major medical or surgical services may provide for continuation coverage after the death of the insured person; a person who is covered by a group policy and whose hours are reduced to less than the minimum required for coverage may continue coverage for up to a year with the consent of the employer; a person whose coverage is discontinued due to discharge may convert to an individual policy if the person has been insured for three months, as long as the person pays the premium within 31 days of termination. See Mont. Code Ann. Sections 33-22-503, 33-22-507 and 33-22-508.

Nevada: Applies to employers not covered by COBRA (workplaces with one to 19 employees); Employers must maintain a policy of group health insurance and must permit employees who are terminated or have their hours reduced, and spouses and dependent children, to continue coverage; Employees may continue coverage for up to 18 months for employees, and 36 months for spouses and children; Employees who voluntarily quit, who are terminated for gross misconduct, or who haven't been covered under any group plan for at least 12 consecutive months aren't entitled to continuation coverage. See Nev. Rev. Stat. 689B.245.

New Hampshire: Applies only to employers with 50+ employees and only to group hospital/medical expense policies and group health service plan contracts and HMOs; the state provisions are similar to COBRA's requirements. See New Hampshire Rev. Stat. Annot. 415.18 VII (g).

New Jersey: Applies to small employers with two to 49 employees who must extend health care coverage to employees who are terminated for a reason other than for cause, and to those employees whose hours are reduced to no less than 25 per week. See N.J. Stat. Ann. 34:11B-8, 17B:27-51.12 and 17B:27A-27.

New Mexico: Applies to employers not covered by COBRA; employers must provide six months of continuation coverage and the right to convert to an individual policy; Covered family members have the right to continue coverage, also; Employers must provide insurance company with insured's change of status and last known address; A continuing or converting person must give notice and make payment within 30 days. Coverage will be provided without proof of insurability and without pre-existing condition limits. See New Mexico Stat. Ann. Section 59A-18-16.

New York: Applies to employers with 20 or fewer employees; State law provides for continuation coverage that's comparable to COBRA but applies to smaller workplaces; Continuation is available for 29 months if the employee is determined to be disabled at the time of termination or within 60 day of coverage. In general, employees or dependents cease to be eligible when the employee is covered by another plan, ceases to pay premiums in a timely manner or becomes eligible for Medicare. See New York Ins. Law Section 3221.

North Carolina: Applies to all employers, but not to those with self-insured plans; employees may continue certain hospital, surgical, major medical and other insurance policies for up to 18 months, if the employee has been continuously insured during the three consecutive months prior to date of termination. See North Carolina Gen. Stat. Section 58-53.1 et seq.

North Dakota: Applies to all employers; continuation coverage is available for up to 39 weeks if requested in writing within 10 days after the date of termination or date the employee or dependent is notified of the right to elect coverage, whichever is later. Employees must have been continuously insured under the group plan for the entire three-month period prior to termination. After the continuation period, employees and their dependents can elect a conversion plan. See N.D.C.C. Section 26.1-36-23.

Ohio: Applies to employers with fewer than 20 employees; Ohio law is similar to COBRA but only allows continuation coverage for six months; employees must have been continuously covered for three months preceding the end of employment. Insured persons also have the right to convert group coverage into an individual policy. See Ohio Rev. Code Sections 3923.38, 3923.32, and 3923.122.

Oklahoma: Applies to all employers; employees whose insurance is terminated under a group policy must remain insured under that policy for at least 30 days post termination unless the employee and dependents become eligible under another policies. Group policies must provide for conversion. See Okla Stat. Title 36 Sections 4502.1 and 4509.

Oregon: Applies to all employers; employees may continue coverage for medical expenses under a group health insurance policy for six months after the date of the end of coverage due to termination. Employees are required to pay premiums. Continuation isn't available under the state statute when the employee is covered by another plan, such as federal COBRA. See Oregon Rev. Stat. 743.610 and 743.600.

Rhode Island: Applies to all employers (except certain construction businesses); Employees who lose coverage may continue coverage for up to 18 months. Continuation may not exceed the shorter of the period of continuous employment with the employer or the time at which the employee becomes employed and is eligible for benefits under another group plan. See R.I. Gen. Laws Section 27-19.1-1.

South Carolina: Applies to all employers providing group health insurance that aren't covered by COBRA; Individuals who lose coverage, but have been covered under a group policy for hospital, surgical and major medical insurance continuously for six months, are entitled to continue coverage for six months. See S.C. Code Ann.Section 39-71.770.

South Dakota: Applies to all employers; employees have the right to have coverage continue for themselves and dependents for 18 months; Qualified beneficiaries may continue coverage for 36 months; employee and dependents may continue coverage for 12 months, if coverage ends because the employer ceased operations. Employees can convert to an individual policy without evidence of insurability by applying to the employer within 180 days of continuation coverage and praying the premium. See S.D.C.L. 58-18-7.4, 7.5, 7.12 and 58-18C-1.

Tennessee: Applies to all employers; Employees whose coverage is terminated for any reason are entitled to coverage for the end of the month in which termination occurs and an additional three months as long as the employee has been continuously insured for at least three months prior to termination. Employers may require employees to pay the premium in advance, including any portion of the premium usually paid by the employee; Similar provisions for spouses; when coverage is terminated during pregnancy, the law requires continuation coverage the rest of the month in which termination occurred plus an additional six-months post birth. See TCA Section 56-72312.

Texas: Applies to all employers not subject to COBRA; continuation coverage is required for certain dependents for up to three years if termination of coverage is because of death, retirement or divorce. A dependent must have been covered by the group policy for one year or be an infant one year old. Other requirements for dependent continuation coverage. If employees meet requirements, Texas law requires that when either their job ends or COBRA ends, all group plans must offer the chance to continue group coverage for six months. Before the continuation period ends, employees must be provided with information about the Texas Health Insurance Risk Pool. See Insurance Code Sections 1506.152 and 1506.153, and Texas Admin Code Title 28, Part 1, Chapter 3, Subchapter F, Rule 3.504.

Utah: Applies to all employers; Spouses are entitled to convert coverage to an individual policy after divorce or annulment from the covered employee; State law prohibits an insurer from considering whether the insured is a victim of domestic abuse in refusing to continue insuring or refusing to convert the insured. See Utah Code Sections 31A-22-612 and 31A-21-503.

Vermont: Applies to all employers; Whether COBRA applies or not, continuation coverage is required of all employers offering hospital and medical insurance; any person whose coverage would end is entitled to continuation coverage as long as the covered employee was insured for the three months immediately preceding termination; Continuation coverage not available for employees discharged for misconduct; conversions possible without evidence of insurability. See 8 Vermont Stat. Annot. Sections 4090a and 4090d.

Virginia: Applies to private employers; employees whose hospital and medical policies are terminated must be offered either a conversion policy or a 90-day continuation of coverage at the policy holder's selection. See Va. Code 38.2-3541.

Washington: Applies to all employers; employers with group health plans are required to include an option for employees who become ineligible for coverage to continue group benefits for a period of time at an agreed-upon rate; The law also provides for the right to obtain conversion coverage. See Wash. Rev. Code Sections 48.21.250 through 270.

West Virginia: Applies to all employers with group accident and sickness insurance; policies must contain a provision that permits eligible employees to pay premiums at group rate and receive the same coverage for up to 18 months when an employee is *laid off*. See W. Va. Code Section 33-16-3(e).

Wisconsin: Applies to all employers; terminated insureds are allowed to continue group coverage or convert to individual policies for up to 18 months. See Wis. Stat. Section 632.897.

Wyoming: applies to all employers not covered by COBRA; employees and dependents can continue coverage if they've been covered for the preceding three months or they can convert to an individual policy as long as coverage in the group policy wasn't because of failure to pay any required contribution or because discontinued group policy was replaced by a similar group policy. See Wyo. Stat. Sections 26-19-113 and 26-22-201.

SAMPLE --

Exit Interview Form

_____   _____   _____
Employee Interviewed   Date   Conducted By

1. For what reason(s) are you leaving?

2. What is your understanding of the events that have led to your separation from employment with this organization?

3. What is your opinion of the supervision you received?

4. What did you most like and dislike about this organization and its policies?

5. What do you recommend that the organization change, if anything?

6. What is your opinion of the working conditions at this organization?

7. How do you feel about the pay? Benefits?

8. What is your opinion about the training you received?

9. Do you believe that appropriate opportunities for advancement were available to you?

10. Did you experience or witness discrimination, harassment, or other illegal conduct during your tenure with this organization?

11. Have you obtained a new job? Yes _____ No _____ If yes, please tell us: _____

Employer's name: _____

Address: _____

Position title: _____ Starting salary: _____

11. What do you see as most attractive about your new job? _____

12. Additional Comments: _____

Exit Interviews

There is no legal requirement that employers grant exit interviews to departing employees but it's a prudent risk management strategy to do so. Typically, exit interviews are only requested of employees who leave the nonprofit voluntarily or on good terms. However, because the goals of the exit interview are to give the departing employee formal information about the separation of employment and for the employer to gain information about the employee's work experience, exit interviews are relevant for all departing employees, and should be a consistent part of the separation process with an employee for whatever reason.

Exit interviews can cover a host of issues, but several are paramount. The nonprofit representative should explain the nonprofit's reference policy and the importance of keeping sensitive client or agency information confidential. Many employers request that the departing employee sign a form at this juncture, promising to keep information learned during the course of employment confidential in accordance with the nonprofit's confidentiality policy (*Note:* a better time to obtain an employee's signature on a confidentiality agreement is at the beginning of the employment relationship.) Keys, electronic devices such as a mobile phone and pager, credit card, and other property can be returned, and the employee's emotional reaction to separation can be gauged.

The interviewer, preferably not the employee's supervisor or the person who terminated the employee, may be most successful when posing open-ended questions about the employee's work experience. If the employee is angry about the termination, that anger might be diffused by an opportunity to describe the work experience with the interviewer. Similarly, the nonprofit will benefit from learning about the concerns and issues expressed by the departing employee. This is the nonprofit's chance to probe for internal management problems that might otherwise go unreported. Are supervisors sensitive to employee concerns? Do the nonprofit employees believe that management is fair? Is there an atmosphere of racism or sexism? Do employees feel fairly compensated?

Every employee should be asked during the exit interview whether he or she experienced or witnessed discrimination or harassment or other illegal conduct. A denial by the employee during the exit interview of discrimination or harassment can seriously undercut any future claims raised by the employee. On the flip side, expression of such claims during the exit interview can be helpful in highlighting a hidden problem and preparing the nonprofit for a potential legal challenge.

The interviewer should place copies of any document shown or discussed with the employee during the interview into the employee's personnel file with a summary of the exit interview. An effective exit interview can bring closure to separation, make it easier for the nonprofit to anticipate legal challenges, spot internal issues that otherwise would have gone unnoticed, and create a record that important mandatory notices were communicated to the employee.

Risk Management Checklist for Terminations

- ❏ **Follow closely any internal policies and procedures in the organization's handbook.** Before taking any significant step that will negatively impact an employee's situation, always consult the organization's personnel policies or employee handbook to determine whether or not the situation is covered. If so, *follow your established procedures.* If the procedures really don't make sense in the situation at hand, consult with legal counsel.

- ❏ **Articulate the objective, business-related reason for deciding which employee(s) will be terminated.** Challenge yourself. Write down the business reason. If you can't, that's a signal to you that an aggrieved employee could successfully challenge the termination decision.

- ❏ **Consult with legal counsel, experienced in employment matters.** Terminations create too great a risk to fly solo. In advance of needing to consult with an employment lawyer, identify legal resources in your community where the nonprofit can receive advice from an employment lawyer; ideally one who has worked with other clients in the nonprofit sector.

- ❏ **Consider using a separation agreement and release.** If your organization wants to take the most conservative path, and has assets available to write a check to departing employees, then consider using a *Separation Agreement and Release.* A Separation Agreement and Release is a legally enforceable contract that commits the organization to compensate the departing employee in exchange for a promise by the employee not to bring a legal action against the employer. Such an agreement, if carefully crafted, can document and clarify the terms of the separation, such as the impact to the separating employees on their insurance coverage and the dollar amount of their separation packages. The agreement can also describe other obligations that may be important to the organization, such as the requirement that the departing employees keep certain information confidential, or return the organization's property. The *release* aspect of the agreement (if drafted correctly) can prevent a former employee from bringing a lawsuit against the organization.

    The **benefit** of these agreements is that they provide certainty to an otherwise often uncertain situation.

    The **downside** is that they're costly, both in terms of the additional compensation to the departing employees and because it's unwise to use these agreements without professional legal assistance in drafting the language and in negotiating the agreement, often with the departing employee's lawyer.

- ❏ **Finally: Review your organization's directors' and officers' liability insurance** or consult with your insurance broker/agent to confirm that your organization has coverage for Employment Practices Liability (EPL) claims. Typical coverage will cover the costs of defending an organization when terminations are challenged. If you don't understand the coverage for employment practices claims after reading your policy, contact your agent/broker and request assistance. Describe your circumstances and ask his or her opinion about whether there would be coverage in the event that one of the affected employees brought a future legal claim against the organization. Ask the nonprofit's agent/broker to respond in writing. Armed with that information, the nonprofit can make a business decision about the potential financial costs/risks of the planned action. Note that insurance **won't** cover payments to employees for separation pay.

Separation of Older Workers

Age discrimination is a risk whenever a nonprofit terminates or seeks the resignation of an older worker. Consequently, a sound risk management strategy is to structure the separation of older workers through a *negotiated agreement* with the employee. A negotiated agreement will give the nonprofit the benefit of discharging the older worker, while reducing the risk that the former employee will bring a suit for age discrimination. It will also give the former employee a cushion of compensation to soften the blow of separation.

Even though the negotiated agreement will result in giving severance pay to the older worker, such money will be far less costly in the long run than defending a lawsuit for age discrimination. The nonprofit should involve legal counsel in drafting the separation agreement, which should include a *release* of all claims the employee might bring against the nonprofit. Severance pay in some appropriate negotiated amount is exchanged for the employee's promise to resign and not to bring suit. A recent survey found that the average severance pay-out equation was slightly over one week per year of service. (*Source*: Watson Wyatt Worldwide.) Due to the requirements of the federal legislation protecting older workers, it's advisable to have legal counsel draft all separation agreements with older workers.

The Age Discrimination in Employment Act of 1967 (ADEA) (www.eeoc.gov/policy/adea.html), in conjunction with more recent federal legislation called the Older Workers Benefit Protection Act of 1990 (OWBPA) (www.eeoc.gov/abouteeoc/35th/thelaw/owbpa.html) require that when an older worker (defined in the ADEA as over 40 years old; various state laws define the protected category differently) is separated from employment subject to a release, certain procedures must be followed to ensure that the employee wasn't coerced into signing the release. The ADEA, as amended by OWBPA, sets out specific minimum standards that must be met for a waiver to be considered *knowing and voluntary* and, therefore, valid. Among other requirements, a valid ADEA waiver: 1) must be in writing and be understandable; 2) must specifically refer to ADEA rights or claims; 3) may not waive rights or claims that may arise in the future; 4) must be in exchange for valuable consideration; 5) must advise the individual in writing to consult an attorney before signing the waiver; and 6) must provide the individual at least 21 days to consider the agreement and at least seven days to revoke the agreement after signing it.

These are prudent guidelines to follow for any release. Without a strong showing that the release was voluntary, it won't be valid, and the separating employee would be able to bring suit against the nonprofit for wrongful discharge despite having received severance pay. In fact, recent U.S. Supreme Court rulings suggest that if an older worker disputes the legality of the separation agreement, he or she may still be able to keep the severance payments. *Oubre v. Entergy Operations, Inc.* 52 US 422 (1998).

Separation Pay or Severance Pay

Lay-offs that are motivated by economic or administrative reasons, such as a staff reorganization or loss of funding, are common in the nonprofit sector. Through no fault of their own, employees may find themselves without a job. Because such a termination is often unexpected and not the fault of the employee, many nonprofit employers offer separation pay when termination is a result of economic necessity. There is a risk in having such a policy as a standard procedure: in cases where a severe shortfall necessitates layoffs, there may not be sufficient funding to cover separation payments for all employees, despite expectations or a past practice of paying severance.

Consequently, while softening the blow of a lay-off is a terrific idea, rather than codifying separation pay in personnel policies, it's better to offer it as funding allows, or to make it clear through policy language that separation pay will be offered, "at the discretion of the board, as funding permits."

Downsizing

Technically *downsizing* simply means that an organization is going through a process of reducing the number of staff or volunteers. In other words, the organization is terminating someone's employment or volunteer service. No matter *what* the organization calls it, *how* the organization conducts this process can heighten or lessen exposure to legal claims.

When economics dictate that a staff position be cut, it's critical that the nonprofit have a well-supported business reason to determine which employees are to be terminated. The risk is that the nonprofit will be vulnerable to claims that discrimination played a part in deciding who was to remain and who was to be let go. Whenever a nonprofit is considering lay-offs, alternatives should be considered. Can the objectives of the *reduction-in-force* (RIF) be accomplished through a hiring freeze, salary freeze, reducing hours, or changing some employees to part-time classification? The nonprofit should document that it has considered alternatives to the RIF, and should spell out in a written memorandum to the board, the business reasons for the necessary lay-offs, as well as justification of those positions selected for termination.

Before implementing the terminations/lay-offs, consider the impact on the workforce. Is the downsizing going to affect a particular group of employees more than others? Is the reorganization going to eliminate the only minority in the agency? If so, there are clear liability risks involved in the RIF, even if there are solid business reasons for the selection of that particular position or employee.

The nonprofit can reduce the risks of liability in a number of ways. Ask for voluntary resignations. Offer those who volunteer a severance package with a release. Alternatively, target the position to be eliminated, but offer a severance package to the employee in that position and request that the employee sign a release in exchange for severance pay. Such severance pay offers and the release should be orchestrated with the assistance of legal counsel.

In selecting which employees/positions will be eliminated, it's imperative to use an objective method, such as seniority, or link the positions/job functions to essential parts of the mission or specific goals of the organization, after conducting a needs analysis. Another objective method of selection would be to base retention on a lottery, or on past performance, retaining those employees with the strongest performance, and letting go those with weaker performance ratings. Whatever the method: 1) convene an oversight committee to provide objectivity for the process of implementing the reductions, 2) conduct a needs analysis to determine which positions are critical and which could be eliminated, and 3) identify a legitimate business reason for the reduction/termination(s), and 4) review the termination decisions for discriminatory bias.

A legitimate business reason for a termination is that the nonprofit has fewer dollars for its operating budget, and, therefore, must decrease costs by eliminating a staff position. The decision of which staff position to eliminate must also be based on legitimate, objective business reasons.

Salary shouldn't be a consideration in who goes and who stays, since typically older workers are those both with longer tenure and at the higher end of the salary scale, therefore basing the decision solely on compensation may result in a claim of age discrimination. A legitimate business reason is objective criteria that the organization either has established through policy or precedent, or that the organization states in connection with the termination at hand.

Examples of objective criteria used by employers to successfully justify downsizing decisions include:

❑ **Seniority:** last hired, first fired.

❑ **The Weakest Link:** employees whose performance evaluations demonstrate that they fail to meet the expectations for their performance criteria will be discharged.

❑ **Strategic Positioning:** employees whose job duties are linked to programmatic goals that are no longer a priority for the nonprofit will be terminated.

❑ **Budget Reductions:** employees whose salaries are paid through a grant, contract or other funding that isn't renewed will be terminated.

Once you are satisfied that there is a legitimate business reason for the termination, also ask: "What will the human impact of this termination be on the remaining workforce?" (For example, is the person being terminated the only person over 40 years old in the workplace? If so, this could result in the appearance that the termination was motivated by age discrimination.) Sometimes, even though there is an obvious objective business-related criterion for the termination, the end result is that the workplace is less well-balanced in terms of minority representation. The resulting imbalance can give rise to allegations that the process used to select who would remain, and who would be terminated, was discriminatory.

Wrongful discharge claims in downsizing situations typically allege:

❑ discrimination

❑ retaliation

❑ violation of public policy, violation of whistleblower protection laws

❑ violation of family and medical leave laws

❑ violation of a state or federal WARN Act

It's critical to communicate to the staff the reason for the downsizing. Management or the board should share the economic realities of the situation with the staff, and explain the business justification for the reorganization or downsizing. The nonprofit might express that the downsizing is being carried out reluctantly and only after efforts had been taken to avoid such as result. If possible, the nonprofit might make an effort to network with other nonprofits in the community to identify alternative new positions for those being let go.

In severe downsizing situations, such as a nonprofit closing its doors, the federal Worker Adjustment and Retraining Notification (WARN) Act or a parallel state law may apply. WARN requires employers to give employees 60 days' advance notice when 50 or more employees will be terminated, if that constitutes one-third of the workforce (or when 500 or more employees will be laid off). WARN only applies to those nonprofits with 100 or more full- or part-time employees, who, in aggregate, work at least 4,000 hours per week.

❑ Beware of state laws: the Michigan mass layoff law affects workplaces with 25 or more employees; in Hawaii, Massachusetts, Tennessee, Wisconsin and Maryland, the trigger is 50 employees; and Connecticut and Maine have their own state WARN Acts affecting workplaces with 100 employees. In Minnesota, a nonprofit must immediately notify employees in writing when a petition for bankruptcy is filed.

❑ **Connecticut** law requires employers with more than 100 employees to pay for the continuation of health insurance benefits in full for up to 120 days, or until employees become eligible for group coverage, whichever comes first, in the event of a plant closing or mass layoffs. Conn. Gen. Stat. Sections 31-51n et seq. and 38A-554.

Basic Risk Management Principles to Reduce Liability for Wrongful Termination in Downsizing Situations

1. **Preparation:** Know in advance what criteria the nonprofit would use in the event that the organization is faced with the necessity of downsizing. Make sure the criteria used to determine who is terminated and who remains are objective, legitimate, business reasons. Know whether the organization is covered by the federal or state laws governing plant closings.

2. **Documentation:** It's important to articulate the objective business-related reason(s) for why a certain individual(s) was selected for termination but not another. The reasons should be documented in a management memo at the time the decisions are made. Consider formalizing a practice or internal procedure for managers requiring documentation of their decision making.

3. **Consistency:** Be consistent in the nonprofit's message to employees affected, as well as to any third parties. Make sure that individuals in similar circumstances are treated comparably (Example: If all employees with 10 years or more of tenure are given seniority preference in a downsizing, someone with 7.5 years of tenure *isn't* in the same category as someone with 10 years' tenure.)

4. **Compassionate Communication:** Verbally inform the employee(s) as soon as possible about a planned termination, and explain the business related reason. If the termination is based on performance failures, explain that. Giving employees advance awareness of significant changes in their workplace will ease anxiety (and anger) caused by last-minute announcements, and give affected employees an opportunity to transition into alternate employment.

5. **Remain Receptive to Complaints and Concerns:** When an employee loses his or her job, expect multiple, legitimate concerns ranging from the impact on health insurance to a request for a job reference. Make sure that those affected know that the organization is open to their questions and concerns, and that they've ready access to someone who can answer their questions. Internal grievance procedures can channel complaints about terminations to the organization first, before the aggrieved former employee engages a lawyer.

6. **Provide Help:** Many nonprofits are too small to offer ongoing employee assistance programs, and most organizations have adopted strict rules prohibiting use of the organization's assets (such as, computers, telephones or photocopiers) for personal reasons. Consider relaxing some of the rules for affected employees (for a limited time), in order to provide the assistance an employee may need during the difficult transition period. Before informing affected employees about their separation, conduct research on the availability of job placement services or other forms of support. If reasonably priced, consider paying for these services for affected employees. At a minimum, provide employees with information on any available free resources.

Post-Termination Protocol

After an employee has been terminated, there is always a risk that the employee will claim that the termination, or the way it was conducted, caused damage to the employee's reputation. For this reason, there is a risk of defamation associated with every termination. To guard against this risk and to uphold your commitment to "taking the high road" in your employment practices, there should be no casual discussion with any other staff member about the particulars of any other employee's separation. Discussions of the details of a former employee's termination with staff members, clients, or third parties could result in a lawsuit for *breach of privacy* or *defamation*. Consequently, only minimal information should be shared with the nonprofit's staff and constituency. Beware of written communications that mention the termination in a letter to clients, constituents, funders and board members. Even reports made to the board of directors about a staff member's termination have been known to be the genesis of claims that the report to the board defamed the terminated employee.

Of course, in most situations it's necessary to explain the departure of a staff member. For visible positions, such as top management, it's appropriate to circulate a brief memorandum announcing the termination, but only with prior approval of the employee being terminated. During the termination conference, present the employee with a proposed announcement of the termination/resignation, and make sure the employee is comfortable with the memo that will be circulated. If the employee objects, reach an understanding with the employee as to how inquiries will be handled and what message will be given to co-workers concerning the termination. It's better to have the former employee's blessing on the message than to be sued later for defamation or breach of privacy.

Reference Policies

One of the issues to discuss with employees during a termination conference is how the nonprofit will handle requests from prospective employers making inquiries about the employee's employment history. Many nonprofits have very conservative reference policies, such that when inquiries are made the nonprofit will only respond with the dates of employment, confirmation of job title and compensation. This policy is protective of the nonprofit, because it prevents negative information from being shared with a prospective employer, reducing the risk of a claim of defamation. However, if every nonprofit took this stance on references, it would be difficult if not impossible, to screen prospective employees. References are a valuable and important screening tool. Refusing to provide adequate references also puts the nonprofit at risk for a claim alleging *negligent failure to warn*. As indicated in a prior section of this text, an employer can be held liable for failing to disclose an employee's known propensity to violence. A better policy is to provide more meaningful information to prospective employers after obtaining a waiver and authorization from the former employee. Such waivers are effective to block defamation suits.

Regardless of whether the nonprofit uses a waiver, it must tread carefully to avoid potential liability for defamation any time it provides information about former employees. A claimant alleging defamation, including written defamation (libel) or spoken defamation (slander), must generally prove that:

1. the communication was defamatory (defined as language, spoken or written, that tends to lower an individual in the esteem of any substantial and respectable group);

2. the communication was made in reckless disregard of the truth or with the knowledge of its falsity and with intent to harm the subject of the communication; and

3. injury resulted.

Defamation is actually a difficult claim to prove, however, just the allegation is damaging. The best way to insulate the organization from potential liability for defamation is to have a policy that states: details about a former employee's work history or qualifications from employment will only be provided if the former employee has signed a written authorization/waiver, and that statements about a former employee will be limited to those that can be supported by the nonprofit's written records. For example, informing a prospective employer that, "Mary was occasionally tardy," would be inappropriate unless Mary's personnel file contained information supporting this statement. The most powerful defense against defamation is truth. Therefore, any reference provided by the nonprofit about a former employee should provide truthful, verifiable (supported by documentation) information about the employee.

It's typical for job-seekers to list their supervisor as a reference. As a result, a former employee's supervisor may be contacted by a prospective employer. It's critical to specifically designate through the organization's policies *who* has the authority to give references. Any supervisor or others who are authorized to provide references should receive training about the risks of negligent references and safe practices in reference giving.

An additional emerging state-level protection is legislation insulating former employers from defamation suits by former employees for giving legitimate factual job performance information in the course of providing a reference. These laws are referred to as *job reference immunity laws*. Almost every state has extended immunity to employers for giving information to prospective employers about a former employee's qualifications for employment.

Grievance Procedures and Internal Dispute Resolution

Having an internal mechanism for resolving disputes is like wearing a seat belt—an internal restraint can help the nonprofit avoid harm from a civil lawsuit. Providing an outlet for employees' frustrations at the workplace is a proven safety valve.

Rather than turning a deaf ear to complaints, nonprofits need to provide employees with a credible listener who will also provide an objective review of their grievance. Employees will feel fairly treated if they've had an opportunity to tell their story, and the nonprofit has the benefit of learning, outside of litigation, the details of the employee's concerns so that corrections can be made, if warranted. Insurance carriers and defense lawyers recommend that every employer have some sort of internal procedure for resolving complaints.

Recent decisions by the U.S. Supreme Court concerning sexual harassment have decreed that when there was a complaint mechanism at the workplace that the victim did not take advantage of, the employer has an affirmative defense to a lawsuit. Courts reason that if a plaintiff (employee) truly felt harassed, she or he would have taken advantage of the employer's grievance procedures. This same reasoning is often used to challenge the credibility of plaintiffs' complaints in other types of employment law actions. Therefore, not only is having an internal grievance mechanism effective from an employee relations perspective, but it's a basic risk management strategy that every nonprofit should implement.

There are various types of internal dispute resolution options, ranging from a very formal, binding mandatory arbitration procedure (not permitted in some states, such as Kentucky), to the informal open-door policy favored by most mid-sized and small nonprofits. Some options are: 1) mandatory binding arbitration, 2) a commitment to bring disputes to alternative dispute resolution (ADR), using non-binding arbitration, 3) a formal two- or three-step grievance procedure, with a review committee composed of various board and staff members, 4) referral of the dispute to an impartial party, who may or may not be connected with the nonprofit, to serve as the arbiter of disputes, 5) an open-door policy that encourages employees to bring their concerns to management, and 6) a peer review committee.

Whatever the mechanism, an internal dispute resolution procedure is helpful because it provides an outlet for employees' concerns. A grievance or complaint procedure gives the employee his or her "day in court" and can be helpful for the nonprofit's management, because misunderstandings or unhealthy disputes between staff may be uncovered and addressed before the conflicts spin out of control. Serious concerns can be uncovered and addressed by the nonprofit before a lawsuit is filed. The goal of internal dispute resolution is to solve the problems at the lowest level possible, so that workplace disputes don't escalate into legal actions. It's important that whatever internal dispute resolution procedures the nonprofit uses provide that employees who use the process won't be retaliated against.

Alternative Dispute Resolution

Increasingly employers, including those in the nonprofit sector, are using agreements to require employees to resolve any future dispute using alternative dispute resolution (ADR) methods, rather than proceed directly to court. This requirement is an effort to avoid the large expenses involved with litigating employment law cases. There are ADR firms that provide mediation services to address employment-related disputes. Before establishing a policy that requires mediation of disputes or arbitration, check with the nonprofit's insurance agent. It's likely that alternative dispute resolution costs will be covered under employment practices liability coverage. However, due to the variation in policy forms, confirm the coverage with the nonprofit's insurance agent. If the policy doesn't provide coverage for alternative dispute resolution, it may be available by purchasing an endorsement.

Formal Written Grievance Procedure

Another way to increase the likelihood that workplace disputes will be raised internally in a timely fashion is to implement a formal grievance policy. The basic elements of a written grievance procedure are:

❏ A requirement that employees exercise the grievance procedure by submitting their disputes or complaints to the nonprofit in a timely fashion;

❏ A statement of how complaints are submitted (usually in writing) and to whom (usually there is a choice of two people so that if one of the identified persons makes the complainant uncomfortable, the other is still an option.);

❏ An identification of who will review the complaints and make the determination;

❏ A statement that retaliation against any employee who brings a complaint is prohibited and will subject the retaliator to discipline up to and including discharge; and

❏ A statement that the nonprofit will report back to the complaining party, and that the nonprofit's decision is final.

The use of an internal grievance procedure doesn't eliminate the possibility of a legal claim. If an employee is dissatisfied with the final determination of the internal grievance procedure, the employee can still hire a lawyer to file a lawsuit. However, this risk is greatly reduced in cases where the employee already had his or her case heard internally. Moreover, the nonprofit will be aware of the concerns by that point, and should be prepared to effectively defend the claim.

Advantages of an Ombudsperson

In order for internal grievance procedures to be a success, the panel or individuals who review the grievance must have the respect of the staff and must be perceived as neutral, unbiased, and credible. Sometimes hiring an outside person to serve as *ombudsperson** is an effective method of preserving credibility and objectivity. Appointing an internal ombudsperson from a different division or department might also be an option. The ombudsperson could be selected on a permanent basis, or case by case, as the need arises. The ombudsperson reviews the concern(s), interviews the complainant(s) and issues a determination to the nonprofit's administration or board. When confidentiality is a major concern, an outside consultant or alternative dispute resolution firm is particularly effective serving in this role. If well executed, employees will respect the results, which aren't binding on the employee or nonprofit.

Open-Door Policy

An open door policy implies that when an employee has a concern, he or she should first approach his or her supervisor or even the executive director for an informal discussion and attempt at resolution, and if not satisfied, should write a formal complaint, which the supervisor is obligated to take to the next level of management. Often a policy will spell out the time frames for employee complaints and for the nonprofit's responses. Generally it's best to stay flexible with time frames. Unforeseen circumstances may prevent the nonprofit from responding within the given span. Nevertheless, it's best to respond as quickly as possible to all employee complaints. To address situations when the employee isn't satisfied with the response of a supervisor to a stated concern, many nonprofits permit an appeal to a progressively higher level of management, sometimes including the board of directors in the dispute resolution process. Alternatively, if the nonprofit doesn't wish to involve board members in internal squabbles, the executive director/CEO can serve as the final arbiter. The advantage of an open-door policy is that the nonprofit has numerous opportunities to check itself, to ensure that the Fundamental Fairness Formula was followed, and to correct any deficiencies before a potentially hostile review by external eyes.

Peer Review Boards

Another method of internal dispute resolution is referral of the dispute to a peer review board comprised of a panel of employees who consider the dispute or complaint and determine the outcome. Often the panel will need to be trained by an outside consultant. Those on the panel need to respect the confidentiality of all employees who come before the review board. The nonprofit can limit the authority of the panel to disputes involving only certain types of discipline or particular policy violations and in this way can combine a peer review panel with other methods of internal dispute resolution. In certain workplaces, where there is already a great deal of trust, a peer review panel can be extremely effective.

Employee Complaint? Caution!

Whatever the method used, the secret to success is to respond immediately to an employee's complaint. While the nonprofit's written policy should require employees to put complaints in writing, if a supervisor merely hears about an employee's complaint, the supervisor should remind the employee that no retaliation may be taken against the employee and encourage the employee to put the complaint in writing for further review and investigation.

Red Flag! No Retaliation!

Nonprofits need to be aware that in many instances it's illegal for an employer to retaliate against an employee who files a complaint with either government offices or internally. In more and more states, employees are protected by state *whistleblowing* laws for reporting that their employer or a co-worker is engaging in illegal or unethical practices. Make sure that if an employee has filed any complaint that disciplinary action taken by the employer against that employee is clearly documented to show that the reason for the discipline is unrelated to the complaint filed by the employee.

The Whistleblower

Janet was the bookkeeper at a large nonprofit foundation. Her work habits deteriorated shortly after her six-month work test period. She began coming to work chronically late and using her sick leave as it accrued. The executive director tried talking to her about the problem several times. When there was no improvement, he documented the behavior and began the progressive discipline process outlined in the employee handbook. After the process was initiated, Janet wrote a letter to the foundation's president accusing the foundation's executive director of misusing the organization's credit card for personal expenses. Shortly after this, the disciplinary process was complete and Janet was terminated for cause. Although the executive director was cleared of any wrongdoing, Janet sued the foundation alleging that her termination was related to her charges. The organization prevailed, but spent $15,000 in defense costs just to get the case dismissed.

---

*The term ombudsperson has various meanings in different workplace settings. We use it here to connote an objective third party charged with hearing and resolving internal disputes or the designated person to whom employees should direct their allegations of wrongdoing or concerns about improper conduct at the workplace.

Ten-Step Formal Investigation of Employee Wrongdoing

1. Allow a short but significant time to pass so that all involved can gain perspective and cool down. Waiting any longer than 48 hours to investigate a serious offense or allegation isn't appropriate. Fairness to all concerned dictates that the investigation be started expeditiously and completed efficiently.

2. Gather all physical evidence that might be helpful in the investigation. Secure the evidence and keep it confidential.

3. Obtain written statements, which should be signed and dated, from all involved or who witnessed the conduct/incident. Keep the statements confidential.

4. Review what disciplinary steps have been taken in the past for similar conduct and review the employee's entire personnel record.

5. If the employee is in a protected category, determine whether the employee has been treated differently than others, and whether his or her protected status played a part in the disparate treatment.

6. Get a full statement from the employee including comments that the employee offers as mitigating circumstances.

7. Have the appropriate decision maker document the business-related reason for whatever discipline will be imposed (or not imposed).

8. Ask someone not directly involved with the situation to act as an objective review and final filter.

9. Consult an employment law specialist to ensure that there are no hidden issues and that all steps have been appropriate. An attorney can help project the likelihood of subsequent legal action if the decision to terminate is carried out, or related actions are taken or not taken, and can provide an assessment of the nonprofit's chances of successfully defending its actions. When a potential termination arises, if the nonprofit has followed the preceding steps, a short telephone conference with an attorney may be all that's needed to determine whether the nonprofit has taken appropriate risk management steps.

10. Communicate the final decision to the affected employee in a calm manner, and communicate the result of the investigation to those involved without violating the privacy of the employee or others involved in the investigation. Document the investigation and termination decision in a summary memorandum.

In the next section, Chapter 8, we examine policies for prevention and prudent response to allegations of workplace harassment.

Chapter 8

Illegal Harassment—Policies for Prevention and Prudent Responses

What Is Illegal Harassment?

Harassment is a subsection of discrimination, which is illegal when it's based on a person's characteristics that are protected by law, such as age, race, color, religion, gender, marital status, military status, national origin, or disability. The most common claims of illegal harassment arise in the context of sex/gender and race discrimination, and increasingly, discrimination based on religion. No workplace is immune. Illegal harassment can still be a risk when a workplace is predominantly one gender, one race or one religion.

If the nonprofit doesn't have a written policy prohibiting harassment or doesn't conduct staff training to raise awareness about illegal harassment, it's vulnerable to considerable risk. Liability for harassment may stem from inside as well as outside the organization: staff members, clients, vendors, consultants, board members, or a member of the general public could engage in illegal harassment of staff or clients. Would the nonprofit's employees know how to react? Do the executive staff and supervisory staff know what to do?

When any high level nonprofit representative, such as a board member or a supervisor, engages in harassment, the nonprofit can be vicariously liable, even if the senior management of the nonprofit is unaware of the illegal conduct.[24] Because of this stringent standard, nonprofits must educate all employees, especially supervisors, (and board members), to recognize illegal conduct. Nonprofits also must strive to create an environment where employees are willing to report their concerns directly to management, even if that means filing a complaint about their supervisors. The EEOC's guidance provides that: "An employer's harassment complaint procedure should be designed to encourage victims to come forward. To that end, it should clearly explain the process and ensure that there are no unreasonable obstacles to complaints."

The first step toward reducing the risk of illegal harassment at the workplace is having a policy to prohibit it. Effective risk management continues with training staff and promptly investigating complaints. Harassment is inherently subjective: It is defined as a form of discrimination consisting of verbal or physical behavior/conduct which is:

- ❏ unwelcome,

- ❏ directed towards someone or affecting someone who is a member of a protected class (such as race, sex, age, national origin, veteran status or sexual orientation),

- ❏ severe or pervasive, and

- ❏ has a negative impact or creates a hostile environment.

Examples of conduct that can rise to the level of illegal harassment include:

- ❏ racist or sexist jokes, comments, notes, or e-mails;

- ❏ a computer monitor displaying offensive pictures/photographs;

- ❏ graffiti or offensive words, pictures or symbols that are present at the workplace;

- ❏ subtle or overt pressure for sex or an intimate relationship;

- ❏ unnecessary touching or other unwelcome physical contact; and/or

- ❏ disparaging remarks about one's protected class status (such as race, sex, or disability).

> **California Court Rules That Vulgar Language Alone May Not Create a Hostile Environment**
>
> A recent California Supreme Court case ruled that sexually coarse and vulgar language, standing alone, didn't create a hostile work environment for a writers' assistant who worked on the television show *Friends*. The court stated that the law against sexual harassment "isn't a 'civility code' and isn't designed to rid the workplace of vulgarity." *Lyle v. Warner Brothers Television Prods.*, No. S125171 (Cal. April 20, 2006).

---

24 For a more detailed explanation of an employer's vicarious liability and the procedures the EEOC expects employers to follow to address harassment, see the EEOC's Enforcement Guidance.

The same federal law that prohibits illegal discrimination (Title VII) also prohibits harassment based on the same categories that are protected under federal law. Consequently, nonprofits with 15+ employees can be liable under federal law for illegal harassment. Since many state anti-discrimination laws apply to workplaces with only one employee, and since no nonprofit should tolerate a workplace where hostility or offensive conduct occurs, harassment is an issue that should be at the top of the list for risk reduction no matter how small the nonprofit workplace.

Sexual Harassment

Sexual harassment at the workplace is a form of sex discrimination and has been clearly prohibited by Title VII of the Civil Rights Act since the EEOC issued guidelines defining harassment as discriminatory conduct in 1980. The U.S. Supreme Court first defined sexual harassment in 1986, in the case *Meritor Savings Bank, v. Vinson*, 477 US 57 (1986). In that case the Court held that the employer is responsible for sexual harassment at the workplace when either: a) an employee's conditions of employment are dependent upon the provision of sexual favors, or b) there is a hostile or offensive working environment. Title VII applies to employers with 15 or more employees.

Sexual harassment in its classic form is the request by a supervisor for sexual favors (called *quid pro quo* harassment). However, many other scenarios have been found to constitute illegal sexual harassment on the theory that certain conduct creates a hostile, offensive, or abusive work environment. Sexual harassment isn't just about a male supervisor demanding that a female subordinate perform sexual favors. The U.S. Supreme Court has recognized that same-sex harassment violates Title VII, and that employers are responsible when nonemployees are the harassers.

State anti-discrimination laws, all of which prohibit sex discrimination and some of which specifically prohibit sexual harassment, generally apply to workplaces with fewer than 15 employees. In some states, damages and defense costs of sexual harassment lawsuits may be excluded from a nonprofit's insurance coverage, leaving the nonprofit completely exposed to bear the burden of defending a sexual harassment claim on its own.

To recover under the theory of hostile environment a plaintiff must show that a) the conduct at issue was unwelcome, and b) the conduct was "sufficiently severe or pervasive to alter the conditions of employment and create an abusive working environment." Some examples of conduct which may create a hostile environment are:

❑ workplace graffiti that is derogatory towards a particular race;

❑ sculptures of female nudes in the lobby of an office; .

❑ amorous or sexually suggestive e-mail;

❑ failing to provide adequate bathrooms at a work site.

❑ the circulation of sexually explicit cartoons to various employees' desks;

❑ subjecting an employee to constant questions about his or her love life; and

❑ physical touching or sexual advances.

As you can see from these examples, sexual harassment doesn't have to be physical contact or even expressly aimed at the victim, but if it has the effect of creating a *hostile or offensive environment*, the result can be a finding of illegal sexual harassment.

What constitutes sexual harassment is ultimately subjective because each employee or volunteer may have a different definition of what is unwelcome or hostile. To dispel the potential lack of understanding about what constitutes illegal harassment, nonprofits need to clearly spell out the expectations for conduct at the workplace. Clarity is accomplished through both a written policy and staff training.

Reducing Liability Risks

1. **Employer Exposure to Liability:** If an employee suffers what the court has termed a *tangible employment action* in connection with sexual or other illegal harassment at the workplace, the nonprofit will be legally responsible for damages to the victim on the basis of *strict liability*. (A tangible employment action might be job loss, demotion, a poor performance review, being placed on probation, being transferred to a less desirable position or some other similarly negative impact on the victim's employment.) In these situations, a nonprofit can be responsible for any damages suffered by the victim despite taking reasonable steps in response to a complaint of harassment.

   If the harasser is the victim's supervisor, even when there is no tangible employment action taken, and despite the nonprofit having no knowledge of the harassment, the nonprofit will be vicariously liable for the conduct of the supervisor and responsible for the victim's damages. The nonprofit may raise an *affirmative defense* showing that it had taken reasonable measures to prevent and correct promptly any harassing behavior *and* that the employee had unreasonably failed to take advantage of those measures. Once the employer finds out about the harassment, the law requires the employer take whatever steps are reasonable to minimize harm to the victim and prevent any further harassing behavior. Without a prompt response in an effort to correct the situation, the affirmative defense won't be available.

With respect to harassment between co-workers or by third parties towards an employee, the nonprofit will be liable if it *knew or reasonably should have known* about the behavior, and failed to take reasonable steps designed to end the harassment or protect the employee.

For this reason, the authors recommend that the nonprofit's policy require staff to report observed or experienced harassment at the workplace. It is to the employer's advantage to know that an employee experiences the workplace as a hostile environment. Once the nonprofit knows of allegations of improper conduct, steps can be taken to minimize the potential harm to victims—and in so doing, to minimize potential liability to the nonprofit. By taking swift and effective remedial action, many employers have been able to reduce their liability or eliminate it altogether.

2. **Policies and Training:** Curiously, federal law doesn't mandate that employers have a written policy or conduct training for staff on the subject of illegal harassment—despite the fact that a written policy and training staff are proven to be the most effective ways an employer can prevent and address harassment. In contrast, several states, including California, Connecticut and Maine, require employers to train staff about illegal harassment, and require training on sexual harassment in particular. Recent U.S. Supreme Court cases have demonstrated that having a policy and training staff are considered the minimum steps an employer should take to show reasonable efforts to prevent harassment at the workplace. Educating staff about anti-harassment policies should occur on a regular basis, no less frequently than annually. The EEOC Enforcement Guidelines stress that the staff training should be *interactive*. Many employers incorporate a module on harassment into their new staff orientation, using laptop computers and readily-available commercial software programs. Other nonprofits prefer to use a facilitator to engage staff in discussions during an annual staff meeting where questions can be asked and the nonprofit's own policy can be reviewed.

3. **Prompt Investigation With No Retaliation:** Where a complaint of harassment is brought to the employer's attention, the employer has the opportunity to limit its liability by responding to the complaint appropriately, and by ensuring that no action that could be interpreted as retaliatory is taken against the complaining employee.

The employer needs to show that it did everything in its power to avoid harm to the victim. Having a written policy with appropriate complaint procedures, conducting staff training, and promptly investigating any complaints are key ingredients to demonstrate that the nonprofit responded reasonably.

Anti-Harassment Posting Required in Many States

Title VII and many state laws require that employers **post a notice** explaining that harassment is illegal and providing workers with information on filing a complaint and the prohibition against retaliation. *Note:* A regulation size poster (13 inches x 18 inches) isn't available to print from the Internet, but can be requested from the EEOC Publications Distribution Center via *www.eeoc.gov/posterform.html* or by calling 1-800-669-3362. Many states have their own requirements for mandatory postings about illegal discrimination/harassment or equal employment opportunity/civil rights. Many of these posters can be downloaded from the states' Web sites. States that require postings on the subject of illegal harassment include: **Alaska** *www.gov.state.ak.us/aschr/harassment_ poster.pdf*, **Arizona, California**, *www.dfeh.ca.gov/Publications/postersemp.asp* **Colorado, Connecticut** (applies to workplaces with 3+ employees) *www.state.ct.us/chro/metapages/Education/SexHarassPoster.pdf*, **Delaware, District of Columbia**, *www.ohr.dc.gov/ohr/site/default.asp* **Florida, Georgia, Idaho**, *http://cl.idaho.gov/ftp/requiredposters.pdf*, **Kentucky** (pertaining to wage discrimination based on sex) *www.oet.ky.gov/des/pubs/jobser/wagedis05.pdf* **Louisiana, Maine** *www.maine.gov/labor/posters/* **Massachusetts, Michigan, Minnesota** (pertaining to age discrimination) *www.doli.state.mn.us/posters.html* **Missouri** *www.dolir.mo.gov/hr/* **New Hampshire, New Jersey, New York, North Dakota**, *www.nd.gov/labor/publications/posters.html* **Tennessee**, and **Vermont** *www.labor.vermont.gov/ FormsPublications/WageHour FormsandPublications/tabid/128/Default.aspx/#Mandatory%20Posters*.

Third-Party Harassment

The EEOC's guidelines[25] provide that unless the employer takes immediate and appropriate corrective action, the employer can be responsible for harassment by third parties (such nonemployees as vendors, clients, volunteers or former employees) when the employer, its agents, or supervisory employees, knows or should have known of the improper conduct. Additionally, numerous federal courts have held that an employer may be liable for sexual harassment perpetrated by persons who aren't employees or agents of the employer. You might ask, "How can a nonprofit be liable for third-party harassment when the nonprofit can't control the person who is doing the harassing?" The answer is that the EEOC and federal courts have found that the employer is in the best possible position to **stop** the harassing conduct, and consequently should be legally responsible.

Third-party sexual harassment can occur even when the victims aren't themselves the *target* of the harassment. Third-party sexual harassment claims may be based on the conduct of others at the workplace: either *quid pro quo* harassment or the existence of a *hostile environment*. Men and women may bring such claims. Quid pro quo (something for something) third-party sexual harassment can occur when employees who aren't themselves harassed, are treated less favorably than other less qualified employees who submit to harassment. Hostile environment third-party sexual harassment occurs when employees who aren't themselves harassed must work in an atmosphere where such harassment is pervasive and they're forced to observe it.

What is the appropriate *cure* when the person who is the alleged harasser isn't the employee of the nonprofit? First, no matter who the parties are, an effort should immediately be made to *separate the alleged victim from the alleged harasser to reduce the risk of a continuing hostile environment.* Document these steps, and all steps taken both to investigate and correct the situation. Some examples of corrective action follow:

1. *Investigate:*

    ❏ The purpose of the investigation is to test the credibility of the complaining party. This is accomplished by interviewing the alleged victim, and then separately interviewing the alleged harasser, as well as any other individuals who might have knowledge about the situation(s) complained of, or the conduct of the alleged harasser.

    ❏ Don't promise complete confidentiality—it may not be possible to keep all allegations completely confidential. During any investigation it's possible that someone's identity will have to be disclosed. The nonprofit can tell employees that it will do everything possible to maintain confidentiality, and to limit the people who know the details of the allegation(s). Ask those involved with the investigation similarly to be sensitive to the need not to disclose allegations that may later turn out to be false.

    ❏ Document the steps taken to investigate the allegations. Keep notes of interviews with other employees. Ask those who witnessed the harassment to submit a written statement.

2. *Determine appropriate corrective action, which depends on who the alleged harasser is:*

    ❏ **Vendors:** If the harasser is an employee of a vendor to the nonprofit, file a complaint with the vendor. Use the nonprofit's leverage as a consumer. Tell the vendor that another person must be assigned to service the account immediately, while an investigation is under way. Find out what procedures the vendor has for filing complaints about the vendors' employees and use them.

    ❏ **Board Members:** Contact the chair of the board and enlist the chair's assistance in determining next steps. The board member who is the alleged harasser shouldn't have any contact with the alleged victim of the harassment.

    ❏ **Clients:** Reassign the alleged victim so that she or he doesn't have continuing contact with the client who is the alleged harasser. Does the nonprofit have guidelines for client conduct? Can the client be terminated if his or her conduct warrants it?

3. *Take Action:*

In some cases, following the investigation it will be obvious that a policy violation has occurred. In those cases, termination of any relationship with the nonprofit may be the most appropriate, albeit the most severe, step to take. If the harasser is a board member, ask for his or her resignation; if it's a vendor, terminate the business relationship and require a different representative to be on site at the nonprofit in the meanwhile. Less severe options include freezing the salary of an employee, requiring the offending party to attend sensitivity training, or at the very least, ensuring that the alleged harasser doesn't have contact with the alleged victim(s) in a work-related capacity in the future.

In other cases, the investigation may reveal a situation where someone acted unprofessionally, but it isn't clear whether the conduct justifies the most severe discipline. In such cases, the offending party must at least be reprimanded and made aware of the impact of his or her actions on the victim. In many cases an apology is called for. Sometimes arranging for a counseling session with a mediator is appropriate to ensure that the parties don't continue to have conflicts in the future.

---

25 29 C.F.R. § 1604.11(e) (2004).

Remember that third-party harassment could also arise when discriminatory attitudes and conduct exists that are based on age, race, color, religion, disability, national origin, military status or a protected category other than sex.

How Can I Protect My Nonprofit From Liability?

The best thing a nonprofit can do is to have clear policies and communicate those policies to its staff and volunteers. Make sure the staff knows that the nonprofit's harassment policies cover conduct by nonemployees, such as vendors, suppliers, clients, service recipients, and the general public. Provide ways of reporting all types of harassment, including third-party harassment.

Policies and procedures can shield the organization from liability. They can establish a forum for open communication at an early stage so that a misunderstanding or insensitivity can be corrected before it explodes into a legal complaint. Not only may policies help a nonprofit avoid costly litigation, they may prevent escalation to more serious assaults. In one case, after a supervisor disregarded a serious sexual harassment complaint, the alleged harasser attacked a co-worker after an office party and was later convicted of attempted rape.

The nonprofit must create an environment where its policies are respected and followed. If a victim doesn't complain, the court may conclude that the organization discouraged the victim from raising the issue. The suggestions offered here can help you develop appropriate policies and procedures. The following section lists critical items for inclusion in policies addressing prohibitions against harassment.

❑ **Start at the Top.** The board of directors plays an important role in eliminating harassment. It can create a healthy workplace by emphatically stating a commitment to creating and maintaining a harassment-free workplace—regardless of the rank or position of the alleged harasser. The board can demonstrate its commitment by supervising the implementation of the organization's policies and procedures, rather than merely asking the executive director to write something down to please the lawyers. A *zero tolerance* policy will set the tone, discourage inappropriate behavior, and encourage open communication.

❑ **Policies and Procedures.** Policies should prohibit both harassment and unfounded accusations of misconduct, as well as retaliation against those who invoke the policy's reporting procedures. Violation of the policies should result in appropriate disciplinary action. The policies should be backed by a procedure for investigating allegations that protects the privacy of all parties to the extent possible.

❑ **Commit the Policies to Writing.** The nonprofit's policy on harassment should be prominently placed in the employee handbook. Employees can be required to sign an agreement stating that they've read the written policies and will adhere

---

Harassment and Volunteers

Although most anti-discrimination laws address only harassment affecting *employees*, there is no reason to limit the nonprofit's policies to protection of employees if volunteers are also a component of the workforce. Volunteers are also owed a workplace that's harassment-free. The nonprofit's good will is at risk when volunteers are treated poorly. Policies should foster and encourage a culture where volunteers are respected and their rights protected.

Volunteers can also create risks to the nonprofit if they're insensitive or unaware that their conduct is creating a hostile environment for employees or other volunteers. Consequently, volunteers should either be included with other staff during training on harassment, or provided with their own sensitivity-awareness training.

Anti-Discrimination/Harassment Postings Required

Alaska law requires employers to post notices concerning sexual harassment. Alaska Stat. Section 23.10.40

Connecticut law requires employers with 50+ employees to post notices explaining the illegality of sexual harassment and the remedies available; training is required of all supervisory personnel.

Louisiana requires a posting to alert employees that discrimination based on: sickle cell, age and genetic characteristics are illegal. Copies of the posters may be obtained by contacting the Louisiana Department of Labor.

Maine requires a posting on sexual harassment. Posters can be downloaded from the following Maine state Web site: *www.maine.gov/labor/bls/posters*.

Massachusetts requires a poster on maternity leave, fair employment law and harassment.

Minnesota's required posters, including one of age discrimination, can be downloaded from the Minnesota Department of Labor and Industry's Web site, www.doli.state.mn.us/posters.html.

Missouri requires a posting on discrimination in employment, available from the following Web site: www.dolir.state.mo.us/posters2.htm.

Nevada's Equal Rights Commission requires a posting on discrimination in employment, housing and public accommodations.

New Hampshire requires a posting on employment discrimination, which can be obtained from the New Hampshire Human Rights Commission, e-mail: human-rights@nhsa.state.nh.us.

New Jersey requires a poster telling employees about the employer's anti-sexual harassment policy.

New York's posting requirements include discrimination.

Tennessee's required poster on the prohibition of discrimination is available from the Tennessee Human Rights Commission.

to them. Written policies can be referred to as needed and used to document your organization's position should an allegation be made.

- ❏ **Spread the Word.** Policies and procedures that go no farther than the written page are of limited value. Cover your organization's policies at staff orientations and provide ongoing communication, through written memos or training sessions, to make the policies widely known.

- ❏ **Supervise for Compliance.** Require notification of the executive director, or other top manager, of any and all complaints and ask the board of directors to hold that individual accountable for the resulting investigation and course of action.

- ❏ **Make changes as necessary.** Solicit staff feedback, through interviews or surveys, to assess the adequacy and effectiveness of your organization's policies and procedures. Review your policies and procedures periodically to ensure that your organization is still in compliance with applicable laws.

Policies Prohibiting Harassment

All nonprofits should draft a written policy prohibiting illegal harassment at the workplace. The written policy should:

- ❏ define harassment in general (both hostile environment and quid pro quo), and sexual harassment specifically (court cases have held that the employer's policy needs to include a description of what constitutes illegal sexual harassment). Sexual harassment happens to be the most notorious form of illegal harassment. It's also illegal to tolerate harassment based on age, religion, race, color, or disability, and numerous other characteristics protected by state statutes. Know the categories in the state(s) where the nonprofit resides and draft the nonprofit's policy to address all such categories of illegal harassment.

- ❏ require all employees (and volunteers, if applicable) to attend sensitivity training on harassment.

- ❏ encourage reporting of any offensive conduct *before* it rises to the level of a hostile environment.

- ❏ designate at least two people to whom complaints of harassment must be reported, ensuring that the alleged victim doesn't have to report to the alleged harasser.

- ❏ explain the rights of victims under the policy (such as not to be retaliated against and to have complaints, and the investigation file, maintained in confidence).

- ❏ describe procedures for the investigation of complaints.

- ❏ include a short description of the consequences for breach of the policy such as: "policy violations may result in termination, salary freezes or other appropriate discipline."

SAMPLE---

Prohibition of Harassment Policy

Harassment Prohibited

[Name of Nonprofit] is committed to maintaining a work environment that's free of discrimination and harassment based on a person's sex, race, age, color, creed, religion, disability, ancestry or national origin or any other classification protected by state or federal laws. All employees should respect the rights, opinions, and beliefs of others. Harassment, because of sex, race, age, color, creed, religion, disability, ancestry, national origin or [*list here any other categories addressed in the state's anti-discrimination laws*] whether conducted by, or affecting an employee, vendor, client, volunteer, board member, or any other individual connected with [Name of Nonprofit] is strictly prohibited. Examples of conduct prohibited by this policy include using racial and ethnic slurs, making offensive references to stereotypes, or making jokes about characteristics protected by law. Any such harassment is prohibited by this policy, whether or not the conduct also violates federal or state law. This policy applies to all employees, directors, officers, volunteers, and agents of [Name of Nonprofit], including the chief executive officer and the board of directors.

Sexual Harassment Prohibited

No one may threaten or imply that an employee's submission to or rejection of sexual advances will in any way influence any decision about that staff member's employment, advancement, duties, compensation, or other terms or conditions of employment. No one may take any personnel action based on an employee's submission to or rejection of sexual advances.

No one may subject another employee, volunteer, or client to any unwelcome conduct of a sexual nature. This includes both unwelcome physical contact, such as touching, blocking, staring, making sexual gestures, and making or displaying sexual drawings or photographs, and unwelcome verbal conduct such as sexual propositions, slurs, insults, jokes, and other sexual comments. An employee's conduct will be considered unwelcome and in violation of this policy either when the employee should have known that the conduct was unwelcome, or when the person subjected to the conduct voiced his or her objection.

Examples of sexual harassment are: demanding sexual favors in return for employment conditions; unwelcome physical touching; sexual remarks, innuendos and jokes; graphic, obscene or sexual posters or calendars or other print material; e-mail, voice messages or similar communications that are persistent and unwelcome and sexual in nature; and lewd suggestive comments regarding a staff member's style of dress, appearance, body or personal life.

Making Complaints—Mandatory Reporting

If you believe you are the victim of harassment you must immediately report this fact to _____ (person or position designated to receive complaints) or _____ (second person or position designated to receive complaints). Also, if you observe harassment you should bring the offensive conduct to [Name of Nonprofit's] attention. You should make any complaint about harassment directly to one of the two persons previously listed. Complaints of harassment don't need to be in writing, however, in order for [Name of Nonprofit] to properly investigate the complaint, they may not be anonymous. It's the policy of [Name of Nonprofit] that no reprisal, retaliation, or other adverse action will be taken against any complainant for making a good faith report of harassment, or for assisting in an investigation of harassment.

Investigation of Complaints

[Name of Nonprofit] will promptly and thoroughly investigate all alleged violations of this policy assuming the allegation is in good faith and made in sufficient detail for [Name of Nonprofit] to conduct a confidential but thorough investigation. The investigation will generally consist of interviews with witnesses to the event/conduct including the complainant and the alleged harasser. Every effort will be made during the course of the investigation to protect the confidentiality of those involved and of the information gained during the investigation; however, information will be disclosed as necessary to conduct a thorough investigation. The investigation may take several weeks. During the time period following a complaint of harassment, the alleged harasser and alleged victim aren't permitted to have one-on-one unsupervised contact at the workplace. The results of the investigation will be reported to the complainant and the alleged wrongdoer.

Penalties for Violations

[Name of Nonprofit] will take prompt disciplinary and remedial action in response to policy violations, including breach of confidentiality, retaliatory action, or bad faith allegations. Disciplinary action may include termination of employment.

If you have questions about this policy, contact _____ for additional information.

Clients as Victims

It's important for nonprofits to discuss with staff their clients' possible perceptions of inappropriate conduct. For instance, child-serving agencies and schools must address the issue of peer-to-peer harassment and potential allegations of child abuse in cases where an adult caregiver's words or actions are interpreted by the child (or parent) as inappropriate sexual conduct. What avenues does the nonprofit provide for clients to report perceived harassment? While clients don't have the same remedies as employees or volunteers for recovery of damages under state discrimination laws or Title VII, their allegations, generally based on a claimed violation of state tort law, can be equally disastrous for the nonprofit. The same principles of risk management that apply to an investigation of allegations of harassment by employees, should also be applied to protect the nonprofit when allegations of sexual harassment are raised by clients.

The Importance of Staff Training

Training is critical. Since harassment is ultimately subjective, the opportunity to actively discuss what is prohibited is fundamental to the nonprofit's ability to discipline a staff member who violates the policy. An orientation for new employees should include a review of the nonprofit's policy prohibiting harassment. All staff should be required to review the policy periodically in discussions that stress the mandatory complaint procedure, the confidentiality expectations, the prohibition against retaliation, and the consequences for breach of policy. Frank discussions among staff about what constitutes illegal harassment are helpful to raise awareness about inappropriate, unprofessional conduct in general and sexual harassment in particular. Such discussions should always remind staff that retaliation against someone who has made a good faith allegation, or cooperated with an investigation, is prohibited.

The goal of training should be to raise the staff's awareness about what constitutes illegal harassment. Each employee should be able to answer:

- ❏ "What is unwelcome behavior?" (*anything related to a person's characteristics, which the person objects to…*)

- ❏ "What language is inappropriate at the workplace?" (*profanity, gender-based slurs or derogatory comments about a person because of his or her religion, gender, sexual preference, color, race, obesity, or any other disabling physical conditions…*)

- ❏ "What subjects are simply taboo for discussion at work?" (*dating, one's sex life, private body parts, remarks about physical characteristics or disabilities…*)

Also, it may be helpful to have staff role-play what they would do if they believed they were being harassed, or what they would do if another employee told them he or she was being harassed. Make sure that employees know that no retaliation is permitted for either making a complaint, or participating in an investigation of a complaint. Employees will have legitimate questions about what will happen in the event they're wrongfully accused of harassment, and whether the investigations will be confidential. The investigation procedures can be described and the point made that one of the reasons for an investigation is to test the credibility of the complainant. Employees should be assured that those who make false allegations will be disciplined up to and including termination, and that both the allegations and the results of the investigation will be kept reasonably confidential, but that information will be disclosed as necessary in order to conduct an effective investigation.

Complaint Procedures

Foremost among the training topics should be to stress the policy's requirement that complaints of harassment be reported to the nonprofit. The staff should be reminded that complaints are to be addressed to one of several administrative staff, including, but not limited to, the employee's supervisor. An effective complaint procedure doesn't require complaints to be made in writing, since some courts have determined that requiring a written complaint creates an unnecessary barrier. Moreover, once a management level employee hears about a complaint, that knowledge, whether it comes to the nonprofit in writing or verbally, should be acted on.

To make the complaint procedure user friendly, make sure that both a female and male management level employee are designated as the individuals to whom complaints of sexual harassment should be made. Since the executive director is a special case, the policy may state that in cases where the executive director alleges harassment, his or her complaint should be made to one of two predesignated board members, such as the chair of the board's human resources committee and the board chair.

Basic Risk Management Steps to Reduce Liability for Harassment

1. *Communicate a clear policy that the nonprofit won't tolerate harassment.* Make sure all employees and volunteers are familiar with the organization's harassment policy, not only by including the written policy in any handbook of personnel policies, but also by holding periodic employee/volunteer trainings on the topic.

2. *Have a clear reporting procedure.* Give employees/volunteers options about who to report harassment to in case the person harassing them is the person they're supposed to report to.

3. *Take all complaints of harassment or discrimination very seriously.*

4. *Investigate allegations* by speaking with the complaining party, and then the alleged harasser, and any witnesses who could lend information to test the credibility of all parties.

5. *Determine appropriate action and take action.*

6. *Report back to the complaining party* so that she or he knows that the allegation was taken seriously and appropriate action taken.

7. *Don't retaliate* against anyone for filing a complaint of harassment.

What to Do if an Allegation of Illegal Harassment Is Made

Step 1. Investigate Every Allegation.

In order to preserve a potential legal defense the nonprofit must take every allegation of harassment very seriously, and the nonprofit's reaction must be immediate to curtail potential further harm. The nonprofit should document all the steps taken from the moment the allegation was made through the completion of the investigation, to the final resolution of the incident. The first responsive step after receiving a complaint of harassment should be to determine who the appropriate person to conduct an internal investigation is. (It doesn't have to be an attorney, although this may be optimal. Sometimes your insurance carrier will suggest a lawyer or provide counsel for this purpose.) In some cases, a nonprofit may be in position to identify a suitable investigator well in advance of the first allegation, and ensure that the designee has the training and experience necessary for this important assignment.

Step 2. Separate the Alleged Victim From the Alleged Harasser.

After receiving a complaint of harassment, it's important to take immediate remedial action to prevent further harm to the victim. Simultaneously with beginning the investigation, the nonprofit should consider how it will address personnel matters at the workplace to allow both victim and harasser to continue their jobs but not have unsupervised one-on-one interaction with each other. If necessary, one of those involved should be transferred or their job duties temporarily changed, making sure that such actions aren't interpreted as *retaliation* against the complainant.

In cases where the harasser isn't under the nonprofit's control, such as where a vendor is coming on-site and harassing an employee, the nonprofit should take reasonable steps to prevent future harm to the employee(s). Such steps may require cancellation of the vendor's relationship with the nonprofit, requesting a replacement representative be named, or permitting the employee special privileges to take time off whenever the vendor is on site.

Step 3. Interview Witnesses.

Once the investigator is selected, immediately arrange for an interview with the complainant and the alleged harasser, and others who may have first-hand knowledge of the complained-of conduct. It's important to get the facts quickly, while they're fresh in everyone's mind. Evidence of harassment is usually provided by witnesses' statements about who said or did what to whom. Obtaining timely and complete statements from everyone with knowledge of the allegedly harassing conduct is critical to give the investigator an accurate picture of the workplace environment and to document the thorough and objective nature of the nonprofit's investigation.

Step 4. Protect Confidentiality.

Protecting the confidentiality of the investigation is critical from its initial stages. Everyone involved in the investigation should be reminded how serious the allegations are, and that disclosure of any of the questions asked or responses provided would be a breach of the policy. Those involved in the investigation and the substance of their interviews should be treated as highly confidential information, with access provided only to those administrators with a need to know. Additionally, the very fact that an allegation of illegal harassment was made against an employee is potentially explosive and damaging for that employee. Often, the employee will ask for assurances of confidentiality. They should understand that, ultimately, identities may have to be disclosed either to effect discipline or to test the credibility of allegations.

Involving outside legal counsel can, in many cases, result in protection of the findings of the investigation because of the attorney-client privilege. However, more and more courts are scrutinizing the employer's reasonableness and timeliness in conducting the investigation itself, thereby making it unlikely that the investigation file will be entirely protected from disclosure. Consequently, the fact that the internal investigation file may be disclosed in subsequent litigation should be foremost in the minds of those documenting the investigation. Always seek the advice of a lawyer before making any statements in the investigation file that could be interpreted as admissions of wrongful conduct.

Step 5. Document the Investigation.

Both the steps taken by the nonprofit to implement an investigation and the factual *findings* resulting from the investigation should be documented. A well-documented investigation file will be critical to justify a finding of *no harassment* and can make-or-break the nonprofit's defense that it reacted reasonably when faced with an allegation of harassment. Moreover, accurate and complete documentation of the investigation is necessary to justify the nonprofit's actions post-investigation. If the alleged harasser is terminated as a result of the investigation, there is always the risk that the discharged harasser will file charges of wrongful termination. It's essential to have a well-documented file to support the discharge.

Step 6. Evaluate Whether Inappropriate Conduct or a Violation of Policy Occurred.

The end result of the investigation should be a determination that the complained-of conduct either was or wasn't a violation of the nonprofit's policy or that the evidence is inconclusive, and that discipline either is or isn't appropriate. All that's necessary is for the nonprofit to determine whether a policy violation occurred, not whether the conduct was technically *illegal*. Even so, the nonprofit may want to share the results of the investigation with an employment lawyer to obtain an independent opinion as to whether the complained-of conduct would rise to the level of illegal conduct.

Step 7. Take Remedial Action to Address the Wrongdoer's Conduct.

If a violation of the policy is found, prompt, appropriate remedial action is required. The wrongdoer should be disciplined according to the severity of his or her conduct, taking into consideration that the prohibition against harassment at the workplace is absolute. If there is any risk that the wrongdoer will repeat the conduct, accepting the wrongdoer's resignation or discharging the wrongdoer is the only prudent option. For incidents that are less serious, a written warning, one day's suspension, or a salary freeze plus further training may be effective disciplinary measures.

Step 8. Promptly Share the Results of the Investigation With the Complainant and Address the Complainant's Needs.

The victim shouldn't be left in the dark about the results of the investigation or the actions the nonprofit intends to take to address the concerns raised by the complaint. If communication doesn't occur, the victim may get restless and assume that the employer hasn't taken appropriate steps to address his or her allegations. This can result in distrust, which in turn can result in the victim calling an attorney or filing an action with the state civil rights division or the EEOC. After considering the results of the investigation, the conclusion may be that the alleged harasser behaved unprofessionally, but didn't actually violate the policy. This conclusion should be shared with the complainant, as well as whatever disciplinary actions the nonprofit will take to address the unprofessional conduct of the alleged harasser. Consider whether it's possible to separate the alleged harasser and victim either through work assignments or physical transfer. Ask them if they're willing to engage in a facilitated mediation process to repair their working relationship. However, never transfer the victim unless the victim specifically requests transfer. If separation is appropriate, the alleged harasser should be moved to avoid an allegation of retaliation.

Remedial action shouldn't be limited to the wrongdoer. Consider what action should be taken to address any ongoing or past concerns of the victim: Provide time off for psychological counseling? Transfer of duties to another work site? When sexual harassment results in the need for psychological counseling of the victim, the nonprofit may offer to cover the costs or reimburse the employee, in return for a release from the employee promising not to bring any employment action against the nonprofit as a result of the harassing conduct.

What remedial action is needed for the nonprofit as a whole? Surviving an illegal harassment investigation often motivates employers to be more diligent about staff training and to clarify the existing policy against illegal harassment.

SAMPLE ---

Managing the Risk of Illegal Harassment—A Checklist

Use this checklist to ensure that the nonprofit is ready to respond to allegations of sexual harassment:

- ❏ A written policy prohibiting harassment was distributed to all staff and volunteers.
- ❏ The employees who received the policy signed an acknowledgement of receipt.
- ❏ A complaint procedure is in place which is communicated to the employees and volunteers.
- ❏ The complaint procedures make reporting harassment mandatory.
- ❏ Complaints don't have to be in writing, and employees have several choices among administrative staff members to whom complaints should be made.
- ❏ Staff training on harassment is conducted regularly.
- ❏ There is documentation of who attends the training and follow-up with those staff who miss the training.
- ❏ During an investigation, the nonprofit will document all complaints and the steps taken by the nonprofit in response to the complaint(s).
- ❏ Those involved in any investigation are reminded of the policy of confidentiality, which should provide that confidentiality will be reasonably maintained but that information will be disclosed as necessary in order to conduct an effective investigation.
- ❏ A thorough investigation is initiated promptly after any complaint is made.

❏ The victim is separated from the alleged harasser during the period of the ongoing investigation to prevent any further harm.

❏ Remedial action for the alleged victim is considered and implemented.

❏ The victim is informed of the status and results of the investigation in a timely fashion.

❏ Appropriate discipline is imposed on the wrongdoer.

❏ Follow-up monitoring occurs to ensure that the victim hasn't suffered retaliation and that harassment hasn't resumed.

❏ The nonprofit conducts a self-assessment: What went wrong? What can the nonprofit do to prevent illegal harassment at the workplace in the future?

- -

In the next section, Chapter 9, an employer's obligations under the Americans with Disabilities Act is addressed as well as prudent risk management strategies to address accommodations of employees.

Chapter 9

The Obligation to Make the Workplace Accessible

The Americans with Disabilities (ADA) Act of 1990 (ADA), 42 U.S. Code 12101 ✐ and the Rehabilitation Act of 1973, 29 U.S. Code 791 ✐ , as well as state laws in almost every state, require nondiscriminatory and unbiased treatment in all aspects of employment towards qualified applicants and employees with a disability.

The ADA has two important provisions: one requires places of *public accommodation* be accessible, and the other protects persons who meet the minimum qualifications for employment but who:

❑ are disabled,

❑ have a record of a disability in the past (such as past drug abuse), or

❑ are perceived as having a disability (for example, someone with cosmetic disfigurements).

Illegal discrimination under the ADA exists where an employer fails to make a *reasonable accommodation* that would allow the employee to perform the essential functions of the job. A reasonable accommodation is one that can be made without undue hardship on the employer (administrative or financial).

❑ The ADA limits an employer's right to ask questions about disabilities and also the right to require applicants or employees to undergo physical examinations.

❑ Employers may not require applicants to undergo prehire physical examinations, or ask any questions during the hiring process that would elicit whether or not an applicant has a disability.

❑ Employers may only require physical examinations after a job offer has been made, and only then if all applicants for similar positions are treated alike.

❑ During employment, employers may only ask an employer's physician questions about an employee's medical condition or require the employee to undergo medical examinations when the employer has a reason to believe that there is a medical explanation for changes in the employee's performance, or that the employee's condition poses a safety threat.

The ADA requires employers to keep a separate file, distinct from the employee's personnel file, in which all medical, health insurance and related information is maintained. This medical file must be a confidential file, with access only by other employees and supervisors with a business-related *need to know*. (For instance, a supervisor or manager who needed information to negotiate an appropriate accommodation or to apply appropriate first aid.)

Most significantly, the ADA requires employers to offer a *reasonable accommodation* for qualified individuals with a disability to enable them to perform the essential functions of their job. A reasonable accommodation could be a leave of absence, a re-arranged work schedule, a different computer monitor, or a fan and a window that opens. What is *reasonable* in each situation will be different. Employers need to explore the accommodation options with the affected employee/applicant.

Plaintiffs in ADA actions are entitled to a jury trial and can receive an award for punitive and compensatory damages, as well as equitable relief which may include:

❑ back pay,

❑ hiring,

❑ promotion,

❑ reinstatement,

❑ front pay (or advance),

❑ reasonable accommodation, or

❑ other actions that will make an individual *whole* (in the condition she or he would have been but for the discrimination).

Remedies also may include payment of:

❑ attorney fees,

❑ expert witness fees, and

❑ court costs.

Individuals can't be liable under the ADA, so if an individual manager discriminated against a person with a disability, the nonprofit would be legally responsible.

The EEOC has developed a detailed publication that answers common questions about the ADA. The booklet is available at: www.ada.gov/q%26aeng02.htm.

Who Is Protected Under the ADA?

Title I of the ADA provides that employers may not discriminate against, and are required to make *reasonable accommodations* in employment for *qualified persons with a disability*. The ADA's accommodation provisions apply to workplaces with 15 or more employees (computed by determining the number of employees on the payroll 20 or more weeks in a year). Almost all nonprofits are covered except for tax-exempt private clubs. In addition, almost all state laws prohibit discrimination on the basis of disability. (State laws may have a lower threshold than 15 employees.)

The ADA defines *disability* as a physical or mental impairment that substantially limits a major life activity. Most disorders, both physical and mental, which have a long-lasting effect on a person's ability to perform major life functions will meet the criteria of a disability. Depression, cancer, morbid obesity, epilepsy, severe and chronic back pain, and learning disabilities have all been found to be disabilities affording employees protections under the ADA. Current use of illegal substances isn't a protected disability, but prior drug use by a recovering or former drug abuser triggers the protections of the ADA.

Individuals whose impairments substantially limit a major life activity, as well as those who *are perceived as being disabled,* are protected under the ADA. The ADA also provides protections for individuals who aren't themselves disabled but are discriminated against *because of their association with someone who is disabled*— family members, friends, or anyone else. Example: An individual with a disabled child applies for a job and during the interview mentions his or her child's disability. The applicant isn't hired because the employer believes that the applicant won't be a dependable employee because he or she will miss work to care for the child. The applicant is protected from discrimination at the workplace under the ADA, but not entitled to accommodation.

If an individual doesn't have the minimum qualifications, or can't accomplish the essential functions of a position, with or without an accommodation, the individual isn't a protected person under the ADA. Correctable or temporary disabilities don't qualify for protection under the ADA, although several states' disability protections are broader than the ADA on this point. Individuals recovering from substance abuse are considered to be disabled for purposes of the ADA, but, individuals who are currently using illegal controlled substances, or whose use of alcohol prevents the performance of their job duties, aren't protected by the ADA. A third exception exists in cases where the disabled person's conduct poses a risk of harm to self or others. Mental illness is generally a protected disability requiring accommodation, with the exception of disorders that pose a risk of harm to others such as: pedophilia, exhibitionism, compulsive gambling, kleptomania, and pyromania.

Mental Illness and Intellectual Disabilities

The ADA provides protection for mental as well as physical disabilities. Court cases in various jurisdictions have found that individuals with attention deficit disorder, bi-polar disorder, agoraphobia, and obsessive-compulsive disorder were each protected by the ADA. Individuals with lower-than-normal IQs (below the 70-75 range) or those with significant adaptive abilities (basic skills needed for everyday life, such as communication, self-care, home living, social skills, functional academics for example, reading, writing and basic math) are protected under the ADA if the individual's impairments substantially limit a major life activity, or if the individual *is perceived* as having a disability that limits a major life activity.

Drinking, Drugs and the ADA

Courts have held that employers are free to take disciplinary action against employees whose drinking or drug abuse causes conduct at the workplace that's unacceptable. Similarly, where alcohol or drug abuse causes an employee's work performance to be a risk of harm to others, the nonprofit is generally permitted to terminate the employee, but such cases are determined not on the fact of drug or alcohol use, *but on the employee's conduct*. When faced with a drug or alcohol abuse concern, nonprofits should always treat the issue from a work-performance perspective, imposing suitable discipline on the employee, which could range from suspension without pay until his or her condition improves, (A leave of absence is generally considered an appropriate accommodation under the ADA) or immediate termination. Care should be taken not to jump to conclusions about a former or current alcoholic's ability to perform the job: in one case, a current alcoholic who was capable of performing job requirements, and didn't pose a risk of safety to others, recovered damages from his employer under the Rehabilitation Act for wrongful termination (*Altman v. New York City Dep't of Health & Hospital Corp.* 903 F. Supp. 503, S.D.N.Y. 1995).

Accommodation: A Three-Step Process

First Step: Is the Employee Entitled to Accommodation?

When a nonprofit is faced with whether or not a duty of accommodation exists, it's useful first to determine whether the worker is a *qualified person* under the ADA. Qualified persons are those who meet all the prerequisites for employment (all the minimum qualifications) except for functional limitations because of a disability, and who can perform all the essential functions of the job *with or without* an accommodation. There are thus two parts to the analysis of whether an applicant or employee is a *qualified* person protected by the ADA:

1. Does he or she meet all the minimum qualifications?

2. Can she or he perform the essential functions of the job—if not on his own, then can he perform the essential functions with an accommodation?

If the answer to these questions is "No," the individual isn't protected by the ADA, and no accommodation is required by the employer. If the employee can't perform the essential functions of the position, with or without an accommodation, the nonprofit may terminate the employee. Caution: An employer may not know the answer to number two above, unless and until possible reasonable accommodations are explored, and the employee tries them out.

Second Step: Recognizing That an Accommodation Is Required

As a general rule, employers aren't required to accommodate an employee until the employee requests an accommodation or informs the employer of a disability. However, a request doesn't have to be *formal*, and can be made in a discussion without mentioning the word *accommodation*. Requests for accommodation can be made orally or in writing, and come from someone other than the employer, such as from a family member.

Harassment-Based Disability Discrimination

At least four federal circuit courts have acknowledged a cause of action for hostile work environment under the ADA. Disabled employees claiming harassment due to a hostile environment must show that 1) they're a qualified person with a disability; 2) they were subjected to unwelcome harassment; 3) the harassment was based on their disability; 4) the harassment was sufficiently severe or pervasive to alter the terms, conditions or privileges of employment; and 5) some basis exists to hold the nonprofit responsible, such as the fact that the harassment continued with the knowledge of a supervisor.

When an employee complains of being harassed based on his or her disability, the nonprofit should treat the situation just as if the complaint were about sexual harassment: separate the alleged victim from the alleged harasser, investigate, and determine what corrective or disciplinary action is applicable.

Nonprofits are usually familiar with the *public access* provisions of the ADA, which require all places of public accommodation to be accessible to persons with disabilities. Generally all nonprofits are places of public accommodation and are therefore subject to the ADA's public access requirements. *Note:* Churches are exempt, but religious schools aren't. The public access provisions require *barrier-free* workplaces, and mandate such structural changes to facilities as adding ramps and lowering drinking fountains. The public access provisions also require places of public accommodation to provide auxiliary aids to permit individuals with vision or hearing impairments or other disabilities, to enjoy the full benefits of programs offered to the public. These public access provisions have been widely commented on in other forums, and aren't the subject of this book.

Third Step: What Accommodations Are Reasonable in the Circumstances?

When the nonprofit offers an accommodation, it must keep in mind that the goal is to enable the employee to perform the essential functions of the job, but it doesn't have to involve sophisticated technology, or even be the same accommodation as that suggested by the employee. The accommodation need only be *reasonable*.

A *reasonable accommodation* could include restructuring the employee's job duties, moving the employee's work area, modifying a work schedule, or changing desk chairs. The definition of *reasonable* takes into consideration the financial, as well as the administrative, result of an accommodation. Employers aren't expected to spend enormous sums to make accommodations for staff, nor are employers required to reschedule all the other employees to accommodate one worker. On the other hand, if an accommodation is financially inconsequential, or would have no appreciable effect on other employees, the accommodation probably will be considered reasonable. What is *reasonable* will be determined on a case-by-case analysis, depending on the size of the workforce, budget, administrative needs and mission of the nonprofit. Most often accommodations cost less than $100 and can be implemented with relative ease and a bit of creative thinking, greatly aided by the person with the disability who, after all, knows what is needed.

The U.S. Department of Labor offers several resources on its Web site to assist employers determine appropriate accommodations. See *www.dol.gov/dol/topic/disability/jobaccommodations.htm*.

Making the Application Process Accessible

Barriers to employment can be intangible or concrete. Nonprofits should examine their application procedures to ensure that persons with disabilities have the same opportunity to apply for employment as those without disabilities. Accessibility becomes an issue from the moment an applicant sets out to apply for a position through the time the person separates from employment. The very act of applying for a job must be accessible. Consider how candidates learn about job openings at your nonprofit. To be truly accessible, information about a job opening must be made available in nontraditional formats. This is easily accomplished by making a staff person available to help applicants fill out an application upon request or review job descriptions with a candidate. Additionally, the application itself should include a statement requesting applicants to notify the nonprofit if accommodations are required during the hiring process.

The Duty to Negotiate a Reasonable Accommodation

The ADA and similar state laws demonstrate that compliance will require a nonprofit to engage in an *interactive process* with the employee, to determine what accommodation is reasonable. See 29 C.F.R. 1630.2(o)(3). California law makes it a violation to fail to engage in a "timely, good faith, interactive process with the employee or applicant." The obligation to negotiate could be triggered by a request from an employee for time off to attend therapy sessions or by a doctor's note stating that an employee shouldn't be lifting more than 20 pounds. As soon as it comes to the employee's attention that an accommodation may be needed, the employer should start a conversation with the employee about what accommodation options exist.

It's dangerous to ignore or deny an employee's suggestion (or an employee's doctor's suggestion) for an accommodation, because a unilateral decision by the employer won't satisfy the *interactive process* requirement. Instead, the employer should literally sit down with the employee and go through the options, explaining what options are feasible and why—and which aren't feasible.

If the requested accommodation or the most obvious accommodation would cause *undue hardship* to the nonprofit, there is no obligation to implement the requested accommodation. If another accommodation would work, alternatives to those requested should be considered. Whenever a nonprofit is weighing whether an accommodation is financially and administratively *reasonable*, the organization is well advised to carefully document (that means in writing!) the financial and administrative consequences of the requested accommodation and of the accommodation eventually offered. The paper trail should demonstrate that the nonprofit engaged the employee in a dialogue and considered alternatives, and how the nonprofit determined what was reasonable. In the end, the nonprofit has the right to determine that an accommodation would cause *undue hardship*, and, therefore, that the employee's disability can't be accommodated.

How the ADA Affects Pre-Employment Screening

The ADA prohibits employers from using any criteria that would tend to screen out individuals with disabilities. This means that pre-employment testing, the blanks to be filled-in on applications, and the questions posed in interviews, if they would elicit information about an individual's disability, are all subject to challenge under the ADA. Medical examinations are absolutely prohibited prior to an offer of employment. (Post-offer qualifying examinations are allowed if: 1) the examinations are required of all those offered a job in that position, and 2) the information resulting from the examination is treated confidentially. An offer of employment may be withdrawn based on a disability only if the exclusionary criteria are job-related, and consistent with business needs (related to the essential functions of the position, or to avoid a direct threat to the safety of the employee or others).

The key is to prohibit any questions that seek to elicit information about a disability, or about the severity or extent of an obvious disability.

Questions such as the following shouldn't be posed on applications or in interviews:

❏ Have you ever had a major illness or been injured?

❏ Did you file any workers' compensation claims with your previous employer?

❏ Do you take any prescribed drugs? Have you ever been in therapy?

❏ Are any of your family members disabled?

❏ Do you have asthma?

❏ Have you ever been treated for alcohol problems? Mental illness?

❏ Do you have any physical or mental conditions that would affect your ability to work?

The ADA *doesn't prohibit* questions such as the following:

❏ Do you use illegal drugs?

❏ Can you meet the attendance requirements of this position?

❏ Can you perform all the essential functions listed on the job description?

If the employee answers "No" to the last question, the nonprofit may follow up and ask whether the employee requires any accommodation to perform the tasks. Additionally, if the employer asks all applicants to do so, the applicant may be asked to demonstrate how he or she would physically accomplish a particular task.

> ### Job Description: Important Tool in Avoiding Disability Discrimination
>
> Every job description should include a list of the position's essential functions. During an interview with an applicant the interviewer may not ask whether there is anything that would prevent the applicant from accomplishing the job duties, (because that question is designed to elicit whether or not the applicant has a disability) but the interviewer may show the applicant a list of the position's essential functions (such as lifting a child, sitting for several hours at a time in front of a computer monitor or driving a van) and ask the applicant whether he or she can accomplish all the essential functions listed on the job description. If the applicant answers, "No," then the interviewer can explore whether an accommodation would enable the applicant to accomplish the essential functions.

Your Right to Ask Current Employees About Disabilities and to Submit to a Medical Examination

When an employee is returning to work after a medical leave, or when it appears that there is something preventing the employee from conducting the essential function of a job, a nonprofit may require that the employee submit to a medical examination (generally at the employer's cost, except for employees out on leave who may see their regular health professional and then submit the results to the employer). An employer's right to require a medical examination has been upheld in cases where it's apparent that an employee's health problems were causing a *substantial and injurious impact* on the employee's ability to perform necessary job functions.

In such cases, the results of the examination may help the employer determine whether the employee has a covered disability requiring accommodation, or whether a leave of absence would be appropriate under the Family and Medical Leave Act. Instead of the employer speaking directly with the employee's physician, the employer may want to provide the employee with a letter to give to the physician, including a copy of the employee's job description, and request that the physician provide an opinion whether or not the employee is capable of performing the essential functions of the position.

Employers may only conduct medical examinations of current employees (the employer foots the bill) and ask employees about their disability status if the examination and inquiry are shown to be job-related (such as the employer trying to design a reasonable accommodation for a disabled employee). The employer also must keep the results of such inquiries and examinations confidential by maintaining the results in separate, confidential files and only allowing access on a need-to-know basis. Best practice is to keep these files physically apart from regular personnel files, to minimize the risk that supervisors seeking performance history will consult the medical information files as well.

An employer may ask questions or test an employee at any stage for current illegal drug use without violating the ADA. However, other state laws or constitutional rights may be violated by requiring employees to submit to drug tests.

ADA Policies and Posting Requirements

The ADA requires that employers notify employees of their rights under the act. This is most easily accomplished by posting a notice (the U.S. Department of Labor will supply the poster) and by including a **written policy** in conjunction with an employee handbook. The nonprofit's written policy should state that the nonprofit:

Evacuating Employees With Disabilities

Every nonprofit employer should establish a plan to safely evacuate employees in the event of an emergency. The plan may differ based on the nonprofit's predictions about likely causes of a crisis, from fire, to a flu pandemic or incident of workplace violence. Although the details of the plan may differ from one nonprofit workplace to the next, every suitable plan should consider the special issues that arise with regard to evacuating employees with disabilities.

Risk Management Steps for a Safe and Inclusive Evacuation Plan:

❏ Prior to hiring a staff member with a disability (but after making a job offer), the employer may ask the prospective employee whether he or she will need assistance during an emergency.

❏ Publish the evacuation plan and communicate the overall evacuation strategy, as well as specific instructions, to the employees and volunteers through periodic briefings. Remember that paid and unpaid staff will need to know your plan before they can evaluate their needs for special assistance.

❏ Don't assume that every employee with a disability known to management will require special assistance.

❏ Survey staff members from time to time to identify whether any current employees will require special assistance during an evacuation.

❏ Identify personnel who are willing and able to provide assistance to disabled staff. Such assistance may take the form of removing physical barriers, carrying others, or simply accounting for disabled staff members.

❏ Purchase, install and maintain equipment and tools that will support the nonprofit's goal of effectively notifying all personnel about the need to evacuate. Examples of such equipment include alarms with visual signals and maps placed strategically along planned escape routes.

❏ Protect confidentiality. While no employer can or should promise complete confidentiality under any circumstances, a nonprofit should pay careful attention to safeguarding personal information. Personal information about employees should be released on a need-to-know basis only, such as to co-workers who have been selected to assist persons with disabilities or key personnel who will manage the evacuation.

❏ Conduct periodic mock drills involving the evacuation team in order to identify and remedy glitches in your plans.

❏ Adheres to the principles of nondiscrimination stated in the ADA and applicable state and local laws;

❏ Won't discriminate against an applicant, employee or volunteer on account of disability, provided that the employee/applicant is otherwise qualified for employment;

❏ Won't administer medical examinations to applicants until after conditional offers of employment have been made;

❏ Will segregate all medical information in employee/volunteer files and maintain the confidentiality of such information;

❏ Will provide applicants and employees/volunteers with disabilities with reasonable accommodation, except where such an accommodation would create an undue hardship on the nonprofit; and

❏ Will notify individuals with disabilities that the nonprofit provides reasonable accommodations to qualified individuals with disabilities, by: a) including a copy of the nonprofit's written policy in any handbook or personnel manual circulated to staff, and b) by posting the Equal Employment Opportunity Commission's poster conspicuously throughout the nonprofit's facilities.

The policy itself doesn't need to be more extensive than the list above. However, there should also be a clear description of the procedures for employees (and applicants) to follow in the event they require an accommodation (some nonprofits use a form that employees or their physicians fill out), as well as procedures for the nonprofit to follow when analyzing whether a requested accommodation is reasonable.

Here's a list reminding you of the ADA's prohibitions:

Don't ask applicants any question which is designed to draw out information about a past or current disability, such as, "Are you disabled?" "Have you ever used drugs or abused alcohol?"

Don't ask an applicant's references any question which you aren't permitted to ask the applicant directly.

Don't take any notes at any time concerning an applicant's physical characteristics or mental limitations. Focus on job-related skills, experience and capabilities.

Don't ask applicants for the same position different questions, or ask one applicant to physically demonstrate something, but not the others.

Don't require applicants to undergo a medical examination prior to a conditional offer of employment.

Don't terminate a employee because she or he suffers from a disabling condition if the worker would be able to perform the job with a reasonable accommodation.

Don't reject an employee's request for an accommodation without negotiating with the employee and carefully considering the financial and administrative burden of the requested accommodation, and documenting the decision to either accept or reject the accommodation request, or to implement an alternative accommodation.

Don't permit other employees or third parties (including clients) to harass, make fun of, or intimidate persons with disabilities.

Don't treat persons with disabilities differently from similarly situated employees in any term or condition of employment, solely because of their disability.

Summary of ADA Compliance

Here's a summary of the nuts and bolts of ADA compliance:

❏ Include an ADA policy in written personnel handbooks and post the U.S. Department of Labor notice that informs employees of their rights under the ADA.

❏ Determine the essential functions of every job at the nonprofit, distilling job duties into the bare essentials, and paying particular attention to physical requirements such as, lifting a child up to 60 pounds off of playground equipment, and mental requirements such as ability to work well with others.

❏ Maintain written job descriptions for every position and list the essential functions to show to any applicant and ask the question, "Can you perform all the essential functions on this job description?" This is the appropriate way to draw out whether the applicant has any limitations that would impact job performance.

❏ Relate to the applicant all the job-related expectations, including such obvious expectations as getting to work on time, and ask whether the applicant can meet those expectations.

❏ Educate staff who conduct interviews and check references to know what questions not to ask of applicants and references.

❏ Ask all applicants for the same position the same questions, and document the interview with an outline showing the same script for each interview.

❏ Make sure that all supervisors know that applicants and employees may request an accommodation and the requests can be made orally, in writing, or by someone else on the person's behalf. Emphasize that the applicant or employee requesting accommodation doesn't have to use specific terms such as *reasonable accommodation*.

❏ Maintain separate files for medical information, results of medical examinations, and requests by employees for family and medical leave. The separate files are necessary to maintain the privacy of any employees with a disability, and to minimize the possibility that awareness of fellow employees' disabilities will negatively impact performance evaluations and disciplinary actions by supervisors.

❏ Develop a protocol for handling confidential information relating to employees' medical information.

❏ Always offer the employee the opportunity to explain that she or he has a disability and requires an accommodation, but don't always take the employee's word for it. Unless it's an obvious disability, send the employee's written job description to the employee's treating physician and request the physician to certify what portions of the job the employee is capable of performing. If the employee is no longer capable of performing even one of the essential functions of the position, with or without an accommodation, the employee is no longer *qualified* for the position, and no further protections are afforded by the ADA.

❏ Engage in an *interactive negotiation* with employees over accommodations and document the process and the ultimate decision concerning whether and what accommodation is determined to be reasonable.

Procedures for Ensuring That There Is an Interactive Process to Explore an Accommodation

Qualified individuals with disabilities may make a request for reasonable accommodation to the [Name of position] with [Name of Nonprofit]. Upon receipt of an accommodation request, the [Name of position] will meet with the requesting individual to discuss and identify the precise limitations resulting from the disability, and the potential accommodation that the [Name of Nonprofit] might make to overcome those limitations.

The responding staff member in conjunction with the executive director and, if necessary, appropriate supervisory staff identified as having a *need to know* will determine the feasibility of the requested accommodation, considering various factors, including, but not limited to, the nature and cost of the accommodation, the availability of tax credits and deductions, outside funding, the nonprofit's overall financial resources and the accommodation's effect on the operations of the nonprofit, including impact on other staff and clients, and on [Name of Nonprofit]'s overall ability to [provide services to the public.]

The responding staff member will inform the employee requesting the accommodation of the organization's decision on the accommodation request or on how accommodation will be accomplished. If the accommodation request is denied, the employee will be advised of his or her right to appeal the decision [using the nonprofit's internal grievance procedure]. The employee desiring to appeal should submit a written request to the nonprofit along with the reasons for the appeal. [The nonprofit will review the request for appeal in accordance with its internal grievance procedures.]

The next section, Chapter 10, explores issues related to privacy in the workplace.

Taking the High Road—A Guide to Effective and Legal Employment Practices for Nonprofits

Chapter 10   Workplace Privacy

The Fourth Amendment of the United States Constitution creates a right for an individual's person and property not to be subjected to an *unreasonable search or seizure*. Though not explicit in the constitution, case law has conferred a constitutional right to privacy on all individuals. Therefore, the following each raise potential privacy law issues: searching a staff member's desk, videotaping staff in action with clients, listening to an employee's voice mail, accessing computer files or requiring an employee to take a drug test. However, court cases have consistently held that in the right conditions, an employee of a private employer (as opposed to the government) doesn't have a right to privacy at the workplace. Therefore, nonprofits can conduct monitoring activities with a staff member's consent—or even without consent, when warranted—and especially if the right to inspect or monitor is supported by a clear written policy.

On the other hand, employees have a personal life away from their work. They have hobbies, (perhaps blogging or bar-hopping) relationships, (perhaps with a co-worker) and even other jobs (perhaps with another nonprofit). If you are nervous after reading the prior sentence, you should be. What the employee does during nonworking hours is governed by a right to privacy and can't be controlled by the nonprofit—or can it? Risks can be created by employees' or volunteers' conduct, either during work hours or outside of work. Employees may engage in conduct during nonworking hours that isn't consistent with the best interests of the nonprofit. As discussed later in this chapter, when a volunteer or employee's conduct, even if occurring outside of work hours, is in conflict with the nonprofit's best interests, ignoring the conflict creates a significant risk.

Changing World, Changing Risks

Employee conduct has changed with the explosive growth of technology in the workplace. In the early 1990s, a growing number of nonprofits welcomed the introduction of e-mail addresses and the creation of promotional Web sites. While dramatically increasing the productivity of paid and volunteer personnel, new technologies have increased— exponentially—the risks facing employers. From the ease with which harassing messages can be sent to fellow employees, contractors, clients and the general public, to the threat of unauthorized disclosure of the nonprofit's confidential information, the magnitude of risk requires careful attention on the part of nonprofit leaders. Along with new exposures to claims against the nonprofit, emerging technologies offer possible tools for preventing and addressing misuse of a nonprofit's systems and equipment. Examples of tools that can help an employer safeguard its vital property and information assets while assuring compliance with essential workplace rules include screening and blocking software, and keystroke logging. In organizations that deploy paid and volunteer staff to distant locations, global positioning satellite (GPS) systems may be installed in nonprofit-owned vehicles to provide a means of tracking employee whereabouts.

The Right to Privacy at Work

An employee might have the impression that his computer files, telephone messages, work area, and desk drawers are *private*. The courts have consistently recognized the right of private employers to monitor their employees' use of computers and related equipment owned by the employer or used for the employer's business. To protect and safeguard this right, nonprofit employers should reduce any expectation of privacy at the workplace through a written policy that reminds staff that work areas, including desks, computers, software, and the contents of filing cabinets or storage closets, don't belong to the employee, but are the property of the nonprofit. Another way to reduce expectations of privacy and maintain the nonprofit's option to search employee work areas is to gain all employees' written consent to searches. If employees have provided written consent, and been warned not to expect that their desks, work areas, computer files or voice mail are *private*, the employer will prevail if the employee raises a legal challenge.

An employee's right to privacy is also impacted when an employer seeks to monitor telephone conversations or voice messages, read e-mails sent or received, or conduct video surveillance. The Federal Electronic Communications Privacy Act of 1986 (ECPA), 18 U.S.C. 2510 et seq. ⟵ extended traditional privacy principals to a new set of technologies: e-mail, cellular phone calls and paging devices. The ECPA prohibits the interception of electronic communications without the consent of one party to the communication. The majority of state laws also require consent of at least one party to a communication. However, once a communication has been received and is stored via a voice message or e-mail that has been listened to and/or read and is still present in a phone or computer, the communication can no longer be *intercepted*, so accessing voice messages and reading e-mails that have been received and read isn't a violation of law.

An employee's (and client's) consent to monitoring will remove the federal and state law obstacles that regulate interception of electronic communications. Many nonprofits, such as child care centers and those offering telephone hotlines, routinely monitor employees' conduct with surveillance videotapes or by taping hotline conversations. These nonprofits in particular should obtain employees' (and clients') consent and have written policies to notify staff of monitoring activities. Nonprofits offering hotline services would be well advised to put a message on the telephone service such as: "For your protection and to enable [Name of Nonprofit] to monitor quality of service, this conversation may be recorded." A nonprofit's right to videotape staff is strengthened if the cameras are in plain sight and if the taping occurs in areas at the workplace where the staff have no reasonable expectation of privacy. (Videotaping employees using the women's restroom wouldn't be acceptable because employees have a reasonable expectation of privacy in the restroom.)

Eavesdropping on Employees: Proceed With Caution

The general rule is that if one party to the communication is aware of or has consented to the interception, then there is no invasion of privacy. However, several states have laws that completely *prohibit* an employer from *eavesdropping* on employee conversations or that require *all parties* to a conversation to provide consent.

California: See Cal. Penal Code Sections 631, 632 and 636 : No person other than an authorized law enforcement officer may wiretap or eavesdrop on confidential communications.

Georgia: See O.C.G.A. Sections 16-11-61 and 16-11-62 requires consent of all parties.

Illinois: The Illinois Eavesdropping Act, 720 ILCS 5/14-1 et seq. makes it unlawful to knowingly intercept in person, by telephone or electronically, another person's conversations, regardless of whether one or more of the parties is aware of the eavesdropping;

Louisiana: The Louisiana Electronic Surveillance Act, La. Rev. Stat. Ann. Section 15-1301 et seq. makes it unlawful to intercept or try to intercept or procure someone to intercept any wire or oral communication.

Michigan: requires consent of all parties. See MCL 750.539c and 750.539d.

Minnesota: State law prohibits intentionally intercepting any wire, electronic or oral communication and using any device to intercept oral communication; Employers may use video surveillance, but cameras the record sounds are restricted under the wiretapping statutes. M.S.A. Section 626A.02.

Montana: requires the knowledge of all parties to a conversation. See Mont. Code Ann. Section 45-8-213.

Nevada: requires consent of all parties. See Nev. Rev. Stat. 200.620.

New Hampshire: requires consent of all parties. See N.H. Rev. Stat. Ann. 570-A-2.

Pennsylvania: Intentionally intercepting a wire, electronic transmission or telephone call is prohibited. See 18 Pa. C.S. Sections 5701 et seq.

Washington: requires all parties to consent. See Wash. Rev. Code Section 9.73.030.

Two states, **Massachusetts** and **New Jersey**, have a business necessity exception that permits employers to use telephone recording devices in the course of business where there is a legitimate business reason to do so.

The rapid evolution of technology creates its own challenges relating to violation of privacy. Given the nature of the Internet and e-mail, and how easy it is to access, download, print and transmit information using a variety of electronic and wireless devices, employees are constantly able to view, send and receive nonwork related communications. Many do so while at work, at times resulting in abusive situations where employees spend more time e-mailing friends and surfing the Internet than drafting a funding proposal. The widespread use of social networking Web sites, and the prevalence of blogging will only grow in the future, making it crucial for nonprofits to clarify that personal use of the nonprofit's computers, e-mail and the Internet should be limited. Policies on the use of technology should address:

❏ the appropriate use of technology, including e-mail, instant messaging and Internet access and use,

❏ that e-mail and instant messages are stored on the nonprofit's servers and all computer hard drives are subject to search at any time, passwords notwithstanding,

❏ that posting, accessing, downloading, printing, or transmitting inappropriate, unprofessional, pornographic or obscene information is contrary to the nonprofit's values,

❏ that employees are expected to respect copyright and trademark laws, and

❏ that a violation of policy that will subject the employee to discipline, up to and including discharge.

Whether or not the computer used at work is owned by the nonprofit, if the employee uses the computer for work-related tasks, the nonprofit's e-mail and Internet policy should apply to the hardware and software in use. Also keep in mind that an effective policy must reflect the employer's awareness of new technologies, including those that the organization might introduce and adopt in the months or years ahead, as well as those that an employee may bring to the workplace. Many employers were surprised by their lack of readiness for the risks associated with the use of camera-phones. The rapid development and widespread use of portable high-tech devices has brought a new perspective to the way that employers must consider and address technology-related risks in the workplace. In the years ahead, devices whose misuse could threaten the nonprofit and its workforce will continue to shrink in dimensions, while growing in sophistication and functionality.

Risks Relating to E-mail and Internet Use

The use of e-mail at work raises the possibility that an employee will send or receive e-mail tainted with bias, discriminatory or defamatory language, obscene or pornographic material. For this reason it's essential that an employer's broad policy on technology use or specific policy concerning e-mail defines inappropriate communications as anything which is illegal, obscene or which violates copyright laws or infringes on a trademark.

Personal communications sent internally to another employee via e-mail can result in liability for the employer. In one instance an e-mail communication which was presumably deleted came back to haunt the employer. In that case, one employee sent another a crude, racially biased joke about a co-worker via e-mail, which was deleted by the recipient. However, the employee who was the subject of their humor heard about the joke, and used this fact as evidence of a hostile environment at the workplace in a sexual harassment trial. The plaintiff was able to enter a hard (printed) copy of the *deleted* message into evidence at trial, since the employer's computer system had backed it up. The employer was ultimately held responsible for the employee's biased e-mail message.

Other risks relating to the improper use of technology include:

❏ copying software that's licensed to the nonprofit for the employee's personal use (theft or at the very least a violation of license agreements);

❏ using the telephone, facsimile, or e-mail systems for the dissemination or solicitation of information about for-profit ventures, religious beliefs or political causes, or any non job-related business;

❏ viewing obscene material (for example, child pornography or material that might be child pornography) that triggers a duty by the employer to investigate the employee's activities and possibly take action to stop unauthorized activity*;

❏ uploading or downloading any protected, copyrighted, or proprietary software, which can put the entire nonprofit's computer system at risk for computer viruses;

❏ harassing or intimidating co-workers or third parties, through the use of the nonprofit's computers.

*In a recent New Jersey case, a company was sued by the wife of a former employee who alleged that the company was on notice of the employee's use of the Internet to view obscene material. The appellate court held that the Restatement (Second) of Torts 317 places a duty to control an employee when the employee is acting outside the scope of his employment to prevent the employee from "intentionally harming others or from so conducting himself as to create an unreasonable risk of bodily harm to them."

Developing a Technology Policy

Protecting your nonprofit against misuse of property and other assets and exposure to liability claims begins with articulating a clear policy of do's and don'ts. Your employees need to know the ground rules before they can comply. An effective technology policy can be helpful on two fronts: it provides a defense to claims that the nonprofit unlawfully

Tech Terms You Need to Know

Blog—A Web log or diary. Millions of Americans *publish* details of their personal lives in blogs available for public consumption. Bloggers include those who wish to make their opinions known, share their creative talents, or vent with kindred spirits in cyberspace. Given the growing number of active bloggers, it's likely that some of the nonprofit's employees have created blogs. And they may be publishing blog content during the workday. Worse, they may be disclosing confidential or inappropriate information about the nonprofit in their online diaries.

Cyberslacking—Neglecting one's job in order to surf the Web for pleasure. Every employee with Internet access may be guilty of occasional *cyberslacking*, but in some workplaces violations seriously impair workplace productivity. Cyberslacking can be dangerous on several fronts, particularly if an employee is visiting sites whose content violates the nonprofit's rules or offends nearby co-workers.

Instant Messages and E-Mails Sought in Litigation

According to the *2004 Workplace E-Mail and Instant Messaging Survey* conducted by the American Management Association and The ePolicy Institute, one in five employers have had employees' e-mail and instant messages (IM) subpoenaed in a lawsuit or regulatory proceeding (Source: *www.epolicyinstitute.com/survey*). The same survey reported that 79 percent of employers surveyed had adopted e-mail policies, and 25 percent of survey respondents reporting dismissing an employee who had violated the organization's policy concerning e-mail or instant messaging.

Although the prevalence of specific policies restricting use of e-mail and the Internet is significant, only a relatively small percentage of employers have incorporated restrictions on the use of instant messaging in their technology policies. Adding to an employer's risk is the tendency of IM users to correspond in an informal style when sending instant messages. This reality calls attention to the need for a broadly written technology policy that cautions employees about the appropriate use of IM, while putting staff *on notice* that the nonprofit maintains the right to monitor use of instant messaging.

monitored employee communications and it may prevent inappropriate uses of the nonprofit's systems and equipment. An appropriate policy should incorporate the elements listed below. In addition, it should be tailored to reflect the culture and resources (including the ability to monitor communications) of the nonprofit. Although sample policies are offered in this text, remember that it's never appropriate to simply copy and use the policy of another organization without first customizing the policy template to meet your needs.

When developing a technology policy in the organization, or revisiting an existing policy, consider whether the policy:

❏ broadly defines the nonprofit's property—don't limit your description to *computer systems* or *office equipment*—consider all of the mobile equipment, software, and systems now in place, as well as systems that may be purchased for the nonprofit's benefit in the years to come. One approach is to define systems as "any electronic device used to communicate or transmit information internally or externally." (Source: "Emerging Technology in the Workplace," 21 *The Labor Lawyer* 1 (2005).

❏ informs employees of the nonprofit's right and intent to monitor employee communications to protect the interests of the organization and its vital assets.

❏ notifies employees that they should have no expectation of privacy when using the nonprofit's technology resources and assets, including when using personal equipment to access the nonprofit's resources or accounts.

❏ is distributed to all staff with an opportunity given for review and questions. Employees should be required to sign to acknowledge receipt, understanding and their willingness to abide by the policy.

❏ is sufficiently flexible to permit management to further update the policy at management's discretion.

❏ defines permissible personal use of the nonprofit's equipment. Advances in technology have made it impossible, if not impractical, to fully prohibit personal use of the nonprofit's equipment. A more practical approach is to permit limited personal use, while providing guidance on what constitutes excessive use.

❏ cautions employees about the prohibition on inappropriate internal or external disclosure of confidential information concerning employees, volunteers, donors or clients/service recipients.

❏ strictly prohibits use of the nonprofit's systems, electronic devices, etc. for any inappropriate conduct, including retrieving, viewing or transmitting sexual content, or sending harassing, discriminatory or defamatory messages.

❏ reminds employees that any messages transmitted with the nonprofit's equipment or systems are stored and subject to retrieval by management for any reason.

Technology Policy

[Name of Nonprofit]'s information technology systems (including, but not limited to network servers, PCs, telephones, mobile phones, PDAs, or copiers) are tools that are provided to employees to enhance productivity and performance on the job. Although limited nonbusiness use is permitted, employees understand that any use of the nonprofit's systems, equipment or subscriptions should create no expectation of privacy to any data, information, or files that are created, accessed or stored on or through the organization's systems. [Name of Nonprofit] reserves the right to access and monitor use of its systems, software and equipment as necessary to protect the assets of the organization.

Employees are expected to exercise good judgment in their use of e-mail, instant messaging, and the Internet and understand that access to these media is a privilege, not a right.

Examples of Inappropriate Uses of Technology

❏ Any use violating law or government regulation

❏ Any use promoting disrespect for an individual, discrimination, or constituting a personal attack, including ethnic jokes and slurs

❏ Any use intended to cause embarrassment or other harm to another person, including fellow employees, volunteers, or representatives of a vendor, partner organization or other organization with which [Name of Nonprofit] conducts business

❏ Viewing, copying, or transmitting material with sexual content

❏ Transmitting harassing or soliciting messages

❏ Using copyrighted material without legal right

❏ Any use for personal financial gain, or in a manner that creates a potential conflict of interest for [Name of Nonprofit]

❏ Defamatory, inflammatory, or derogatory statements about individuals, organizations, companies or their personnel, products or services

❏ The failure to use good judgment or to abide by this policy may result in suspension of privileges or other discipline, up to and including termination.

I have read and agree to abide by the Technology Policy described above. I am aware that violations of this policy may subject me to discipline, up to and including termination of employment.

_____   _____
Signature   Date

Internet/Computer Use Policy

This policy applies to all employees when they're using computers or Internet connections supplied by [Name of Nonprofit], whether or not during work hours, and whether or not from the organization's premises.

No Privacy

[Name of Nonprofit] provides computers and Internet connections (*facilities*) to further its business interests. You should use those facilities only for the organization's business. The organization has the right, but not the duty, to monitor all communications and downloads that pass through its facilities, at its sole discretion. Any information retained on the organization's facilities may be disclosed to outside parties or to law enforcement authorities.

Improper Activities

You may not disseminate or knowingly receive harassing, sexually explicit, threatening or illegal information by use of the organization's facilities, including offensive jokes or cartoons. You may not use the organization's facilities for personal or commercial advertisements, solicitations or promotions.

Nature of E-Mail

E-mail resembles speech in its speed and lack of formality. Unlike speech, e-mail leaves a record that's often retrievable even after the sender and recipient delete it. If you wouldn't want your mother to read your message on the front page of the newspaper, don't send it by e-mail.

Regular Deletion of E-mail

[Name of Nonprofit] strongly discourages storage of large numbers of e-mail messages. As a general rule, you should promptly delete each e-mail message that you receive after you have read it. If you need to keep a message for longer than a week, save it to your hard disk, or print it out and save the paper copy. The systems administrator will regularly purge all messages in employee inboxes and all copies of sent messages that are older than 30 days.

Intellectual Property of Others

You may not download or use material from the Internet or elsewhere in violation of software licenses or the copyright trademark and patent laws. You may not install or use any software obtained over the Internet without written permission from the systems administrator.

Report Violations

If you observe or learn about a violation of this policy, you must report it immediately to your supervisor, or to the systems administrator.

Acknowledgment

By signing on the line below, I acknowledge that I have read, understand and agree to comply with the foregoing Internet/Computer Use Policy. I understand that, if I don't comply with the Internet/Computer Use Policy, I may be subject to discipline, including loss of access to the organization's facilities and discharge from employment. I may also be subject to legal action against me for damages or indemnification.

Signature _____ Date: _____

This sample policy was prepared by Gutierrez, Preciado & House, LLP, 200 S. Los Robles, Ste. 210, Pasadena, CA 91101-2482.

Confidentiality

Proprietary information (such as donor lists) and private, confidential information about clients and employees must be kept secure in order to protect against violations of privacy, as well as violations of federal and state laws that govern the disclosure of personal, confidential information. Electronic transmission raises challenges to maintaining confidentiality which merits thoughtful discussion among paid and unpaid staff, and may require the nonprofit to customize internal operating procedures to maintain client and employee confidentiality. Nonprofits with social workers and medical health professionals on staff need to be aware of special ethical obligations relating to maintaining confidentiality that mental health and healthcare professionals must observe to avoid liability for malpractice or the loss of professional licenses.

Because of the nature of their work, nonprofits may have obligations to maintain confidential communications stemming from funding sources or contracts with government agencies to provide specialized services. Many nonprofits with state funding from disability and human services agencies will find that they're required to have extensive policies and practices to protect the confidentiality of personal health information about clients because they're *business associates* under the Health Information Portability and Accountability Act (HIPAA) P.L. 104-191 (1996) . ☞ Business Associates must protect the privacy of certain identifying health information in the same manner as *covered entities* under HIPAA. A sample business associate contract is provided by the U.S. Department of Health and Human Services on its Web site. ☞ Employees who regularly work with the types of information that are protected from disclosure, or with clients whose personal information the nonprofit maintains, should be well versed in the nonprofit's obligations, so that violation of privacy rules doesn't occur. Employees should also know that due to the seriousness of privacy rules and the need to be respectful of clients' confidential information, violation of the nonprofit's confidentiality policies is a serious offense, with consequences including termination of employment.

Disciplining Employees for Off-Duty Conduct

As a general rule, a nonprofit employer shouldn't discipline or discharge employees for participating in lawful activity, off premises, during nonworking hours, unless the conduct is in direct conflict with the essential business-related interests of the employer or in direct conflict with the best interests of the employer. Most state laws addressing this issue prohibit employment decisions that are based on lawful, off-premises use of tobacco products during nonworking hours. Several state laws also provide that employers may not control or direct the political activities or affiliations of employees. However, there are also public policy considerations: It could be considered a violation of the public policy in some states to discharge an employee for exercising his or her legal rights to free speech or free association, even if the employee's off-duty conduct is inconsistent with the nonprofit's values.

In general, HIPAA doesn't apply to employment records; however, some nonprofits are themselves covered entities under HIPAA, and thus required to have various privacy policies in place in accordance with federal law. The Department of Health and Human Services (www.hhs.gov) offers a decision-tree tool on its Web site to assist organizations determine whether they're a *covered entity* under HIPAA. The tool is available at: *www.cms.hhs.gov/apps/hipaa2decisionsupport/default.asp*. If your nonprofit electronically transmits health-protected information about clients, HIPAA may require that your organization implement a privacy policy and authorization procedures to clarify *how* and *when* a client authorizes disclosure of protected health information. Check with an attorney knowledgeable about HIPAA compliance to determine if and how the nonprofit should implement policies and procedures to comply with HIPAA.

The First Amendment and the Real World

The reality is that sometimes an employee's personal life spills over and negatively affects his work performance, or an employee of the organization may engage in outside work, causes or hobbies that are plainly contrary to the values of the nonprofit. The risk of potential outside conduct by an employee causing embarrassment or harm to the nonprofit's reputation varies depending on the mission and scope of the organization. Many organizations that have a high level of concern about this risk have found that establishing a written code of conduct, document describing Guiding Beliefs and Principles, or Code of Ethics help in putting all employees *on notice* about the nonprofit's expectations. Employees whose personal values conflict with the nonprofit's may choose not to work at the nonprofit. In instances where there is a conflict in values with respect to a current employee, the existence of a code of conduct may offer the nonprofit solid grounds on which to terminate an employee whose conduct outside of work is in conflict with the nonprofit's stated values.

Summary of State Laws Concerning Outside Conduct

The state laws noted here are subject to constant review and revision in state legislatures. This summary should therefore be used for reference purposes, rather than as a definitive guide.

Arizona: Employers may not discipline employees for the exercise of their civil rights.

California: Employers may not discipline or discharge employees for any lawful conduct occurring during nonworking hours.

Connecticut: Employers may not discharge or discipline employees for smoking or using tobacco products. Employers with 25+ employees may not discriminate against, discharge or discipline any employee who runs for, or takes time off to serve in, state public office.

District of Columbia: Employers may not discipline employees for smoking or using tobacco products.

Illinois: Employers may not discipline employees for the use of lawful products outside work, during nonworking hours.

Indiana: Employers may not require that employees refrain from off-duty tobacco use.

Kentucky: Employers may not make employment decisions based on an employee's status as a smoker and may not restrict employees freedom to smoke during off-duty hours.

Louisiana: Employers are prohibited from discriminating against employees or applicants for using tobacco outside the workplace. Employers may not control or direct the political activities or affiliations of employees.

Maine: Employers are prohibited from discriminating against employees or applicants for tobacco use outside the workplace.

Michigan*: Employers may not keep records of employees' associations, political activities, publications or communications about nonwork activities. *Note:* this law could restrict an employer from disciplining an employee who **blogs**.

Minnesota: Employers may not refuse to hire or discharge employees because they engage in or have engaged in the lawful consumption of food, alcoholic or nonalcoholic beverages and tobacco, while off the premises.

Mississippi: Employers may not make employment decisions based on off-duty, off-premises use of tobacco.

Missouri: Employers may not discriminate based on the lawful use of alcohol or tobacco.

Montana: Employers may not make employment decisions based on an employee's use of lawful products away from the job **but** employers may make decisions based on the fact that the employee's lawful use affects the employee's ability to perform job-related responsibilities, the safety of other employees, or conflicts with a bona fide occupational qualification that's *reasonably related* to the employee's job. **Nonprofits with a primary purpose of discouraging the use of a lawful product are excepted.**

Nevada: Employers may not have policies that prevent employees from engaging in politics or becoming candidates for public office. Employers may not discipline or discharge or discriminate against employees or refuse to hire those that engage in the lawful use of any product outside the premises during nonworking hours.

New Hampshire: Employers may not require employees or applicants to refrain from tobacco use outside the course of employment.

New Jersey: Employers may not refuse to hire or take adverse action against employees because they do or don't smoke or use tobacco products unless the employer has a rational reason related to employment.

Blogging: New Danger Zone for Employers

The use of personal blogs—the term referring to Web logs or diaries—has skyrocketed in recent years. Often containing highly personal information, blogs are readily accessed by Internet users. In a survey conducted in 2004, the Pew Internet & American Life Project estimated that 8 million American adults maintain a blog (Source: The State of Blogging, Pew Internet & American Life Project, January 2, 2005). ☞ The popularity of blogging poses several risks for nonprofit employers. First, many active bloggers readily admit to posting to their blogs at various times during the business day. Coupled with the time spent reading the work of other bloggers, this represents a potentially significant misuse of the nonprofit's financial assets. A second perhaps more ominous risk concerns the content of employee blogs. The content of an employee's blog could prove embarrassing to the nonprofit employer or cause other harm. To address these risks, a nonprofit should first be prepared to strictly enforce its technology policy. Misuse of any asset should be addressed through appropriate discipline, up to an including termination. Second, an organization should give careful consideration to whether it's desirable to monitor blogs maintained by employees, although doing so could unduly stretch the limited resources of the organization.

New Mexico: Employers may not require, as a condition of employment, that employees or applicants abstain from smoking or using tobacco products during nonworking hours.

New York: Employers may not discriminate against employees for the following off-premises and outside work hours: 1) engaging in political activities, 2) legal use of consumable products, 3) legal recreational activities or (4) membership in a union.

North Carolina: Employers may not discharge or discriminate against employees or refuse to hire them because they engage in the lawful use of lawful products off premises, during nonworking hours and as long as the conduct doesn't adversely affect job performance or the safety of other employees. *Exception:* when the employee's off duty, off premises conduct conflicts with the fundamental objectives of the organization.

North Dakota: Employers may not discriminate against employees for participating in lawful activity off premises during nonworking hours that isn't in direct conflict with the essential business related interests of the employer.

Oklahoma: Employers may not discharge or discriminate against individuals based on their smoking or use/non-use of tobacco products. Employers may not require that employees refrain from smoking during nonworking hours.

Rhode Island: Employers may not require employees to refrain from smoking outside the course of employment; **however, nonprofits with the primary purpose of discouraging tobacco use are excepted.**

South Carolina: Employers are prohibited from taking employment actions based on an employee's use of tobacco products outside work, or because of political activities.

South Dakota: Employers may not discharge employees because of their tobacco use off-premises during nonworking hours unless the restriction relates to a bona fide occupational requirement and is rationally related to the employment or required to avoid conflict of interest.

Tennessee: Employers may not discharge employees for off-duty tobacco use or any other lawful agricultural product.

Utah: Employers **may** make employment decisions based on off-duty conduct concerning alcohol or illegal drug use because there is a state law that provides guidelines for employers to make decisions and take action based on employees' private activity.

Washington: Employers may not discipline or discharge employees for the exercise of their rights to be politically active or support candidates.

West Virginia: Employers may not discriminate against employees for off premises use of tobacco during nonworking hours.

Wisconsin: Employers may not take adverse job actions against employees based on their use or nonuse of lawful products off premises during nonworking hours. *Exception:* nonprofits that discourage the use of certain lawful products may refuse to hire employees who use those products.

Wyoming: Employers may not prohibit employees from tobacco product use outside of employment.

Personnel Files

One of the areas where employees typically have an expectation of privacy is in their own personnel files. Personnel files contain personal information that employees expect to be kept confidential. The nonprofit should develop a clear policy defining when and how an employee may have access to his or her files. Conventional wisdom tells us that what is contained in an employee's file shouldn't be a secret from the employee, so it doesn't make sense to prohibit an employee from reviewing his or her file. However, it wouldn't be prudent to permit employees free access to their files, just as it wouldn't be appropriate for anyone to have free access to any of the many other business records of the nonprofit. It also doesn't make sense to permit an employee to take the contents of the file home, or even to the copier machine or the employee's work station because of the risk of inadvertently violating the employee's confidentiality or losing the contents of the file. An employee who is reviewing a personnel file should do so in a controlled environment, with his or her supervisor or the human resource manager present to ensure that the file is kept intact. If the employer has done a good job documenting the employee's performance, nothing in the file should be a surprise to the employee.

A minority of state laws require an employer to give an employee access to personnel files and to provide the employee with a copy of the file. Absent a statutory right to access personnel files, employers are free to determine their own policies. As with all policies at the workplace, care should be taken to implement the personnel file policy consistently, ensuring that all employees are treated equally with respect to access to their files.

Summary of State Laws Governing Access to Personnel Files

The state laws noted here are subject to constant review and revision in state legislatures. This summary should therefore be used for reference purposes, rather than as a definitive guide.

Alaska: Employers must allow employees to inspect and copy their personnel files and other personnel information maintained by the employer concerning the employee. Employers may require employees to pay the reasonable cost of copying. Alaska Stat. 23.10.430. See 8 Alaska Admin. Code 15.910(d).

California: Employers must permit an employee to inspect his or her own file (defined as records, wherever maintained that employers use to assess the employee's performance) at reasonable intervals. A copy of the employee's file must be maintained at the workplace. See Cal. Lab. Code Section 1198.5.

Connecticut: Employers have a reasonable time to provide employees and former employees a copy of all or part of their file, when the request is in writing. The employer may require employees to pay the reasonable cost of copying. Employers don't have to comply with requests more than twice a year. See Conn. Gen. Stat. Sections 31-128b, 31-128g and 31-128h.

Delaware: Employers must permit employees to inspect their personnel files at least once every year. Employers don't have to allow employees to make copies. See 19 Del. C. Section 730-735.

Illinois: Employers with at least five employees must provide employees with a copy of their file. Employers may require employees to submit a written request to view their file. Employers must grant at least two requests for inspection in a calendar year when made at reasonable intervals. Former employees have the right to inspect their file for one year from the date of separation of employment. See 820 ILCS Section 40/1 et seq.

Iowa: Employer must permit employees to examine and copy personnel files upon mutual agreement as to the time. Employees aren't permitted to access references written for them. Employers may require employees to pay the reasonable cost of copying. See Iowa Code Ch. 91B.1.

Maine: Employers must permit employees and former employees to review and copy personnel files within 10 days of the employee's written request. Employers must provide one copy of the entire file at no cost to the employee upon request in each calendar year. See 26 Maine Rev. Stat. Ann. Section 631.

Massachusetts: Employers must permit employees and former employees to review their file at their workplace during normal business hours, or provide a copy of their file, within five days of receiving a written request. Employees have the right to submit written statements to be added to the file that explain their disagreement with the contents of their personnel file. See Mass. Gen. L. c. 149 Section 52C.

Michigan: Employers must provide employees and former employees, upon written request, an opportunity to review their personnel file at reasonable intervals, generally not more than twice a year. Employees are entitled to copies, but the employer may require employees to pay the reasonable cost of copying. See MCl 423.503 and 423.504.

Minnesota: Employers with 20+ employees must permit employees and former employees the opportunity to review their personnel files once every six months, and for up to a year post separation. Employers have seven working days to respond to the request if the record is within the state and 14 days if the record is stored out of state. Employers may not charge for copying the file. See Minn. Stat. Ann. Sections 181.961.

Nevada: Employers must provide a reasonable opportunity for employees to inspect their records on employee qualifications and discipline. Confidential reports from previous employers and information concerning the employee's prior criminal history doesn't need to be made available. Employers may charge the actual cost of copying the file. Employees have the right to submit written statements to be added to the file that explain their disagreement with the contents of their personnel file. If they're correct, the records must be changed. Former employees who were employed 60+ days have the right to inspect records if requested within 60 days of termination. If requested, employers must furnish copies at cost. See Nev. Rev. Stat. 613.075 and 618.370.

New Hampshire: Employers must permit employees and former employees an opportunity to inspect their personnel files and may charge a reasonable copying fee unless the employee is subject of a pending investigation and the disclosure would prejudice law enforcement, or if the information relates to a government investigation. Employees have the right to submit written statements to be added to the file that explains their disagreement with the contents of their personnel file. See New Hampshire Rev. Stat. Ann. 275:56.

Ohio: Only medical records are affected. Employers must furnish a copy of any medical report pertaining to the employee or former employee, and may require the employee to pay the copying cost. See Ohio Rev. Code Section 4113.23.

Oregon: Employers must permit employees and former employees to inspect records used to assess the employee's performance or concerning disciplinary actions. Employees have the right to request a certified copy of the records. See Oregon Rev. Stat. 652.750(2) and 652.750(3).

Pennsylvania: Employers must permit current employees to examine their own files used by their employer to assess performance or disciplinary action, but there isn't right to make copies. See 43 P.S. Section 1322, 1322 and 1323.

Rhode Island: Employers must permit current employees to examine their own files three times a year provided that the employee gives at least seven days' notice. Employees don't have the right to make copies or remove the file from the employer's place of business. Employers may, at their discretion, provide the employee with a copy and charge a reasonable amount for copying. See R.I. Gen. Laws Section 28-6.4-1 et seq.

South Carolina: Only records of exposure to toxic substances are affected. Employers must provide access to records of exposure. See S.C. Code Ann. Section 41-15-100 et seq.

Washington: Employers must permit employees to inspect any or all of their personnel file at the employee's request. Employees may also request an annual inspection to verify that the information in their file is correct and if not, to have it removed or submit a statement for the file expressing the employee's disagreement with the outcome. The state law doesn't explicitly permit employees to obtain copies of their file. See Wash. Rev. Code. Section 49.12.250.

Wisconsin: Employers must, upon request, permit employees to inspect documents used to assess performance and disciplinary actions and any medical records unless specifically excepted. If an employee disagrees with information in the file, the employee may agree with the employer to revise or remove the information from the file, or attach a written statement to their file. Employees have the right to copy records and employers may charge a fee that may not exceed the actual cost of copying. See Wis. Stat. Section 103.13.

Drug Testing and Suspected Drug Abuse

It's always a challenge to know what to do when an employee is suspected of drug abuse. One option is to demand that the employee take a drug test on the spot. There are practical, as well as legal, problems with this approach. A safer option is to treat the suspected drug use as a performance issue and discipline the employee based on performance failings, rather than suspected drug use. Nevertheless, there are times when knowing for certain whether an employee is abusing drugs or alcohol is best. In those cases, suspending the employee and requiring the employee to be tested for substance abuse prior to making a determination whether the employee should return to work is the advisable practice.

Recovering drug addicts and alcoholics are considered individuals with a disability under the Americans with Disabilities Act of 1990 (ADA) (See full text of the law, Section 510.) ✏ and must be given *reasonable accommodation* in the workplace. Therefore, once a nonprofit knows that an employee has had a drug or alcohol problem in the past and is still in recovery, that individual must be considered *disabled* and the nonprofit must consider reasonable accommodations for the employee. A common accommodation in such cases would be to suspend the employee pending rehabilitation. In contrast, current use of illegal substances or coming to work under the influence of alcohol is legitimately grounds for immediate termination with no accommodation requirement since current illegal drug use isn't protected by the ADA, and being under the influence of alcohol at work is clearly inappropriate, unprofessional conduct.

The Drug-Free Workplace Act of 1988, U.S. Code Title 41, Section 701 et seq. ✏ requires *some* federal contractors and grantees (those receiving $25,000+ in federal funding) to agree that they will provide drug-free workplaces as a condition of receiving a contract or grant from a federal agency. Failure to adhere to the requirements of the act may cause the nonprofit to lose the federal contract or grant and/or be unable to qualify for federal funding in the future.

The Drug Free Workplace Act requires a covered nonprofit to:

❑ Publish a statement (written policy) notifying employees that the unlawful manufacture, distribution, dispensation, possession, or use of a controlled substance is prohibited in the person's workplace. The statement should also notify employees of any punitive actions that will be taken. There is also a posting requirement.

❑ Establish a Drug-Free awareness program to inform employees about—

   (i)   the dangers of drug abuse in the workplace;

   (ii) the policy of maintaining a drug-free workplace;

   (iii) any available drug counseling, rehabilitation, and employee assistance programs; and

   (iv) the penalties that may be imposed upon employees for drug abuse violations.

❑ Make it a requirement that each employee be given a copy of the workplace substance abuse policy.

Under the act, employees are required to inform their employer of any drug-related criminal conviction or sentencing within five days. The act doesn't require drug testing.

Drug Testing

Requiring an employee to take a drug test is a risky issue unless the state law where the nonprofit is located has provided specifically that private employers may require employees to take a drug test. A drug test is often considered a violation of constitutional privacy rights because it's akin to a body search. To justify a drug test, a nonprofit must be very certain that there is either a supportive state law, or a strong suspicion of illegal substance use combined with a risk to human safety. Even with strong support in the state's law or with factual evidence, there are practical difficulties with drug testing due to *false-negative* and *false-*

Random drug testing is mandatory for employees with commercial drivers' licenses

Federal law, The Omnibus Transportation Employees Testing (OTET) Act of 1991, 49 C.F.R Section 382 (1994), requires employers to randomly yet periodically test employees who drive vehicles and hold commercial drivers licenses (CDLs). Random testing is required because driving is considered a *safety sensitive* position. Since most nonprofits only have a few employees who hold CDLs, many nonprofits have joined with other organizations to form a cooperative testing collaboration, resulting in less expensive testing.

Is the Nonprofit Covered by the Drug Free Workplace Act?

❑ Does the nonprofit have a federal grant?

❑ Does the nonprofit have a federal contract valued at $25,000 or more?

❑ Does the nonprofit have any subcontracts that include a drug-free workplace requirement?

❑ Is the nonprofit subject to any federal agency regulations, such as those of the U.S. Department of Education, U.S. Department of Housing and Urban Development, or the U.S.Department of Health and Human Services?

If you answered "Yes" to any of these questions, your nonprofit should develop a policy that adheres to the requirements of the Drug Free Workplace Act. Even if your nonprofit isn't required to comply with the act, the act provides guidelines for developing a drug-free workplace policy.

positive tests. Consequently, most employment lawyers advise clients to treat suspected drug or alcohol use as a performance issue, and to discipline employees on that basis. In many states, if suspected substance abuse results in an accident or injury at the workplace, the employer is on stronger grounds to require a drug or alcohol test as a condition of continued employment. In other states, having a *reasonable suspicion* of drug use is sufficient to require an employee to undergo a test. It's important to know what the state law or court cases in the nonprofit's state have decreed with respect to drug testing.

Many states permit testing but only if the employer has a written policy in place ahead of time to notify employees about testing procedures. In some states, employers with comprehensive written policies may be eligible for discounts on workers' compensation insurance premiums.

Summary of State Laws on Drug Testing

The state laws noted here are subject to constant review and revision in state legislatures. This summary should therefore be used for reference purposes, rather than as a definitive guide.

Alabama: Employers participating in the state's drug-free workplace program are required to test applicants (post offer) and when there is a reasonable suspicion of drug use, as well as follow-up testing on employees entering an employee assistance or rehabilitation program. Employers implementing a drug-free workplace program can qualify for a 5 percent discount in workers' compensation insurance premiums. See Ala. Code Sections 25-5-330 et seq.

Alaska: An employer may require drug testing as long as it's pursuant to a written policy and is conducted for a job-related reason consistent with a business necessity. The written policy must address: (a) employees subject to testing, (b) circumstances when testing is required, (c) what substances may be tested for, (d) consequences of refusal to be tested, (e) consequences of positive result, (f) right of the employee to obtain the result, and (g) explain a positive test result, and (h) a statement of confidentiality. The testing must be paid for by the employer and is considered working time. No cause of action may be brought against an employer for adverse employment actions taken in good faith based on a positive drug or alcohol test. See Alaska Stat. 23.10.600-699.

Arizona: Employers are required to have and distribute a written policy outlining the employer's procedures for drug tests. An employer may require drug testing for any job-related purpose consistent with business necessity. Random testing is permitted. The employer is responsible for the costs of testing and testing is considered work time. No cause of action may be taken against an employer for adverse employment actions taken in good faith based upon a positive drug test. Employers implementing a testing program must include all compensated employees and must keep all communications about drug or alcohol test results confidential. See Ariz. Stat. Ann. Sections 23-493.

Arkansas: Arkansas has a voluntary drug-free workplace program for employers covered by the state's workers' compensation law that choose to be part of the program. Participating employers may test applicants for alcohol/drugs. Employees who aren't in safety-sensitive positions may only be tested when there is reasonable suspicion. See Ark. Code Annot. Sections 11-14-101 through 112.

California: No state law; however, the City of San Francisco has its own restrictions: testing is permitted if the employer has reasonable grounds to believe an employee is impaired on the job and there is a clear and present danger to the physical safety of the employee or others. Random, periodic and post-accident testing aren't permitted. See San Francisco, Cal. Code Part II, ch. VIII, art. 3300A.1111(1993).

The City of Berkeley has adopted a city ordinance which prohibits all drug testing within city limits.

Colorado: No state law prohibits or permits drug testing, however, the City of Boulder has adopted an ordinance applicable to employees with supervisors in the City of Boulder that requires that employers have a reasonable suspicion, based on specific, objective and clearly expressed facts, that the employee is under the influence of drugs on the job or the employee's job performance is currently adversely affected by drugs. Employers in Boulder are required to adopt a written policy that is made available to employees prior to the administration of any drug test. The Boulder ordinance also requires employers to notify applicants personally at their first interview, and by posting a notice, if drug screening is part of any pre-employment screening process. See Boulder Colo. Ordinance 5195 Sections 12-3-1 to 5 (1993).

Connecticut: Employers may test **applicants** for drug use but only if the employee is informed of the test in writing when the employee applies for employment and if a reliable methodology is used for testing. The applicant must be given a copy of any positive test results. All results must be kept confidential. Employers may not require **employees** to submit to a drug test unless there is a "reasonable suspicion" that the employee is under the influence of drugs or alcohol that could affect job performance. Random drug testing is only permitted when authorized by federal law as a safety-sensitive or high-risk position, which are further defined in the Connecticut law. See Conn. Gen. Stat. Section 31-51t to 31-51aa.

Delaware: No state law prohibits or permits drug testing, but pre-employment drug testing is required for employers covered by the Handicapped Persons Employment Protection Act, which may test for drug use to ensure that applicants or employees aren't engaging in illegal drug use. See 16 Del. C. Section 1142.

District of Columbia: No state law prohibits or permits drug testing. Testing may be found discriminatory under the D.C. Human Rights Act.

Florida: All drug testing must occur in compliance with written procedures defined by statute. Pre-employment and for-cause testing is required. Random, periodic testing and post-accident testing is permitted, with supporting facts. Employers that don't have an existing drug testing written program must give employees 60 days notice prior to testing. Workers' Compensation discounts available to employers that maintain a certified drug-free workplace program. See Fla. Admin. Code Ann. 440.01 et seq.

Georgia: Workers' Compensation discounts available to state contractors who receive $25,000+ and meet the qualifications of the Drug Free Workplace Act. See Ga. Code Ann. Sections 34-9-413 through 415.

Hawaii: Employers may test employees but prior to testing, the employer must provide the employee with a written statement of the substances to be tested for, and a statement that over-the counter medications or prescribed drugs may result in a positive test result. Employees are permitted to disclose any prescribed drugs taken within 30 days. The statute requires employers to use state-licensed laboratories for testing. All information about test results is to be kept confidential. See Chapter 329B Hawaii Rev. Stat., Hawaii Substance Abuse Testing Law.

Idaho: The Idaho Employer Alcohol and Drug-Free Workplace Act establishes voluntary drug/alcohol testing guidelines. The state law specifically permits employees to test applicants or employees for drug use in accordance with a written policy that must include a) a statement of the consequences of violation of the policy, b) the types of testing that will be conducted, and c) an explanation of the procedures. Employers must pay for testing costs, and testing is considered work time. Employers may discharge or suspend employees who test positive for drug use, or send them for rehabilitation. Employees who test positive have the right to explain the result and request a retest. See Idaho Code Sections 72-1701 to 1716.

Illinois: Employers applying for state grants of $5,000+ must meet the requirements of The Illinois Drug Free Workplace Act, 30 ILCS 580/1 et seq. in order to be eligible for the grant. Prospective grantees or contractors must certify that they will provide a drug-free workplace by complying with requirements similar to the federal Drug Free Workplace Act.

Indiana: Employers applying for state grants or contracts must certify their drug-free status and compliance with the Drug Free Workplace Act (federal) and Indiana Executive Order 90-5.

Iowa: Drug/alcohol testing is permitted for applicants and employees provided that the employer follows statutory requirements, including the creation of a written drug/alcohol program that among other things requires that test results be confirmed at the employer's expense, annual supervisory training, and confidentiality of test results. Employers may test when there is a reasonable suspicion of drug use and post accident, as well as unannounced testing of select employee positions (safety-sensitive). Test results may be used to determining whether an employee qualifies for continued employment. See Iowa Code Section 730.5.

Louisiana: Applicants may be required, as a condition of employment, to submit to testing and if they test positive, may be rejected. Test results may be used for discipline or discharge but employees testing positive for the first time must be offered rehabilitation rather than being disciplined. Current employees may also be required to submit to testing: 1) post accident, 2) upon reasonable suspicion, or 3) to ensure compliance with a rehabilitation program. Random testing is permissible only for employees in safety sensitive positions. Employers must pay for testing and the results must be kept confidential. See La. Rev. Stat. Ann. Sections 49-1001-1012.

Maine: Only employers with 20+ employees and a state approved employee assistance program may test. Employers must pay for all costs. The employer's written policy must address 1) the consequences of voluntary admission of substance abuse, 2) when testing may occur, 3) the manner of collection of specimens, 4) substances to be tested for, 5) cut-off levels, 6) consequences of a confirmed positive-test result, or a refusal to submit to testing, 7) opportunities for rehabilitation, and 8) procedures for contesting a test result. Testing of current employees may occur based on "probable cause" which is defined as a "reasonable grounds for belief" that an employee is under the influence of drugs or alcohol. Probable cause findings should be in writing with a copy given to the employee. Random testing is permitted where drug use would jeopardize the health or safety of co-workers or the public. Testing of applicants is permitted if part of a conditional offer of employment. Employers may refuse to hire an employee who tests positive and may discharge, transfer or discipline an employee unless she or he agrees to undergo rehabilitation. See Me. Rev. Stat. Ann. tit. 26 Section 681 et seq.

Maryland: Employers may test applicants or employees or contractors as long as the testing is in accordance with procedural requirements and pursuant to a written policy, and as long as the testing is in accordance with legitimate job-related reasons. An employee who tests positive must be given a copy of the results, a copy of the employer's policy, a notice stating the right to independent verification of the test results, and must receive a notice of the employer's intent to take disciplinary action. See Md. Code Ann. Health-Gen. 1 Section17-214.

Massachusetts: There is no state law on drug testing for **employers**; however, court cases have held that random testing, which doesn't distinguish between employees holding safety sensitive positions and those who don't, violates employees' privacy rights. **Applicants** may be tested. See Privacy Act, Mass. Gen. L. c. 214 Section 1B. Certain state contractors must certify that they have a drug-free workplace.

Minnesota: Employers must have a written policy in place and give employees notice of it. *Applicants* may be required to undergo testing if job offers have been made, and if all applicants are tested as a condition of employment. *Employees* may be tested as part of an annual routine examination, provided two weeks' notice is given. Testing can occur when 1) there is a reasonable suspicion that an employee is *under the influence* of drugs or alcohol 2) there has been a workplace accident, or 3) employees have violated written work rules on drug use. Random drug testing is prohibited except for safety-sensitive positions. *Employers* may not discharge, discipline or refuse to hire an applicant testing positive for drugs until the test has been confirmed and the applicant or employee told of the test results and given an opportunity to dispute the result. Employees must be given the opportunity for rehabilitation prior to dismissal. See Minn. Stat. Ann. Sections 181.950 et seq.

Mississippi: Employers may test applicants as a condition of hiring, or employees as a condition of employment but only if they give written notice of the testing beforehand (30 days in the case of employees). Employers are generally authorized to conduct testing of employees 1) if the employer has a "reasonable suspicion" that the employee has used drugs in violation of the employer's policy, or 2) on a random basis. An employer may not take any adverse employment action on the basis of an unconfirmed test result. The employer's policy must state: a) the grounds upon which an employee may be required to submit to a test, b) actions the employer may take on the basis of a positive result, c) consequences for refusing to submit to a test, and d) the employee's right to contest the results. See Miss. Code Ann. Sections 71-7-1 to 33.

Missouri: Drug and alcohol tests are treated as medical tests; therefore, they require the employee's consent.

Montana: The Montana Workforce Drug and Alcohol Testing Act allows employers to test certain employees who are engaged in the performance, supervision or management of work in a hazardous work environment or position of public safety. The act permits pre-employment, reasonable-suspicion, post accident, random and follow-up testing, but only if the employer adopts a detailed testing plan and gives employees 60-days' notice of adoption of the plan. See Mont. Code Ann. Section 39-2-205 et seq.

Nebraska: Employers with six or more employees may conduct drug tests. Positive tests must be confirmed before any adverse employment action may be taken. Test results are confidential and subject to release under statutory guidelines. Any employee who refuses testing may be disciplined up to and including discharge. See Neb. Rev. Stat. Sections 48-1901 to 1910.

Nevada: No state law prohibits or permits drug testing, however, a court case upheld an employer's right to terminate an employee who refused to sign an agreement giving consent to post accident, for cause, and post-rehabilitation drug testing. *Blanketship v. O'Sullivan Plastic Corp.*, 866 P. 2d 293 (Nev. 1993). Another court case held that requiring drug tests is appropriate as long as the testing methods are reliable. See *Koch v. Harrah's Club*, (1990 WL 448060 CD.Nev. 1990).

New Jersey: No state law prohibits or permits drug testing. Court cases have held that random drug testing, and testing with the consent of the employee isn't in violation of public policy. See *Hennessey v. Coastal Eagle Point Oil*, 589 A.2d 170 (N.J. Super. Ct. App. Div. 1991), aff'd, 609 A. 2d 11 (NJ 1992).

North Carolina: The North Carolina Controlled Substances Examination Regulation Act establishes procedural requirements for conducting drug testing. Applicants and employees may be tested. Employers must maintain the confidentiality of test results. See N.C. Gen. Stat. Sections 95-230 et seq.

North Dakota: No state law prohibits or permits drug testing, but employers must pay for any medical examination required as a condition of retaining or obtaining employment. See N.D.C.C. Section 34-01-15.

Ohio: Testing employees and applicants is permitted. Workers' compensation premium discounts are available for employers that comply with the state's regulations. Employers must have a written policy which addresses: 1) details of the program, 2) a statement that the program applies to all employees, 3) the types of testing that will be conducted, 4) rehabilitation options, 5) confidentiality protections, and 6) the consequences of a positive test or the refusal to be tested. Employees may not be required to pay for medical examinations. See Ohio Rev. Code Section 4112.02(Q) and 4113.21.

Oklahoma: The Oklahoma Standards for Workplace Drug and Alcohol Testing Act provides for testing of applicants and employees who aren't covered by federal drug-testing statutes. Before testing, employers must have a written policy that's uniformly applied and an employee assistance program in operation. Employees must be given 30 days notice of a first-time policy or changes to the policy. The policy must include: 1) who is subject to the policy, 2) the circumstances under which testing will occur, 3) substances tested, 4) testing methods, 5) consequences of refusing testing, 6) the right to explain positive results, and 7) a statement on confidentiality of test results. Applicants may be tested only after a conditional job offer. Employers may reject applicants who refuse to be tested or whose test results are positive. Employees may be tested as part of a routine check-up, upon "reasonable suspicion" that the employer's policy has been violated, or if property is damaged. Positive results must be confirmed prior to adverse employment action. See Okla. Stat. Title 40 Sections 551 through 565.

Oregon: Drug testing isn't regulated for applicants or employees but alcohol testing is covered by statute. Breath tests of applicants or employees are generally prohibited unless the individual consents to the test or the employer has reasonable suspicion. See Ore. St. Section 659A.300.

Pennsylvania: No state law prohibits or permits drug testing. One court case upheld an employer's right to dismiss an employee after she refused drug and alcohol testing. *Muse v. Philadelphia Electric Co.*, 1996 WL 309971 (E.D. Pa 1996). A 3rd Circuit case held that testing could result in the common law tort of invasion of privacy depending on the procedures used. See *Borse v. Piece Goods Shop, Inc.*, 963 F.2d 611 (3d Cir. 1992).

Rhode Island: Employers may request or require employees to submit a sample of urine, blood, bodily fluid or tissue for testing as a condition of continued employment if the employer has "reasonable grounds" to believe that an employee's use of controlled substances impairs job performance. The employer must provide the employee with the opportunity to have the results confirmed by a lab of the employee's choosing. The employer must keep results of testing confidential. See R.I. Gen. Laws Sections 28-6.5-1.

South Carolina: Employers may test applicants and employees and all employers must maintain a drug-free workplace. Written policies are recommended. Test results must be kept confidential. Employers establishing a drug-free workplace get a deduction on their workers' compensation insurance premiums provided their policy meets requirements. See S.C. Code. Ann. Section 41-1-15.

South Dakota: No law prohibits or permits drug/alcohol testing, but it's a misdemeanor for any employer to require an employee to pay for medical tests, or records, as a condition of employment. SDCL 60-11-2.

Tennessee: The Supreme Court has approved drug testing, including random testing. Employers following state-specific requirements for drug testing are entitled to a reduction in workers' compensation premiums. Employers must notify all employees that testing is a condition of employment. See Tenn. Code. Ann. Sections 50-9-101 to 9-114.

Texas: Employers with 15 or more employees must adopt a written drug free policy to comply with the workers' compensation commission rules. The policy must include statements on: 1) the scope of the policy, 2) the consequences of violating the policy, 3) a description of and the requirements and availability of participation in any treatment, rehabilitation, or employee assistance, and 4) a description of any drug-testing program that the employer has in effect. The policy must be distributed to employees on or before their first day of employment or within 30 days of the adoption of the policy. Covered employers that don't have a drug abuse policy may be subject to a Class D Administrative violation and penalty of up to $500. See Tex. Labor Code 21.120. 28 Tex. Admin. Code Sections 169.1 and 2.

Utah: Applicants and current employees may be tested as long as management also submits to periodic testing. There is no requirement of reasonable suspicion, but before testing the employer must prepare a written policy and distribute it to employees and make it available to applicants. All positive results must be confirmed prior to adverse employment action. Employees/applicants who refuse to be tested may be fired, suspended with or without pay, denied employment, or otherwise disciplined. Employers must pay all costs of testing, including transportation if testing is done off site. Testing is considered work time and must be done during or immediately after work shifts. All information relating to testing is confidential and is the property of the employee. See Utah Code Section 34-38-1 et seq.

Vermont: There must be a written policy in place prior to testing applicants or employees. The policy must specify: 1) the circumstances under which testing will occur, 2) the substances tested for, 3) the testing procedures used, 4) a statement that a positive test result may be produced by over-the-counter medications and other substances. **Applicants** may be tested only when a conditional offer of employment has been made and when written notice is provided at least 10 days in advance of testing or when the test is part of a comprehensive pre-employment/post-offer physical. **Employees** may be tested only when probable cause exists to believe that the employee is using or under the influence of drugs. Test results are confidential and positive initial results must be confirmed. Employees must be permitted to explain positive results at an informal meeting. See 21 Vt. Stat. Ann. Sections 511 to 520.

Virginia: No state law prohibits or permits drug testing. Employers may not require employees to pay for medical tests. A court case has been held to imply that drug testing doesn't generally violate state law. See *Weaver v. Coca-Cola Bottling Co.*, 805 F. Supp. 10 (W.D. Va. 1992).

West Virginia: No state law prohibits or permits drug testing, however, it's contrary to public policy to require employees to submit to drug testing unless the employer has a "reasonable good faith objective suspicion" of drug use or the employee's job is in a safety sensitive position. See *Twigg v. Herctiles Corp.*, 406 S.E. 2d 54 (W. Va. 1990). Reductions in workers' compensation premiums are possible for employers who successfully complete a loss-prevention program that includes the establishment of a drug-free workplace. See W. Va. Code Section 23-2-4.

Wyoming: No state law prohibits or permits drug testing, however, numerous court cases have established a right to test employees as long as the testing is reasonable, which could be in accordance with established written policy or as a result of reasonable suspicion or because the employee is in a safety sensitive position. Urine tests aren't a violation of privacy. See *Greco v. Halliburton Co.*, 674 F. Supp. 1447 (D. Wyo 1987).

Drug Testing: Practical Challenges

Even assuming constitutional issues are obviated by obtaining an employee's written consent to a drug test, there are practical issues relating to the reliability of testing and what do to with the results. What will the nonprofit do if the employee tests positive? What if the results are a *false positive* or *false negative*? Does the nonprofit have a reliable testing service which preserves the chain of custody of the sample so that the validity of the results won't be challenged? How will the confidentiality of test results be maintained? These and other issues have caused many employers to move gingerly into the realm of drug testing.

Since the federal ADA protects recovering drug abusers and alcoholics, even if the nonprofit were to find that an employee tested positive for illegal substances, there is a good chance that the nonprofit would be obligated to accommodate the employee rather than fire him or refuse to hire him. The bottom line is what policy is going to result in the least harm, and the least risk? Most nonprofits err on the side of caution: after confirming that their directors' and officers' liability insurance policy covers employment law claims, they prefer to face the risk of a lawsuit for wrongful discharge or failure to hire, than the aftermath of employee misconduct as a result of substance abuse.

Best Practices and Risk Management Strategies to Address Privacy in the Workplace

The issue of privacy is a moving target in the nonprofit workplace. Each employee brings a unique perspective on the topic. The nonprofit employer's job is to accurately state the nonprofit's policies and expectations, and then hold employees accountable. The five strategies discussed below can help the employer assure that the organization has a solid footing as it moves forward in this difficult arena.

1. **Prepare:** Know in advance that the invasion of privacy rights can lead to sticky constitutional challenges to employees' privacy rights. Anticipate that employees will **not** always share the employer's values and perspective.

2. **Manage Employees' Expectations** about privacy in the workplace. Though unwarranted, it's safe to assume that most employees will believe that some aspects of their workspace (desk drawers, folders marked *personal* on their PC or laptop) are private and off limits to the employer. The employer must be explicit in dispelling this erroneous assumption. It's essential to do so at the beginning of the employment relationship and to remind employees about management's right and intent to monitor the workplace to protect the mission of the nonprofit.

3. **Document:** Consider what written policies will assist the nonprofit if it's ever necessary to discipline or terminate an employee due to conduct outside work, or inappropriate conduct while at work.

   The nonprofit should consider the value of written policies addressing:

   ❏ compliance with copyright laws

   ❏ prohibition against viewing, downloading or transmitting pornographic material from the Internet

   ❏ prohibition of the use, sale, distribution or being under the influence of illegal drugs or alcohol while at work

   ❏ the obligation to inform the nonprofit about outside work and the nonprofit's policy that outside work is permitted as long as it doesn't conflict with the best interests of the nonprofit, in which case the employee will be asked to either cease the outside work, or resign from employment, or otherwise satisfactorily address the conflict.

4. **Be consistent:** Apply all human resources policies consistently, making sure that similar situations result in similar disciplinary actions.

5. **Investigate, don't assume.** Remain receptive to suggestions or shared concerns about the conduct of an employee outside of work, but don't jump to conclusions. Investigate thoroughly, especially allegations of drug or alcohol use, or anything that could be especially damaging to the reputation of the employee.

Outside Work Policy

Although it is discouraged, employees of NONPROFIT may hold outside jobs as long as they also continue to meet all performance standards of their position with NONPROFIT. All employees will be expected to meet NONPROFIT's performance expectations and scheduling requirements, regardless of outside work obligations. All outside work should occur while the employee is not working for NONPROFIT – either before or after, but not during the primary work day. This includes business calls about the outside work, which should be conducted on the employee's own time.

If NONPROFIT determines that an employee's outside work interferes with performance or the ability to meet the job requirements of NONPROFIT, the employee may be asked to terminate the outside employment if he or she wishes to remain employed by NONPROFIT.

Employees who are engaged in outside employment must notify the Executive Director in writing of the name of the employer and the nature of the work. If this work is deemed by NONPROFIT to create a conflict with NONPROFIT's best interests, the employee will be notified of the conflict in writing. In this case, the employee will cease this outside employment or address the conflict of interest to the satisfaction of NONPROFIT, or the employee will be terminated from employment with NONPROFIT.

Chapter 11

Safety and Violence at the Workplace

Workplace Safety

It's a basic tenant of employment law that the employer is responsible for the safety of employees while they're at work. Federal and state laws require employers to maintain a safe work environment and to report unsafe conditions and educate employees about hazards and dangerous substances that they might encounter at the workplace. The federal Occupational Safety and Health Act of 1970 (OSH Act) ☜ requires all employers to report workplace accidents and deaths to the local or regional office of the Occupational Safety and Health Administration (OSHA) and to provide safety training to employees (notably on hazardous substances, bloodborne pathogens and communicable diseases) and engage in safe practices in all aspects of the employer's work. An overview of the OSH Act and compliance assistance, as well as a notice that is required to be posted in the workplace, are available from the U.S. Department of Labor's Web site. ☜

Many state laws mirror the OSH Act's requirements. A few states have requirements that go beyond or are different from the federal requirements. All states that have their own version of the OSH Act prohibit retaliation against employees for filing a grievance or otherwise *blowing the whistle* on their employers for unsafe working conditions. Some of the states provide authority to the state Department of Labor for inspections and monetary penalties for safety code violations.

Of course, many municipalities also have fire and health codes and general safety codes, and many nonprofits are regulated by their own accreditation or certification requirements for safe work conditions to ensure employee or client safety. Nonprofits with kitchens or where food is prepared generally have specific health codes to meet. Consequently, safety is a highly regulated area. A nonprofit's legal obligations will depend on the type of workplace/industry, as well as the particular state law(s) that may impose compliance with safety standard obligations.

Policies on workplace injuries and illnesses should require employees to bring injuries or illnesses or unsafe conditions to a supervisor's attention immediately so that the employer can address dangerous situations in a timely fashion and also so that the employee can file a claim for workers' compensation insurance. Most workers' compensation policies require a claim to be filed promptly, and some specify *within 24 hours*. Consequently, most nonprofits have a policy that requires employees to report work-related health concerns or injuries immediately.

The *best practice* safety standard for all nonprofits is best summed up by Wisconsin's The Safe Place Act, which provides that employers "shall do every…thing reasonably necessary to protect the life, health, safety and welfare of employees and others who frequent the work area."

Violence at the Workplace

Violence is a reality in many workplaces. Nonprofits, like other employers, need to educate staff to be aware of the risk of workplace violence. Relevant policies depending on your nonprofit circumstances may include:

❏ zero tolerance for violent, abusive conduct, threats of violence, or violent language;

❏ a requirement that employees report suspicious or unusual behavior that could put others at risk;

❏ emergency procedures in the event of any serious act of workplace violence;

❏ designation of management personnel and security personnel who will be responsible to investigate complaints of violence and who will be responsible in the event of an emergency;

❏ screening of applicants for past criminal conduct; and

❏ reservation of management's right to review employee e-mail, voice mail, and computer files.

Summary of State Safety and Health Laws

The state laws noted here are subject to constant review and revision in state legislatures. This summary should therefore be used for reference purposes, rather than as a definitive guide.

Alaska: State law generally tracks federal requirements. See Title 18 of the Alaska Statutes, AS 18.60.101 through 18.60.890 and Title 8 of the Alaska Administrative Code, 8 Alaska Admin. Code Section 61.010 through 61.1960.

Arkansas: Requires employers to furnish safety devices and safeguards. See Arkansas Code Annot. Section 11-5-101 through 115.

California: California has its own Occupational Safety and Health Act. See Cal. Lab. Code Section 6300 et seq. ; Also employers are required to establish, implement and maintain an "illness and injury prevention program." Cal. Lab. Code Section 6401.7.

Georgia: State law requires that employers uphold a general duty to provide a safe workplace and working conditions for employees. See O.C.G.A. Section 34-2-10(a) .

Hawaii: Hawaii's requirements are based on federal requirements but, with respect to some safety issues, are broader than federal requirements. See Hawaii Rev. Stat. Chapter 396 and Hawaii Reg. Ch. 12.

Illinois: Employers with 5+ full time employees or 20 employees in total are required to comply with the Toxic Substances Disclosure to Employees Act. See 820 ILCS 255.

Kansas: Kansas hasn't implemented its own OSHA law, but has a program that uses OSHA regulations as guidance and gives the Kansas Department of Labor the authority to enter any workplace to inspect for dangerous or unsanitary conditions. The program has no enforcement powers but can help employers comply with OSHA regulations. See Kansas Stat. Ann. 44-636.

Massachusetts: The Attorney General has the authority to investigate complaints of hazardous substances, asbestos, and communicable diseases, occupational use of lead and specific health concerns. See Mass. Gen. L. ch. 149 Sections.

Michigan: Michigan has its own Occupational Health and Safety Act. See MCL 408.1001 et seq.

Minnesota: State law provides extensive regulation on safety and health, particularly concerning employer responsibilities for hazardous substances and training obligations. See M.S.A. Section 182.653.

Missouri: Missouri doesn't have a law that mirrors OSHA but, instead, has laws addressing worker safety on topics such as restrooms, use of ladders and hepatitis. See Rev. Stat. Mo. Chapter 292.

Montana: The Montana Safety Act (Mont. Code Ann. Section 50-71-101 et seq. requires employers to provide safe workplaces, safeguards, safety devices, and protective clothing under certain conditions; to employ any means to protect the life, health, and safety or employees (Mont. Code Ann. Section 50-7-201). The act authorizes the Montana Department of Labor to establish safety codes for every workplace. The state DOL has adopted a Safety Culture Act, which requires employers to meet extensive requirements for training, awareness development of safety risks, self-inspections and self-assessments, and documentation for three years that the employer has met all requirements. Employers also must have a system for reporting, investigating and taking corrective action on all work-related injuries, illnesses and unsafe working conditions or practices.

Nevada: Upon hiring, all employers with 11+ employees must provide employees with a document or videotape outlining the rights and responsibilities of employers and employees to promote safety in the workplace. Employees must sign an acknowledgment, which must be placed in their personnel file, that they received the document or viewed the video. Nev. Rev. Stat. 618.376. Employers must assign at least one person to be in charge of occupational safety and health. Nev. Rev. Stat. 618.374(4).

New Jersey: The New Jersey Worker and Community Right to Know Act is almost identical to federal standards regarding procedures for employers to handle hazardous substances. See N.J.S.A. 34:5A-1 et seq.

New York: N.Y. Labor Law Sections 200 et seq. sets forth employers' duties to protect employees' health and safety.

North Carolina: North Carolina follows federal OSHA standards with some exceptions.

Ohio: Ohio Rev. Code Section 4101 et seq. governs safety at the workplace.

Oklahoma: Oklahoma has an Occupational Safety and Health Act. See Okla. Stat. Title 40 Sections 401 through 425.

Oregon: Oregon Safe Employment Act: See ORS 654.010 et seq.

Pennsylvania: The General Safety Law. See 43 P.S. Sections 25-1 et seq. and the Worker and Community Right-to Know Act, 43 P.S. 35 Sections 7301 et seq.

Rhode Island: State law provides for employee safety, recording keeping requirements, and workplace inspections. See R.I. Gen. Laws Chapter 20, Title 28.

South Carolina: State law addresses occupational health and safety concerns. See S.C. Code Ann. Sections 41-15-10 et seq.

South Dakota: Employers are required to post a notice promoting safety; employees in safety sensitive positions are required to remain free of illegal drug and substance use; under the state's workers' compensation laws, workers who fail to use protective safety devices can lost benefits. See S.D.C.L. 62-2-11.

Tennessee: Tennessee has its own Occupational Safety and Health Act. See TCA Sections 50-3-101 through 50-3-919.

Texas: All employers must provide and maintain a workplace that's reasonably safe and healthful; and install and use methods of sanitation and hygiene that are reasonably necessary to protect the life, health, and safety of employees and take other actions reasonably necessary to make the employment and place of employment safe. Texas Labor Code 411.103. Employers must file reports on injuries on-the-job that result in an employee's absence for more than one day and/or occupational diseases of which the employer has knowledge. See Texas Labor Code Section 411.032.

Utah: Utah has an Occupational Safety and Health Act. See Utah Code Section 34-6-101 through 307.

Vermont: Vermont has an Occupational Safety and Health Act. See 21 Vt. Stat. Annot. Section 201 through 232 and 18 Vt. Stat. Annot. Section 1416 through 1428.

Virginia: Most state standards are identical to federal OSHA. The state Web site provides a list of those provisions of Virginia law that are different from federal OSHA standards.

Washington: The primary state law that protects safety and health is the Washington Industrial Safety and Health Act, Wash. Rev. Code Ch. 49.17 which, as its name implies, applies more specifically to industrial workplaces, but does have a general requirement that employers: "Shall furnish to each of his employees a place of employment free from recognized hazards that are causing or likely to cause serious injury or death to his employees."

Wisconsin: Under the Wisconsin Safe Place Act, all employers must furnish a safe workplace and must do "everything reasonably necessary to protect the life, health, safety and welfare of employees and others who frequent the workplace." See Wis Stat. Section 101.11.

Wyoming: The Wyoming Occupational Safety and Health Act generally track federal law and requires employers to furnish employees with a place of employment free from recognized hazards that are likely to cause death or serious physical harm. See Wyo. Stat. Section 27-11-101. Employers must post a notice explaining the law.

SAMPLE ---

Sample Policy Prohibiting Workplace Threats and Violence

The safety of our employees, clients, and visitors is an important concern to [Name of Nonprofit]. Threats, threatening behavior or acts of violence against employees, clients, visitors or others while on [Nonprofit's] property, conducting business or receiving services from [Name of Nonprofit] won't be tolerated. Violations of this policy will lead to disciplinary action, possible dismissal, and criminal prosecution as appropriate.

Any person who engages in violent or threatening behavior on [Name of Nonprofit's] property shall be removed from the premises as quickly as safety permits, and shall remain off [Name of Nonprofit's] premises pending the outcome of an investigation. Subsequent to the investigation, [Name of Nonprofit] will respond appropriately. This response may include, but isn't limited to, suspension and/or termination of any business relationship, reassignment of job duties, suspension or termination of employment, and/or the pursuit of criminal prosecution of the person or persons involved.

Reporting of Potential Threats

All personnel are responsible for notifying management of any threats that they've witnessed, received, or have been told that another person has witnessed or received.

Even without an actual threat, personnel should also report any behavior they've witnessed that they regard as threatening or violent, when that behavior is job related.

Employees are responsible for making this report regardless of the relationship between the individual who initiated the threat or threatening behavior and the person/persons who were threatened or were the focus of the threatening behavior.

Employees should report the presence of a weapon immediately to a manager, a supervisor, or if appropriate, to the police by calling 911.

Negligence and the Duty to Prevent Foreseeable Harm

The legal theory of negligence holds that if a nonprofit has knowledge, or should have knowledge, about an employee's dangerous attributes, the nonprofit should act to prevent foreseeable harm to others. If a nonprofit hires an employee with a criminal record or past history of violence, which the nonprofit either knew about or *should have known* about, and that employee causes injury while working for the nonprofit, the organization could be legally responsible under the theory of *negligent hiring*. The basic elements of a cause of action for negligent hiring are:

1. An employment relationship exists between the nonprofit and the employee who caused the injury.

2. The employee was dangerous, incompetent, unprepared, ill-trained or otherwise unfit.

3. The employer *knew or should have known* through reasonable investigation that the employee was unfit or a danger to others.

4. The employee's wrongful actions, whether negligent or intentional, caused harm to another.

In the majority of states, there is case law which holds that an employer who negligently hires or retains an individual who is unfit or incompetent may be liable to a third party who is injured by that employee's conduct. A nonprofit will be liable for *negligent retention* if an employee had previously acted violently or threatened violence, but the nonprofit did not discharge the employee. A nonprofit may also be liable for acts of workplace violence that the nonprofit should have avoided through adequate training and supervision under the theory of *negligent supervision*. Finally, a nonprofit can be liable under the theory of *negligent failure to warn* when the nonprofit has knowledge of the dangerous attributes of an employee, but takes no steps to warn other employees or specific identifiable persons who might be harmed by the employee. The duty to warn is especially critical in the context of providing references for former employees. In several recent cases employers were found responsible for giving negligent references because they failed to disclose dangerous attributes of their former employees to prospective employers seeking reference information.

While policies and raising awareness can't completely insulate any nonprofit from the risk of workplace violence, the nonprofit that has undertaken good faith efforts to educate and prepare staff for emergencies, and has acted promptly to address concerns of the incompetence of staff or threats of workplace violence, conveys the message that safety is a primary concern.

Bibliography

Amalfe, Christine A. and Eileen Quinn Steiner, "Forced Ranking Systems: Still a Potential Legal Target," *New Jersey Law Journal*, April 1, 2005.

Andler, Edward C., *The Complete Reference Checking Handbook: Smart, Fast, Legal Ways to Check Out Job Applicants*, American Management Association, New York, 1998.

Employers Counsel Network, 2006 *50 Employment Laws in 50 States*, M. Lee Smith Publishers, Brentwood, Tennessee, 2006.

Flynn, Nancy, *2004 Survey on Workplace E-Mail and IM Reveals Unmanageable Risks—55% Lack Retention Policies, 21% of E-Mail Subpoenaed*, ePolicy Institute, www.epolicyinstitute.com/survey

Fried, Gil, *Employment Law: A Guide for Sport, Recreation, and Fitness Industries*, Carolina Academic Press, Durham, N.C. 1998.

Kaplan, Andrew, *The EPL Book: A Practical Guide to Employment Practices Liability and Insurance*, Griffin Communications, Inc. Newport Beach, Calif., 1997.

Lewis, Shari Claire, "Internet Monitoring: Wide Implications in Ruling on Employee Visits to Pornographic Sites," *New York Law Journal*, February 14, 2006.

London, Sheldon I., *How to Comply with Federal Employee Laws: A Complete Guide for Employers Written in Plain English*, VIZIA Group, Rochester, New York, 1998.

Maatman, Gerald L., Jr., *Safeguarding Your Future: A Practical Employment Guide for Nonprofits*, Triumph Books, Chicago, 1996.

Nobile, Robert J., *Guide to Employee Handbooks*, Warren, Gorham & Lamont, Boston, 1999.

NonprofitAlert, Gammon & Grange, P.C., McLean, VA (Subscriptions are $75 per year. Call (703) 761-5000 or contact npa@gandglaw.com)

Panaro, Gerard P., *Employment Law Manual*, Gorham & Lamont, Boston, 1990.

Steingold, Fred S., *The Employer's Legal Handbook: A Complete Guide to Your Legal Rights and Responsibilities*, Nolo Press, Berkeley, 1994.

The Labor Lawyer, Volume 21, Number 1, Summer 2005, American Bar Association

Web Sites

www.dol.gov (U.S. Department of Labor)

www.eeoc.gov (Equal Employment Opportunity Commission)

www.shrm.org (Society for Human Resource Management)

www.workforceonline.com (Workforce Management)

Additional Resources Available From the Nonprofit Risk Management Center

Books and e-Books

• *A Golden Opportunity: Managing the Risks of Service to Seniors*
A valuable resource for front-line service providers that care for seniors, and for managers of service agencies. This user-friendly book explains risk management principles in the following areas: seniors as a client group; strategies for protecting

seniors from harm, health, transportation, crime; confidentiality; communal housing; and laws and court rulings. A comprehensive resource list gives online sources for more information.
2003 / ISBN 1-893210-12-X / 92 pages 8.5x11 / $20.00

• Coverage, Claims and Consequences: An Insurance Handbook for Nonprofits
Nothing in the marketplace does a better job of clearly explaining what insurance can and can't do to protect a nonprofit organization's mission. You'll be able to: explain the role of an insurance professional (broker, agent or consultant), feel comfortable with your role and responsibilities as an insurance buyer, evaluate the services you're receiving, put your insurance out to bid, answer the question: Do I need D&O (or other specific types of) coverage?, read your insurance policies and understand the coverage, and see how insurance fits into an overall risk management program.
2002 / ISBN 1-893210-11-1 / 218 pages / 8.5x11 / $30.00

• Enlightened Risk Taking: A Guide to Strategic Risk Management for Nonprofits
Traditionally risk management is about safeguarding against loss, but it can also be about seizing the opportunity for gain. Addresses how to identify the five steps of a risk management process, evaluate the risks associated with a nonprofit's mission, determine potential for loss from a variety of sources, isolate opportunity for gain from seemingly risk business, and put the five steps into action. Also includes a glossary of risk management terms, diagrams, charts and lists of solutions.
2002 / ISBN 1-893210-09-X / 112 pages / 8.5x11 / $25.00

Enlightened Risk Taking: The Workbook
This companion piece to *Enlightened Risk Taking* contains sample forms and checklists to formulate a risk management program from scratch, expand a current program, take advantage of opportunities for gain, and translate theory into practice.
2002 / ISBN 1-893210-10-3 / 54 pages / 8.5x11 / $15.00

• Full Speed Ahead: Managing Technology Risk in the Nonprofit World
Technology affects every aspect of a nonprofit.Written in plain English for those who supervise the IT function of write policies. Includes: security policies and procedures, special consideration for young users, supervising computer backup and testing, database privacy and confidentiality issues, monitoring employee communications, telecommuting, software and hardware inventory, and selecting and managing vendors.
2001 / ISBN 1-893210-07-3 / 122 pages / 8.5x11 / $25.00

• Managing Facility Risk: 10 Steps to Safety
Protecting the organization's buildings and grounds can be as simple as trimming bushes and replacing burned-out light bulbs. This books also covers: duties if own, lease, loan, rent, borrow or operation out of a home; physical and mental capabilities and ages of services recipients; selection or creation of mission-appropriate space; meeting codes; scheduling maintenance and repair; monitoring visitors; and limiting liability and providing risk financing. Addition online resource URLs, sample forms and checklists round out the information.
2003 / ISBN 1-893210-16-2 / 121 pages / 6x9 / $15.00

Managing Risk in Nonprofit Organizations: A Comprehensive Guide
The executive director of the Nonprofit Risk Management Center and three co-authors address how to minimize the negative and maximize the positive consequences to risk-taking through identifying and prioritizing risk; selection and implementing risk management techniques; monitoring risk management for the long term; leveraging risk management in a time-sensitive manner; and recognizing myriad pressures and competing concerns. Diagrams, glossary and resources add to the value of this comprehensive guide.
2004 / ISBN 0-471-23674-8 / 322 / 6x9 / $20.00

• More Than a Matter of Trust: Managing the Risks of Mentoring
Educate your senior management and staff about the risks inherent in a mentoring program. This book also covers fundamental mentoring risk management, legal liability, liability shields and 10 keys to mentoring risk management.
1998 / ISBN 0-9637120-9-8 / 59 pages / 8.5x11 / $15.00

• No Strings Attached: Untangling the Risks of Fundraising & Collaboration
Practical framework for boards, CEOs and others engaged in fund raising for a nonprofit. Addressed are budgeting, raising money from foundations, soliciting individuation donors, obtaining corporate support, negotiation collaborations and partnerships, and restricted funding challenges. Also includes related codes, standards and resources.
1999 / ISBN 1-893219-04-9 / 95 pages / 6x9 / $15.00

• *No Surprises: Harmonizing Risk and Reward in Volunteer Management, 4th edition*
A short, practical handbook for directors of volunteer programs, covering: volunteer risk management basics, volunteer supervision, volunteer protection laws, insuring volunteers, senior volunteers, young volunteers, pet volunteers and corporate volunteers.
2006 / ISBN 1-893210-20-0 / 133 pages / 6x9 / $15.00

• *Pillars of Accountability, 2nd edition*
One of the most important contributions that a nonprofit board makes to the organization's overall risk management effort is managing its own affairs properly. Slippage in this area has been the substance of major news stories and ongoing legal battles for several of our colleagues. Protect your mission by investing in the practical and affordable suggestions in the Center's latest book.

This book offers advice and action steps to build and strengthen the foundation of a nonprofit organization. The book borrows some of the advice from the Nonprofit Risk Management Center's online tool, *Pillars of Accountability in the Nonprofit World* (http://209.61.210.11/pillars.htm). The online tool is intended to help nonprofit CEOs and other senior managers craft an accountability To Do list, while the book is written specifically to provide nonprofit board members with practical ways to reduce the consequences of risk and thus model commitment to excellent management.

2006 / ISBN 1-893210-22-7 / 74 pages / 6x9 / $12.00

• *Playing to Win: A Risk Management Guide for Nonprofit Sports and Recreation Programs*
General direction to protect the child or teen athlete, the organization, and the spectators from harm. Addresses the coach's legal duties; informed consent, waiver and release forms; facility inspection protocol; differences among employee, independent contractor and volunteer status; and staff screening. Includes resources for sports and recreation management; sport-specific associations; federal and state labor departments; and criminal history background checks.
2003 / ISBN 1-893210-14-6 / 89 pages / 8.5x11 / $20.00

• *Ready in Defense: A Liability, Litigation and Legal Guide for Nonprofits*
Written for nonattorney managers, this practical guide walks the read through key legal terms and concepts, contract development, privacy protection, defamation, intellectual property, employment obligations, and board liability. A special section addresses surviving a lawsuit. Sample form, policies and letters are included.
2003 / ISBN 1-893210-13-8 / 109 pages / 8.5x11 / $20.00

Risk in Perspective: Insight and Humor in the Age of Risk Management
If your responsibilities include teaching others in your organization about risk and risk management, you'll find the humor, wisdom and insights by skilled risk analyst Dr. Kimberly Thompson, Harvard School of Public Health, invaluable. Included are quotations, cartoons and stimulating questions about risk and its management.
2004 / ISBN 0-9727078-2-4 / 325 pages / 8.5x11 / $40.00

• *The Season of Hope: A Risk Management Guide for Youth-Serving Nonprofits*
Every youth-serving program must take special care to protect the children who receive services from the program. This book shows you how to develop policies and procedures and train and supervise staff members to: differentiate needs, skills and abilities of children of different ages; identify program-inherent risks; protect children from harm by employees, volunteers, peers and visitors; adhere to strategies to reduce risk from violence, health, injuries and accidents and Internet access; and know how and to whom to report suspected abuse.
2002 / ISBN 1-893210-03-0 / 156 pages / 8.5x11 / $30.00

• *Staff Screening Tool Kit—3rd Edition*
A must for senior staff and boards who are wrestling with the adequacy of a nonprofit's screening process   . Practical, pointed advice on: legal issues, record and reference checks, selection criteria and position descriptions, recruitment and applications and interviews. Lists of state criminal records agencies and state online sex-offender registries. Easy-to-use checklists, sample forms and tip sheets.
2004 / ISBN 1-893210-18-9 / 137 pages / 8.5x11 / $30.00

• *Vital Signs: Anticipating, Preventing and Surviving a Crisis in a Nonprofit*
Prepare to address the symptoms, diagnosis and treatment methods and phases of a crisis from natural forces or manmade. Learn how to target preventable situations, pinpoint crisis and minimize loss, employ time and people wisely, and establish a protocol to increase the odds of survival. Worksheets are included to develop a crisis management plan.
2001 / ISBN 1-893210-06-5 / 83 pages / 8.5x11 / $20.00

• Available as e-books. To order these or other publications from the Nonprofit Risk Management Center, visit www.nonprofitrisk.org or call (202) 785-3891.

On Line Tools

Risk Management Classroom

Affordable risk management training tailored for nonprofit personnel. Available 24/7 on line. Designed for busy nonprofit staffers, 14 courses include quizzes and final tests with immediate scoring. Users who complete the course can generate a certificate of completion to show their mastery of the material.

Single course $29.00 / 14-course subscription saves 50%.

My Risk Management Plan

A user-friendly Q/A format, affordable online program to help you transform good intentions into a risk management plan.Collate existing policies, add new ones, edit/update older ones. Proceed module by module (15 topics); share tasks among several staffers. Export final report into M.S. Word or WordPerfect; edit and format; and share with staff, funders or insurers as proof of your risk management strategy. Return any time to update or add to the plan.
www.MyRiskManagementPlan.org

2005 / online tool / $139.00 one-time licensing fee

Nonprofit CARES™, Computer Assisted Risk Evaluation System

Having access to CARES is like having a risk management consultant on your computer desktop. The interactive question/answer program is easy to navigate, compiles a custom report with recommendations specific to the response you provide, offers specific advice about strategies, is reusable and enables multiple users to access through a single log-on.
www.nonprofitcares.org
(PC or Mac users)

2001 / online tool / one-time licensing fee / $89.00

Sample Forms

center for nonprofit advancement

STRENGTHENING NONPROFITS IN GREATER WASHINGTON
EDUCATION • NETWORKING • ADVOCACY • BUYING POWER

Emergency Succession Plan

for

_____

(Organization Name)

Leadership plays an essential role in the success of a nonprofit organization. And a change in Chief Executive leadership is as inevitable as the passing of time.

This document will help a nonprofit organization recognize that planning for unplanned or temporary leadership change is a best practice—in line with other plans nonprofits regularly complete (e.g., strategic plan, communications plan, fundraising plan). An Emergency Succession Plan can bring order in a time a time of turmoil, confusion and high-stress.

This is a template. Feel free to adapt to make it appropriate for your organization. Action items or areas for tailoring are noted with a __line_____ or a ☞ symbol.

The term "Executive Director" is used throughout this document to address the Chief Paid Staff Member. Should your organization use a title other than Executive Director, feel free to use the title as directed by your organization's bylaws or practice.

May this process bring your organization peace of mind in your day-to-day work.

Disclaimer Statement: This document is provided as guidance for a nonprofit organization facing a change in leadership. It shouldn't be regarded as a substitute for legal advice or counsel. The advice of a competent attorney should be sought any time a nonprofit is considering policy changes or activities that may affect the legal status or liability exposure of the organization.

The Board of Directors of _____ (Organization Name) recognizes that this is a plan for contingencies due to the disability, death or departure of the Executive Director. If the organization is faced with the unlikely event of an untimely vacancy, _____ (Organization Name) has in place the following emergency succession plan to facilitate the transition to both interim and longer-term leadership.

The Board of _____ (Organization Name) has reviewed the job description of the executive director. The job description is attached. The board has a clear understanding of the Executive Director's role in organizational leadership, program development, program administration, operations, board of directors relationships, financial operations, resource development and community presence.

Succession Plan in Event of a Temporary, Unplanned Absence: Short-Term

A temporary absence is one of less than three months in which it's expected that the Executive Director will return to his or her position once the events precipitating the absence are resolved. An unplanned absence is one that arises unexpectedly, in contrast to a planned leave, such as a vacation or a sabbatical. The Board of Directors is authorized (or authorizes the Executive Committee) of _____ (Organization Name) to implement the terms of this emergency plan in the event of the unplanned absence of the Executive Director.

In the event of an unplanned absence of the Executive Director, the Deputy Director (or other highest ranking staff member) is to immediately inform the Board Chair (or highest ranking volunteer board member) of the absence. As soon as it's feasible, the Chair should convene a meeting of the Board or Executive Committee (☞ choose one) to affirm the procedures prescribed in this plan or to make modifications as the Committee deems appropriate.

At the time that this plan was approved, the position of Acting Executive Director would be: _____ Name, _____ Title.

Should the standing appointee to the position of Acting Executive Director be unable to serve, the first and second back-up appointees for the position of Acting Executive Director will be:

(1) _____ Name _____ Title

(2) _____ Name _____ Title

If this Acting Executive Director is new to his or her position and fairly inexperienced with this organization (less than _____ months/years), the Executive Committee or Board of Directors (☞ circle one) may decide to appoint one of the back-up appointees to the acting executive position. The Executive Committee or Board of Directors (☞ circle one) may also consider the option of splitting executive duties among the designated appointees.

Authority and Compensation of the Acting Executive Director

The person appointed as Acting Executive Director shall have the full authority for decision-making and independent action as the regular Executive Director.

The Acting Executive Director may be offered:
(☞ check one)

❏   A temporary salary increase to the entry-level salary of the executive director position

❏   A bonus of $_____ during the Acting Executive Director Period.

❏   No additional compensation.

Board Oversight

The board member(s) or board committee (circle one) responsible for monitoring the work of the Acting Executive Director shall be _____ _____ (list by name or office).

The above named people will be sensitive to the special support needs of the Acting Executive Director in this temporary leadership role.

Communications Plan

Immediately upon transferring the responsibilities to the Acting Executive Director, the Board Chair (or highest ranking Board member) will notify staff members, members of the Board of Directors and key volunteers of the delegation of authority.

Taking the High Road—A Guide to Effective and Legal Employment Practices for Nonprofits

As soon as possible after the Acting Executive Director has begun covering the unplanned absence, Board members and the Acting Executive Director shall communicate the temporary leadership structure to the following key external supporters of _____ (Organization Name). This may include (but not be limited to) government contract officers, foundation program officers, civic leaders, major donors and others (please specify): _____.

Completion of Short-Term Emergency Succession Period

The decision about when the absent Executive Director returns to lead _____
(Organization Name) should be determined by the Executive Director and the Board Chair. They will decide upon a mutually agreed upon schedule and start date. A reduced schedule for a set period of time can be allowed, by approval of the Board Chair, with the intention of working their way back up to a full-time commitment.

Succession Plan in Event of a Temporary, Unplanned Absence: Long-Term

A long-term absence is one that's expected to last more than three months. The procedures and conditions to be followed should be the same as for a short-term absence with one addition:

The Executive Committee or Board of Directors (☞ circle one) will give immediate consideration, in consultation with the Acting Executive Director, to **temporarily** filling the management position left vacant by the Acting Executive Director. This is in recognition of the fact that for a term of more than three months, it may not be reasonable to expect the Acting Executive Director to carry the duties of both positions. The position description of a temporary manager would focus on covering the priority areas in which the Acting Executive Director needs assistance.

Completion of Long-Term Emergency Succession Period

The decision about when the absent Executive Director returns to lead _____
(Organization Name) should be determined by the Executive Director and the Board Chair. They will decide upon a mutually agreed upon schedule and start date. A reduced schedule for a set period of time can be allowed, by approval of the Board Chair, with the intention of working the way up to a full-time commitment.

Succession Plan in Event of a Permanent Change in Executive Director

A permanent change is one in which it's firmly determined that the Executive Director won't be returning to the position. The procedures and conditions should be the same as for a long-term temporary absence with one addition:

The Board of Directors will appoint a Transition and Search Committee within (☞ add number) _____ days to plan and carry out a transition to a new permanent executive director. The Board will also consider the need for outside consulting assistance depending on the circumstances of the transition and the board's capacity to plan and manage the transition and search. The Transition and Search Committee will also determine the need for an Interim Executive Director, and plan for the recruitment and selection of an Interim Executive Director and/or permanent Executive Director.

Checklist for Acceptance of All Types of Emergency Succession Plans

❏ **Succession plan approval.** This succession plan will be approved by the Executive Committee and forwarded to the full Board of Directors for its vote and approval. This plan should be reviewed annually.

❏ **Signatories.** The Board Chair, the Executive Director, the deputy director or human resources administrator and the Acting Executive Director shall sign this plan, and the appointees designated in this plan.

❏ **Organizational Charts.** Two organizational charts need to be prepared and attached to this plan. Prepare and attach an organizational chart reflecting staffing positions and lines of authority/reporting throughout the organization. Prepare and attach a second organizational chart that reflects how that structure will change within the context of an emergency/unplanned absence of the Executive Director.

❏ **Important Organizational Information.** Complete the attached *Information and Contact Inventory* and attach it to this document.

❏ **Copies.** Copies of this Emergency Succession Plan along with the corresponding documentation shall be maintained by The Board Chair, the Executive Director, the Acting Executive Director Appointee, the human resources department, and the organization's attorney.

Information and Contact Inventory

for _____

(Organization Name)

Knowing where your organization's key information is located is critical so that if an emergency succession should occur, your organization would be able to quickly continue work in the most efficient and effective way.

	Onsite Location	Offsite Location	Online URL
Nonprofit Status			
IRS Determination Letter	❏ _____	❏ _____	❏ _____
IRS Form 1023	❏ _____	❏ _____	❏ _____
Bylaws	❏ _____	❏ _____	❏ _____
Mission Statement	❏ _____	❏ _____	❏ _____
Board Minutes	❏ _____	❏ _____	❏ _____
Corporate Seal	❏ _____		

Financial Information

Employer Identification Number (EIN) #: _____

	Onsite Location	Offsite Location	Online URL
Current and previous Form 990s	❏ _____	❏ _____	❏ _____
Current and previous audited financial statements	❏ _____	❏ _____	❏ _____
Financial Statements (if not part of the computer system and regularly backed-up)	❏ _____	❏ _____	❏ _____
State or District Sales-Tax Exemption Certificate	❏ _____	❏ _____	❏ _____
Blank Checks	❏ _____	❏ _____	❏ _____
Computer passwords	❏ _____	❏ _____	❏ _____
Donor Records	❏ _____	❏ _____	❏ _____
Client Records	❏ _____	❏ _____	❏ _____
Vendor Records	❏ _____	❏ _____	❏ _____
Volunteer Records*	❏ _____	❏ _____	❏ _____

Note: Nonprofits that are heavily volunteer-based may need to know the following information about their volunteers who they are, how to contact them (home/work phone, e-mail, cell, etc.), where they live/work, expertise, special skills, or any information related to their usefulness or willingness to help the agency (for example, volunteer Jane Doe can walk to our satellite office, lift heavy boxes and knows CPR).

Auditor

Name: _____

Phone Number/E-mail: _____

Bank

Name(s): _____

Account Numbers: _____

Branch Representative(s): _____

Phone Number: _____

Fax: _____

E-mail: _____

Investments

Financial Planner / Broker Company _____

Representative Name: _____

Phone Number: _____

E-mail: _____

Who is authorized to make transfers? Who is authorized to make wire transfers? Are there alternatives?

_____

_____

Who are the authorized check signers?

_____

Is there an office safe? Who has the combination/keys?

_____

Legal Counsel

Attorney

Name: _____

Phone Number: _____

E-mail: _____

Human Resources Information

	Onsite Location	Offsite Location	Online URL
Employee Records/ Personnel Info*	❏ _____	❏ _____	❏ _____

Names, home addresses, phone numbers, e-mail, emergency contacts, etc.

I-9s	❏ _____	❏ _____	❏ _____

Payroll

Company Name: _____

Account Number: _____

Payroll Rep: _____

Phone Number: _____

E-mail: _____

Facilities Information

Office Lease (for renters)	❏ _____	❏ _____
Building Deed (for owners)	❏ _____	❏ _____

Building Management

Company Name:_____

Contact Name: _____

Phone Number/E-mail: _____

Office Security System

Company Name:_____

Account Number _____

Representative Phone Number/E-mail:_____

Broker Phone Number/E-mail: _____

Insurance Information

General Liability / Commercial Umbrella

Company/Underwriter: _____

Policy Number _____

Representative Phone Number/E-mail:_____

Broker Phone Number/E-mail: _____

Directors' & Officers' Liability

Company/Underwriter: _____

Policy Number _____

Representative Phone Number/E-mail:_____

Broker Phone Number/E-mail: _____

Health Insurance

Company/Underwriter: _____

Policy Number _____

Representative Phone Number/E-mail:_____

Broker Phone Number/E-mail: _____

Unemployment Insurance

Company/Underwriter: _____

Policy Number _____

Representative Phone Number/E-mail:_____

Broker Phone Number/E-mail: _____

Workers' Compensation

Company/Underwriter: _____

Policy Number _____

Representative Phone Number/E-mail:_____

Broker Phone Number/E-mail: _____

Disability Insurance (short-term)

Company/Underwriter: _____

Policy Number _____

Representative Phone Number/E-mail: _____

Broker Phone Number/E-mail: _____

Disability Insurance (long-term)

Company/Underwriter: _____

Policy Number _____

Representative Phone Number/E-mail: _____

Broker Phone Number/E-mail: _____

Life Insurance

Company/Underwriter: _____

Policy Number _____

Representative Phone Number/E-mail: _____

Broker Phone Number/E-mail: _____

Dental

Company/Underwriter: _____

Policy Number _____

Representative Phone Number/E-mail: _____

Broker Phone Number/E-mail: _____

Long Term Care

Company/Underwriter: _____

Policy Number _____

Representative Phone Number/E-mail: _____

Broker Phone Number/E-mail: _____

Retirement Plan

Company/Underwriter: _____

Policy Number _____

Representative Phone Number/E-mail: _____

Broker Phone Number/E-mail: _____

Date of Completion for Information and Contact Inventory: _____

Name of Person Completing Document: _____

The Emergency Succession Plan and the supporting documents (the information and contact inventory, job descriptions, and organizational charts) should be reviewed and updated annually.

Signatures of Approval _____
                                            Organization Name

Board Chair _____ Date _____

Executive Director _____ Date _____

Dep. Dir/HR Dir/Other staff member _____ Date _____

Individual Selected as Acting Executive Director _____

Acting Executive Director's Current Title _____ Date _____

We acknowledge the leadership of Transition Guides (notably Tom Adams and Don Tebbe, as well as plan guidance from Karen Gaskins Jones, and Victor Chears) in guiding The Center for Nonprofit Advancement in grasping the impact of Succession Planning and Executive Transitions. Additional thanks to Troy Chapman of the Support Center for Nonprofit Management of New York City, Tim Wolfred of CompassPoint Nonprofit Services for their guidance on the development of this document. The Information and Contact Inventory document is adapted by permission from the Nonprofit Coordinating Committee of New York City.

Required Federal Law Notices

Minimum Wage (English and Spanish) Required for all employers [U.S. Dept of Labor, Wage and Hour Division]

It's the Law OSHA Notice (English and Spanish) Required for all employers [U.S. Occupational Safety and Health Administration]

Equal Employment Opportunity (English and Spanish) Required for all employers [U.S. Equal Employment Opportunity Commission]

Employee Polygraph Protection (English and Spanish) All employers subject to the Employee Polygraph Protection Act [U.S. Dept of Labor, Wage and Hour Division]

Family and Medical Leave Act (English and Spanish) Required for all employers of 50 or more employees [U.S. Dept of Labor, Wage and Hour Division]

Uniformed Services Employment and Reemployment Rights Act Required for all employers [U.S Dept. of Labor & Veterans' Employment and Training Service]

Notice to Workers with Disabilities (English and Spanish)* Required for all employers of workers with disabilities [U.S. Dept of Labor, Employment Standards Administration]

Earned Income Credit* Recommended for all employers [Internal Revenue Service]

Check Your Withholding* Recommended for all employers [Internal Revenue Service]

The requirements for individual state law notices may generally be obtained from individual state's Department of Labor Web site. Some sites also provide downloadable copies of the required posters, in Spanish and English:

California: *www.dfeh.ca.gov/Publications/postersemp.asp; Effective Date of Latest Change: 5/1/2006*

The Department of Fair Employment & Housing has added several points to their *Discrimination notice.* It now states employers with 50 or more employees and all public entities must provide sexual harassment prevention training for all supervisors. It requires employers to reasonably accommodate an employee or job applicant's religious beliefs and practices. It also now states employers are prohibited from retaliation against a person who opposes, reports or assists another person in opposing unlawful discrimination. It also expands the amount of time a victim under the age of 18 has to report their discrimination/harassment until one year after that person's eighteenth birthday.

Idaho: *http://cl.idaho.gov/ftp/requiredposters.pdf*

Maryland: Posters required at the workplace can be ordered via the Internet from the following Web site: *www.mchr.state.md.us/Orders/newposterorders.html*

New Jersey: *Effective date of Latest Change: 3/1/06*

Specific individual state poster that has changed: Conscientious Employee Protection Act—"Whistleblower Act": Poster refers to expanded protection to employees reporting perceived criminal or fraudulent activity by adding lines protecting employees who do the following:

❏ Provides information involving deception of or misrepresentation to, any shareholder, investor, client, patient, customer, employee, former employee, retiree or pensioner of the employer or any government entity; and

❏ Provides information regarding any perceived criminal or fraudulent activity, policy or practice of deception or misrepresentation which the employee reasonably believes may defraud any shareholder, investor, client, patient, customer, employee, former employee, retiree or pensioner of the employer or any government entity.

New Mexico: *Effective Date of Latest Change: 5/1/2006*

OSHA—They've totally revised the OSHA notice, changing to the "plain language" version. It explains employee's rights to notify the employer or OSHA about workplace hazards, to request an inspection, to see citations issued to an employer and to file a complaint for discrimination for filing a complaint. This new version is also in Spanish now.

Workers' Compensation has created an Ombudsman notice to let employees know how to get help with a workers' compensation Claim.

North Carolina: *Effective Date of Latest Change: 4/30/2006*

There have been a number of changes, most significant is the addition on Right-to-Work Laws and Employment Discrimination. Although they created this new version last November, they did not require people to have the new version and in fact did not start distributing the new version until April. Now that they're distributing the new version, they're requiring employers use the new version so we are updating the poster.

Utah: *Effective Date of Latest Change: 6/1/2006*

Utah Job Safety and Health Protection. The notice requires employers not to remove or destroy any tools, equipment, materials or any other evidence that might pertain to the cause of injuries or illnesses to workers until so authorized by the Labor Commission or one of it's Compliance Officers.

Virginia: *www.doli.state.va.us/infocenter/publications/reqposters_p1.html.*

Checklist for Reference Checking

(Consider adapting this form for use in your nonprofit as a means to keep track of information received during reference checks. Use one form for each employer contacted.)

Candidate's name: _____

Candidate's Previous Employer: _____

Job Title: _____

Contact Name and Title: _____

Contact Telephone Number: _____

Dates Employed: From:_____ to: _____

According to this employer's records, the Candidate left the organization for the following reason(s):

_____

_____

Were there any disciplinary actions taken against this employee? _____Yes _____No

If so, how did the previous employer explain the reason for the discipline?_____

_____

Employer above Would ___ Would Not ____ re-employ this individual (check one)

Employer's Assessment: _____

Check the rating that reflects how this reference described/evaluated the Candidate in each area below:

	Exceptional	Satisfactory	Unsatisfactory
Attendance			
Punctuality			
Professionalism			
Work Quality			
Timeliness of work			
Cooperation			
Supervision (if applicable)			
Teamwork skills			

(Add other categories as applicable)

Other remarks from this reference about the employee's job performance:

_____

_____

_____

Additional sample forms are featured in the online version of this text.